THE ADVENTURES OF A CELLO

University of Texas Press ⌄ *Austin*

CARLOS
PRIETO

The Adventures of a Cello
Revised Edition, with a New Epilogue

TRANSLATED BY ELENA C. MURRAY
FOREWORD BY ÁLVARO MUTIS

PUBLICATION OF THIS BOOK WAS MADE POSSIBLE THROUGH
THE GENEROUS SUPPORT OF THE FOLLOWING DONORS:

Jeanne and Michael Klein
  in honor of Bob Freeman
Ellen Randall
  in honor of Elle Alexander Middleton
and Lowell Lebermann.

THE LIBRARY OF CONGRESS CATALOGED THE FIRST EDITION AS FOLLOWS:

Prieto, Carlos, 1937–
[Aventuras de un violoncello. English]
The adventures of a cello / Carlos Prieto ; translated by Elena C. Murray ;
foreword by Álvaro Mutis.
        p.   cm.
Includes bibliographical references (p.   ), discography (p.   ), and index.
ISBN for the Revised Edition: 978-0-292-72393-1 (cloth : alk. paper)
1. Violoncello. 2. Prieto, Carlos, 1937– I. Murray, Elena C. II. Title.
ML910.P7513 2006
787.4—dc22   2006001346

To María Isabel

To the memory of my parents, Cécile and Carlos

To my brother, Juan Luis

To Carlos Miguel, Isabel, and Mauricio

To the Prieto Quartets

CONTENTS

The Adventures of a Cello
and the Stories and Memories of
Its Happy Owner ÁLVARO MUTIS

As far as I recall, seldom has the word "exhaustive" been so appropriately used as when describing this delightful book, whose title alone promises a good read. *The Adventures of a Cello,* by the renowned cellist and writer Carlos Prieto, thoroughly lives up to our expectations. However, before going any further, it is worth noting that the very concept of this book is highly unusual. To the best of our knowledge, none of the great musicians or composers, past or present, has ever thought of telling the story behind the instrument that has so loyally accompanied them for so many years. What is the reason for this deliberate, inexcusable oversight? I will not attempt to elaborate on this subject. This chronicle, by Carlos Prieto, a world-famous cellist and a cultured, sensitive man with the inexhaustible curiosity of the sages, has succeeded in solving this mystery so completely that I am finally at peace.

Before actually telling the dramatic story of his Piatti, which, incidentally, Alexander Dumas, Eugene Sue, or Sir Walter Scott would have gladly claimed as his own, Prieto introduces us to the world of violin making and the history of its remote and honorable origins, in a style that is both entertaining and scholarly. This introduction is fundamental to the perilous journey undertaken by this cello, known as the Piatti, a journey that began in 1720 and continues to the present day. After almost 300 years that witnessed the most radical, turbulent changes in Western history, the Piatti still prevails, vibrant as ever, still undergoing countless adventures and misadventures.

This historical survey prepares us for the tours that the Piatti and its current owner and devoted ally have made throughout the world, a musical odyssey that fills us not only with envy, but also with an insatiable curiosity about their experiences in countries undergoing unpredictable transformations.

However, Prieto does not stop there. He then presents us with a comprehensive description of music written for the cello from the seventeenth century to the present.

Finally, in order to ascertain the role of the cello today, Prieto provides brief profiles of the great contemporary cellists. To reinforce the rich contents of this comprehensive work, Carlos Prieto's book provides readers with two indispensable repertoires: the first on the principal works written for the cello in this century, classified by country and author, while the second refers to Latin America, Spain, and Portugal.

Consequently, the reader now possesses a book of unprecedented value and importance in the history of music. The author combines a highly personal, moving tribute with outstanding historiographic work in the field of music, his cello acting as his motivator and guide throughout their life together. This book is unquestionably a beautiful love story. Let us thank Carlos Prieto for filling such a great void in the lives of all us inveterate music lovers.

ACKNOWLEDGMENTS

To my wife, María Isabel. Her support and encouragement have always been fundamental to me. She has accompanied me on numerous concert tours and has collaborated with me on countless expeditions in search of information on the Piatti cello, the protagonist of this book.

To my brother, Juan Luis Prieto, who revised the original manuscript in Spanish and whose perceptive suggestions played a vital role in the final version.

To Elena C. Murray, for her fine translation.

To Dr. Robert Freeman, dean of the College of Fine Arts and Effie Marie Cain Regents Chair in Fine Arts, University of Texas at Austin, for his advice and guidance on the publication of this book.

To Joanna Hitchcock, director of the University of Texas Press, for her wholehearted support and interest in the publication of this book.

The Origin and Purpose of This Book

My cello, the protagonist of this book, was born in 1720 in the northern Italian city of Cremona.

In 1720, thirty-five-year-old Johann Sebastian Bach, then kapellmeister at the prince of Anhalt-Cöthen's court, was composing his six suites for unaccompanied cello, among other works. At that time, when Philip V was king of Spain, the sun never set on the Spanish dominions. The viceroyalty of New Spain extended from the Panamanian border region to Louisiana, east along the Atlantic coast, and west to what later became the territory of Oregon on the Pacific.

The cello in question, created in 1720 by Antonio Stradivari, has changed hands several times during its 286 years of life. While in the possession of various cellists in different countries, it has witnessed peaceful, turbulent, and tragic times.

Since 1979, I have had the privilege of being the temporary trustee of this cello, known as the Piatti. I say "trustee" because I believe that a work of art—like this instrument—cannot be considered property, like a house or any other material object at one's disposal. Those of us fortunate enough to play instruments that are genuine works of art must take the responsibility for treating them as such, with the utmost care, so as to transmit them to their future "trustees" in the best condition possible.

Since the day that the Piatti came into my hands, I started investigating its history, and soon it occurred to me that it might well be material for a book. The "biography" of a cello may perhaps seem like a trivial, rather dreary subject, whereas the biographies of great men and women appeal to us for many obvious reasons. However, rarely do we stop to think that some objects, like certain musical instruments, also lead a life filled with dramatic episodes and exciting adventures that reflect certain unique aspects of evolving societies and cultures. My research has taken me several years, and I hope to continue with this pursuit, even after the publication of this book. The history of the Piatti, its life and miracles—and there have certainly been many during its long and almost tercentarian life—are discussed in the second part of this book.

Since I believed that the biography and the adventures of the Piatti might be better understood if they were preceded by a brief history of violin making, Part One of the book is devoted to this subject. Here I explore the remote origin of stringed instruments, the birth of the various members of the violin family, the history of the great Italian violin makers—headed by Antonio Stradivari and Giuseppe Guarneri del Gesù—and the evolution of the violin, viola, and cello.

The birth of the Piatti took place during the same period that the cello began to figure more prominently in the history of music. In fact, it coincides with the dates when J. S. Bach composed the six solo suites for cello (c. 1720), the first fundamental work in the history of this instrument.

Part Three of this book is titled "A Brief History of Cello Music from Stradivari to the Present." Here I refer to such subjects as the gradual incorporation of the cello into the category of a great solo instrument, the cello works of the principal composers, the musical treasures found in its repertoire, and the roles and contributions of some of the most outstanding cellists of the past and present.

Part Three highlights only the main features in the history of cello music, without entering into great detail or attempting a comprehensive, in-depth analysis of this complex subject.

I must clarify a few additional points regarding Part Two, devoted to the history of the Piatti. Although its existence from 1720 to 1979 has been the subject of my research ever since it came into my hands, its life has been intimately linked to mine. Therefore, this story contains many autobiographical elements. I include, for example, a brief account of the adventures that the Piatti and I have experienced during our travels around the world. I certainly wish I had come across similar anecdotes written by its former owners!

In addition to describing several of our tours throughout Europe, Asia, and the Americas, I also refer to one of the subjects that has most absorbed me over the past twenty-six years: celebrating and promoting the music of Mexico and of the Spanish- and Portuguese-speaking countries from both sides of the Atlantic. Through the years I have met many distinguished personalities in the world of Mexican, Latin American, Spanish, and Portuguese music in general, and without professing to have made substantial contributions to Latin American or Iberian musicology, I describe my encounters with some of these musicians—some are close friends who have dedicated numerous works to me. I discuss the music and musicians of Latin America, Spain, and Portugal, the works that I premiered (almost always with the Piatti), the often picturesque circumstances characterizing these premieres, and my tours and musical adventures with this cello.

The painting and literature of Latin America are better known than its music, although the quality of the latter is certainly on the same level. We, the people from Spanish- and Portuguese-speaking countries, have the obligation, as far as possible, to promote and honor our artistic legacy (in my case, music), especially in these times when most First World nations view our countries through a distorted lens of misconceptions and oversimplifications, focusing only on the most negative aspects of our reality and minimizing the importance and merits of our extremely diverse and rich ancestral cultures.

The instruments created by the great violin makers are often named after some famous musician or prominent collector who has owned them. They are also sometimes identified with a distinctive trait or a particular aspect of their life. Thus, for example, the Stradivari viola once owned by Paganini is known as the ex-Paganini or simply as the Paganini, whereas his Guarneri violin was dubbed Il Cannone for its extraordinarily potent sound. A Montagnana cello that spent an entire century untouched and immobile in its case in England was nicknamed Sleeping Beauty. My cello, when it was in Ireland and England between 1818 and 1900, was known as the Red Stradivari. Shortly after 1900 it became the Piatti, or ex-Piatti, after the prominent Italian cellist Alfredo Piatti, who owned it from 1867 till 1901.

THE ADVENTURES OF A CELLO

Part One

A BRIEF HISTORY OF
VIOLIN MAKING

CHAPTER I

Observations on the Origin of Violins and Cellos

THE ANCIENT ORIGIN OF STRINGED INSTRUMENTS

The origin of music and musical instruments is lost in the mists of time. Since this is neither the time nor the place to explore the evolution of musical instruments, for our purposes we need only state that in the third millennium before Christ there was already, in both Sumer and Egypt, evidence of stringed instruments such as zithers, lyres, lutes, and harps. In the *Iliad*, Homer mentions the lyre and the zither, basic Greek instruments that were adaptations of more ancient instruments.

From Greece and Rome, musical instruments followed two main routes. The first led to the Middle East via the Arabs, who cultivated music with great refinement and brought to Spain instruments like the lute (from *ud* in Arabic), the Moorish guitar, and the *rebec* (or *rabel*), a small stringed instrument played with a bow, a direct ancestor of our violin. The second route was from Byzantium to the north, by way of Italy. Later on, these instruments of common origin would meet again, after having evolved differently. For example, the Latin guitar, the Moorish guitar, and the Moorish lute are plucked with a bird feather, whereas the European lute, the rebec, and its European equivalent, the *giga* (or *geige*), are strummed with the fingers. In fact, the duality of giga and rebec still exists to this day. A violin is still called a *Geige* in German, and a certain type of violin is a *rebeca* in Portuguese. However, one must not confuse the rebec or the geige with the violin. As Adolfo Salazar points out, "The semantic evolution loses its connection with the instrument: the ancient rabel . . . although it might have been the violin's ancestor, today has become a different instrument."[1] The same could also be said of the giga or the geige.

In ancient times, the words *kytara* in Greek and *fidicula* in Latin applied to the same common ancestor of the Greek lyres and zithers.

The kytara engendered a series of instruments such as the guitar. The Latin term *fidicula* is a philological goldmine. In the Romance languages, *fidicula* dropped the *d* and evolved into the medieval French *fielle* or *vielle* and subsequently into *viole*; in Italian it became *viola*; and in Spanish, *viela*, *viola*, and *vihuela*. In the Germanic languages, *fidicula* evolved into the Anglo-Saxon *fidele* and eventually to *fiddle* in English; in High German it became *fiedel* and *videl*. In Spain, *vihuela* was a generic term applied to stringed instruments with a flat back and neck and with strings that were plucked with the fingers, a plectrum, or a feather, or else played with a bow.

The introduction of the bow was a turning point in the evolution of stringed instruments from ancient times to the Renaissance. The sound produced by plucking the string is brief and tends to fade. On the other hand, the bow allows for continuous sounds of variable duration and intensity. The bow, unknown to the cultures of Egypt, Mesopotamia, Crete, and Greece, came from the Orient. The earliest evidence of its existence is found during the ninth century in Central Asia, which was probably where the distant ancestor of the European and Chinese bows originated. I will return to this subject in another chapter.

THE VIOLIN FAMILY AND THE BIRTH OF THE CELLO

The cello's first appearance in the music world was in sixteenth-century Italy, a few years after its siblings, the violin and the viola, had arrived. The earliest record of its existence is a fresco painted in 1535–1536 by Gaudenzio Ferrari in the Church of Santa Maria dei Miracoli in Saronno, near Milan. The fresco, which also includes the violin and the viola, depicts an angel playing a primitive version of the cello.[2]

It is common knowledge that the violin, the viola, and the cello belong to the violin family, which arose just as another family of stringed instruments, the violas da gamba, or viols, reached its height of popularity.

From its Italian name, the viola da gamba may be thought to have originated in Italy. However, according to some fifteenth-century paintings, it seems that the oldest of these instruments actually came from Spain—from Valencia, to be more precise. A Renaissance viol is depicted in a *Virgin and Child*, dated around 1475, in the chapel of St. Félix, in Játiva, Valencia.[3] From Valencia, the viola da gamba, or *vihuela de arco*—as it was also known in Spain—spread throughout the Mediterranean to the Balearic Islands, Sardinia, and Italy. Although none of these primitive violas da gamba has survived, in 1658 Vincenzo Galilei, Galileo's father, confirmed their Spanish origin: "In Spain one finds the first music ever written for violas, but the most ancient instruments are now found in Bologna, Brescia, Padua and Florence."[4]

Obviously, Renaissance instruments were not born with a perfectly defined shape or with specific names. Furthermore, the initial problems of terminology have led to considerable confusion. The names *violin* and *cello*—*violino* and *violoncello* in Italian—appeared much later than the instruments themselves. By the 1500s, the Italian term *viola* was applied not only to our present-day viola, but also to all stringed instruments played with a bow. In turn, these instruments were divided into two great families: the leg viols, or violas da gamba (so named because they were held between the musician's legs), and the *violas da braccio* (held in the arm).

Both the violas da gamba and the violas da braccio came in different sizes. The individual instruments from each family were named according to their relative musical registers. The most common violas da gamba were the *viola da gamba soprano*, the *viola da gamba tenor*, and the *viola da gamba basso*.[5] The members of the violas da braccio family were also distinguished by their different tessituras. The violin was known as a *soprano di viola da braccio* (or *violone da braccio*), and our present-day viola was an *alto di viola da braccio*; the cello was a *basso di viola da braccio*, and our double bass was called a *contra basso di viola da braccio*, although these last two were not held in the arm.

It is important to clarify a common misunderstanding: the instruments of the gamba family did not give rise to the violin family. While they both had similar ancient origins, they existed simultaneously.[6]

The term *violone da braccio* was applied to the violin at the beginning of the sixteenth century, whereas the definitive, diminutive term *violino* appeared in Italy in 1538. By the seventeenth century in Italy, the *basso di viola da braccio*—our cello—was simply called *violone*. The diminutive terms *violoncino* and *violoncello* appeared in 1641 and 1665, respectively, more than a century after Ferrari's 1535 fresco.[7] By the end of the seventeenth century, the term *violoncello* was already in common use.

No term has had a more curious evolution than *alto di viola da braccio*—our *viola*. In seventeenth-century Italy it was called simply *viola da braccio*, and soon after, the term *da braccio* disappeared and only the word *viola* remained; in German, *alto* and *viola* disappeared and only *braccio* remained, giving rise to *Bratsche*. In France, *alto di viola da braccio* dropped *viola* and *braccio*, so this instrument is known in French simply as *alto*.

The violas da gamba reached their distinctive shape during the fifteenth century, well before the violas da braccio. They were characterized by flat backs, broad necks, gut frets, six or seven thin strings, and a beautiful, though somewhat pale and flat, sound.

In Spain, one of the most remarkable musicians of the sixteenth century was Diego Ortiz, from Toledo. He was a famous viola player, and his *Tratado de glosas* (Rome, 1553) is one of the first masterpieces in the art of variation and fantasy.

In England, the violas da gamba, called viols, were used in small instrumental groups called consorts, a word that has the same origin as *concert*. A viol consort generally included six viols of different sizes. They were also used in the consort songs, which were written for voice and viols and whose most famous composer was William Byrd.

In seventeenth-century Germany, the viola da gamba, still regularly used by J. S. Bach, was on the verge of extinction when the German school of gambists closed down. It disappeared in 1787 after the death of Carl Friedrich Abel, the instrument's last great virtuoso.[8]

In France the popularity of the gambas, called *violes* in French, lasted longer. From 1675 to 1770 the French school of the gamba was the most important in Europe, and its most celebrated exponent was Marin Marais (1656–1728), author of the well-known *Pièces de violes*.[9]

In less than two centuries, the violin family displaced the viola da gamba group and occupied a predominant place in music. Why such a radical transformation? Although this is a fascinating topic, this brief overview is not the occasion for an in-depth analysis. I need add only that art is always a reflection of historical evolution and that, therefore, both music and musical instruments undergo the transformations imposed on them by particular eras.

The Baroque period, which began in 1600, marked the beginning of a musical revolution. The lyrical madrigal of the sixteenth century gave way to musical drama. New generations searched for a deeper emotional content and a more expressive musical style. Logically, the new style was launched with the most flexible of all instruments: the human voice. Italian singers sometimes expressed their emotions with such passion that, for example, at a performance of a Monteverdi opera at the court of Mantua in 1608, many of the spectators barely held back their tears during a scene in which Arianna, abandoned by Theseus, breaks into a heartrending lament.

It is natural that violin makers and violinists would attempt to create an expressive quality in their instruments, one that came as close to the human voice as possible. The newborn violin had three fundamental advantages over the viola da gamba soprano or the pardessus de viole: a more powerful sound, greater expressive capacity, and the possibility for a greater display of virtuosity. We find the same advantages in the cello and the viola in relation to the bass and alto violas da gamba, respectively.

However, this substitution did not take place without fierce opposition. The musical elite and the aristocracy were especially partial to the violas da gamba. The French composer Philibert Jambe de Fer (1515–1556), in his *Epitome musical* (1556), described the differences between both families and consigns the violin to the lowest musical level, regarding it as "suitable only for dances and processions". Claude-François Ménestrier, author of the book *Des ballets anciens et modernes* (1682), described the violin as extremely noisy ("*quelque peu tapageur*").[10] In 1705 Jean Laurent Lecerf de la Viéville, in his *Comparaison de la musique italienne et de la musique française*, wrote that "the violin is not a noble instrument; the whole world agrees."[11]

The attacks against the cello were similar but lasted much longer. In 1740, Hubert Le Blanc wrote a *Défense de la basse de viole contre les entreprises du violon et les prétentions du violoncel*, where he bemoans the fact that the cello, "a wretched, despised poor devil, who instead of starving to death as could well be expected, now even boasts of replacing the bass viola da gamba."[12] He adds that since the screeching sounds of the violin and the cello cannot possibly rival the delicacy and elegance of the violas, they must resort to huge halls, totally unsuitable to the violas da gamba. This comment actually reveals the disadvantage of the violas da gamba: their weak sound made them almost inaudible in the great concert halls. Ironically, and everything being relative, those "huge halls" were, in fact, the court salons, whose small size is now considered ideal for chamber music.

THE ANATOMY OF THE CELLO

The anatomy of stringed instruments is described in almost human terms. We refer to the instrument's head, neck, body, ribs, waist, and even its "soul." The cello, like the violin and the viola, comprises over seventy different parts. Figure 1 displays the principal pieces of this instrument.

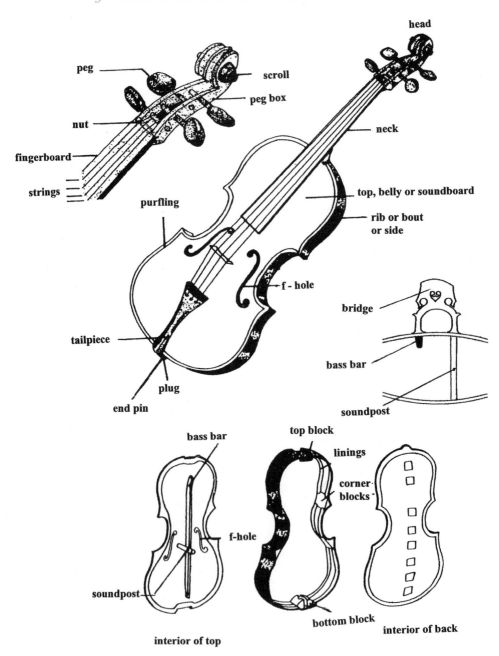

1. The anatomy of a cello.

First, let us examine the exterior.

The top (belly or soundboard) generally consists of two pieces of spruce or pinewood attached to the entire length of the central line.

The back is generally made of two matching pieces of maple and, sometimes, poplar.

A very fine triple line called purfling runs parallel to the two edges of the top and back. There are two inlaid outer strips of black-tinted wood and an inner strip of black poplar. The purpose of the purfling is not merely aesthetic, since it also prevents cracks in the edges.

The ribs (or bouts), also maple, are attached to the top and the back. There are six altogether, three on each side. The first, or upper, bout runs from the neck to the beginning of the waist; the second, or middle, bout is the waist itself (also called *C* because it is shaped like the letter); the third runs from the waist to the lower central part of the instrument. The interior is reinforced with narrow wooden strips called linings, which reinforce the structure of the ribs.

The head, made of maple, ends in the scroll, which is often very beautiful. The function of the head is to house the pegbox: its four pegs, usually made of ebony, hold the upper end of each string, and the tension of a string is adjusted by turning its peg.

The neck is the piece that joins the head to the body of the instrument. In the past, both the neck and the head were made of a single piece of maple. Since today longer necks are required, new ones have been inserted into the original heads of old instruments. The rest of the instrument consists of modern-day pieces that can be changed with relative ease.

Attached to the neck is the ebony fingerboard, along which the strings run lengthwise. The fingerboard provides the surface against which the fingers press the strings and determine the notes to be played.

The bridge, made of maple, transmits the vibrations of the strings to the top, or soundboard. Selecting a well-carved bridge made from the right kind of wood is indispensable for obtaining optimal sound from the instrument. The bridge, an exterior piece, is not attached to the top, but is held in place by the pressure of the strings.

The instrument's interior serves as a sounding board or sound amplifier: sound waves are emitted through two openings, called f-holes because of their shape, on both sides of the bridge.

The tailpiece is the section attached to the lower ends of the strings. It was formerly made of ebony, and sometimes of boxwood or rosewood, though today plastic is generally used. The tailpiece is fastened to the plug by a strap that was usually a cord of catgut, but today is either a steel wire or a synthetic filament.

The four strings of the cello are, in descending order, A, D, G, and C. Originally, the strings were made of catgut. Today they tend to be steel or a synthetic material wound with steel, aluminum, tungsten, or other metal.

The end pin is a cylindrical piece, generally made of steel, with a sharp point and an adjustable length; it allows the player to conveniently set the cello on the floor.

The mute (not illustrated), is a comb-shaped rider that, when placed on the bridge, reduces the vibrations of the bridge and produces a muffled sound.[13]

Let us now examine two vitally important pieces in the interior of the cello. The bass bar is a long narrow piece of pine attached to the interior of the top and running underneath the foot of the bridge, next to the lowest string—hence the name *bass bar*. Its function is to make the top more resistant to the strong pressure exerted by the strings over the bridge.

Finally, there is a piece so sensitive and vital that it is called the "soul" in all Latin languages.[14] In English, it is called the soundpost. It is a small cylindrical bar of spruce, perpendicular to the top and the back, near the foot of the bridge, and opposite the bass bar. It is not attached; rather, it is held fixed to the back by the pressure of the bridge on the top. Its purpose is to transmit the vibrations of the top to the back and then to send them resounding throughout the entire interior of the instrument. Its precise placement is fundamental to producing a good sound, and the slightest change in its position will alter the quality and volume of the sound. The ideal placement depends not only on the instrument but also on the musician.

THE BOW: ITS ORIGINS

The importance of the bow is such that even the finest instrument cannot reach its tonal potential—in both volume and quality—if it is not played with a good bow.

The earliest literary and artistic references to the existence of a primitive bow date as far back as the ninth century in Central Asia—in Transoxiana Sogdiana, Khwarizm, and Khorasan—in what today would approximately be Uzbekistan and Turkmenistan. In the Arabic and Byzantine empires, the use of the bow was already common during the tenth century, as corroborated by certain Byzantine illustrations and Arabic documents.[15]

As in the case of stringed instruments, it was the Arabs who introduced the bow to Europe through the double route of Spain and Byzantium. A Spanish manuscript dated 920–930, a copy of a work by Beatus of Liébana, contains one of the most ancient Spanish representations of a bow. The manuscript, written in the time of Abd ar-Rahman III, caliph of Córdoba, includes a beautiful colored illustration depicting seven angels and four musicians playing bowed instruments.[16]

THE MODERN BOW: FRANÇOIS TOURTE, THE STRADIVARI OF BOW MAKERS

The great modern bow-making tradition began in the eighteenth century with François Tourte (1747–1835), the most brilliant bow maker in history—the Stradivari of bow makers. He was born ten years after the death of Stradivari and, like him, lived a long life, dying at the age of eighty-eight. His life was characterized by an unflagging dedication to his art, from which he retired at the age of eighty-five when his sight began to fail. He worked all day in his small workshop in Paris, located at 10 Quai de l'École, overlooking the Seine. His only pastime was fishing on the river at sunset after a long day's work.[17]

The bows that existed prior to Tourte, even those made by Arcangelo Corelli, did not succeed in extracting the instruments' full range of rich sounds. To familiarize himself with musicians' particular requirements, Tourte worked with the greatest virtuosos of the time, especially with the violinist Giovanni Viotti. Although Tourte did not invent the bow, he established the ideal model by standardizing the dimensions, weight, and balance, and, most particularly, by introducing or reintroducing pernambuco wood from Brazil, the only kind of wood that provides the optimum combination of flexibility, elasticity, resistance, and weight. Tourte paid meticulous attention to the horsehair for his bows, selecting each of the 200 hairs for its perfect roundness and uniform length; he was assisted by his daughter, who, it is believed, added the tiny label with the following text found in one of his bows: *Cet archet a été fait par Tourte en 1824, âgé de soixante-dix-sept ans.* (This bow was made by Tourte in 1824, at 77 years of age.)[18] Tourte's bows were genuine masterpieces, not only because of their incomparable beauty and perfection, but also from the tone they produce in great instruments when played by an artist.

The French school of bow making prevailed in this art, just as violin making had been dominated by the Italians. Among Tourte's successors we should mention François Lupot (1774–1837), Nicolas Eury (1810–1835), Dominique Peccatte (1810–1874), who today is regarded almost on the same level as Tourte, François Nicolas Voirin (1833–1885), and others. There were also outstanding bow makers from other countries: John Dodd (1752–1839) and James Tubbs (1835–1919) from England, and Nicolas Kittel (1839–1870) from Russia.

Figure 2 shows the principal parts of the bow. The thickness of the stick is not uniform: its dimensions are determined by a precise mathematical formula. The stick's curved shape is obtained through an ap-

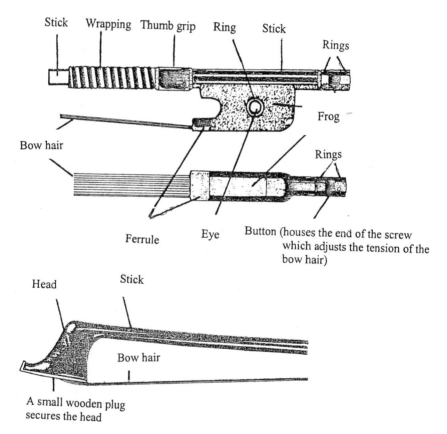

2. *The anatomy of a bow.* BOTTOM: *The head of the bow.* TOP: *The frog of the bow (side and bottom view).*

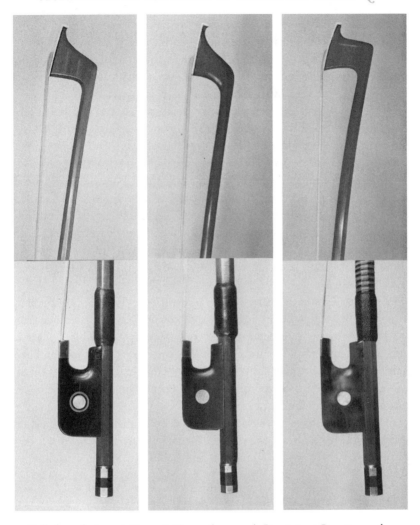

3. Cello bows by (LEFT) *Francois Tourte,* (CENTER) *Dominique Peccatte, and* (RIGHT) *William Salchow (a modern bow). Photos by Isaac Salchow.*

plication of dry heat, requiring a highly developed sense of touch on the bow maker's part.

It is curious that few violinists and cellists ever stop to think about the extraordinary number of materials required to make a bow. As I have already mentioned, the stick is made of a wood called pernambuco, the finest grade of brazilwood. This wood, which comes from a tree called *pau-brasil* in Portuguese and *palo brasil* in Spanish or *brasilium* in Latin, had been known in Europe since the eleventh century, since it also grows in other places. This was the tree that gave its name to Brazil (and not the other way around) when the Portuguese discovered great forests of these reddish trees in the territory later known as Brazil.

The frog is made of ebony (a wood from the central regions of Africa), tortoiseshell, or ivory; use of the latter two is severely restricted today to prevent the extinction of turtles and elephants. Mother-of-pearl is used for the eye of the frog and for the ring that sometimes surrounds it. Silver or gold is generally used for the ferrule. Just above the frog, where the fingers touch the bow, there is a protective wrapping; once made of whalebone, it is now leather, silver wire, or gold wire. A steel screw adjusts the tension of the hair. Finally, bow hair comes from the tails of white horses, preferably those from cold regions. Since the hairs tend to break with use, they must be replaced every two or three months; that is, the bow must be rehaired.

For years I have used an excellent bow made by François Tourte and a modern bow by William Salchow, a renowned New York bow maker whose cello bows are exceptionally good. Whenever possible, I always entrust Salchow with rehairing my bows, since the quality of the bow hair is fundamental. Salchow generally obtains hair from Russian or Mongolian horses: they are raised on the cold steppes, and their thick hair ensures optimal quality.

Figure 3 illustrates three cello bows: one by François Tourte, another by Dominique Peccatte—the model called *tête de cygne* (swan's head) because of its delicately shaped point—and the last by William Salchow.

ROSIN

If one places new hairs in a bow and then glides them across a string, no sound will be produced, since the contact of the clean hairs with the string does not produce any vibrations. To produce sound, the hairs need to be coated with hundreds of diminutive solid particles, which, upon coming into contact with the strings, create a rapid succession of shocks and a continuous vibration, resulting in the emission of sound. This is the function of rosin, which must be frequently applied to the bow. The rosin for bows is obtained from the sap, or resin, of certain kinds of pine trees. When refined through various processes, the sap is used for medicinal, commercial, and artistic purposes. In ancient times, the resin from Colophon in Greek Ionia (in Asia Minor) was regarded as the very finest, so rosin is called *colophane* in French, *colofonia* in Italian, and *kolophon* in German, whereas the Spanish name is *resina*. Good rosin is obtained only after a careful selection of the best raw material and a manufacturing process that adheres to the strictest quality-control standards. Certain kinds of rosins are more appropriate for violins or violas, and other, slightly different, types are more suitable for cellos and double basses.

CHAPTER 2

Amati, Stradivari, Guarneri del Gesù, and the Great Italian Violin Makers

The city of Cremona in northern Italy plays a prominent role in the history of music. Indeed, for over two hundred years, beginning in the sixteenth century, Cremona was the violin-making center par excellence. Most of the instruments played by the most famous musicians in the world originated in its workshops. Two of its illustrious names were destined to elevate the art of violin making to its most sublime expression: Antonio Stradivari and Giuseppe Guarneri del Gesù.

Cremona, part of the duchy of Milan, was the town of second-greatest political and economic importance after the capital. Seventy-five kilometers southeast of Milan, it was also near Venice and the domains of the Gonzaga and the Farnese families (Mantua and Parma, respectively). In 1559, the duchy of Milan was incorporated into the Spanish crown territories, as were the kingdoms of Naples and Sardinia.

Its proximity to Venice was extremely important to Cremona. During the seventeenth century and into the eighteenth, Venice was virtually regarded as Europe's musical center. It was the only city where opera was presented as a profitable commercial enterprise, completely independent of the court or the whims of some nobleman. In 1637 Venice opened its first opera house. Naples, which during the eighteenth century would rival Venice as an operatic center, did not present a single opera until 1651, when a Venetian company performed an opera by Monteverdi.

Monteverdi, the first great opera composer and the most prominent musical figure of his time, was born in 1567 in Cremona, where he studied and lived until around 1590, when he departed for the court of Mantua. By 1613 he was living in Venice, and that same year he was appointed *maestro di cappella* (the person in charge of all music for a religious institution) of St. Mark's Cathedral.

Monteverdi, who availed himself of all the musical innovations of his time, was the first composer to specify the use of violins and cellos in his compositions.[1] For example, in his opera *Orfeo* (1607), the score stipulates the use of cellos (called *bassi di viola da braccio*) and violas da gamba. During the third act of the same piece, he demanded certain highly unusual effects from the violins, such as tremolos, and extreme dynamic expressions like *morendo* (dying away); such notations indicate that the art of violin playing began its development with this composer.

When *Orfeo* premiered in Mantua in 1607, the composition of the orchestra greatly depended on the musicians Monteverdi had managed to find. Shortly thereafter, when Venetians started performing operas profitably, it became necessary to systematize the integration of the orchestra by creating a nucleus consisting of a string quartet: two violins, a viola, and a cello. The ever-increasing passion for opera gave rise to a considerable demand for stringed instruments. Furthermore, the advent of great violinists like Arcangelo Corelli (1653–1715), the most eminent figure among the earliest composer-violinists, called for instruments having a more resonant quality. This and the abovementioned factors serve to explain the extraordinary development of violin making, not only in Cremona, but also in cities such as Brescia and Venice itself.

ANDREA AMATI AND THE AMATI DYNASTY

History's first great violin maker was Andrea Amati, born around 1511 in Cremona, where he died in 1581. He is the creator of the oldest violins, violas, and cellos that we know of, although Amati did not invent these instruments. As mentioned in the previous chapter, they had existed since the early sixteenth century, but it was Amati who perfected their form and provided them with the basic characteristics that they still preserve to this day.

Andrea Amati's fame was such that shortly after 1560, Charles IX of France ordered thirty-eight stringed instruments for the French court, including eight cellos, several of which are now lost.[2] I once had the opportunity to examine one of them, dubbed "The King," built around 1572. This instrument features several paintings on its ribs and on the back, which bears the letter *K* (for *Karolus*, the Latin name for the king of France) with a crown painted above it. A fleur-de-lis, symbol of the French royal family, appears on each corner of the back.

Corelli himself owned a violin made by Andrea Amati in 1578; he probably used it for playing his own violin compositions, including his famed sonatas for violin, cello, and harpsichord. He also possessed a "modern" violin, built by his contemporary Mathias Albani, and this was the one he used when conducting orchestras from his position as concertmaster.[3]

Out of Andrea Amati's vast production, very few instruments—perhaps only fifteen or seventeen—have survived.[4] Regarding an exhibition of Amatis held in Cremona, Charles Beare remarked: "Those who saw these instruments in 1982 were struck by the elegance of their form, the neatness of the hand that made them, and the beauty of their varnish."[5]

Andrea Amati created a dynasty of great stringed-instrument makers, all born in Cremona (see genealogy).[6] Antonio and Girolamo continued their father's work and made numerous violins of exceptional quality, a good number of large violas, tenor violas, and large cellos (or bassettos), most of which were reduced in size during the eighteenth and nineteenth centuries. A smaller version of the viola, the viola contralto, was introduced in Brescia by Gasparo da Salo and his apprentice Giovanni Paolo Maggini. However, the large-sized viola and the cello continued to be the norm until the appearance of Stradivari, around 1700. Because Antonio and Girolamo always worked together, their instruments bear labels with both their names.

The last member of the dynasty, Nicolo, born in 1596, became the most famous of the Amatis. As was the custom at that time, he must have started working when still a child. By 1620 he was the principal

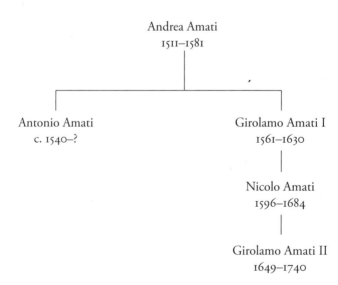

THE AMATI DYNASTY

Andrea Amati
1511–1581

Antonio Amati
c. 1540–?

Girolamo Amati I
1561–1630

Nicolo Amati
1596–1684

Girolamo Amati II
1649–1740

violin maker in the Amati family workshop. In 1628, his instrument production suffered an abrupt suspension that was to last for an entire decade: a dreadful famine, followed by a plague, devastated the region of Cremona and caused the death of a considerable part of the population. Although Nicolo survived, his parents and two of his sisters died. Since Giovanni Paolo Maggini also died, in Brescia, the destiny of Italian violin making remained in the hands of Nicolo. Without Nicolo, it is possible that the violin-making tradition would have been extinguished before Stradivari and Guarneri del Gesù achieved their glories, and that the evolution of stringed instruments would have been entirely different. Perhaps Nicolo left Cremona during those grim years; but a decade later he resumed his activity, as corroborated by the labels appearing on several of his violins.[7]

By 1640, in response to the ever-increasing demand for instruments, Nicolo started hiring assistants and apprentices. The first was Andrea Guarneri, who, in turn, became the founder of another dynasty destined to play a dazzling, fundamental role in the history of violin making. Other outstanding apprentices were Francesco Ruggieri and Giovanni Battista Rogeri.

Finally, it is quite likely that Antonio Stradivari was also once an assistant to Nicolo Amati, although the only possible proof of this assumption is a particular Stradivari violin bearing the following label: *Antonius Stradivari Cremonensis Alumnus Nicolaij Amati, Faciebat Anno 1666.*[8]

THE BRESCIA SCHOOL: GASPARO DA SALO AND GIOVANNI PAOLO MAGGINI

Brescia's violin-making tradition is even more ancient than Cremona's. Luthiers in this small city near Cremona and Venice had already started making these instruments, especially lutes and violas da gamba, during the fifteenth century. Although the names of some of Brescia's earliest violin makers are known to us, like the legendary Giovanni Kerlino (1310–1451) and Zanetto di Montichiaro (1488–?), not one of their instruments has survived.[9]

It is possible both that Brescian violin makers influenced Andrea Amati and that he might have even worked as an apprentice in this city. However, the only established fact is that Andrea Amati worked in Cremona around the year 1540.

The Brescians Gasparo da Salo (1542–1609) and Giovanni Paolo Maggini (1580–1630) built magnificent violins and, above all, incomparable violas, not inferior to those few created by Antonio Stradivari a century and a half later.

JACOB STAINER

Stainer was born in 1617 in Absam, in the Austrian Tyrol.[10] He probably studied in Venice, although some experts believe that he studied for a time under Nicolo Amati in Cremona. Around 1638 he returned to Absam, and his prestige soon extended throughout Europe, as confirmed by the series of instruments built around 1658 on order from the Spanish crown. During his lifetime, he was acknowledged as a master equal to Nicolo Amati, his instruments commanding higher prices than those of Stradivari and much more than those made by Guarneri.

However, his fame gradually declined, although no one has ever questioned the sound quality of his instruments, their beauty, or their excellent workmanship. Their decline in value, according to Jacques Français, is due to the mistaken impression that their sound lacks the power required by the great concert halls of today.

THE GUARNERI DYNASTY

The Guarneri dynasty, which raised Cremona's violin making to new and glorious heights, began with Andrea Guarneri.[11] This particular section will cover Andrea and his sons Pietro of Mantua and Giuseppe. We will discuss his grandson, Pietro of Venice, later on when we discuss the Venetian school of violin making, whereas in view of his importance, we will devote a special section to his grandson Guarneri del Gesù.

ANDREA GUARNERI

Andrea, the founder of the dynasty, was born in 1626, and at the age of ten began working as an apprentice in Nicolo Amati's workshop. The earliest sample of his work is a violin dated 1638, built when he was twelve years old. Andrea lived in the Amati workshop until 1654, and probably created his instruments under the supervision of his teacher, who added finishing touches such as the varnish and the labels.

Andrea Guarneri was no innovator. He continued the tradition of his illustrious teacher by producing excellent instruments that never quite attained Nicolo's levels of perfection and beauty. However, he made two major contributions: beautifully designed violas and a smaller-sized

THE GUARNERI DYNASTY

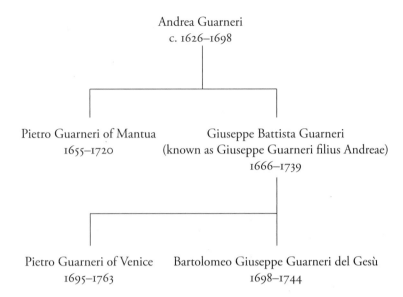

Andrea Guarneri
c. 1626–1698

Pietro Guarneri of Mantua
1655–1720

Giuseppe Battista Guarneri
(known as Giuseppe Guarneri filius Andreae)
1666–1739

Pietro Guarneri of Venice
1695–1763

Bartolomeo Giuseppe Guarneri del Gesù
1698–1744

cello. This new type of cello undoubtedly exerted a strong influence on Stradivari when he conceived his ideal model.

Andrea was not prolific. Perhaps because he worked for Nicolo until the age of twenty-eight, the number of instruments attributed to him is relatively small, since, according to the Hills, they total 250 violins, 14 cellos, and 4 violas.[12]

PIETRO GUARNERI OF MANTUA

Pietro Giovanni Guarneri, better known as Pietro (or Petrus) of Mantua, was born in Cremona in 1655. From a very young age he worked in his father's workshop, where, before long, his exceptional gifts—as well as his original, highly personal touch—came to the fore.

Pietro of Mantua was the only great violin maker who was both a great violinist and viol player. His abilities led him in 1685 to Mantua, where he was appointed master of the violins to the court of the duke of Gonzaga, Ferdinando Carlo.

Mantua was a musical center of greater importance than Cremona. In 1568, the Duke of Gonzaga had founded an academy specializing in poetry and music in that city, where his descendants also became generous patrons of the arts. As mentioned previously, the great Monteverdi, another distinguished citizen of Cremona, joined the Mantuan court in 1583 as a violist, and was subsequently appointed *maestro di cappella*.

While in Mantua, Pietro undoubtedly combined his services as a musician with his activity as a violin maker, which explains the fact that he actually produced few instruments: about fifty violins, and no violas or cellos that we know of. It is unfortunate indeed, because, as the Hills point out, Pietro of Mantua's craftsmanship was superior to that of all his relatives, including his exceptionally gifted nephew Giuseppe Guarneri del Gesù.[13] The varnishes applied to his violins are of incomparable beauty, and the maple and pinewood he selected were always of the finest quality.

GIUSEPPE GUARNERI

Giuseppe Giovanni Battista Guarneri, younger brother of Pietro of Mantua, was later known as Giuseppe Guarneri filius Andreae ("son of Andrea"). He was born in 1666 in Cremona and became an apprentice in his father's workshop, where he worked for a number of years. One of his earliest violins was built in 1690, and another is dated 1696. After Andrea's death in 1698, Giuseppe inherited the workshop. His production was not too extensive, since he is credited with about 250 violins and perhaps 20 cellos.

His instruments adhere to the high standards of craftsmanship so characteristic of that family, and in general his finish was quite good, though the quality of the varnish was irregular. In his best instruments, however, the varnish was superior to that of Andrea, even rivaling that of his brother, Pietro of Mantua, although occasionally the texture tends to be slightly dry and lackluster. His selection of wood also varied considerably in quality. The pine was generally excellent, but the maple was not exceptional, and sometimes he used less attractive poplar and beech. It is possible that the finest wood was reserved for his neighbor Antonio Stradivari, who, with his exceptional talent and unrelenting diligence, undoubtedly eclipsed all his colleagues.

Giuseppe's instruments, and those of the Guarneri family in general, brought prices considerably lower than those commanded by instruments made by Stainer, Amati, or Stradivari, which perhaps explains why Giuseppe produced few instruments during the last twenty years of his life and why he died penniless and in debt.

Giuseppe had two sons, the remarkable del Gesù and Pietro Guarneri of Venice. I will refer to their work after discussing Antonio Stradivari.

*4. Allard violin by Antonio Stradivari,
1715.* CLOCKWISE FROM TOP LEFT:
*Front view, back view, and scroll.
Photos by Stewart Pollens.*

ANTONIO STRADIVARI AND THE ZENITH
OF VIOLIN MAKING

Antonio Stradivari (1644–1737) represents the highest point in the history of violinmaking.[14] No one has ever surpassed the sheer quality of the tone, beauty, and perfect craftsmanship of his instruments.

At a very young age he worked as an apprentice and assistant under the great Nicolo Amati in Cremona, but soon began working on his own. Not only did he inherit the great Cremona tradition and incorporate the Brescian virtues of violin making, but he was also a great innovator who never ceased to experiment in the search for the perfect instrument.

His contemporaries were in awe of his tremendous capacity for hard work and of his talent. He must have had an iron constitution, since he worked indefatigably for seventy years until his death at the age of ninety-five. One of the very few surviving descriptions of him is extremely eloquent: "He was tall and thin in appearance, invariably to be seen in his working costume, which rarely changed, as he was always at work."[15] It is not surprising, therefore, that he left such a large number of instruments. In their fundamental book on Stradivari, the Hills estimate a total of 1,500 instruments, of which 600 violins, 60 cellos, and 10 violas still remain. Of course, it is impossible to determine the exact number of instruments that have been either lost or destroyed over these past three centuries.

STRADIVARI'S VIOLINS

Although one must be wary of generalizations, Stradivari's violins can be divided into three categories. His earliest violins, built between 1666 and 1690, reflect the influence of Nicolo Amati in their shape (featuring a distinctive arch in the central section), in their relatively small size, and in the yellowish gold varnish. For these reasons, this type of violin bears the French name *amatisé*.

By 1690, feeling the need to venture into uncharted territory, Stradivari designed a new type of violin. It was much longer and larger, combining the distinctively smooth sound of the Amati with the darker, more potent sound of the Brescian instruments, like Maggini's. Since practically all of Stradivari's violins from 1692 to 1697 tended to be longer, they are known as *longuets*. After 1699 he never made them again.

One exceptional violin, dated 1704 and called the Betts, indicates that Stradivari had attained his objective in regard to tone: except for a few minor details, from then on he never deviated from the building principles underlying this particular instrument. Of an intermediate size between the amatisés and the longuets, the violins of Stradivari's last period are distinguished by their velvety though powerful sound.

STRADIVARI'S CELLOS

Stradivari's cellos can also be divided into three groups. The first thirty, built between 1684 and 1700, are all large. These cellos were perfectly suited to the cello music repertoire prior to 1700, but their size made them too cumbersome for the new cello compositions that called for a singing tone in the upper registers of the A string. Therefore, most of the Stradivari cellos from that period, with one exception, have been reduced in size. Although the "surgery" was properly performed in some cases, several of those majestic old cellos are now mere shadows of their former splendor because of the botched efforts of inexperienced or irresponsible violin makers.

Two magnificent cellos from 1700 clearly indicate that Stradivari was striving for a new, smaller type of instrument: the Cristiani and the cello at the Royal Palace in Madrid, both smaller than their predecessors.

TABLE I

Name of cello and year constructed	Current owner
Castelbarco, 1707	Aurora Nátola-Ginastera
Gore-Booth (or Rothschild), 1710	Rocco Filippini
Mara, 1711	Heinrich Schiff
Duport, 1711	Mstislav Rostropovich
Romberg, 1711	Private collection
Davidov, 1712	Private collection, assigned to Yo-Yo Ma
Bass of Spain, 1713	David L. Fulton
Batta, 1714	Evan Drachman
Suggia, 1717	Private collection
Piatti, 1720	Carlos Prieto
Hausmann, 1724	Private collection
Baudiot, 1725	Evan Drachman
Chevillard, 1725	Museum of Music, Lisbon
Vaslin, 1725	Private collection, Hong Kong
Marquis de Corberon, 1726	Royal Academy of Music, London

In 1707, Stradivari broke with tradition by presenting us what the Hills have described as the *ne plus ultra* of perfection, the ideal type of cello.[16] Although no two cellos are identical, the basic model did not change between 1707 and 1727. Table 1 shows instruments from this period.

Toward the end of his life, Stradivari made five much smaller cellos. The finest of these, the De Munck from 1730, became famous because it was the favorite of Emanuel Feuermann and was later owned by Aldo Parisot.

The last cello attributed to Stradivari, dated 1736, bears its original label that reads *D'Anni 92*, which means that its was built when its creator was ninety-two years old. Curiously enough, this cello reverts to the old pattern from the 1707–1726 period as if, after experimenting with five small cellos, Stradivari had finally decided that the previous model was the ideal after all; it is also possible that this cello was specially commissioned.

STRADIVARI'S VIOLAS

When Stradivari embarked on his long career, violas were relatively large, in accordance with the models created by Andrea Amati, Gasparo da Salo, and Maggini. However, several violin makers, particularly the brothers Antonio and Girolamo Amati, Stainer, and Andrea Guarneri had built smaller violas.

Stradivari, who was such a prolific instrument maker, devoted so little time to violas that we only know of ten. His first viola, dating from 1772, is quite small, even smaller than the aforementioned instruments. Later, in 1690 and 1696, he created two very large violas and two others of intermediate size for two quintets, each comprising two violins, two violas (the large one was a tenor and the other a contralto), and one cello. All the rest of his violas are of an intermediate size. Although one cannot help admiring the beauty and sound of these instruments, Stradivari's genius was most clearly evident in his violins and cellos rather than in his violas.

The small number of violas he made is probably because his life coincided with a transition period in the role of violas in music. We must bear in mind that Corelli's earliest compositions, the twelve trios for two violins and bass written in 1681, do not include a part for viola, and that the first works where the viola played an important part were Corelli's twelve concerti grossi published in 1714. However, these concertos could also be performed in a version without violas. Furthermore, the parts for viola in the concerti grossi, as well as in later works by Handel and Bach, rarely require a player to move from the first position in order to play the higher notes. This music could be easily played on the large violas, such as those by da Salo, Andrea Amati, and Maggini, whose tone is truly incomparable. Perhaps the first work that accords the viola a solo role is Bach's Sixth Brandenburg Concerto, whose instrumentation is highly unusual. Two violas and one cello constitute the solo group—with a marked predominance of the violas—and two violas da gamba, a contrabass, and a cembalo form the *ripieno*, or main body of the orchestra, which, along with the soloists, plays the ritornellos. The virtuoso role played by the violas in the first and third movements, as well as their melodically expressive role in the second movement, were regarded as a genuine innovation.

We must recall that it was Haydn and Boccherini who, after Stradivari's death, transformed the viola into a vital instrument for their string quartets. The first of Haydn's quartets dates from 1755, and the first of Boccherini's quartets was published in Paris in 1768. It was probably for these reasons that Stradivari received very few commissions for violas and why he decided on the intermediate-sized violas, whose smaller dimensions and lighter weight made them more comfortable to play.

Among Stradivari's most famous violas, we can mention the 1701 Macdonald, played for several decades by Peter Schidlof, the violist of the Amadeus Quartet, and the 1731 Paganini, similar in character to the Macdonald.

On Paganini's first visit to England in 1832, when he became acquainted with the 1731 viola, he purchased it to complete a quartet of Stradivari's instruments. Paganini was so enthusiastic about his viola, and there were so few compositions for this instrument, that he commissioned Hector Berlioz to write a symphony with a major solo part for the viola, for which he paid 20,000 francs. Berlioz describes the encounter as follows: "Paganini came to me and said 'I have a marvelous viola, an admirable Stradivari, and I wish to play it in public. But I have no music *ad hoc*. Will you write a solo piece for the viola? You are the only one I can trust for such a work."[17] The result was *Harold in Italy*, a symphony for viola and orchestra. However, Paganini, displeased with the work, refused to perform it because it was excessively orchestral and did not give the viola an opportunity to shine as much as Paganini had intended.

FRANCESCO STRADIVARI (1671–1743) AND OMOBONO STRADIVARI (1679–1742)

The circumstances surrounding the sons of Stradivari, Francesco and Omobono, are mysterious indeed. We know that they were both excellent violin makers who worked in their father's workshop. Compared to the approximately 1,000 instruments produced by Antonio, the number of instruments built by his children seems meager indeed: twenty-six instruments by Francesco and six by Omobono.[18]

The two brothers were considerably overshadowed by their father's dazzling virtuosity as a violin maker, although they probably made many more instruments than those actually attributed to them. Although they undoubtedly collaborated with their father in repairing instruments and preparing materials for new instruments, it is also true that a good number of instruments were erroneously credited to Antonio. From the late eighteenth century onward, the increasing fame and value of his particular instruments must have constituted powerful incentives for merchants and violin makers to place labels bearing Antonio's name on instruments actually produced by Francesco and Omobono.[19]

In some of the instruments that Antonio made after turning eighty, one can detect a helping hand. Some instruments may have been collaborations, whereas others were probably made entirely by Francesco and Omobono. A case in point is the magnificent 1732 Stuart cello, which, according to Simone Sacconi, is the work of Francesco and Omobono and not of their father, to whom it has been attributed.[20]

THE EXTRAORDINARY CASE OF
GIUSEPPE GUARNERI DEL GESÙ (1698–1744)

Giuseppe Guarneri del Gesù was born in Cremona in 1698, when Stradivari was already fifty-four years old.[21] He learned the craft from his father, Giuseppe, while his coworkers in the workshop were his brother Pietro of Venice and Carlo Bergonzi, another future great violinmaker.

Before long, del Gesù started working on his own. His earliest violins still reflect the influence of his family, of his colleague Bergonzi, and, naturally, of Stradivari. Although they also express his outstanding craftsmanship and strong personality, no one in 1730 could possibly have predicted his astonishing originality or the incomparable quality of his future instruments.

In 1737, Stradivari, who for sixty years had outshone the Guarneri family, died at the age of ninety-three. Perhaps del Gesù was aware that, from that moment on, he was Stradivari's only possible heir. His contemporaries, however, did not seem to agree, since they clearly preferred instruments made by Stainer, the Amatis, and Stradivari, in that order.

The work of del Gesù, the most enigmatic of the great violinmakers, characterizes, along with that Antonio Stradivari, the most glorious peak in the art of violin making. His name, del Gesù, was inspired by a cross and by the initials *IHS* that appear next to his name on the labels placed in his instruments' interiors. IHS may be an abbreviation of the Greek transliteration of the Hebrew name for Jesus, IH (ΣΟΥ)Σ, or perhaps the abbreviation of *Iesus Hominum Salvator* (Jesus, Savior of Man).

The life and work of del Gesù are enveloped in mystery and legend. It was said that toward the end of his life he spent several years in prison for having killed a fellow violin maker in a street brawl, and even that the jailer's daughter, moved by his plight, provided him with tools and materials so he could continue working behind bars. Apparently these imputations have been disproved, the source of these rumors and the identity of the actual violin maker who killed a colleague having been discovered in Milan.

Del Gesù, unlike the long-lived, highly prolific Stradivari, died at the age of forty-six, leaving a relatively small production. Whereas Stradivari made an estimated 1,500 instruments of different types, del Gesù's legacy amounts to no more than 150 violins, only one cello, and not a single viola. During his lifetime, his violins were not highly sought after. Guarneri's clients were not kings, princes, or noblemen, but rather modest local musicians. This situation, however, changed during the early nineteenth century, largely thanks to the Mantegazza brothers, violin makers and instrument merchants in Milan, and perhaps the first to detect the unique character and quality of Guarneri's violins.

It was Niccolò Paganini who brought about a dramatic reassessment of del Gesù's reputation, since throughout his dazzling career he performed with one of del Gesù's most remarkable violins. This instrument, dubbed Il Cannone by Paganini himself for its extremely potent sound, is now also known as the Paganini. According to the Hills, a Frenchman named Monsieur Livron gave this instrument to the fifteen-year-old Paganini, who had lost his violin to gambling debts. Although Paganini owned many violins in his lifetime, Il Cannone always remained his favorite. At his death, he bequeathed it to his native city of Genoa on the condition that it be preserved there forever: *Legio il mio violino alla cittá di Genova onde sia perpetuamente conservato.*[22]

A great many illustrious violinists have fallen in love with del Gesù's violins. Since I have already mentioned Paganini, I will also add the names of Joseph Joachim, Henri Vieuxtemps, Henryk Wieniawski, Eugene Ysaÿe, Jascha Heifetz, Fritz Kreisler, Itzhak Perlman, Isaac Stern, Henryk Szeryng, Pinchas Zukerman, Gidon Kremer, and Elmar Oliveira.

Toward the end of 1994, I had the good fortune to attend an exceptional exhibition organized by Peter Biddulph at the Metropolitan Museum of Art in New York. For the first time, under the same roof, twenty-five of Del Gesù's most important violins were exhibited to the public. The event took place on the 250th anniversary of Del Gesù's death. For purposes of simplification, I will list only ten of the violins on display:

The Stretton (1726), one of the earliest of the del Gesù violins, now the property of Elmar Oliveira

The Kreisler (1733), which for many years belonged to Fritz Kreisler, who subsequently donated it to the Library of Congress

The marvelous Violon du Diable (1734), one of the most perfectly preserved del Gesùs

The Joachim (1737)

The Ysaÿe (1740), which belonged to Isaac Stern

The Heifetz, or David (1740), which Jascha Heifetz used until his death and which he bequeathed to the Fine Arts Museum of San Francisco

The Vieuxtemps (1741)

The Sauret (1742), currently the property of Itzhak Perlman

The Paganini (Il Cannone), Paganini's favorite, dated 1742, one of two del Gesù violins still preserving their original necks

The Leduc (1743), covered with a rare reddish varnish, its narrow scroll and elongated *F*'s characteristic of Del Gesù's last period; owned by Henryk Szeryng until his death

THE VENICE SCHOOL AND THE EXCELLENCE OF ITS CELLOS

I have already referred to the intense musical activity that distinguished Venice from other cities.[23] The first opera house was founded in Venice in 1637. By the end of that century, it had added eleven more opera houses, evidence, in a city of 140,000, of a genuine passion for music and opera.

Monteverdi, appointed *maestro di cappella* of St. Mark's Cathedral in 1613, doubled the size of his orchestra, from twelve to twenty-four musicians. His successor, Giovanni Legrenzi (1626–1690), not only increased the number to thirty-four but also decided to replace the gambists with violinists and cellists.

Undoubtedly, it was the establishment of the four *ospedale* that considerably influenced the development of Venetian music. The ospedale were institutions where poor, abandoned, or orphaned girls were taught science, philosophy, and music in order to prepare them for marriage. However, some of the female students who opted to stay in the ospedale became excellent music teachers of future virtuosos.

Antonio Vivaldi, born in Venice in 1678, was a teacher at the Pio Ospedale della Pietà from 1703 to 1740. In addition to being a great violinist, he composed 27 cello concertos, among the first ever written for this instrument, as well as 250 violin concertos. Benedetto Marcello (1686–1739) was another well-known Venetian composer who accorded the cello a particularly prominent role.

All the above factors account for the development of violin making in Venice. Its founder was a German, Martin Kaiser, known for his superb lutes. However, it was Matteo Goffriller (1659–1742) who actually initiated the great Venetian violin-making tradition. Goffriller, a student of Kaiser's, was born in Bressanone, a small Italian town near the Austrian border. He arrived in Venice in 1685, and for the next twenty-five years he was its only violin and cello maker. His cellos are highly regarded. Pablo Casals himself played a Goffriller during his entire career, claiming he had never found a cello as well suited to his hands. Pierre Fournier and Janos Starker also played cellos made by this master.

Domenico Montagnana (1687–1750) arrived in Venice as a child and was trained in Goffriller's workshop. Around 1711 he opened his own shop, where he received numerous commissions for cellos, an increasingly popular instrument in Venice. His wide robust cellos bear his distinctive personal touch (Figure 4), and their characteristics, entirely different from those of instruments made by his contemporaries from Cremona or Venice, produce a marvelous tone, distinguished by its power and masculinity. Gregor Piatigorsky for many years played a famous Montagnana before purchasing two Stradivari cellos: the Batta (1714) and the Baudiot (1726). Yo-Yo Ma owns a Montagnana and plays a Stradivari (the Davidov, 1712, which is owned by a foundation that has assigned it to Ma) and selects one or the other, depending on the particular composition he is performing.

Pietro Guarneri of Venice (1695–1762) was the brother of del Gesù and the son of Giuseppe Guarneri, from whom he learned the craft in his native Cremona. He is considered a prominent member of the Venetian School because he left Cremona in 1717 and moved to Venice,

*5. Cello by Domenico Montagnana, Venice (front and back views).
Photos by Stewart Pollens.*

where he worked until his death. Consequently, he is known as Pietro Guarneri of Venice. In a market dominated by the name Stradivari, the Guarneri house in Cremona understandably received few commissions. Pietro Guarneri was especially attracted to Venice's intense musical activity and the greater opportunities it offered. When he started working in his adopted city, it was first with Montagnana and later on with Carlo Tononi, and before long he went on his own. Naturally, his earliest instruments bore the distinctive Cremona touch, though later on he developed his own personal style. His cellos in particular are veritable jewels of elegance, beauty, and tone.

When Pietro Guarneri died in 1762, the great violin-making tradition in Venice came to an end, as had occurred in Cremona after the death of his brother del Gesù in 1744. However, gifted violin makers from other countries soon came to the fore: Nicolas Lupot and Jean-Baptiste Vuillaume in France; José Contreras, "El Granadino," in Spain; William Forster in England; and the Guadagnini dynasty in Italy. Nevertheless, the death of Pietro of Venice in 1762 marked the end of violinmaking's glorious golden age.

SEASONING OF THE INSTRUMENTS

It is interesting to note that during Stradivari's and del Gesù's lifetimes—and even for several decades after their deaths—older instruments, such as those by Amati or Stainer, were in far greater demand. Whereas in 1775 Amati's violins were valued at forty *gigliati* (the gold currency of that time), Stradivari's were worth a third of this price, from twelve to fifteen gigliati.[24] Del Gesù's instruments commanded an even lower price. One great collector, Count Cozio de Salabue, even claimed that prior to 1800 one could acquire "several del Gesù instruments for two or three gigliati."[25]

TABLE 2

Violin maker	Instrument detail	Seasoning period (years)
Stainer	all	10–15
Nicolo Amati	average sized	20–25
Nicolo Amati	large	30–35
Stradivari	made before 1710	30–50
Stradivari	made from 1710 to 1736	50–60
Guarneri del Gesù	representative	50–80

6. Cello by Pietro Guarneri of Venice, 1726.

One particular factor that might explain this phenomenon is the "seasoning" of the instruments, that is, the period required for them to reach their fullest tonal potential. The length of this period depends on the nature of the instrument and on the quality of the wood. The Hills, a celebrated family of London dealers and violin makers, devised a table, reproduced here in an abbreviated form (Table 2), regarding the relative maturing or seasoning period required for violins made by the most renowned violin makers.[26]

This phenomenon had been common knowledge for quite some time. In 1720 the Italian violin maker and composer Francesco Veracini (1690–1750) was appointed violin soloist to the private orchestra of Augustus II, king of Poland. Five years earlier, Jean Baptiste Volumier, the conductor, had arrived in Cremona to await the completion of twelve violins, which the king had especially ordered from Stradivari. Hart observed, "Though they were new, their tones were doubtless rich and beautiful. Veracini, it may be assumed, saw, heard, and played upon these comparatively new Stradivari violins. He, however, whilst fully alive to their sterling merits, played, in all probability, upon his Stainers with more pleasure, from their being fully matured."[27]

THE IMPORTANCE OF VARNISH

The varnish used by Cremona's violin makers is legendary. Although it was Stradivari who accorded varnish its greatest splendor, as Charles Beare points out, "its basic magic was already applied to the productions of Andrea Amati, and to those of his Brescian contemporaries."[28]

Varnish was a liquid applied to the exterior of the instruments after they were finished, and once it dried, endowed both the wood and their tone with incredible beauty. The purpose of varnish was also to preserve the wood in prime condition and protect it from insects.

Not all varnishes were the same. In the instruments made by the Amati family, for example, there was a predominance of beautifully golden yellow tones. Stradivari, on the other hand, used several colors ranging from gold to orange and even to dark red. The Guarneri family also used a variety of varnishes. However, they all had the same magical effect. These varnishes were not the result of a jealously guarded secret formula. Probably one very simple ingredient in these varnishes is now unfamiliar to us, which is perhaps why the secret of the varnish has been lost. Without a doubt, the varnish was among the key factors behind the incomparable quality of the instruments produced in Cremona, Venice, and Brescia.

SOME OBSERVATIONS ON MODERN INSTRUMENTS

I am familiar with several outstanding modern cellos, most of them copies of Stradivaris, Montagnanas, Amatis, or Goffrillers. They have a magnificent tone and have earned their rightful place among musicians. Of course, we have no way of predicting how well those instruments will fare in the future and how the seasoning process will affect them. The very fact that contemporary violin makers tend to model their instruments on the masterpieces of the past is an indication that the art of the Cremonese, Venetian, or Brescian makers of the seventeenth and eighteenth centuries is still considered the epitome of perfection.

THE HYPERCELLO AND THE SOUND BUGS

I wrote in the preceding chapter that "art is always a reflection of historic evolution and that, therefore, music and musical instruments undergo the transformations that every era imposes upon them." The reader will recall how the violin family displaced the viols in the eighteenth century. In our era of unprecedented technological and scientific progress, many radically new instruments and means of producing music have already emerged. Tod Machover and his teams have created fantastic new instruments at the Media Lab of the Massachusetts Institute of Technology. Machover calls his musical-computer creations "hyperinstruments." Among them, there is an instrument called the hypercello, which he created in collaboration with Yo-Yo Ma. There are also hyperviolins, hyperpianos, "sound bugs," and other instruments that merge the sounds of traditional instruments and synthesizers with easy-to-control computer interfaces.

Will these and other and other inventions gradually displace traditional instruments from the central place they occupy in music? Will our violins, violas, and cellos still have a vital role in the music of the twenty-second or twenty-third centuries? Will the music of Bach, Beethoven, Debussy, Bartók, or Shostakovich be as close to the hearts of the music fans of the future as it is to those of today?

Part Two

∫ THE ADVENTURES OF A
STRADIVARI CELLO FROM
1720 TO THE PRESENT

CHAPTER 3

∫ The Adventures of a Stradivari Cello: From Cremona in 1720 to New York in 1979

THE BIRTH OF THE PIATTI CELLO

In 1720, at the age of seventy-six, Stradivari made fourteen violins and only one cello, the protagonist of this book, later to be known as the Piatti. Despite Stradivari's age, his capacity for hard work and his craftsmanship remained unaltered. His second wife, Antonia Maria Zambelli, by whom he had five children, managed his household at No. 1 Piazza San Domenico, thus enabling him to devote all the daylight hours to his instruments. Not even the death of his daughter Francesca Maria in 1720 seems to have affected his work.[1]

MATERIALS AND CHARACTERISTICS OF THE 1720 CELLO

Stradivari took great pains in selecting the wood for his new cello. The maple for both the back and the head came from a stock of wood obtained that same year from a tree native to the Balkans. He liked that kind of maple because of its acoustic qualities—a rich, resonant sound—and for its beautiful delicate markings. The back consists of two pieces. The head, with its exquisitely sculptured scroll, is, in itself, a work of art. The sides are also made of maple, with rich broad markings. They come from a different tree, whose wood was also used for subsequent cellos. The top, or belly, is made from two pieces of pine from the Dolomites; its grain is fine and uniform. The softly textured varnish is a deep reddish color. (See Fig. 5) It took Stradivari slightly over a month to make this cello. Once finished, it was hung in front of a large window in his workshop so that the sun would dry the marvelous varnish.

This cello was to be one of the finest he made during his long life. Many years later, in their book about Stradivari, the Hill brothers observed, "The Piatti bass is indeed an admirable example, by itself a worthy monument of the maker. . . . As a whole, it is above reproach and the more one contemplates such an instrument, the more one is struck by the complete harmony which reigns throughout."[2]

UNCERTAINTY ABOUT WHO ORDERED THE PIATTI

The disparity between the number of violins and cellos made by Stradivari was obviously due to the greater demand for violins. Many of his violins were commissioned, specifically destined for the palaces of the nobility and for the church. Such is the case, as mentioned earlier, of the twelve violins commissioned from Stradivari by Augustus II of Poland in

1715.[3] However, Stradivari also built violins on his own, since they were easy to sell.

Cellos were an entirely different story. Stradivari only sold one or two cellos a year, and almost always on commission, since making a cello takes much longer to complete and is physically more demanding than making a violin. Those who ordered his cellos included Cardinal Orsini (the future Pope Benedict XIII) in 1685; the Duke of Modena, Francesco II, in 1686; Prince Ferdinand of Tuscany in 1690; the Duke of Toralba ordered one as a gift for the Duke of Alba in 1702; and the Marquis Desiderio Cleri in 1707, for the royal court of Spain.[4] Although this also appears to be the case of the 1720 cello, I have been unable

7. Piatti cello by Antonio Stradivari, 1720. FROM LEFT: Front view, back view, side view, and scroll. Photos by Stewart Pollens.

to find concrete data in this regard; tracing its history has been an extremely complicated task. Stradivari's instruments did not have the fame or value that they acquired later. We know the complete history of only very few instruments. Although the price of these instruments was not as high as those paid for Stainers or Amatis, few musicians could afford to purchase Stradivari's cellos or violins, and there is no record of any cello commissioned in 1720 either by the French or Spanish courts or by the aristocracy. England still had little contact with Stradivari, whereas in Vienna and in the German cities, Italian instruments were not yet fully appreciated. The excellent orchestra conducted by Bach in Cöthen, precisely at the time when the 1720 cello was made, possessed several Stainers but not a single Italian instrument.

Therefore, we may logically assume that the special order for the Piatti came from an Italian city like Mantua, Milan, or Naples—but not from Venice. Although the latter was certainly a widely recognized musical capital, the demand for cellos there was fulfilled by three prominent local violin makers distinguished precisely for the excellent quality of their cellos: Matteo Goffriller, Domenico Montagnana, and Pietro Guarneri of Venice (see Fig. 6 for an example of Pietro's work).

THE PIATTI'S EARLY YEARS: 1720–1762 IN CREMONA

It is of little consequence who actually ordered this cello. It is quite possible that Antonio Stradivari and Francesco and Omobono, his sons and collaborators, did not sell it in 1720 but rather decided to keep it. At Stradivari's death in 1737, his son Francesco inherited all the instruments that remained in the workshop: ninety-two violins, five violas, and the following three cellos: a decorated instrument made prior to 1700 for the king of Spain, the 1720 cello, and another heretofore unidentified cello from Stradivari's last period.

Stradivari was born a Spanish subject. In 1644, the year of his birth, Cremona and the duchy of Milan belonged to the Spanish crown. In 1702, the king of Spain, Philip V, happened to be in Italy, fighting against the Austrian and British troops during the War of the Spanish Succession, in which he also successfully defended the kingdoms of Naples and Sicily. When he passed through Cremona in July and October of 1702, Stradivari wanted to take advantage of the occasion to solemnly present him with the special set of instruments he had ordered. However, Stradivari was prevented from doing so by the municipal authorities, probably because of the increasing political differences generated by the war.

After Antonio's death in 1737, Francesco sold some of the instruments remaining in the workshop, including the cello from Stradivari's last period. Consequently, at his own death, barely five years later, it was his younger brother Paolo who inherited the vast collection of instruments, impressive not only for its quantity but for its quality as well.

On many of the instruments, though not all, Paolo wrote the initials *ps* (Paolo Stradivari) on the mortise of the head, as in the case of such remarkable violins as King Maximilian (1709), Soil (1714), Allard (1715; see Fig. 7), Lady Blunt (1721), and Sarasate (1724). However, that inscription did not appear on the ornamented instruments, on the famous 1716 Messiah, or, for that matter, on the Piatti.

Around 1760, a cellist by the name of Carlo Moro approached Paolo with the intention of buying one of the two cellos. I have been unable to find out much of anything about Moro's time in Italy except that he was protected by the dukes of Mantua and was an acquaintance of Paolo Stradivari's. Paolo refused to sell him the decorated cello that formed part of the quintet created for the Spanish crown. He would only sell only the entire quintet.[5] With the support of the Mantuan court, Moro succeeded in convincing Paolo to sell him the other cello, that is, the Piatti. Shortly after, this instrument left Cremona, the town where it had remained practically untouched for forty years.

Moro was a young musician obsessed with the idea of seeking his fortune in Spain. He was dazzled by the wonderful stories about the musical activities in Spain and about the warm reception accorded there to Italian musicians like Farinelli, Scarlatti, and Boccherini, among others.

THE PIATTI IN CÁDIZ, 1762–1818

In 1762 a certain impresario asked a group of musicians, including Moro, to join an opera orchestra scheduled to begin its activities in Cádiz that same year. Moro and his 1720 Stradivari traveled by coach, first from Cremona to Milan, and from there to Genoa. The passengers were crammed together in the small space, and the cello, in a heavy wooden box, had been placed on the top rack along with the rest of the baggage. This was to be the first of many voyages undertaken by the 1720 Stradivari during its long life. Along with another group of musicians, the party sailed from Genoa, a port that maintained close ties with Cádiz. They arrived a few days later, and immediately joined the Italian Opera Theater.

Cádiz is an exceptional city because of its location: an island and a port city at one of the world's major international maritime crossroads. Its position as an Atlantic seaport was a decisive factor in the prosperity it achieved during the Spanish colonization of the New World. Cádiz's remarkable wealth throughout the seventeenth century increased considerably during the eighteenth. As Maria Pemán pointed out, "The customs duties collected at the Cádiz customhouse were four times greater than that of Barcelona and far superior to the total collected in the rest of Spain."[6] At the same time, Cádiz developed a refined, cultured lifestyle. Excellent libraries and painting collections were established, along with an increasing taste for music.

Several thousand foreigners were living in Cádiz when Moro arrived, mostly French or Genoese involved in commercial activities. Moro was certainly not the first Italian musician to settle in Cádiz; during the early part of the eighteenth century, many prominent Italian musicians also lived and worked there. There was, for example, Ignacio de Jerusalem, a composer and violinist born in Italy in 1710, regarded by his contemporaries as a "musical marvel," who frequently performed at the Coliseo de Cádiz. In 1742, a new theater in Mexico City received authorization to hire music and dance teachers from Cádiz. Consequently, Jerusalem departed for Mexico City, where he remained until his death.

Although Moro was constantly working, he could not afford any luxuries. In 1773, eleven years after his arrival in Cádiz, his financial situation worsened when operatic activity in Cádiz ceased and he was suddenly deprived of his main source of income. It was not until 1787 that operatic activities in Cádiz were resumed.

Fortunately, Moro had become acquainted with several prominent figures in the Cádiz of the Enlightenment era. The first was Father José Sáenz de Santa María, who in 1773 helped Moro obtain a position in the cathedral's orchestra and who was destined to play a decisive role in the lives of Moro and the 1720 Stradivari. Father Santa María also made sure that Moro participated in the chamber-music sessions held in the salons of Cádiz's most enlightened aristocracy. It was under these circumstances that Moro met the Marquis of Méritos, with whom he established a linguistic and musical rapport. The marquis spoke perfect Italian, since his father, an Italian-born magnate, had sent him to Geneva, Florence, Bologna, and Naples for two years. Furthermore, he had a passion for music and was a friend of Haydn's.[7]

Moro also knew the Marquis of Ureña, an outstanding amateur musician, who, according to Pemán Medina, "mastered several instruments like the violin, viola, bassoon, flute, clavichord and organ. He composed some pieces, commendable for their good taste and elegance, which he played in the company of his friends, both amateurs and professionals."[8] Moro was one of the professional musicians most frequently invited by the marquis.

FATHER SANTA MARÍA, THE SANTA CUEVA, AND *THE SEVEN LAST WORDS* OF HAYDN

The first documented concert featuring the 1720 Stradivari was held on Good Friday 1787 in the Santa Cueva de Cádiz.[9] Let us briefly review the background.

Since 1730, a certain religious brotherhood had been meeting every Good Friday to practice the rites known as the Passion of Our Lord. In 1756, a cave discovered next to the Church of the Rosary was subsequently adapted as a place for the members of the brotherhood to celebrate their rituals, and ever since it has gone by the name of Santa Cueva (the Holy Cave; see Fig. 8).

After being ordained in 1761, Father Santa María had moved from Cádiz to Madrid, where he fulfilled his priestly duties. One morning in May 1764, in response to an invitation from a distinguished member of the court, he set out for the Royal Palace, but suddenly refused to go any further, deeply distressed over the sharp contrast between the opulence he had observed there and the sheer poverty of many churches in Cádiz. Father Santa María vowed, then and there, to improve the conditions of at least one church in which he hoped to render his religious services. Father Santa María returned to Cádiz in 1766, and in 1771 became the director of the brotherhood, which "prospered considerably thanks to his apostolic zeal and exceptional virtues."[10]

On Good Friday 1774, Father Santa María invited Carlo Moro to the spiritual exercises at the Holy Cave. Moro was profoundly impressed by the spirituality of the ceremony: every wall and window of the cave was draped with black cloth, and only a dim light illuminated the area. At midday the doors were closed and the ceremony began. It included, as always, a reading of Christ's utterances on the cross, traditionally known as the Seven Last Words of Christ. After reading each utterance, the priest reflected briefly on it, and then proceeded to read the next, and so on.

When Santa María's father died in 1778, he inherited the title of marquis of Valde Íñigo along with a substantial fortune. Father Santa María, now the marquis of Valde Íñigo, knew immediately what he would do with his newfound wealth. In 1781 he financed the total renovation and

8. Santa Cueva (Holy Cave), Cádiz. Photo by Arenas.

expansion of the Santa Cueva. On Good Friday 1783, the Passion services were conducted in the newly refurbished Santa Cueva.

It is interesting to note that the liturgy for celebrating the Passion, also known as the "Three-Hour Devotion," originated in the New World—in Peru, to be exact. According to Robert Stevenson, it was the Peruvian Jesuit Francisco del Castillo (1615–1673) who introduced this practice by congregating the faithful of Lima on Good Friday from midday until three in the afternoon to meditate on the Seven Last Words.[11] Alonso Messia Bedoya (1655–1732), another Peruvian Jesuit, came up with the idea of incorporating musical passages into the meditations, and established this devotion in a book posthumously published in Seville, in 1757.

In view of the above, and in order to accord greater significance to this devotion, Father Santa María decided to commission a musical piece from the most eminent composer of the time. Moro suggested his compatriot, Boccherini, who had been living in Spain since 1768 and had acquired considerable fame. However, Father Santa María had set his sights much higher, on Franz Joseph Haydn, no less. Haydn was the most famous and admired composer of the period, particularly in Spain and the Spanish-speaking world. He lived near Vienna, in the Esterháza palace, where he was kapellmeister of the superb orchestra that played in Prince Nikolaus Esterházy's chapel.

For Moro, who was a modest cellist, the very thought of commissioning a work from Haydn seemed sheer lunacy. However, Father Santa María knew exactly how to go about it. To contact Haydn, the priest requested the intercession of his friend and fellow brotherhood member, Francisco de Paula María de Micón, marquis of Méritos, mentioned above. He was a cultured noble, an accomplished musician, *maestro de capilla* of the Cádiz Cathedral, and a friend of Haydn's. The Marquis of Méritos commissioned the work by means of a letter he sent Haydn in 1785, including a detailed description of this composition's principal characteristics. Haydn accepted the commission and in 1786 proceeded to compose *Die sieben letzten Worte unseres Erlösers am Kreuze* (*The Seven Last Words of Our Savior on the Cross*).

According to Haydn, the explanations contained in the Marquis of Méritos's letter were extremely helpful to his composition process. It is a shame that Haydn's correspondence with the marquis was lost in Spain, but one of Haydn's nephews recalled that in the letter enclosed with his work, Haydn wrote that "the composition owed more to the explanation that he had received in writing from Sr. de Micón than to his own creation because in its own unique fashion, it led him through every step of the way, to the point that, while reading the instructions from Spain, it seemed as though he was actually reading the music."[12]

A friend of Haydn's, Albert Christoph Dies, wrote numerous accounts of his visits to the composer. In one particular case, undoubtedly echoing Haydn's own opinion, he says the following about de Micón's letter: "The succinct explanation is a great credit to the Spanish author. He must have had the sensitivity of a great poet to realize that a few brief words, so vividly uttered, can touch the heart. Furthermore, in order to make them plainly understandable, they were not expressed in song but rather in words, further clarified by a brief sermon."[13]

Haydn himself wrote the following description:

The walls, windows and pillars of the church were hung with black cloth, and only one large lamp hanging from the center of the roof broke the solemn obscurity. At midday the doors were closed and the ceremony began. . . . The bishop ascended the pulpit, pronounced the first of the seven words (or sentences) and delivered a discourse thereon. This ended, he left the pulpit and prostrated himself before the altar. The pause was filled with music. The bishop then in like manner pronounced the second word, then the third, and so on, the orchestra following on the conclusion of each discourse. My composition was subject to these conditions, and it was no easy matter to compose seven adagios to last ten minutes each, and succeed one another without fatiguing the listeners.[14]

The original instrumentation consisted of two flutes, two oboes, two bassoons, two trumpets, four English horns, two timpani, and strings. Haydn's score arrived in Cádiz early in 1787. Its complete title is *Musica instrumentale sopra le sette ultime parole del Nostro Redentore in croce, ossiano Sette Sonate con una introduzione, ed alfine un Terremoto* (*Instrumental Music on the Seven Last Words of Our Redeemer on the Cross, namely, Seven Sonatas with an introduction, and an Earthquake at the End*). Both the Introduction (*maestoso ed adagio*) and the sonatas are written in slow tempos (three largos, two graves, one adagio, and one lento). Only the "Earthquake" is of an entirely different nature: a *presto e con tutta la forza* (rapidly and very forcefully).

Its world premiere was held on Good Friday 1787 in the Santa Cueva. It goes without saying that Father Santa María spared no expense for such a grand occasion. He was acquainted with the finest musicians in Cádiz—among them, Carlo Moro, whose cello, along with the many other Stradivari instruments in Spain, was acquiring certain renown. Thus, the 1720 Stradivari was both an eyewitness and a protagonist at the premiere of Haydn's *Seven Last Words*. —

The participation of the Piatti at this premiere was not my only surprise when I was researching its history. The second was the discovery that Don José Sáenz de Santa María, that distinguished member of Cádiz's enlightened community, was not from Spain but from Mexico, or rather from New Spain, since he had been born in the port of Veracruz in 1737. His parents were Don Pedro Saénz de Santa María, a Spaniard "from the most ancient and distinguished aristocracy of La Rioja"[15] and Doña Ignacia Sáenz Rico, who, according to some sources, was a native of Veracruz, although others claimed she also originally from La Rioja. José's mother died when he was twelve, and his father, a wealthy merchant, decided to return to Spain and settle in Cádiz. At that time its thriving trade with the new continent had raised the city to the height of its prosperity. His father wanted to train him as a merchant, but young

José, inspired by a profound religious vocation, decided to become a priest.

It is extraordinary to think that the 1720 cello had, through Father Santa María in 1787, its first indirect contact with Mexico, where so much of its musical life would be centered two centuries later.

A short time after the premiere of *The Seven Last Words*, Father Santa María made sure that Haydn received the promised honorarium, though he did so in a highly unusual manner. One day the composer received a small box from Cádiz. When he opened it, he found nothing but a chocolate cake. Extremely irritated, he sliced the cake and discovered that it was filled with gold coins.[16]

The composition was an immediate success. Haydn himself accorded considerable importance to the work: a short time later he adapted it as a string quartet (op. 51), besides also revising and approving the piano transcription submitted by a colleague. Years later, he even wrote another version for vocal quartet, chorus, and orchestra.

In an admirable persistence of tradition, *The Seven Last Words* has been performed at the Santa Cueva every Good Friday since 1787. Manuel de Falla, who was born in Cádiz in 1876, had heard it there as a child and attributed the awakening of his musical vocation to the profound impression created by this composition.

The munificence of our Veracruz-born priest, Don José Sáenz de Santa María, was not solely restricted to reconditioning the Santa Cueva and commissioning music from Haydn. At his own expense, he ordered the construction of an oratory above the Santa Cueva, to be dedicated to the Blessed Sacrament, and also commissioned a series of paintings from none other than Francisco de Goya: *The Last Supper*, *Miracle of the Loaves and Fishes*, and *Parable of the Guest without a Wedding Garment* (all from 1796–1797).

To make contact with the painter, he turned to his friend Sebastián Martínez, a renowned collector of paintings and engravings. Goya knew Sebastián Martínez well: during a long illness in 1792 and 1793 he had been tended by Sebastián and his daughters at their house in Cádiz. As proof of his friendship, he painted a magnificent portrait of Sebastián Martínez in 1792, now exhibited in New York's Metropolitan Museum of Art (Fig. 9).

I have visited the Santa Cueva several times and have contemplated the portrait of Don José Saénz de Santa María painted by the German artist Franz X. Riedmayer (see Fig. 10), as well as the painting of the Virgin of Guadalupe over his tomb. The young José had brought it with him

9. DON SEBASTIÁN
MARTÍNEZ Y PÉREZ,
*Francisco Goya, 1792. Oil
on canvas, 36⅝ x 26⅝
in. (93 x 67.6 cm). The
Metropolitan Museum of
Art, Rogers Fund, 1906
(06.289). Photograph, all
rights reserved, Metropolitan
Museum of Art.*

10. JOSÉ SÁENZ DE SANTA
MARIA, *Franz Xavier
Riedmayer. Santa Cueva,
Cádiz. Photo by Arenas.*

from New Spain, as if this remarkable man from Veracruz—who had played such a vital role in the cultural life of Cádiz and in the creation of masterpieces by Haydn and Goya—had never forgotten his roots.

Around 1791, Carlo Moro, who was getting on in years, was forced, like Boccherini later on, to consider parting with the Stradivari that had accompanied him for thirty years. Moro was acquainted with the Italian violinist Vaccari, who played in Charles IV's court in Madrid. Knowing that Boccherini, Brunetti, and other Italian musicians in Madrid also owned Stradivari instruments, Moro set off for Madrid around 1791. Recalling Charles's days in Naples, when he was a young prince who enjoyed the violin at the court of his father, the future Charles III, Moro thought of selling his cello to a member of the nobility through his friend Vaccari.

Vaccari knew Charles IV well, since they both participated in the chamber-music sessions at the palace. The king played first violin; Vaccari, second; Dámaso Cañada, viola; and Francesco Brunetti, cello. Vaccari, who did not have a high opinion of his majesty as a violinist, related to his friend Moro two anecdotes that he believed clearly illustrated the king's musical abilities. Before playing with Vaccari, Charles IV met regularly with professional musicians to play string quartets. The first violin was the renowned French violinist Alexandre Boucher. The king, who was second violin, had trouble counting the rest bars and sometimes entered at the wrong bar. Once, when the king was told to wait until the end of his rest bars, his response was totally adamant: "The King of Spain waits for no one!"[17]

The second incident took place years earlier and involved Vaccari's compatriot Luigi Boccherini, known as Luis Boquerini in Spain, where he had lived for many years. Boquerini was a cellist and composer for Prince Luis's court orchestra. The prince, who was the brother of Charles III and, therefore, uncle of the Prince of Asturias, the future Charles IV, had great respect for Boccherini and was his principal patron in Spain. One day Prince Luis invited Boccherini to the Royal Palace so that his nephew Charles, then Prince of Asturias, could play the quintets he had just composed.

Prince Charles played first violin, and the following disaster occurred:

> His part contained a series of monotonous bars: do, si, do, si. Exasperated, the prince suddenly sprang to his feet and exploded, "This is intolerable! Even a beginner could do better. Do, si, do, si!" Boc-

cherini then explained, "Sir, pay attention to the modulations of the second violin and the viola. . . . This apparent monotony disappears when the other instruments join in the dialogue."

"Do, si, do, si! And this for a full half hour. A delightful dialogue indeed. A beginner's music and a poor beginner at that," the prince repeated.

"Sire, before expressing such an opinion, one must first know something about music," Boccherini retorted.[18]

The reaction was immediate. The prince, whose irascible temper was accompanied by tremendous physical strength, lunged at the composer, and only the terrified shrieks from the Princess of Asturias saved him from a severe beating. From that day forward, Luis Boquerini never again set foot in the Royal Palace.

Moro's idea of selling his Stradivari in Charles IV's court seemed highly unrealistic to Vaccari, since during the reign of Charles III, the court had acquired the legendary decorated Stradivari quintet. Furthermore, at that time the court was a hotbed of intrigue and petty quarrels. Everyone was plotting against everyone else, so there was little interest in purchasing a cello. Charles IV, though irascible, was rather naïve and totally oblivious of what was going on, including the infidelities of his wife, María Luisa of Parma.

In court, Vaccari brought up the matter of the 1720 cello, but just as he had predicted, there was not even the slightest interest. Cellists Boccherini and Brunetti had arrived in Madrid with magnificent Stradivari instruments, but Boccherini was now thinking of selling his own. At that time there were at least eight Stradivari cellos in Spain, most of them in Madrid, so Moro decided to return to Cádiz, where he hoped to find more favorable conditions for selling his instrument.

There is little further data on Carlo Moro, except that he was finally able to sell his cello in Cádiz, and that he died around 1794.

According to the information provided by María Pemán Medina, the buyer was probably Don Sebastián Martínez, the friend of Goya's mentioned earlier. He was the proprietor of a sherry company known as Compañía de Vinos de Jerez de Martínez y Cía., with cellars located in Jerez de la Frontera and Sanlúcar de Barrameda, both very near Cádiz.[19] He also possessed a remarkable library and a collection of priceless musical instruments, which afforded the Marquis of Ureña the opportunity to "satisfy the urge of every amateur musician: to play fine instruments."[20] Thus, the 1720 Stradivari became the crown jewel in his collection of musical instruments. In 1792, Don Sebastián, who had also made a name for himself in the world of finance and economics, was appointed chief treasurer of the kingdom, a position that he held until his death in 1800.

The contents of Sebastián Martínez's artistic collection are verified with considerable precision by a document registered in the Public Records of Cádiz.[21] It contains the inventory of his possessions to be distributed after his death to his daughters (and sole beneficiaries), Josefa and Catalina. Each of them inherited numerous paintings, sculptures, images, engravings, books, pieces of jewelry, and properties—as well as a collection of musical instruments. Each instrument collection was valued at 2,550 *reales* in coins. (Goya's portrait of Don Sebastián was valued at 750 reales in coins.) These collections included a harpsichord, a pianoforte, a psaltery, several guitars, a flute, and a musical treatise. However, the Stradivari cello was not included in the list of his assets.

What has been definitely corroborated is that in 1818 the Piatti was still in Cádiz, in the hands of an Irishman named Allen Dowell.[22] It is quite likely either that Dowell acquired the cello directly from Sebastián Martínez, or that having been registered in the inventory of Martínez's sherry company the company itself sold the cello to Dowell—who was also a sherry merchant.

In 1801, more that 100 Irishmen were living in Cádiz, mostly merchants.[23] Let us now take a look at Dowell, the colorful Irishman who became the owner of the Piatti.

Allen Dowell—or "Don Alonso Dowell," as he appears in several local documents of the period—was a sherry merchant.[24] According to the testaments registered in Cádiz, he was born in Roscommon, Ireland, in 1774, the son of Edmund Dowell and Catherine Plunckett.[25] Although a "subject of His Britannic Majesty," he had lived in Cádiz since at least 1809. During the Peninsular War (1808–1814), he was a contractor for the British army. With Don Alonso Fallow he established a commercial establishment that went by the name of Alonso Dowell y Compañía. Both his home and his place of business were located at no. 136 Calle de las Cinco Torres.[26]

Dowell, who played the violin, was a great admirer of Stradivari's instruments. In 1809, he sold a Stradivari violin to John Betts, a prominent London instrument merchant, and shipped it from Cádiz.[27] Over the next few years, he took advantage of the increasing chaos in Spain by purchasing at least five additional Stradivari violins, all of which he subsequently sold in England at considerably higher prices.[28]

A BRIEF HISTORICAL ASIDE

After 1800 the political and economic situation in Spain deteriorated quickly. In 1805 Admiral Nelson destroyed the Hispano-French armada at Trafalgar, and in 1808 a rebellion in Aranjuez forced Charles IV to abdicate in favor of his son Ferdinand VII, who was unable to ascend the throne because Napoleon (Spain's recent ally) had lured him, his father, and his wife to Bayonne, and then kidnapped them. Napoleon then placed his brother Joseph Bonaparte on the Spanish throne and imposed a liberal constitution, abolishing the Inquisition and proclaiming the rights of man. The Spaniards, forced to choose between the freedom offered by the French invaders and the despotism of the Bourbons, cried, "Long live the chains!" and fought against the imperial troops.

The political and economic turmoil in Spain, the French invasion, the War of Independence, the return of Ferdinand VII, and the defeat of the liberal forces marked the beginning of several decades of profound decline after the most glorious era in Cádiz's history. It is no accident that this period also marked the exodus of many fine musical instruments from Cádiz and from Spain in general, all sold by collectors and artists anxious about the wars and the increasing political turmoil. Joseph Bonaparte returned to Paris. Two instruments from the decorated Stradivari quintet were stolen from the Royal Palace, probably concealed in Bonaparte's baggage.

In 1818, Allen Dowell and his 1720 Stradivari, which by then was ninety-eight years old, abandoned Spain and set out for Ireland.

THE "RED CELLO" IN IRELAND: 1818–1853

Dowell retired from the sherry business and remained in Dublin with his cello. Three years later, in 1821, he decided to sell it. To this end, he contacted his friend Paul Alday, a French composer and violinist. A resident of Dublin since 1809, Alday had opened a music academy, and was also acknowledged as one of the city's leading music publishers. Alday, who was well acquainted with Irish musical circles, suggested that Dowell sell the cello to the Reverend Booth, an amateur cellist who lived in the small county of Carlow, some sixty-two miles south of Dublin. A letter from Alday to the Reverend Booth, discovered in the clergy's archives in Dublin, informed him that the Stradivari cello had made its way from Cádiz, where it had "participated" in the church music concerts of the Santa Cueva since 1787.[29] Although a young Dublin cellist, Samuel J. Pigott, had also expressed his interest in the Stradivari, in the end it went to Reverend Booth, who acquired it for the sum of 300 guineas in 1821. After Booth's death, his heirs decided to sell the cello and turned it over to Cramer & Beale's, a London firm specializing in string instruments, to obtain the best price.

Pigott, meanwhile, had done well in the music business. In 1823, he founded his own company, Pigott & Co., Musical Instrument Importers and Music Publishers, located on Dublin's Westmoreland Street. The business flourished, becoming the most important company in its field in Ireland. In 1831, Cramer & Beale's sold the Stradivari; the buyer turned out to be none other than Samuel J. Pigott, who finally realized his dream of acquiring the cello. Pigott was undoubtedly a shrewd businessman. By 1833 the Westmoreland Street building was too small for his business, and the establishment moved to 112 Grafton Street, in the heart of Dublin.

At that time, Dublin was the scene of an extremely active musical life, whose origins dated back to the eighteenth century. Francesco Geminiani had gone to Dublin in 1731, and Handel, who had arrived in 1741, conducted the Dublin premiere of the *Messiah* the following year. One of the central figures in the Irish music world was composer and pianist John Field, born in Dublin in 1782. Field and his family moved to London in 1792, where he studied with Muzio Clementi. Field's romantic, dreamy style (he was the creator of the nocturne) made him one of the most popular pianist-composers during the first half of the nineteenth century, especially in Russia, where he died in 1835.

In 1844, Alfredo Piatti, an Italian, and one of the most acclaimed cellists of the nineteenth century, embarked on his first concert tour of England and Ireland. In Dublin, as can be expected, he met Pigott, who showed him the Stradivari. Piatti, always avidly interested in good instruments, left us the following account of his first encounter with the cello: "Great was my astonishment to see such a noble example, and I must confess I greatly envied its owner, who, I may add, seemed to thoroughly appreciate his treasure."[30]

Piggott's business continued to flourish even though Ireland was undergoing catastrophic times: from 1845 to 1849 a dreadful famine resulted when a potato blight ruined the potato crop, the Irish population's primary food source. Almost one million people died of hunger, typhoid, and cholera. Another million immigrated, mostly to the United States.

When Samuel Piggott died in 1853, he bequeathed the company to his widow and subsequently to his son John. A document from the Piggott establishment, written twenty-five years after Samuel's death, provides a fascinating insight into the personality of its founder:

> The name of Pigott has long been familiar in the ears of the Dublin musical public as an old-established and highly respectable house connected with the sale and hire of pianofortes and other musical instruments. The firm of Pigott was originally established in Westmoreland Street, Dublin, by Mr. Samuel J. Pigott, the father of the present proprietor, Mr. John A. Pigott. . . . When Samuel J. Pigott died in 1853, Dublin sustained the loss of not only a kind-hearted and good business-man, but of a thorough musician and a celebrated violoncellist. He was the owner of the Antonius Stradivarius celebrated "red" cello, dated 1720, now in the possession of Signor Piatti.[31]

THE RED CELLO IN ENGLAND: 1853–1867

When Samuel J. Piggott died, his widow, Mary, decided to sell it. She then turned over the instrument to Sir Robert Gore-Booth, a close friend of her late husband's. Sir Robert, an amateur cellist, also owned a Stradivari cello, dating from 1710. Since Sir Robert was a friend of Alfredo Piatti's, he invited Piatti to see the instrument, thinking he would be the ideal client. Once again, the words of Piatti himself:

> I was agreeably surprised on immediately recognising my former acquaintance, and great was my chagrin at not being in a position to purchase it; I simply had not the means to do so.
>
> Happening to call upon Maucotel, the violin-maker, I talked about the instrument, and strongly urged him to see it and try to buy it. He followed my advice, and after some bargaining became its owner at the very modest figure of £300. It remained only a short time in his hands, as at my suggestion he offered it for £350 to Colonel Oliver, who accepted it; this took place in 1853.
>
> A short time afterwards J. B. Vuillaume [the greatest French violin maker of the time] came to London, and hearing through Maucotel of the cello, called upon its owner and there and then made an offer of £800 for it, but the Colonel refused to sell.[32]

11. Italian cellist Alfredo Piatti with the 1720 Stradivari cello, c. 1880.

Colonel (later General) Oliver was a fine amateur cellist who lived in London. He was a friend of Piatti's and kept the Stradivari for fourteen years, from 1853 to 1867. In 1867 there occurred a totally unexpected event, which Piatti describes as follows:

> I was a frequent visitor at the [Colonel Oliver's] house, and often played upon the Stradivari. I used to restring it; in fact, looked upon

it as if it had been my own child! One day—a day graven in my memory—in 1867, I was as usual at the Colonel's house, and was playing on and comparing the three violoncellos he possessed: an Antonio and Hieronymus Amati, a Montagnana and the Stradivari. The Colonel suddenly said to me: "Which do you prefer?" Laughingly I answered: "One cannot have a doubt—the Stradivari." "Take it home" was his rejoinder. I felt so embarrassed by what appeared to me a sudden resolve that I politely declined, and in due time took my leave and went home. To my astonishment, though—and I must say it was of a joyful nature—the Stradivari followed in my wake.[33]

THE GREAT CELLIST ALFREDO PIATTI, OWNER OF THE CELLO FROM 1867 TO 1901

After that, Piatti always played the Stradivari. He owned numerous cellos during his long career: an Antonio and Girolamo Amati, a gift from Franz Liszt; a Pietro Giacomo Rogeri, his favorite for many years; two Matteo Goffrillers (one dating from 1697, which later belonged to the great American cellist Leonard Rose, and the other from 1700, once owned by Niccolò Paganini); and several others. With unusual insight, Piatti observed:

> I have at times become enamoured at the sight of a fine instrument, have been impressed by its beauty, and when I have become its owner I have tried to believe that its tone equalled that of my Stradivari. Time, however, has invariably seen me return to my old friend with a feeling of satisfaction difficult to explain. True, the differences of tone between my Stradivari and other recognised fine instruments are subtle, but I can only say that I obtain from the former a depth and nobility of tone which ever affords me a sense of contentment; in fact, there is a something unattainable elsewhere.[34]

A short time after receiving his unexpected and extraordinary gift, Piatti arrived in Paris. Since he had been informed that Vuillaume was eager to see the instrument, Piatti arranged for an appointment, described as follows by W. E. Whitehouse, his favorite pupil:

> The magnificent Stradivarius violoncello was a very perfect specimen; it even had the original Strad neck. . . . Vuillaume was lost in admiration of it and after examining every detail minutely, he said

to Piatti, "It is a dream of beauty and grandeur. There are a few signs of wear—marks and impressions of where the bridge has stood indenting the table—and the edge is badly worn (where the left hand comes against the ribs [of the cello]. I can easily remove the marks of the bridge, and touch with varnish, and put a new edge on it where it is worn, so that you will not see it." Piatti politely thanked him, but took good care not to allow him to have it! Piatti was very proud of the cello's pristine originality.[35]

Alfredo Piatti was born in Bergamo in 1822. He began studying the cello at the age of five with his great-uncle Gaetano Zanetti, who played first cello in the opera's orchestra. Piatti's remarkable progress astonished everyone who heard him play. When barely seven years old, he was allowed to join Bergamo's opera orchestra. A few months later, when Zanetti died, Alfredo was appointed his successor as the lead cellist of the opera, despite his young age.

When he was ten, he was admitted to the Milan Conservatory, where he studied for five years under Professor Vincenzo Merighi. It was at his teacher's house that Piatti saw a Stradivari cello for the first time. This instrument had been acquired under peculiar circumstances. One day in 1822, while strolling through the streets of Milan, Merighi spotted a worker pulling a cart filled with a pile of discarded objects, including a dilapidated cello. Merighi approached the man and ended up buying the cello, which turned out to be an authentic Stradivari from 1707. It was in such deplorable condition that it cost next to nothing. Sometime between 1834 and 1835, Merighi sold it to Paganini, who in turn sold it to the great violin maker Vuillaume, who probably restored it and sold it to Count Stanlein in 1854.[36]

In 1838, the young Piatti, age sixteen, gave a recital at the Teatro alla Scala in Milan.[37] He created such a sensation that he was invited to play the following year in Vienna, with phenomenal success. In 1843 he played in Munich for Franz Liszt, who presented him with an Antonio and Girolamo Amati cello.

In 1844 Piatti traveled to England. In May he gave his first concert in London, at Her Majesty's Theater, where he was instantly acclaimed as an extraordinary artist. Subsequently, when he played at the Athenaeum, the critics praised his flawless precision and, above all, his cantabile, which according to one critic, "he had obviously formed under the influence of singers from his own country." It was precisely in reference to this concert, that Piatti "thought he had played rather well and was pleased with the impression he had made, when a little fat boy with ruddy cheeks and a short jacket stepped on to the platform and played the violin in a way which completely cast his own performance into the shade." The young musician turned out to be Joseph Joachim, the legendary violinist, who would frequently play with Piatti in the future.

Piatti's debut with the Philharmonic Society of London took place on June 24, 1844, also under peculiar circumstances. The piece immediately preceding Piatti's appearance was Beethoven's Piano Concerto no. 4 in G Major, with Felix Mendelssohn himself as soloist. It was one of Mendelssohn's favorite concertos, and his interpretation was especially brilliant. Most likely, Piatti would not have agreed to play had he known that he would follow Mendelssohn, one of the greatest, most popular musicians of the day. However, Piatti's performance was a resounding success. He played a fantasia by Friedrich August Kummer, and the critic from the *Morning Post* wrote, "Piatti's magnificent violoncello playing won universal admiration, by the perfection of his tone and his evident command over all the intricacies of the instrument."

After the concert, the pianist Ignaz Moscheles informed Piatti that Mendelssohn would like to play a sonata with him. When they met at Moscheles's house, Mendelssohn took out the manuscript of his Cello Sonata in D and played it with Piatti. The composer was so enthusiastic about it that he sent Piatti the following note, "*À M. Piatti avec mille remerciements du plaisir qu'il m'a fait en jouant ma sonate ce matin et avec l'admiration la plus sincère de son beau talent. Felix Mendelssohn Bartholdy. Londres, 8 Juillet, 1844.*" [To Mr. Piatti with many thanks for the great pleasure of playing my sonata with him this morning and with my sincerest admiration for his great talent. Felix Mendelssohn Bartholdy. London, July 8, 1844.]

Soon after, Mendelssohn began composing a concerto for cello and orchestra; he dedicated it to Piatti and completed the first movement. Unfortunately, the manuscript was lost in the mail, and Mendelssohn never tried to rewrite or finish the piece. Piatti, who had seen this manuscript, later remarked that "the work was not remotely up to par with his violin concerto."

By 1846, Piatti was spending a considerable amount of time in London. In fact, England became his second home. In addition to his concerts as a soloist in England and on the continent, Piatti frequently participated in chamber music concerts with such great artists as Joseph Joachim, Henri Vieuxtemps, Camillo Sivori, Heinrich Wilhelm Ernst, and others.

In 1858 a series of reasonably priced concerts in London called "Popular Concerts," or "the Pops," were made available to less affluent music lovers rather than only to small groups of aristocrats or wealthy dilettanti. At the inaugural concert Henryk Wieniawski played first violin; Louis Ries, second; C. W. Doyle, viola; Alfredo Piatti, cello; and Charles Halle, piano.

At the final concert of the 1885–1886 season, Clara Schumann joined Joachim, Ries, Ludwig Straus, and Piatti in Robert Schumann's splendid piano quintet. The cello selected for this event was the Stradivari. The music critic from the *Times* wrote, "Who is to take the place of Madame Schumann and Herr Joachim and Signor Piatti when these artists retire from the platform is as difficult to foresee as it is to name the composer of the rising generation who is to write our operas and symphonies and quartets of the future."

During Piatti's declining years, Robert von Mendelssohn, a nephew of the composer's and an amateur cellist, attempted on several occasions to purchase the cello. Piatti rejected an offer of £2,000, which prompted Mendelssohn to offer him a blank check. Nevertheless, Piatti refused to part with his instrument.

He so enjoyed admiring its noble beauty that even when he fell ill and was no longer able to play, he would ask his faithful housekeeper Miss Freeman, to bring him the case and open it so that he could at least contemplate it.

Piatti retired in 1898 and spent his last few years in his native Bergamo with his daughter, Rosa. He died on July 18, 1901. In accordance with his wishes, the andante from Schubert's String Quartet in D Minor was played during his funeral.

After his death, Piatti's daughter, the Countess Lochis, decided, albeit with great reluctance, to part with the cello. She believed that it would be worse to condemn this instrument to silence. In 1901, she finally accepted an offer from the persistent Robert von Mendelssohn and sold it to him for £4,000. It was then that the cello had a new neck grafted on it. As Whitehouse wrote: "I am sorry to say that I heard Mendelssohn did not resist the temptation to have it 'restored' and that he had a new neck grafted on it. I wonder what became of the old Strad neck? I hope it was placed with the cello, perhaps comfortably ensconced somewhere in the case."[38]

The old neck has never been found, as is the case for almost all Stradivari instruments.

THE PIATTI IN GERMANY: 1901–1936

Robert and his brother Franz von Mendelssohn were descendants of the Jewish philosopher Moses Mendelssohn (1729–1786) and nephews of Felix Mendelssohn. Moses's children had converted to Christianity, and his descendants, like Felix and the brothers Robert and Franz, were Protestants. Franz and Robert were prominent Berlin bankers and outstanding amateur musicians. Robert, as noted earlier, played the cello, and Franz the violin. Their palatial mansions contained Goyas, El Grecos, Rembrandts, and between them they possessed an extraordinary collection of musical instruments, including a Stradivari septet.

Since the Mendelssohns were also great patrons of chamber-music activities, their homes were often visited by many of the outstanding musicians of the time: pianists Artur Schnabel and Rudolf Serkin; cellists Pablo Casals, Gregor Piatigorsky, Emanuel Feuermann, Gaspar Cassadó, and Hermann Busch; violinists Adolf Busch, Bronislaw Huberman, Nathan Milstein, and many others.

12. Francesco Mendelssohn, c. 1925. Photo courtesy of Dr. Christoph Bernoulli and Thomas Blubacher.

13. LEFT TO RIGHT: *Francesco Mendelssohn, cellist Gregor Piatigorsky, and pianist Vladimir Horowitz. Switzerland, 1930. Photo courtesy of Jean Fonda Fournier.*

Robert von Mendelssohn married an Italian, Giulietta Gordigiani, by whom he had two children, Francesco and Eleonora. Giulietta, whom everyone called "Contessa," was an accomplished pianist, and she frequently participated in these musical sessions. The diary of Arthur Hill, the famous violin expert and dealer, had this to say about Robert, upon his death in 1917:

> The death of Robert Mendelssohn removes a fine amateur violon-cellist. He and his brother, Franz, who played the violin, were very wealthy men, so when we heard that the Countess Locchis [*sic*] had received an offer of £4,000 for her father's cello, and now that our competitor was Mendelssohn we had not a look in! The Stradivari

cello, therefore, was transported to Berlin where it has been since Piatti's death. I remember Robert Mendelssohn calling upon us with Piatti and noted that his execution, for an amateur, when he played, was quite exceptional. He struck me as being a big, stoutly built German. He married an Italian lady who, Sir Edward Goschen told us, was quite Italian in her sympathies, this, and the anxieties arising in consequence of the War may have served to hasten his end.[39]

Young Francesco, born in 1902, studied the cello and received guidance from Casals and Cassadó, among others. Piatigorsky recounts an anecdote that best describes the prevailing atmosphere at the Mendelssohns' home:

> My great wish was to hear Pablo Casals. One day my desire was almost fulfilled and I met him. But ironically, however, it was I who had to play. It was in the home of the Von Mendelssohns, a house filled with El Grecos, Rembrandts and Stradivaris. Francesco von Mendelssohn, the son of the banker, who was a talented cellist, telephoned and asked if he could call for me; they had a guest in the house who would like to hear me play.[40]

We have no idea which cello Piatigorsky played for Casals, but most likely it was the Piatti.

At this point the young Spanish cellist, Gaspar Cassadó appeared on the scene. Cassadó, born in 1897, had been a pupil of Casals in Paris, and in 1918 launched his brilliant international career. He arrived in Italy in 1923, fell in love with the country, and soon took up residence in Florence. Shortly after, when he was in Berlin on a holiday, he was invited to the Mendelssohn home. There he met Giulietta, her son Francesco, and the Piatti. At this point Giulietta had been a widow for six years, and it is anybody's guess whether Cassadó fell in love with her, the Piatti, or both. In any event, they all got along well. During his vacation, Cassadó often played chamber music with Giulietta and even participated in trios with Giulietta at the piano and Alfred Einstein on the violin. Exhilarated by the experience, he set about composing a trio for violin, cello, and piano.

After that, Giulietta became Cassadó's frequent piano accompanist. The Piatti, on loan to the cellist, became the instrument of choice for the majority of his concerts throughout the 1920s and the early 1930s. In 1925 or 1926, he premiered his own *Sonata en el estilo antiguo español*

(Sonata in the Old Spanish Style) in Venice. In December 1936, Cassadó made his debut in New York during a concert with the New York Philharmonic. The *New York Times* published an enthusiastic review ("Cassadó triumphs at Carnegie Hall. Haydn Concerto offered."), noting that "His cantilena would inspire envy in singers . . . his tone is very sonorous and rich."[41] A few days later, Cassadó played his own transcription of Carl Maria von Weber's Clarinet Concerto no. 2, and once again the *New York Times* sang his praises: "Cassadó performs brilliantly. . . . Tone as living, humanly expressive and voluminous as his in this work is rarely met with among cello players."[42]

During the period between the two world wars, the Mendelssohn family sold most of the instruments collected by Franz and Robert Mendelssohn, with the exception of the Piatti.[43]

In the meantime, Francesco and his sister Eleonora continued to live in Berlin, where Francesco was a member of the Klinger String Quartet from 1926 to 1928. He also occasionally worked as a theater producer, and directed several of Brecht's plays, though rather unsuccessfully. In 1928, his passion for the theater led him to pay his first visit to the United States, where he remained for several weeks, dazzled by Broadway and the New York theater. He also went to Hollywood, as a result of his friendship with the German movie director Berthold Viertel, who worked both in Germany and in Hollywood, and was introduced to Greta Garbo, a close friend of Salko Viertel, the director's wife. When Francesco returned to the United States in 1933, he directed Kurt Weil's *Threepenny Opera* at Broadway's Empire Theater. It was such a dismal failure that it closed after twelve performances. Eleonora, on the other hand, became a well-known actress and had a successful career in the theater.[44]

Francesco's relationship with his mother was not excessively cordial. Although the "Contessa" was the legitimate owner of the Piatti, Francesco regarded himself as having been stripped of his inheritance. Irritated by the loan of the cello to Cassadó, he took revenge by accusing his mother of having turned over the Stradivari to a "fascist" (because Cassadó, although totally apolitical, lived with Giulietta in Mussolini's Italy). "There are three things I detest," his mother used to say. "Jews, Communists, and homosexuals." To which Francesco responded, "Well, I happen to be all three!"[45] Nevertheless, the "Contessa" ended up giving the cello to Francesco.

Francesco, or "Cesco," as he was called, was a very close friend of the Busch family: violinist Adolf Busch; his wife, Frieda; his brother Hermann, a cellist; and pianist Rudolf (Rudi) Serkin, who later married

Irene Busch, Adolf and Frieda's daughter. Cesco was extremely generous to his friends. In 1929 he gave the Busch family an automobile as a gift. In a letter to a friend, Frieda mentioned that she and Rudi Serkin were taking driving lessons.[46]

Adolf Busch was very active in all areas of music. In 1918 he had founded the Busch String Quartet, whose cellist, after 1930, was his brother Hermann.[47] He was also the founder of the Busch Trio, with Hermann and Rudi Serkin.

By the 1930s, the political situation in Germany had become positively sinister. The Nazis' rise to power in 1933 sent out alarm signals that were not immediately perceived by many intellectuals and artists—Jews and Gentiles alike. However, the government soon began dictating measures aimed at controlling the arts, artists, and performers, much in the way that Stalin was doing in the Soviet Union.

The Busch Trio had been originally scheduled to perform at the Brahms centennial celebrations in Hamburg in May 1933, but after the new regime came into power, they received a letter informing them that Serkin's appearance would be unwelcome, since "the Fürher planned to be present." Busch replied: "Outraged by your impertinence. Will naturally not play either."[48]

When Busch gave a concert in Germany in April of that same year, he witnessed the brutality and inhumanity of the first anti-Jewish boycott. He then cancelled all further engagements and never returned to his homeland. The Busch family then made their home in the Swiss town of Basel, near the German border.

In 1933, Wilhelm Furtwängler, conductor of the Berlin Philharmonic Orchestra, had refused to expel five Jewish musicians from his orchestra: the concertmaster and eminent violinist Szymon Goldberg, cellists Nikolai Graudan and Joseph Schuster, and two violinists.[49] However, there was no power on earth to contain the anti-Jewish hatred. Fortunately, thousands of Jewish and Gentile intellectuals and artists either managed to leave the country or were expelled before 1938. This was the case of prominent musicians like Arnold Schönberg, Alban Berg, Paul Hindemith, Ernst Krenek, Kurt Weill, Fritz and Adolf Busch, Emanuel Feuermann, Artur Schnabel, Bruno Walter, Otto Klemperer, Erich Kleiber, Nikolai Graudan, and Joseph Schuster.

The infamous Joseph Goebbels exercised strict control over literature, art, and the press. In 1937, he organized an art exhibition in Munich entitled Entartete Kunst (Degenerate Art) with the most representative examples of "decadent art." The exhibit included works by Pablo Picasso,

Oskar Kokoschka, Vassily Kandinsky, Paul Klee, and other painters of a "similar ilk."[50]

In 1938, Goebbels sponsored a festival called Days of German Music in Düsseldorf. Running parallel to the festival was an audiovisual exhibition of "degenerate music": patterned on the Degenerate Art exhibition, it was intended to illustrate how such barbaric, pernicious elements had infected German music. The exhibition, consisting of music scores, programs, posters, and other "evidence" of musical degeneration, provided individual booths where visitors could listen to the recorded works of Mendelssohn, Mahler, Schönberg, Krenek, Hindemith, and other "degenerates," performed by such equally "degenerate" musicians as Bruno Walter, Otto Klemperer, Emanuel Feuermann, and Fritz Kreisler. This exhibition of "degeneracy" was such an astonishing success, an outcome diametrically opposed to its objective, that Goebbels prohibited the press from even mentioning the event.[51]

The Mendelssohns, though of Jewish origin, had converted to Protestantism. Furthermore, the Nazi government had accorded them a title that purportedly protected them from anti-Semitic persecution: they were designated *Ehrenarier* (Honorary Aryans). Nevertheless, this did not prevent the authorities from banning the music by Felix Mendelssohn, Francesco and Eleonora's uncle, in 1934. Although, in addition to being "Honorary Aryans," Francesco and Eleonora were the children of an Italian mother, it goes without saying that Nazi Germany did not inspire them with a great deal of confidence. However, in 1936, when they decided to emigrate, they discovered that it was forbidden to leave the country with any works of art. The Nazi government would confiscate them without hesitation.

The Mendelssohns tried to do so anyway. Eleonora was the first. She took down many of her priceless paintings, removed their frames, and packed them into a bundle. The paintings, wrapped in newspaper, were piled on top of one another. Dressed in rags, she arrived in Hamburg where she was to board a ship. When a group of Gestapo agents inquired about the contents of the package, she replied that they were old family portraits. "Open it!" barked one of the agents. Eleonora then lifted a corner of the newspaper, exposing the first painting. It happened to be a self-portrait of Rembrandt, no less. Without blinking an eye, Eleonora exhibited her exceptional skills as an actress. "That's the portrait of my poor uncle, the rabbi," she said, bursting into such disconsolate weeping that the officials themselves—whose artistic training was fortunately nil—even helped her tie up the bundle and wished her bon voyage.[52]

Francesco, for his part, left Berlin and temporarily moved to the village of Lörrach, near the Swiss city of Basel, where the Busch family lived. Francesco managed to cross the border frequently to play chamber music with them. At a ridiculously low price, Francesco had purchased a mass-produced cello—both ugly and poorly made—a coarse canvas bag, and a bicycle. Duly equipped, he made his first attempt to cross the border. The border guards detained him and asked where he was going. Francesco replied that he was going to play chamber music with some Swiss friends. The guards carefully examined his appalling cello and allowed him to pass. In the evening, Francesco returned to his village. This episode was subsequently repeated countless times, until the guards deemed it unnecessary to keep inspecting the contents of the canvas bag and merely waved—albeit somewhat jeeringly—to their eccentric friend. One day, Francesco placed his Stradivari in the bag and, barely concealing his extreme nervousness, greeted the guards in the usual manner as he crossed the border on his bicycle. Once in Switzerland, he kept on pedaling, but his nerves got the better of him: he started shaking so much that he almost keeled over, cello and all. That is how the Piatti left Nazi Germany.[53]

Eleonora's and Francesco's departures could not have come at a more providential moment. Their status as "Honorary Aryans" was no reliable guarantee, as was shown by the experience of Max Friedländer (septuagenarian, legendary art historian, former director of the Kaiser Friedrich Museum in Berlin) and his colleague Vitale Bloch. Like many intellectual German Jews, they lived in Nazi-occupied Holland; both were arrested and sent to the Osnabrück concentration camp. Reichsmarschall Göring immediately dispatched Walter Hofer, his specialist in artistic affairs, to Holland. Hofer issued a memorandum to the authorities in charge of the Nazi occupation, whereby "due to their profound knowledge of German and Dutch painting, Reichsmarschall Göring wishes Friedländer and Bloch to remain in The Hague and, therefore, should not be affected by orders from the Reichsmarschall for Jewish Affairs."[54] Friedländer and Bloch were declared "Honorary Aryans" on the condition that they become appraisers for Nazi collectors acquiring European art works in Holland. Their imprisonment was deemed a bureaucratic "error" and they were "set free."[55] (Other "Honorary Aryans," however, were not granted such clemency in the face of the horrifying Nazi anti-Jewish onslaught.)

After spending some time in Switzerland, Francesco decided to immigrate to the United States.

THE PIATTI IN THE UNITED STATES

In 1939 Francesco and the Piatti arrived in New York. At the end of the war, Francesco lent the Piatti to his dear friend Hermann Busch, the cellist from the Busch Quartet. Adolf Busch wrote that in 1947, when the quartet played in London, they visited the legendary firm of Hill and Sons: "The people are unchanged, and to a person like me it seems as though time has stood still. The same salespeople in the shop who appeared to be 90 ten years ago. They're still 90. . . . Mr. Phillips-Hill was very kind, and all three of them from the quartet immediately bought bows. . . . They properly admired the Piatti, which Francesco von Mendelssohn had lent Hermann."[56]

Soon after, the Busch family moved to the United States. In 1951, along with Rudolf Serkin, they founded the Marlboro School of Music, which rapidly became a key institution in American musical life.[57]

Eleonora, Francesco's sister, also lived in New York. According to some sources, she and Arturo Toscanini were a little more than just friends. She was also acquainted with David Sarnoff, president of the Radio Corporation of America (RCA) and the National Broadcasting Company (NBC), and his representative Samuel Chotzinoff; the two men cofounded the NBC Symphony Orchestra, which Toscanini conducted for seventeen years, until 1954.

The Mendelssohn family had established a trust fund that assigned a monthly allowance for Francesco. However, since Francesco usually ran out of funds, he lived on loans from his friends. Although he squandered his money, he was also extremely generous to the many artists and intellectuals who arrived in New York, fleeing the war.

Francesco was a likable bohemian with a great sense of humor. From the moment of his arrival in New York he struck up a close friendship with Rembert Wurlitzer, the most renowned violin expert and merchant of the time, and with his wife, Anna Lee.

Once in a while, the Piatti was a guest at the Wurlitzer instrument workshop on 42nd Street. Here the great violin maker, Fernando Sacconi, would make adjustments and repairs to the cello as needed. I remember Wurlitzer and Sacconi very well, since I occasionally visited them during my student days at the Massachusetts Institute of Technology (MIT).

All those who knew Francesco agreed with Piatigorsky, who once wrote that he was a talented cellist and that his playing was considerably above average. However, he studied little and his public concerts were rare. An ardent theater lover, he liked to impress his friends with his stentorian renditions of Shakespeare's monologues.

Francesco led a disorderly life that became increasingly dissipated and sad. His recurrent drinking bouts occasionally landed him in the hospital. However, Francesco never lost his sense of humor. Rembert Wurlitzer was one of the friends he turned to when he needed money. Once Eleonora begged him to stop giving money to her brother, since he was undergoing rehabilitation but still could not resist spending the money on alcohol. When Francesco arrived, Rembert informed him that he didn't have "even a nickel and, therefore, could lend him nothing." The next day, Wurlitzer received a bank draft for five cents![58]

One Sunday morning Francesco stopped by Rembert and Anna Lee Wurlitzer's house. Anna Lee, who was very fond of him, greeted him warmly, but did not awake her husband since he liked to sleep late and also because she suspected that Francesco was visiting from ulterior motives. Francesco leisurely sipped his coffee, showed her some family photographs, and then began reciting passages from Shakespeare. After a considerable amount of time had passed, Anna Lee finally said, "I'm sorry, Francesco, you must be getting quite impatient, but Rembert is still sleeping." "I'm in no hurry," Francesco replied. "By now, though, the one who must be impatient is the taxi driver who brought me here and is still waiting at the door!"[59]

Since, as we have seen, Francesco was a sporadic cellist and had no ongoing need for the instrument, he sometimes lent it to several re-nowned musicians. Cassadó, an old friend of the Piatti, still lived in Italy with Francesco's mother and had occasion to use it again in that country and in Spain.[60] Hermann Busch gave many concerts in Europe and the United Sates with the Piatti, including several recitals in New York with Yehudi Menuhin. The cello was also lent to the Italian virtuoso Luigi Silva, who later taught at the Juilliard School of Music.

Pablo Casals himself also played it on several occasions. In the sum-mer of 1964, Casals had left his famous Goffriller cello with Sacconi for extensive repairs. He needed another instrument for his recitals and classes at the Marlboro Festival in Vermont. At that time the Marlboro Festival was directed by Rudolf Serkin, who in his youth had known the Mendelssohn family in Berlin. Francesco naturally consented to lend the Piatti, and Marianne Wurlitzer, Rembert and Anna Lee Wurlitzer's daughter, removed it from the vault in her father's workshop and flew with it to Vermont. Rudolf and Irene Serkin met her at the airport, and all three of them delivered the cello to Casals.[61] The Piatti was certainly no stranger to Casals, who remembered admiring it at the Mendelssohns' home in Berlin. Casals played the cello at Marlboro, and he was so pleased with it that a year later he played it again during the same festival.[62] At that time, Casals even attempted to purchase it, but Francesco and Eleonora refused his offer.

The principal player of the cello was, naturally, Francesco. However, his bohemian lifestyle, his amorous escapades, and his abuse of alcohol often placed the Piatti in great peril. One night after playing in a concert with this instrument, Francesco had one too many, and when the taxi left him at his home on East 62nd Street, Francesco couldn't quite manage to open the door to his house. Realizing he had the wrong building, he deposited the case containing the cello on the sidewalk while he looked for the right door. He finally entered his house, fell into bed, and went promptly to sleep. The next morning, when the maid came in she had a hard time waking him up. "Isn't this your cello?" she asked. "I found it lying in the street just as the garbage truck was about to pick it up!"[63]

More than once the Piatti spent the night in New York bars, left as a guarantee until Francesco could pay off his debts.[64] Under these circumstances, it is quite understandable that Eleonora deemed it prudent, and imperative, to remove the Piatti from Francesco's presence and to remove Francesco himself from New York's many temptations. At Eleonora's and Arturo Toscanini's recommendation, Max Reiter, the conductor of the San Antonio Symphony Orchestra, invited Francesco to form part of the cello section in his orchestra. Texas, far more conservative than New York and largely a "dry" state, perhaps would provide a more wholesome environment for Francesco. Rembert Wurlitzer owned a cello that he had made himself during his apprenticeship with Dieudonné in France. Wurlitzer and Sacconi persuaded Francesco to take it with him and leave the Piatti in the 42nd Street workshop vault.

At that time, the great violin expert René Morel was working with Sacconi. René, who, as we shall see later, has been closely involved with the Piatti since 1979, clearly remembers the Wurlitzer cello as well as every repair Sacconi performed on the Piatti. The former instrument was by no means a work of art, but rather the clumsy attempt of an inexperienced apprentice.[65]

Francesco left for San Antonio to play in the city's orchestra, though his stay, to say the least, was far from uneventful. Jascha Heifetz, who

was the soloist during one concert, was infuriated at Francesco's irresponsible, derisive behavior. Only Max Reiter's indulgence saved him
from being expelled.[66]

A short time after arriving in San Antonio, Francesco got drunk in
his room. He fell asleep with a lighted cigarette in his hand and started a
huge fire. Although Francesco was unharmed, his apartment was totally
destroyed. All that was left of the Wurlitzer cello was a pile of ashes.[67]
Thanks to Toscanini, it was not the Piatti!

Francesco returned to New York, where he was occasionally allowed
to use the Piatti. His last few years were pathetic. When he wasn't in
the hospital, he would return to his apartment at 91 Central Park West,
where he was tended by a nurse. His most frequent visitors were a group
of expert bridge players, especially hired to play cards with him, and two
Juilliard students, who played violin, cello, and piano trios with Francesco and his Piatti. Francesco died on September 22, 1972, at St. Clare's
Hospital on West 51st Street. The Piatti was later discovered under the
piano in his Central Park West apartment.[68]

Several years after the death of Francesco Mendelssohn, Pablo
Casals described his impressions of the Piatti during a conversation with
José María Corredor:

> *Casals:* I have never felt attracted to a Stradivarius. In my opin-
> ion, these admirable instruments have too much personality. When
> I play them, the only thought that comes to mind is that I am hold-
> ing a Stradivarius in my hands, which bothers me to no end. . . . As
> I said once to a friend about these instruments: "Let's see if Their
> Majesties grant me permission to play them."
>
> *Corredor:* Nevertheless, you were on the verge of acquiring one
> of the most magnificent cellos bearing the label of the celebrated
> violin maker.
>
> *Casals:* That's true. A long time ago I was fascinated by Mr. Men-
> delssohn's Stradivarius, regarded as Number One. I proposed to buy
> it from him, but he did not accept my offer. Later on, I was glad I
> had not bought it, for the reasons I have just mentioned and because
> the cello was too big for me. I would have had to reduce its size,
> which might have ruined it. During the early years of the Nazi per-
> secution, Mr. Mendelssohn immigrated to the United States, where
> he met a tragic end. His cello is currently in the hands of a well-
> known violin maker in New York.[69]

RUDOLF SERKIN AND THE MARLBORO FOUNDATION

In his will, Francesco left the Piatti to the Marlboro Foundation, then headed by his old boyhood friend, the great pianist Rudolf Serkin, who, as Francesco's guest, had played with Piatigorsky for Casals half a century before at the Mendelssohn's home in Berlin. Serkin and the Piatti were old friends. Serkin first laid eyes on it at the Mendelssohn's home during the 1920s. In 1964, he and Marianne Wurlitzer had delivered the (loaned) cello to Pablo Casals in Marlboro.

For the second time, the Piatti changed hands without a sale-purchase transaction. In 1867 Colonel Oliver had presented Alfredo Piatti with the cello as a gift. In 1972 Francesco Mendelssohn bequeathed it to the Marlboro school.

In 1973, on behalf of the Marlboro Foundation, Serkin lent the Piatti to a brilliant young cellist, Paul Tobias, highly recommended by his colleague and friend Gregor Piatigorsky. Paul Tobias enjoyed the use of the cello for several years until Serkin decided to reclaim it.[70]

In 1978, the foundation decided to put it up for sale, since its directors agreed that, instead of keeping it, it was preferable to take the income generated by its sale and assist talented young musicians. The foundation's only condition was that the cello should be sold neither to a museum nor to a collector, but rather to a cellist who would play it all over the world.[71]

The foundation offered the Piatti to Mstislav Rostropovich, who declined the offer because he had already purchased the marvelous Duport Stradivari from Mrs. G. Warburg. Serkin then contacted Jacques Français, the most important stringed-instrument dealer in New York.

MY FIRST CONTACTS WITH THE PIATTI

The date September 7, 1978, is forever engraved in my memory. I was having an early breakfast in a Mexico City restaurant when I received a call from my brother, Juan Luis, with sensational news: our good friend Jacques Français was urgently trying to contact me because it was highly probable that the Piatti would be sold in the very near future. For me the Piatti had always been a legendary instrument that I had learned about through hearsay and from books. I immediately contacted Jacques. It was true: Rudolf Serkin, artistic director of the Marlboro School, had practically arrived at the decision to sell the cello. Since Jacques and I had been close friends almost all our lives, I was the first person he called.

I replied that naturally I was interested, but that obviously I would have to see the instrument and try it out at my leisure. Furthermore, in this particular case, I first had to sell the cello I already owned to raise the necessary funds for the purchase. We agreed to talk again if Serkin definitely confirmed his decision to sell the Piatti.

A few days later I received another call from Jacques. He knew I had to stop over in New York in October, and Serkin had offered to lend him the cello for a few hours so I could see it and play it.

On October 20, 1978, my wife and I arrived at Jacques Français's workshop on West 57th Street, near Carnegie Hall. At 10:15 a.m. Jacques showed up with a case containing the cello. Barely able to contain myself, I eagerly tried to open it, but it was locked. After ten interminable minutes, the key finally appeared, and at last we had the opportunity to cast our eyes on the famous cello. Although it was marvelously preserved, it was rather filthy and in need of repair. I was left alone to try the cello. A few minutes later I left the room and said to Jacques: "I am truly disappointed. This cello has no tone. It's anemic, dull, and opaque. Is this the tone of the famous Piatti?"

Since Jacques was totally mystified, I asked him to listen to it with René Morel, one of his closest collaborators and an undisputed expert in these matters. While I played, I couldn't help noticing the bewildered expressions on their faces.

"You are absolutely right," observed René. "It has no sound. However, this is not due to the cello itself, but to the fact that it is poorly adjusted. I have no doubt whatsoever about its potential tone. The cello must be adjusted, and we must move the sound post and perhaps change the angle of the neck and fingerboard. Then you will see the genuine marvel that the Piatti can be."

Jacques was in total agreement. "This cello is on loan to cellist Paul Tobias until the end of the year. At the end of December the Marlboro Foundation will give it to us, and then we can adjust and repair it. We will call you early next year, and then you'll change your mind—you'll see."

Deeply discouraged and somewhat skeptical, we left Jacques Français's workshop. I had a particularly hectic, concert-packed year ahead of me: seventy-nine concerts, to be exact. With the intense preparation for so many performances, which included, besides, a great many works that were entirely new to me, I temporarily forgot the Piatti.

In May 1979 I stopped over in New York again en route to Europe, and on the 16th I had my second encounter with the Piatti. It had undergone a complete transformation. Thanks to René's work and adjustments, it had partially recovered its lost voice, and the wood on the top (or table) was no longer quite as grimy, although it still needed a more thorough cleaning job. Furthermore, the angle of the neck still had to be adapted to the present-day style of playing, which required opening up the cello. If the sound has improved to this extent, I thought to myself, Jacques and René are undoubtedly right in saying that that the instrument has indeed an extraordinary potential. Right then and there I decided that Jacques should make an offer to Serkin on my behalf, on the condition that Jacques sell the cello I would leave him for that purpose.

A short time later, Jacques notified me that he had found a buyer for my cello and that Serkin had received my offer. He wanted to make sure that the Piatti would not end up in a museum showcase, condemned to silence, nor in a collector's mansion, but rather in the hands of someone who would play it all over the world. To reassure him, I promptly sent Serkin a copy of my concert schedule for 1979: almost 100 concerts in Mexico, Poland, Bulgaria, the Federal Republic of Germany, the German Democratic Republic, Russia, the five Soviet Central Asian republics, Japan, and the People's Republic of China.

On July 17, 1979, I received a call from Jacques Français announcing that Serkin had accepted my offer. On July 23 the transaction was completed. The Piatti was mine!

CHAPTER 4

A Brief Autobiographical Note

I must now introduce the new owner of the Piatti, that is, myself.

I have often remarked that I owe my very existence to music. This apparently trite comment is neither an exaggeration nor a romanticized idea: it is the statement of a fact.

THE PRIETO QUARTETS

My father was an excellent amateur violinist. As a law student in the Spanish city of Oviedo, he played with the local symphony orchestra for several years. However, what he really desired with a passion was to form his own string quartet. At that time in Oviedo there was a French family that was also extremely fond of music. Maurice Jacqué, my maternal grandfather, played the viola, and his children, my mother, Cécile, and my uncle Léon, played the violin and the cello, respectively. They happened to be looking for a violinist to complete a quartet.

My mother's family and my father had a friend in common who learned of these reciprocal searches and introduced everyone to one another. It was therefore fate, in the guise of music—or more specifically, in the guise of a string quartet—that brought my parents, Carlos and Cécile, together. The quartet met habitually and soon established the first Prieto Quartet, comprised of four excellent nonprofessional musicians. After a few years my parents were married, and then moved to Mexico. I was born in Mexico City, under the sign of music.

The atmosphere in our home was exceptionally conducive to the cultivation of our musical skills. Even before my birth, my mother had decided I should take up the cello because my uncle Léon lived in France and the family lacked a cellist.

At the age of four, I began my studies with Imre Hartman, a former member of the Léner Quartet of Budapest, which, to the good fortune

14. The Prieto family: (LEFT TO RIGHT) *Cécile Jacqué (mother), Carlos Prieto (father), Maurice Jacqué (grandfather), nanny, and Carlos Prieto (1 year of age). Mexico, 1938.*

of countless music lovers and students, had taken refuge in Mexico during World War II. Then my brother, Juan Luis, two years younger than I, began studying the violin. Before long, when we were still quite young, we started playing quartets. Thus the Prieto Quartet No. 2 was instituted. It consisted of my father and my brother at the violin, my mother at the viola, and I at the cello. The quartet took on a more youthful appearance when my son Carlos Miguel—now a conductor and violinist—and my nephew Juan Luis grew older. Both of them also started playing the violin in early childhood. Naturally, this was the Prieto Quartet No. 3. My brother, who is a businessman, went from the violin to the viola; Carlos Miguel and my nephew Juan Luis take turns on the first and second violins, and I remain at the cello. The Prieto Quartet, therefore, has encompassed four generations. Now in its third version, it constitutes what is probably a highly unusual case of uninterrupted musical family tradition. Unlike the previous Prieto Quartets, which only played in the privacy of their homes, the new quartet has been performing in public concerts throughout Mexico, the United States, and Europe since 1989.

While attending the Liceo Franco Mexicano in Mexico City, I still continued practicing the cello. By the age of sixteen, when I finished my studies at the lycée, I had already given several recitals and concerts as a soloist. It seemed that I was heading toward a musical career. However, it was not until after I ventured into entirely different activities that I became a full-time cellist.

I completed my studies at the lycée with high marks in physics and mathematics. There were two paths open to me: music or a profession linked to my apparent scientific inclinations. I opted for the latter, partly influenced by my parents, who dreaded the hardships and sacrifices of a musical career. Attracted by the reputation of the Massachusetts Institute of Technology (MIT), I prepared for the entrance exams and for its other strict admission requirements. One day I received a letter with the red MIT letterhead: I had been accepted! Looking back on that turning point in my life, I don't know whether to describe it as fortunate. Indeed, although my studies at MIT provided me with a series of fascinating experiences, they also delayed my true vocation—music—by several years.

MIT

In September 1954, at the age of seventeen, I entered MIT, where I obtained degrees in metallurgic engineering and economics. In addition to being one of the leading scientific and technological centers in the world, MIT also accords crucial importance to the humanities, especially music. This fact is demonstrated by the outstanding quality of the performing groups—the symphony orchestra, where I was first cello and soloist, the wind ensemble, the jazz and chamber music groups—and by the excellence of its music faculty.[1] Furthermore, the school has an excellent music library, where I discovered countless works new to me, starting with the works of Dmitry Shostakovich. As we shall see later on, they were to play a definitive role in my life.

THE STEEL INDUSTRY

After graduating from MIT, I returned to Mexico and started work as an engineer at Fundidora Monterrey, one of Mexico's leading iron and steel industrial complexes. In 1964 I moved to Monterrey, having been appointed assistant director of production in the steel plant. Because of my intense work schedule, the cello was relegated to second place, but I managed to practice a few hours every night. Every time I took out my cello I felt a pang of regret at not having devoted myself to music.

A few years passed, and by the mid-1970s, I was a well-established businessman in Mexico. At that time I was already president of Fundidora Monterrey and chairman of several national business organizations. Although I found my industrial activities very stimulating, my misgivings at having abandoned the cello persisted and, in time, grew more intense and bitter. I felt that in failing to follow the dictates of my musical vocation, I had not been true to myself. Finally, in 1975 the day came when I confronted my dilemma: either continue to live with a sense of futility and emptiness at having chosen the wrong path (and soon there would be no other alternative), or take the bull by the horns, renounce my industrial and entrepreneurial activities, and dedicate myself entirely to music.

A DIFFICULT METAMORPHOSIS

Thus, in 1975, after undergoing considerable inner turmoil, I opted for the second path. True, I had studied the cello ever since my earliest childhood, but the profession of soloist generally demands the most absolute, unfailing dedication. When I finally made up my mind to change my career—and my life—I was fully conscious, or so I believed then, of the tremendous risks and obstacles involved. When weighed in the balance, on one hand there was my successful career as a businessman, and on the other, my profession as a cellist with an uncertain future. I could well be headed toward a colorless, mediocre career or even failure, either result having serious consequences for me and my entire family. I had the advantage of my self-confidence, my genuine passion for music, and my fiery determination to work with an intensity that would compensate for those years that, though certainly not wasted, had been lost as far as the cello was concerned.

I spent long months studying with Pierre Fournier in Geneva and several summers with Leonard Rose in New York. As I mentioned before, I had believed myself fully aware of the difficulties ahead. If I had had a crystal ball, perhaps the balance would have tipped to the other side, since the path I chose turned out to be far more hazardous than I had imagined. I really don't know. Fortunately, since I did not consult the supernatural, no one or nothing could dissuade me from making a decision that I have never regretted.

After 1975 I began to play more frequently in Mexico and other countries.

MY LONG RELATIONSHIP WITH RUSSIA,
SHOSTAKOVICH, AND STRAVINSKY

My interest in Russia began during my university days at MIT. I heard a Shostakovich symphony for the first time in 1955, in its music library. It had such a profound impact on me that before long I had listened to every single recorded work by this composer and had read all his scores available in the library.

It was not that I admired all his music; on the contrary, besides the works that filled me with enthusiasm and emotion, there were those whose banality and superficiality both astonished and disappointed me. A great many of his works were shrouded in mystery. After his second and third symphonies and his opera *Lady Macbeth of Mtsensk* were played in the Soviet Union, they were denounced as "formalistic, bourgeois and decadent" and banned from the Soviet repertoire. His Fourth Symphony had been extensively rehearsed, yet on the eve of the premiere, the composer withdrew it without any explanation; it had never been performed in the intervening twenty years. I would eagerly await the announcement of a new composition or the resurrection of previous works, going to great lengths to obtain his new recordings. Sometimes, a new piece proved to be a great disappointment, whereas others were veritable masterpieces that once again kindled my enthusiasm for his music and my curiosity about his personality, both equally enigmatic.

My interest in Shostakovich soon extended to the language, history, and culture of Russia. I enrolled in MIT's Russian Department and took every course offered. (This part of my education is a historical artifact: MIT canceled its Russian-language courses some years ago.) When I was still at MIT, I had my first opportunity to visit the Soviet Union. In 1958, the State Department invited the Russian-language students to apply to be interpreters for a huge exhibit mounted by the United States in Moscow. Although I passed the exam, I was extremely disappointed when I was rejected because I was not a U.S. citizen. Then in 1959 the opportunity arose again, from a series of chance circumstances. That year, an important official Soviet delegation, headed by Anastas I. Mikoyan, then first deputy premier of the USSR, visited Mexico. An extremely shrewd politician, he was one of the few to survive all the purges from Lenin's era to the present. I also met the composers Shostakovich and Kabalevsky, who were part of the delegation.

The official Soviet mission also went to Monterrey, the capital of Nuevo León. The visit included a tour of Fundidora Monterrey, where

I was employed. Because the official interpreter was temporarily indisposed and there was no other option, I replaced him. For several hours, I accompanied Mikoyan, Mr. Bazykin (the Soviet ambassador to Mexico), and other delegates.

When he took his leave, Mikoyan said to me, "You, young Prieto, must visit the Soviet Union. Wouldn't you like to go?" "Of course!" I replied. "Not only would I love to go, but I would like to stay for a while and take intensive Russian courses." Mikoyan then turned to the Soviet ambassador and said, "Comrade Bazykin, you will be in charge of organizing young Prieto's visit to Russia," leaving me absolutely speechless.

Meanwhile, I obtained the necessary leave of absence from the plant. However, several weeks went by without any news of my trip to the USSR. My disappointment increased as the months passed with no word.

After a year, I forgot all about it. However, at that time I was totally unfamiliar with Soviet bureaucracy. Two and a half years later, I received a call from Ambassador Bazykin. The trip, as well as my enrollment in Moscow's Lomonosov University, had been arranged. On September 11, 1962, I arrived in Moscow. It seemed incredible to me that I was actually there.

It was during the era of Nikita Khrushchev, the first reformer after Stalin's terrifying dictatorship. It was a small-scale *glasnost* and an incipient *perestroika*. A series of unprecedented technological and scientific advances—the launching of *Sputnik*, the first artificial satellite, and the flight of Yuri Gagarin, the first human to orbit the earth—had transformed the USSR into a pioneer of space exploration. The prevailing optimism prompted Khrushchev to predict that within twenty years living standards in the USSR would surpass those of the United States and that the Soviet System would lead the United States to its grave. "We will bury you," he had declared. That first sojourn, during which I obtained my diploma in Russian from Moscow's Lomonosov University, was an exhilarating experience for me.

I will only recount three episodes corresponding to that particular period.

THE HISTORIC VOYAGE OF IGOR STRAVINSKY

I had been in Moscow for about three weeks when a sensational event occurred: Igor Stravinsky, who had been away from his homeland for half a century, visited Russia.

Stravinsky, like other Western composers, had been the target of vicious attacks in the USSR. He was described as an "artistic ideologist of the imperialistic bourgeoisie," an "apostle of the reactionary forces of bourgeois music," and a "shameless prophet of bourgeois modernism." "The composer's soul must have been castrated and destroyed in order for him to create such horrendous music as this," wrote a Soviet "musicologist." Stravinsky, for his part, was unsparing in his criticisms and acerbic comments regarding Soviet politics, art, and music.

In light of this, it is understandable that Stravinsky's arrival in the USSR, where he was to remain for four weeks, was an extraordinary, historic landmark. His first concert, scheduled for September 26, 1962, raised tremendous expectations. In response to an official invitation from the same Soviet government that had so maliciously attacked him in the past, one of the greatest composers of the twentieth century—Rimsky-Korsakov's former pupil, a legendary figure who had left tsarist Russia fifty years earlier—was now arriving in Soviet Russia.

Naturally, the tickets for his concerts sold out immediately. Fortunately, Stravinsky himself obtained an invitation for me; I had known

15. (LEFT TO RIGHT): *Poet Carlos Bousoño Prieto, Juan Luis Prieto, Igor Stravinsky, Cecilé Jacqué (mother), Carlos Prieto, composer María Teresa Prieto, and Carlos Prieto (father). 1948.*

16. With Stravinsky (LEFT TO RIGHT): *Carlos Prieto, Cécile Jacqué (mother), Igor Stravinsky, Carlos Prieto (father), and Juan Luis Prieto. (The other individuals in the photo are not identified.) Mexico City, 1952.*

17. With Stravinsky at a bullfight (LEFT TO RIGHT, *starting above the letter* V): *Carlos Prieto, Igor Stravinsky (covering his mouth), Vera Stravinsky, Juan Luis Prieto, and Robert Craft. Mexico, 1961.*

him since my childhood. On every one of his visits to Mexico, he and his wife, Vera, would come to my parents' home for lunch or dinner. A few months before his return to Russia he had visited us in Mexico, where my brother, Juan Luis, and I had the unique experience of accompanying the Stravinskys and their friend, conductor Robert Craft, to a bullfight, which Stravinsky had expressed a desire to attend.[2]

As soon as I learned of his arrival in Moscow with Vera and Craft, I went to see them, and they immediately obtained a pass for me to attend all his rehearsals and his two concerts in Moscow. The evening of the first concert I agreed to meet them at 6:15 in their suite at the National Hotel. Half an hour later, Stravinsky, Vera, Craft, and Ralph Parker—an English friend of theirs—and I left for the Great Hall of the Conservatory.

The audience also included a number of prominent personalities from the Soviet government and the intelligentsia, headed by Ekaterina Furtseva, minister of culture. Tikhon Khrennikov, secretary of the Soviet Composers' Union, who years before had written the most virulent attacks against Stravinsky, was in charge of the official address, welcoming him back to his homeland. When Stravinsky appeared on stage, he was greeted with thunderous applause. The program, which comprised *Ode*, *Le Sacre du Printemps* (*The Rite of Spring*), and *Orpheus*, was a resounding success.

When the concert was over, we returned to the National Hotel for a private dinner in the Stravinskys' suite. The meal consisted of Soviet champagne, caviar, cold chicken, black bread, and butter. Stravinsky was deeply moved—ecstatic—at the Russian audience's warm reception. Unlike Craft, he was delighted with the USSR State Orchestra's playing of *The Rite of Spring*. According to its composer, it had been one of the finest versions of this work he had ever heard. Not only in his euphoria regarding the orchestra, but also in many other details, I perceived how Stravinsky's innate "Russianness" had emerged. He enjoyed everything: the flavor of the bread, the smell of the earth, the Soviet champagne he drank, the fact he could ramble on endlessly in his mother tongue.

Ekaterina Furtseva, in her official capacity as minister of culture, offered both a welcome and a farewell reception in his honor. Here, two natives of St. Petersburg, Stravinsky and Shostakovich, met for the first time. During the farewell dinner party, Shostakovich approached Stravinsky and, in a moving gesture, confided that when he saw the score of the Symphony of Psalms for the first time, he had been so impressed that he made a transcription for two pianos that he wanted to present to Stravinsky as a farewell gift. Shostakovich's generosity sharply contrasted with Stravinsky's attitude toward him. When I asked him, "What do you think of Shostakovich?" he answered, "I never think of Shostakovich; I only think of him when someone asks me: 'What do you think of Shostakovich?'"

Several of Stravinsky's opinions that I jotted down include the following: on Prokofiev's talent as a composer: "Prokofiev was a great pianist"; on Khachaturian's works: (in Russian) "Who needs music like the kind composed by Khachaturian?" adding, in French, "*Toute sa musique est laide et vulgaire!*" [All his music is ugly and coarse!]

After Stravinsky's visit to Moscow, the Great Hall of the Conservatory accorded me special treatment. Since officials had seen me arrive at rehearsals and concerts with the illustrious composer, they must have thought that I was either a celebrity in the music world or a high Party member. I never attempted to find out the real reason. But whenever they were sold out, they always let me enter through the stage door and listen to concerts from the wings.

A GRAVE CRISIS

On October 16, 1962, the world was shaken by an unprecedented crisis: the danger of nuclear confrontation. President Kennedy's government discovered that the Russians were installing military bases in Cuba capable of launching medium-range missiles with nuclear warheads. Although the installation had not yet reached the operational stage, Soviet ships, loaded with rockets and other military infrastructure, were already on their way to Cuba.

On October 22, President Kennedy announced a naval blockade of Cuba and declared that, if necessary, the passage of Soviet ships would be stopped by force. News of the crisis reached me in unusual circumstances that were, at the same time, rather comforting. The night of October 23, I had gone to the Bolshoi Theater to see Mussorgsky's *Boris Godunov*, an opera I did not want to miss under any circumstance. Jerome Hines from the United States was singing the role of Boris.

Present in the official balcony were First Secretary of the Party Nikita Khrushchev; Anastas Mikoyan, who, as I mentioned earlier, was responsible for my presence in the USSR; Frol Romanovich Kozlov and other government officials; and a large Romanian delegation headed by Gheorghiu-Dej. Khrushchev was the picture of tranquility and good humor. I watched as he joked with his companions in the balcony; I could almost hear his guffaws. As he enthusiastically applauded Hines, a great baritone, I never imagined what was occurring at that precise moment.

After leaving the theater I stopped for a sandwich at a cafeteria near the Moskva Hotel. As always, I read the *Moscow Evening News* while I ate. All of a sudden an article on the last page of the newspaper caught my eye. It was a brief news item from the TASS news agency concerning President Kennedy's speech announcing the blockade of Cuba. I also read the editorials indignantly protesting this arbitrary decision. Since there was no mention at all of the Soviet missiles in Cuba, I was completely disconcerted. I could not understand Kennedy's motives or actions. My subsequent attempts to tune in to the news on a shortwave radio in my room proved to be fruitless. The news seemed worrisome, but not enough to alarm me. The image of Khrushchev laughing jovially at the Bolshoi prevented me from imagining a truly alarming crisis.

Although the morning papers provided little concrete information, their numerous editorials reflected considerable indignation at the United States' "provocative actions toward the Island of Freedom." The articles from the foreign press mentioned only that the Western European governments were thoroughly confused and disgusted by the United States' actions.

That evening when I returned to my room, a coded telegram from my father was awaiting me:

TELEGRAM: 22 OCTOBER 10:30 PM
URGENT YOU LEAVE FOR PARIS FOR INTERVIEW WITH YOUR
UNCLE. HE URGENTLY NEEDS TO SEE YOU REGARDING THE
DIFFICULTIES ARISEN WITH YOUR UNCLE JUAN. CARLOS
PRIETO

I immediately understood that my Uncle Juan was John F. Kennedy and that my father was giving me a reason to get out of Moscow. Until I received this message it had not crossed my mind to leave the USSR. I kept recalling Khrushchev at the Bolshoi and thought that if a serious conflict were about to occur, the same danger would follow me anywhere, be it Moscow, Paris, or New York. So I decided to stay, and answered with the following:

MOSCOW: OCTOBER 24. ABSOLUTE CALM. UNCLE JUAN IS
BETTER. WILL STAY HERE. CARLOS

Two days later the Soviet media announced that the problem was resolved: Kennedy declared the end of the blockade, the USSR was removing its missiles, and, in exchange, the United States promised not to invade Cuba.

Throughout the duration of the crisis, I experienced the anxiety resulting from a lack of information, which the Soviets suffered for decades. I perused all the newspapers over and over again, trying to read between the lines, and at night I spent many hours glued to my radio, attempting, sometimes successfully, to catch a broadcast from the West.

AN EMOTIONAL ENCOUNTER:
TWO SISTERS SEPARATED FOR TWENTY-FIVE YEARS

Before my departure from Mexico for the USSR, I went to take leave of my dear friends Masha and Vladimir Kaspé. Vladimir was a great architect, as well as an excellent pianist who had played chamber music with my family on many occasions. Masha, his wife, a woman of exceptional sensibility and culture, had a profound knowledge of Russian poetry and literature. In fact, I began learning Russian from her in 1957 before pursuing my Russian courses at MIT.

When I went to visit Masha and Vladimir, Masha confided that she had a sister in the Soviet Union, Rosa Vikker, with whom she had lost contact before World War II. I asked for additional information in case I was able to locate her in Moscow. Masha did not have an address for Rosa and did not even know if she was still alive. The only information she could provide was the last address in Moscow for her elder sister, Betty Prissman, who had died many years ago: 69 Maroseyka Street. Masha was rather reluctant to give me the address, since she knew the possible dangers of snooping around in the USSR, which was frowned upon by the KGB.

By December 7, 1962, I had been in the USSR for three months and moved about quite freely. I never noticed anyone following me or any microphones hidden in my room. Perhaps I was being watched, but I had reached the conclusion that the KGB surely had more important things to do than investigate the activities of a young Mexican student.

On December 7 I decided to take certain precautions. I memorized the name of Marsha's sister, Rose Vikker, and even her maiden name, Rosa Shapiro. I also memorized the name and address of the deceased sister—Betty Prissman, 69 Maroseyka Street—so as to avoid carrying any piece of paper that could incriminate either Rosa or me if she were still alive.

After taking the metro, I proceeded on foot to 69 Maroseyka Street, which turned out to be a large apartment building. I asked the concierge if she knew a Betty Prissman, but since she was quite young, she obviously could not have known her. The person who might remember, she told me, was Olga Novikova, the building's oldest tenant. Citizen Novikova (the term *Mrs.* had ceased to be used in 1917) was out shopping, and returned twenty or thirty minutes later. She remembered Betty Prissman, but had never known Rosa and, for that matter, was unaware of her existence. I asked if anyone else in the building might remember Betty. At first she said no, but then she suddenly remembered, "Yes, Betty had a cook called Tania. Tania is retired and lives in a building on Novoslobodskaya Street."

I located Tania, who received me rather warily at first, but after we exchanged a few words, she must have decided that I was harmless. In fact, she had been Betty Prissman's cook.

"Did you know Betty's sister, Rosa Vikker?" I asked.

"Of course," she replied. "She is the younger sister."

"Is she alive?"

"Of course. I see her every now and again."

I was filled with emotion. Masha's sister was alive! I only needed the address. Tania remembered it perfectly: 25 Petrovsko Razumovsky Proyezd. I found the building and entered. After searching for several hours, at three o'clock I was standing before Rosa Vikker's apartment. I knocked, and a woman with very white hair opened the door. "I have come from Mexico," I said. "I am Masha and Vladimir Kaspé's friend."

The woman paled, and, without a word, closed the door, leaving me outside. I decided to wait awhile. If the woman who answered was Rosa, then the mention of her sister, who had been lost since 1937, might have been too much for her. Also, the presence of a stranger might have filled her with terror, since contact with a foreigner during the Stalinist regime could have meant that an accusation and the gulag were not that far off.

Less than a minute passed. An elderly man now opened the door and in a low voice asked me to repeat the reason for my visit. He let me in and closed the door carefully. "Excuse me," he said. "But my wife has just received a great shock. She'll be back shortly."

The miracle had occurred. I had found Masha's sister, Rosa Vikker, who was in good health. Rosa emerged shortly, and over tea asked me questions about Masha and Vladimir. As time passed, I noticed the fear perceptively recede from their faces. Nevertheless, the conversation continued practically in whispers. "The walls are very thin, and you can hear everything, well, you know . . ." they explained.

After a while they started describing how terrifying life had been under Stalin. No family had been left intact. Those who had not lost a father had lost a son or a brother. Entire families were completely wiped out. When they mentioned Stalin's name their voices became almost inaudible.

I did not tell Masha and Vladimir Kaspé about this meeting while I was still in Russia, because I knew it could be dangerous for Rosa and her family. However, once aboard the Air France plane that took me to Paris, the first thing I did was to write a long letter to Masha and Vladimir.

The sisters renewed contact. Although Rosa was never able to leave the USSR, her son-in-law, Leonid, managed to visit Mexico during Brezhnev's time as a member of a delegation of architects, and he was able to meet his aunt and uncle.

After that first visit to the USSR, I returned to Mexico and continued to work in the steel industry until, as I explained earlier, I decided to dedicate myself completely to the cello. Later I returned to the USSR on many occasions as a concert cellist. My recollections, spanning three decades in that vast region, are described in my book *From the USSR to Russia*, published in Mexico in 1993 and 1994.[3]

CHAPTER 5

Around the World
with the Piatti

As I mentioned at the end of Chapter 3, the Piatti became officially mine on July 23, 1979. Since I was about to embark on a long concert tour, I stopped over in New York to meet with Jacques Français and René Morel and to decide on the necessary repairs. Besides the fact that René Morel is also my distant relative and a close friend, he is one of the finest instrument restorers and sound adjusters of our time. In his opinion, the Piatti was in exceptionally good condition, but we agreed that the following work should be done:

1. A thorough cleaning to remove all the dust, rosin and other particles that for several decades had stuck to the top, back, and ribs, marring the beauty of the wood and varnish.
2. Retouch the varnish wherever necessary.
3. Open the cello, insert a new bass bar, and adjust the angle of the neck.
4. Repair any obvious cracks.

I returned to Jacques Français' workshop in early February to check up on the progress of the work. Since René had removed the top, its interior was perfectly visible. According to René and Jacques, they had never seen an instrument of that age in such perfect condition. Although barely a few square centimeters of wood had been cleaned, the marvelous original varnish emerged. The cello required no major repairs. René estimated that it would be ready in five or six months. Meanwhile, I continued to use my 1725 Goffriller.

The Piatti was delivered to me early in 1981. René advised me to play it as much as possible. Instruments tend to lose their sound, to become mute, if they spend long periods in silence. This was certainly the case with the Piatti, which had been subjected to a form of surgery and had not been played for nineteen months. The wood needed to vibrate for many hours so that the instrument could recover the full power of its voice. René kept insisting that perseverance was the only secret to restoring the Piatti's former splendor. I followed his advice by devoting countless hours to this cello.

The month of March arrived. The 19th was the date scheduled for a tribute to Joaquín Rodrigo in Mexico City's Sala Nezahualcóyotl, where the composer himself would be present. I was to play, for the first time in Mexico, his *Concierto en modo galante* (for cello and orchestra), as well as the world premiere of a piece for cello solo entitled *Como una fantasía*, which he graciously dedicated to me. Should I choose the Goffriller or the Piatti for such an important occasion? Although the Stradivari sounded better and better each day, I did not hesitate: I chose the Goffriller.

MY FIRST CONCERTS WITH THE PIATTI

My first concerts with the Piatti took place in October 1981, with a series of recitals in Mexico City's Sala Manuel Ponce, at the Palace of Fine Arts. For these recitals I selected a veritable marathon of works for solo cello:

Ricercari by Domenico Gabrielli (1689), one of the first works ever composed for solo cello
J. S. Bach's six suites, the supreme masterwork of cello literature, created in 1720, like the Piatti
Sonata, op. 8, by Zoltán Kodály, one of the twentieth century's fundamental works for solo cello
Como una fantasía by Joaquín Rodrigo
Twelve Caprices by Alfredo Piatti

Although I did not announce this publicly, I included Piatti's caprices as a personal tribute to the great Italian cellist who preceded me in the use and enjoyment of this instrument. Technically, these particular works are extremely difficult, and as I studied them, I reflected that they were undoubtedly very familiar to my cello, since they had been often played by their author. I hoped that, as in the case of horses that always find their way back to the stable, the cello's familiarity with the caprices would guide me through the maze of arpeggios and double stops! However my vain hope was dispelled soon enough, since I had to devote a

18. With famous violin expert René Morel. New York, 1979.

19. With Spanish composer Joaquín Rodrigo. Mexico, 1980.

considerable amount of time to surmounting their intricacies, though not quite as much as the endless hours required by the Bach suites. It was a pantheon of works for solo cello, clearly worthy of the venerable instrument that I was playing in public for the first time.

Nevertheless, I felt that the Piatti had not yet attained its full potential, and in November and December of that same year, 1981, I again decided to take my Goffriller on a long concert tour of Spain, Switzerland, Norway, Sweden, and France.

During the summer of 1982, I spent a few weeks in New York with my good friend and teacher Leonard Rose. We spent hours comparing the sound of his magnificent Nicolo Amati with that of the Piatti and the Goffriller. Rose was dazzled by the Goffriller, which he pronounced a "truly first-rate concert instrument," and somewhat bewildered by the Piatti, which still did not completely respond.

Together we took the Piatti to René Morel so he could listen to it and examine it carefully. René discovered that the changes in climate had affected the adjustment of the cello and that the bridge Leonard had temporarily placed turned out to be counterproductive. The next day I returned to the workshop to try the cello. It was completely transformed. At last, it finally sounded the way we had expected. René was pleased but not surprised. His prediction had come true.

I returned to see Leonard. Once again, we began our comparisons by taking turns playing the Amati, the Goffriller, and the Piatti, string by string, on low, medium, and high registers. That day, the Piatti finally sounded second to none, and since then it has always been by my side. Occasionally, for certain pieces, I prefer the deep, powerful tone of the Goffriller. Cello infidelity—not as serious as marital infidelity—adds variety to the musical experience and allows one cello to rest, which is advisable from time to time.

FIRST CONCERTS IN THE UNITED STATES: 1983 AND 1984

In January 1983 I embarked with the Piatti on my first concert tour of the United States. The excellent pianist Doris Stevenson was my partner, and the program included a Bach sonata, Kodály's Sonata for solo cello, Shostakovich's Sonata for cello and piano, and Tchaikovsky's *Pezzo capriccioso* in its version for cello and piano. We began in New York, playing concerts in Poughkeepsie, Binghamton, Long Beach, Buffalo, and Rochester (at the Eastman School of Music). Then the tour went on to

Cincinnati, Boston's Jordan Hall, Atlanta, Baltimore, and Washington D.C.'s Kennedy Center.

The concerts in Boston—where I had spent over five years as a student—and at the Kennedy Center were particularly emotional experiences for me, and, in the dressing room at the end of the concert, I was delighted to see several of my former MIT professors. The recital at the Kennedy Center and the presence of Marta Casals Istomin, were, of course, major highlights of our tour.

The concerts on the first tour were encouraging, receiving excellent reviews, and thus paved the way for my return the following year.

Once again with Doris Stevenson at the piano, the second tour took place in January and February 1984. It consisted of ten recitals, the most important of which were held in San Francisco, Dallas, Toronto, Union, New Jersey (at Kean College), and New York, where I made my Carnegie Hall debut on February 11, 1984.

Playing in Carnegie Hall was a dream come true. We rehearsed the morning of the concert, and merely stepping onstage before the empty hall was in itself a thrilling experience. We marveled at the theater's acoustics and magnificence as seen from the stage. The program was the same as from the previous year's tour: a Bach sonata, Kodály's Sonata for cello solo, Shostakovich's Sonata, and Tchaikovsky's *Pezzo capriccioso*.

The following day I played in Toronto, and then immediately departed for Bulgaria.

A week later, while still in Bulgaria, I received a phone call from Carlos Lagunas, the Mexican ambassador. He had wonderful news: the *New York Times* had just published an excellent review of my Carnegie Hall recital.

1985: AROUND THE WORLD WITH THE PIATTI

The year 1985 contained a heavy concert schedule: seventy-eight in eight countries: the United States, France, Germany, the Soviet Union (including stops in Estonia, Lithuania, Latvia), Mexico, Colombia, China, and India. The Piatti and I traveled 93,000 miles on fifty-one flights. I spent hundreds of hours aboard airplanes. I made the most of so much free time by taking notes, which eventually became a book published in 1988 and 1989. Entitled *Around the World with a Cello*, it could just as well been called *Around the World with the Piatti*.[1] Here I will refer to only a few of the most interesting highlights of such a hectic year.

20. The six Bach cello suites. Lincoln Center, New York, 1985.

In the first place, 1985 marked the 300th anniversary of Johann Sebastian Bach's birth. I have always believed that Bach's music is one of
the most sublime manifestations of the human spirit. His six suites for
solo cello are a monument without parallel in the entire cello repertoire.
Consequently, many of my concerts that year were either totally or partially dedicated to these works.

BACH'S SIX SUITES AT NEW YORK'S LINCOLN CENTER

On March 18, three days before the tercentennial, I played all six suites in one concert at Alice Tully Hall in New York's Lincoln Center (Fig. 20). It is highly unusual to program the complete suites in one concert. Since they demand exceptional concentration on the part of the public and the cellist alike, they are usually divided into two recitals of three suites each. However, it is a fascinating experience to listen to the complete suites in one sitting and to admire the extraordinarily rich diversity of these masterpieces.

BACH'S COMPLETE CELLO REPERTOIRE IN PARIS

In November I performed a cycle of three concerts, entitled "Bach's Complete Works for Cello," at Paris's Salle Chopin-Pleyel (Fig. 21). In addition to the six suites, the cycle also included the three sonatas for cello and harpsichord. Though originally written for viola da gamba, they can be played just as well on the cello. For these sonatas I was fortunate to have the French harpsichordist Claire Corneloup as my accompanist.

A RECORDING IN BERLIN, AN INCIDENT IN NUREMBERG, AND THE PIATTI IN THE HOSPITAL

In June 1985 I arrived in Berlin with conductor Jorge Velazco. We had been invited to record the first cello concerto ever composed by a Mexican composer, Ricardo Castro, whom I will talk further about in the next chapter. We had one rehearsal, then recorded the following day. Time, as is often the case, turned out to be an inexorable enemy. We had barely an hour and a half to complete the recording. We finished at five o'clock, just as our time was running out.

On my return to Mexico I stopped over in Nuremberg. My recollections of this city are no longer associated with Meistersingers, but rather with its airport and a passenger who was in such a dreadful hurry that she lost control of her baggage cart. It collided with the cello case, which crashed to the ground. The passenger did not even stop, and barely managed to mutter, "*entschuldigen!*" ("Excuse me.") I immediately assumed that something dreadful had occurred. Indeed, I opened the case, and the view was awful: the fingerboard had been detached from the cello's neck. The fingerboard, in case the reader has forgotten the cello anatomy lesson that I presented in Chapter 1, is the long piece of ebony under the strings. It is, of course, impossible to play without it. The next day in New York, I gave the cello to René Morel, who assured me that the only damage—spectacular, though not serious—was the loosened piece. The Piatti was promptly "hospitalized," and twenty-four hours later was given a clean bill of health.

CHINA

I have made two concert tours of China. The first took place in 1979 as a member of the Trío México, together with violinist Manuel Suárez and pianist Jorge Suárez. In twelve days we played thirteen concerts throughout China, from Beijing to Guangzhou (Canton). The country

21. The complete Bach cello works. Paris, 1985.

22. With Isabel Prieto (wife) and Chelo Prieto (the cello). Beijing, China, 1985.

was just emerging from the chaos of the Cultural Revolution and embarking on a new path under the innovative leadership of an extraordinary figure, Deng Xiaoping.

I returned with my wife in 1985 (Fig. 22). This new tour was of particular interest to us, since it enabled us to compare—within obvious limitations—the China of 1979 with the China of 1985. Six years are barely an instant in China's long history. However, we were absolutely astounded at the changes we perceived, at the inexorable drive of its economic progress, and at the general mood of the people. I also witnessed remarkable advances in music.

In 1985, with pianist Bao Hui Qiao, we played and taught master classes in Beijing, Qingdao, Jinan, Qufu, and Shanghai. Two memories from that trip stand out in my mind: the concert in the small village of Qufu and the story of pianist Bao Hui Qiao.

The small village of Qufu had been opened to foreigners in 1985, shortly before our visit. Everything in Qufu revolves around the figure of Confucius (K'ung-Fu-tzu, or "Kung, the Master"), who lived there 2,500 years ago.

Allow me a few brief comments on Confucius and Confucianism. Confucianism establishes five natural relationships: ruler-subject, father-son, eldest son–youngest son, husband-wife, and friend-friend. The basic concept of every social relationship is the Chinese symbol *jen*, which, lacking a precise equivalent in our languages, can be loosely translated as "virtue," "love," and "magnanimity." "Jen is love for your fellow man," said Confucius. Obedience to the laws of justice and morality in personal, social, and public relationships are all derived from jen, as well as respect and affection toward one's ancestors and parents.

The most eloquent illustration of this respect for family—which eventually evolved into ancestor-worship—is Confucius's Forest, a huge private cemetery located within China's largest public park. The tomb of Confucius is located here, as are the graves of his son Kung Li, his grandson Kung Zisi, and seventy-seven generations of his direct descendants. Over 1,000 steles loom majestically among 30,000 trees, and rows of stately old thuja trees and huge stone statues lead to Confucius's tomb, which is flanked by those of his son and grandson. Another large monument marks the grave of the writer Kung Shangren, Confucius's direct descendant, who lived seventy-four generations after the master. The most ancient tomb, dating from the year 479 BC, is Confucius's own. There are places reserved both for those of his descendants who may still be living and for future generations. There are, therefore, 2,500 years of Kung generations laid to rest in this impressive cemetery. Confucius has two living descendants: one in Taiwan and the other in New York. They belong to the seventy-eighth generation, and currently constitute the last link of the most ancient lineage on earth. It is truly mind-boggling to think that these two members of the Kung family can refer to their ancestor Kung-Fu-Tzu, who lived 2,500 years ago. A contemporary of the Persian emperor Cyrus, Buddha, Lao-tzu, and the prophet Jeremiah, he preceded Socrates, Plato, and Aristotle and lived five hundred years before Christ.

The temple of Confucius, partially destroyed by the Red Guards during the Cultural Revolution, is a series of buildings whose magnificence and huge dimensions surpass every other temple and palace in China except for the Imperial Palace in Peking.

The Piatti accompanied me on a visit to the forest and temple of Confucius, and from there we left directly for the auditorium at Qufu Teachers University, where we listened to a concert and then later gave a recital. The auditorium was overflowing with students. First there was a concert performed by pupils and teachers of music and ballet. It turned out to be an extremely interesting experience, since all the instruments were Chinese: *erh-hu* (a type of Chinese violin), *pipa* (a Chinese lute), *yang chin* (which means "foreign zither" or "dulcimer"), *cheng* (zither), and *mu-qin* (a contemporary marimba).

At the end of the Chinese concert, Madame Bao and I played sonatas by Beethoven and Boccherini. However, the audience refused to leave and "demanded" that I play an entire Bach suite. I accepted with pleasure, and thus, during Bach's tercentennial year, I played his sixth suite with the Piatti in the land of Confucius.

Throughout my 1985 concert tour of China I was fortunate enough to have a talented pianist, Bao Hui Qiao, whom everyone called "Madame Bao," as my partner. I believe her case sheds considerable light on the catastrophe known as the Cultural Revolution, which Mao promoted in 1966.

Madame Bao was enveloped in an aura of mystery. Although she was certainly deserving of the admiration and affection of Chinese music lovers for her unquestionable musical ability, her technique, and her personal qualities, both my wife, María Isabel, and I sensed that a peculiar cloud hovered over her. Our attempts to find out something about her background were futile; she would only smile. Nevertheless, I was able to discover some clues. After I left China, I finally succeeded in solving the mystery of Madame Bao by consulting numerous books and articles on the Cultural Revolution. She had studied piano in Beijing, and in 1960 won first prize in the Central Conservatory's annual competition. In 1961 she was a laureate in the George Enescu International Competition in Romania. She then pursued her graduate studies in Beijing and went on to a brilliant career as a pianist and teacher, but this was cut short by the Cultural Revolution.

Between 1966 and 1976 a chaotic and disastrous movement took hold of China: the Cultural Revolution, launched by Chairman Mao as a tool to regain power after the incipient reforms carried out by Liu Shao-chi and Deng Xiaoping. Mao's wife, Jiang Qing, and her group of left-wing extremists, later known as the Gang of Four, were the guiding forces of the Cultural Revolution.

One of the Cultural Revolution's main objectives was to "knock down the old," to "oppose old ideas, old cultures, and old customs," as well as harmful foreign influences.[2] For a country like China, with such a rich and ancient culture, this policy was a disaster. Chinese musicians became a primary target, since many of them played Western music and had even studied outside of China, and therefore were undoubtedly "contaminated" by dangerous viruses. To cure them, they were sent, at best, to perform manual labor in communes or to care for pigs. Others, like the famous pianist Liu Shikun, were not so fortunate. He was arrested and charged with espionage. He spent six years in prison, where Red Guards fractured his right hand. Liu himself estimated that about 100 of the 400 members of Beijing's orchestras had been imprisoned, placed under house arrest, or sent to agricultural communes.[3]

One of the Cultural Revolution's earliest interventions in music took place on a winter day in 1965: when Jiang Qing unexpectedly appeared before the Central Philharmonic Society of Beijing and announced that "the capitalist symphony is dead."[4] To the musicians who objected to her lack of musical expertise, she retorted that she contributed something far more important: revolutionary fervor and purity. Therefore, the authorized repertoire was reduced to a handful of compositions like the *Shajiabang* Symphony, which she herself, with zero musical knowledge, adapted from the opera of the same name, and the *Yellow River* Piano Concerto, based on Hsien Hsing-hai's *Yellow River* cantata, adapted for piano and orchestra by a committee.

All the conservatories and universities were closed. Beijing's famous Peita University was shut down for fifty-one months. Cultural relations with the outside world were completely severed. Beethoven, charged with spreading "bourgeois humanitarian ideas," and Shakespeare headed the list of creators whose works were banned.[5]

It was not until Mao's death in 1976 that Jiang Qing, nicknamed the "White-Boned Demon," and the Gang of Four lost their power and were, in turn, arrested and imprisoned.

Like every Chinese musician I have met, Madame Bao was also subjected to harsh criticism and mistreatment during the Cultural Revolution. However, her case became somewhat more complicated as a result of a bizarre situation involving her husband, Zhuang Zedong.

Zhuang Zedong, Madame Bao's husband, was an expert table-tennis player who had won China's national championship. Since this is a highly regarded activity in China, Zhuang became a celebrity. Jiang Qing was introduced to him; they became romantically involved, and soon they were lovers. Just as quickly, Zhuang Zedong was promoted to the post of sports minister of the People's Republic of China no less.

As a result, Madame Bao suddenly found herself in the peculiar position of persona non grata for two reasons: on one hand, her Western-style musical education, and on the other, as a rival of Mao's wife. She was immediately exiled to a far away commune.

Shortly after Mao's death in 1976, and after the arrest of his widow, Jiang Qing, Zhuan Zedong, the sports minister, suddenly plummeted from the highest-ranking position in the ministry to the lowliest. He was placed in charge of cleaning the bathrooms and latrines.

Madame Bao returned from her commune and has since resumed her activities as a teacher and concert pianist. Therefore, the manifestations of affection and admiration we had observed were due to a double motive. She was acknowledged everywhere both as a great pianist and as a victim of a repressive system, a survivor who had succeeded in rebuilding her life.

INDIA

Our flight from Beijing to Delhi lasted almost seven hours. Two high-ranking members of the Indian Council for Cultural Relations (ICCR) met us at the Delhi airport. A customs officer then informed me that I had to declare the value of the cello. I was somewhat taken aback, but one of ICCR members turned out to be an expert in such matters. "Open the case!" he ordered. I opened it, and for a while he studied the cello and its two bows. "This cello, the case, and the two bows are worth fifty dollars," he proclaimed in a confident tone that admitted of no protest. Inflation has probably increased the value of the Piatti since then.

India thoroughly enchanted us with its beauty, its art, its ancestral culture, and its extraordinary spirituality, which begat many schools of philosophical and religious thought. However, we also witnessed distressing scenes of appalling poverty and human degradation.

From the musical point of view, our concert tour throughout India was quite inconsistent. My concerts in Delhi, Bangalore—dedicated to Bach's suites—and especially Bombay, were extremely well organized, whereas others, such as those in Madras and Goa were, frankly, chaotic.

Goa had belonged to Portugal for 450 years. Vasco da Gama arrived at the Malabar Coast in 1498, on his first trip beyond the Cape of Good Hope. In 1510 Alfonso de Albuquerque, the future viceroy of India, took control of Goa, which soon became the capital of the Portuguese Empire in India. Goa remained a Portuguese colony until 1961, when Nehru, yielding to internal pressure, forcibly seized Goa, Diu, and Daman.

Although the older generations speak Portuguese fluently, it is gradually being replaced by Hindi, English, and Konkani, the local dialect. The former capital, Velha Goa, was a magnificent city of 200,000 inhabitants when Luís de Camões visited it in the sixteenth century and dubbed it the "Pearl of the Orient." Today it is a ghost town where only majestic, though empty, buildings survive. The malaria epidemic of 1760 forced its inhabitants to abandon the city and move the capital to Nova Goa, known today as Panjim.

We arrived in Goa and were taken to the hotel. We waited in vain for the conductor of the Goa Symphony Orchestra, Lourdino Barreto. He was nowhere to be found. In fact, he was at the airport waiting for two flights from Bombay since the ICCR had mistakenly informed him that we would be arriving from that city instead of Bangalore. We finally met, and Maestro Barreto—a tall dark slender man who had studied music and theology in Rome—also happened to be Father Barreto, a Catholic priest at the Nossa Senhora Seminary.

There was also considerable confusion regarding our concert. Since I was scheduled to play Haydn's Concerto in D Major, I breathed a sight of relief when Father Barreto told me he had received the score and the parts, adding that he had conducted "many rehearsals." However, my relief turned out to be premature, as he suddenly asked, "And have you received my concerto?" "What? What concerto?" I replied. "My concerto for cello and orchestra, composed especially for you, so that in addition to Haydn's concerto, we can play its world premiere tomorrow. I sent it to you in Delhi two weeks ago."

Not only had I not received it, I had no idea that it even existed. "Father Barreto, I am terribly sorry, but as a musician yourself, you can understand the impossibility of preparing a work at such short notice. Out of respect to you and the public, I cannot possibly play your concerto."

As I spoke, Father Barreto's face fell. He then showed me the Goa newspapers announcing my participation in the world premiere of his concerto. I promised to take a look at the score and see whether I could play it someday in Mexico.

However, Lourdino Barreto's great disappointment remained engraved in my mind. Out of curiosity, I decided to have a look at his composition. Entitled *Kai Borem Suknem*: Concert Piece for Cello and Orchestra, it is based on a popular Goan melody of the same name. Back in the hotel, I took out the cello and started playing the piece. It contained no insurmountable difficulties, and I continued playing till four in the morning. So as not to awaken my wife, I had placed a lead mute on the bridge, which considerably muffles the sound, but she nevertheless occasionally opened her eyes and muttered, "You are insane!" I finally went to bed, fully decided to play the piece.

The next morning Father Barreto was overjoyed when I told him I would play his piece.

The rehearsal was scheduled for early in the afternoon, so as to have enough time before the concert at 6.30 p.m. I arrived precisely at the appointed time. The musicians were tuning their instruments, which they were holding in a rather peculiar manner. Many of them were young people, and even a few children, though certainly not child prodigies! They had had many rehearsals indeed: not the usual three, but twenty! Since they were extremely nervous, I reassured them by saying that they had worked very hard and we should now try to enjoy playing together.

We devoted several hours to Haydn and the *Kai Borem* piece, and our rehearsal finished shortly before the concert, which began as scheduled. The programs had just arrived, with the unusual last-minute listing:

Suite in D Major for Solo Cello	J. S. Bach
Concerto in D major for Cello and Orchestra	Joseph Haydn
Kai Borem Suknem: Concert piece for Cello and Orchestra	Lourdino Barreto

The master of ceremonies read a few comments on these pieces for the benefit of a public unfamiliar with this type of music, and announced that a Bach cello suite would be performed in Goa for the very first time.

The concert went as well as could be expected, and was enthusiastically received by the audience.

At the end of the concert Father Barreto publicly thanked me for my participation and for my tireless efforts and sleepless nights, which had made the premiere of *Kai Borem Suknem* possible.

My last concert in India, which happened to be my last concert of the year, was a model of organization. It was held in Bombay's jam-packed Parker Hall. I had the excellent pianist Mrs. Dehmi Gazdar as my accompanist. The concert was sponsored by the Time and Talents Club, a group of women from Bombay's distinguished Parsee community. The chairman of the concert committee was Mrs. Ratti Mehta, Zubin Mehta's aunt.

The Parsees are followers of the prophet Zoroaster, or Zarathustra. They first arrived in India from Pars (in Iran) in the eighth century, when Muslim expansion practically annihilated Zoroastrianism.[6] According to several prominent Parsees, it is the oldest monotheistic religion in the history of humanity, born several centuries before the Hebrews proclaimed Yahweh the only God. Today, there are no more than 130,000 Parsees in the world, most of whom live in Bombay. Despite their small number, they have played and continue to play a fundamental role in India's industrial, commercial, and cultural life.

The pianist Dehmi Gazdar, a prominent member of the Parsee community, had perceived our interest in learning more about the Parsees and their religion, and one afternoon, she invited us to a little girl's initiation ceremony. We were among the few Westerners ever to witness the *navjote*, the most important ritual in Zoroastrianism. The ceremony was held outdoors, before sundown, on the grounds of an elegant club in Bombay. The navjote takes place when a boy or girl is between seven and fifteen. With this ceremony, the initiate becomes a full-fledged member of the Zoroastrian community and acquires the obligation to pray periodically and to uphold the high moral standards of their religion.

We left Bombay the following morning at 4:45 a.m. Hours later we landed in Dubai in the United Arab Emirates. The next stop was Frankfurt. At three in the afternoon, local time, we landed in New York, twenty-one hours after leaving Bombay. My Bach year had ended.

TWO EXHIBITS—MEXICO: 30 CENTURIES OF SPLENDOR
AND MEXICO: A WORK OF ART

Between October 10, 1990, and January 13, 1991, the largest, most comprehensive exhibit of Mexican art, Mexico: 30 Centuries of Splendor, was presented in New York City. The exhibit, highlighting a number of Mexico's most outstanding archeological pieces and diverse examples of Mexican art from the past 3,000 years, took place at the Metropolitan Museum of Art with great success. Complementing the exhibit at the

Met were 150 other events, collectively titled Mexico: A Work of Art. These included painting and art exhibitions, concerts, conferences on literary, political, and social subjects, and opportunities for sampling Mexican cuisine.

The musical events consisted of twenty-three concerts featuring Renaissance, Baroque, and contemporary music, two of them mine. I also participated in a third concert that had nothing to do with the exhibit itself, but happened to be scheduled during the same dates: the world premiere of the Concerto for Cello and Orchestra by Mexican composer Samuel Zyman, held at Lincoln Center (Figs. 23 and 24).

The program for my concerts in New York was the following:

November 14, 1990
Alice Tully Hall
Lincoln Center
Doris Stevenson, Piano

Suite in D Major	Bach
Sonata, op. 40	Shostakovich
Three Preludes for Cello and Piano	Ponce
Four Pieces	Enríquez
Pampeana no. 2	Ginastera
Pezzo capriccioso	Tchaikovsky

November 28, 1990
Avery Fisher Hall
Lincoln Center
American Symphony Orchestra
Catherine Comet, conductor

Concerto for Cello and Orchestra	S. Zyman

January 7, 1991
Merkin Hall
Doris Stevenson, piano

Sonatina	Chávez
Sonata	Ponce
Three Tarascan Dances	Bernal Jiménez
Quotations	Lavista
Sonatina	Enríquez
Pampeana no. 2	Ginastera

23. *Three New York concerts, 1990 and 1991.*

24. *With composer Samuel Zyman for the world premiere of his cello concerto. Lincoln Center, New York, 1990. Photo used by permission of Samuel Zyman and Camera 1, New York, NY.*

From November 1990 to January 1991, I played fourteen works in New York, nine by Mexican composers: one was a world premiere and six were premieres in New York.

The premiere of Zyman's concerto was preceded by days filled with suspense, even outright anguish. Before I explain the reasons, I will present a brief overview of Samuel Zyman's remarkable career.

I met him in New York in 1980, when he had just completed his medical studies at the National Autonomous University of Mexico. However, his musical vocation compelled him to abandon medicine and dedicate himself exclusively to music. He studied at the National Conservatory of Music in Mexico City, and when we met, he had just come to New York to attend Juilliard, where he received his master's and PhD degrees in composition. He subsequently joined its faculty. Since our first encounter in New York, I have followed his career very closely.

In 1989, impressed by his excellent piano concerto, I commissioned a concerto for cello and orchestra, which he began writing in early 1990. That March, he mentioned that a New York company, Carillon Importers, was interested in sponsoring artistic activities and would like to share the commission with me. He also wanted to know if the premiere could be held November 28 at Lincoln Center. I agreed on both counts. On April 30 I met with Samuel at Juilliard. He had finished about one-third of the first movement, which he played on the piano for me. Although the opening of the piece made a profound impression on me, I was getting rather nervous, since the date for the premiere was almost upon us, and I had a very heavy workload prior to that concert, including the world premieres of cello concertos by Federico Ibarra (Mexico), Celso Garrido-Lecca (Peru), and Manuel de Elías (Mexico).

The date for the premiere of Zyman's concerto drew inexorably closer. It was not until June that he gave me the first movement. On September 5 we saw each other again at Juilliard, where he handed me the second movement. However, he had only a one-page draft copy of the finale. I was also concerned because classes at Juilliard, which were about to begin, would occupy a great deal of Zyman's time. On September 5, I wrote in my journal: "S. Z. has a lot of work to do if he's going to finish the concerto on time!"

On October 4, I called Samuel. He told me that the third movement was basically finished, and he promised to deliver it to me the following week in New York. I arrived in New York on October 12 and went straight to Juilliard, where I had an appointment with Samuel. Here I will directly quote from my journal, attesting to both Samuel's and my anxiety: "I arrived at Juilliard at 5:40 p.m. Samuel arrived twenty minutes late, drenched from the rain. He had just finished the third movement! He took out two copies, one for the conductor, Catherine Comet, and one for me. Samuel was exhausted. He had barely slept over the past few days. That same day, Samuel gave the score to a copyist, which was enough time to have the orchestra parts ready."

On October 21, I began a series of recitals with pianist Doris Stevenson, and on November 3 I played Elgar's Cello Concerto with the MIT Symphony Orchestra, conducted by David Epstein.

On November 14, I performed at Alice Tully Hall. The program appears on the preceding pages. On the 18th I repeated the same program at Boston's Jordan Hall.

The premiere of Zyman's concert was scheduled for November 28 at Avery Fisher Hall. We were to rehearse on November 23 and 24, and the dress rehearsal was set for November 27. It was during these rehearsals that the suspense reached fever pitch.

The November 23 rehearsal was held at the Manhattan School of Music. I was quite pleased with this first rehearsal, even though it was too short. Catherine Comet was very upset, since she had not yet received the parts for the French horns. The copyist had a reputation for being extremely punctual, and Samuel himself had been supervising the work on the copies. However, inexplicably, the copyist let us down by not finishing the parts. When this brief rehearsal was over, Samuel went in search of the copyist, who was nowhere to be found.

At 9:45 a.m. on the 24th I arrived at the Manhattan School of Music for the second rehearsal. The copyist had not shown up, and Samuel, who obviously had not slept at all, was pale and distraught. Catherine Comet, furious, cancelled the rehearsal—one in which we had hoped to overcome the complexities of the composition. At that moment I was strongly tempted to cancel my participation. Fortunately, at the dress rehearsal at Lincoln Center, on the eve of the concert, the missing parts were put in place. We played Zyman's work nonstop, from beginning to end, compressing the thirty-two-minute concerto into twenty-eight minutes!

Avery Fisher Hall was packed for the premiere. Samuel had to go onstage and acknowledge the applause. Few people there knew about the suspense and anguish undergone by the composer and all the performers. The next day, Samuel bought a computer and a printer. He no longer needs a copyist!

As is often the case after a piece is played for the first time, the composer went back and made significant revisions. Sometime later I premiered and recorded the new version with the National Symphony Orchestra of Mexico, conducted by Enrique Arturo Diemecke, and went on to play it in the United States, Spain, and Argentina.

FROM THE USSR TO RUSSIA

After my first stay in Russia in 1962 as a student, I never lost my interest in this fascinating and often bewildering country. I returned many times as a concert cellist to perform in numerous recitals and orchestral concerts throughout Russia and most of the Soviet republics in Europe and Asia (Fig. 25). I was able to witness the evolution of the Soviet Union under every government—Khrushchev, Brezhnev, Andropov, Chernenko, and Gorbachev—until its final collapse in December 1991. I returned to Russia in 1993, then governed by Yeltsin, and again in 2003, to the vastly changed Russia under Putin. My many experiences in that country resulted in a book entitled *From the USSR to Russia*, published in Mexico in 1993 and 1994.[7]

The observations on the following pages, focusing mainly on the highlights of my different tours, were written after each stay. Although I could have deleted certain conclusions here that time has proved false, I believe the spontaneity of these lines, and their faithfulness to my beliefs at the time, makes up for their lack of accuracy.

My 1979 tour included the five Central Asian republics. We performed in Alma-Ata (Kazakhstan), Tashkent (Uzbekistan), Frunze (Kyrgyzstan), and Dushanbe (Tajikistan)—a few hundred miles from the still-peaceful borders of Afghanistan—in addition to two concerts in Ashkhabad (Turkmenistan), very close to the Iranian border.

I marveled at the historical and artistic riches of Central Asia, dating back to the Persian Empire of Cyrus the Great and, later, to Alexander the Great. These cities are located all along the legendary Silk Road to China. After Mohammed's death, Islam soon spread throughout the entire region. By the eighth century, the vast territory in Central Asia known as Turkestan had been converted to Islam. Eminently mercantile cities like Bukhara and Samarkand established important schools. Arabic was the universal language, as it was in Baghdad, Basra, Córdoba, Granada, and Seville.

These illustrative paragraphs are taken from my diary, dated October 15, 1979:

25. With the Piatti in Moscow, 1985.

I was struck by the absence of mosques in Ashkhabad and in some of the Central Asian capitals and asked whether the Soviet Government had destroyed them, as it had done with thousands of Orthodox churches and with many synagogues. "Oh no! The Government did not destroy any mosques," I was told. "What happened was that we recently suffered a tremendous earthquake. The Government has already rebuilt everything except the mosques, which nobody needed. It is Allah who destroyed the mosques, and not the Government or the Party," our guides added, chuckling rather gleefully.

Near Ashkhabad we saw the enormous Kara Kum Canal, the world's longest canal, along with others that serve to irrigate former deserts now cultivating fruits, rice and 90 percent of the cotton produced in the Soviet Union.[8]

On January 22, 1982, I played a recital with pianist Itzaak Izachik in Leningrad's magnificent Philharmonic Hall (Fig. 26). On the eve of my recital, there had been a concert in that same city devoted to the first public performance of recent works by Alfred Schnittke. Schnittke was one of the most outstanding composers of the post-Shostakovich generation. When they were not banned outright, his works were at best tolerated by the regimes prior to Gorbachev's. María Isabel and I attended the concert, profoundly impressed by the music's beauty and originality, as well as by the enthusiastic response of the audience—comprised mostly of young people—to a type of music that was officially frowned upon because it did not conform to the dictates of Socialist Realism.

Since Schnittke himself was present, we had the opportunity to chat with him for a while. I expressed my great interest in obtaining some of his pieces for the cello. Although they had been published in the USSR,

26. Concert in Leningrad with Itzaak Izachik, January 22, 1982.

ГОСУДАРСТВЕННАЯ ФИЛАРМОНИЯ
ЛАТВИЙСКОЙ ССР

Концертный зал Филармонии, ул. Амату, 6

Четверг, 10 октября 1985 года, в 20.00 час.

Заслуженный коллектив

ГОСУДАРСТВЕННЫЙ СИМФОНИЧЕСКИЙ ОРКЕСТР ЛАТВИЙСКОЙ ССР

Художественный руководитель и главный дирижер
народный артист Латвийской ССР,
лауреат международного конкурса

Василий СИНАЙСКИЙ

Дирижер

Дзинтарс ИОСТС

Солист

Карлос ПРИЕТО

(Мексика) (виолончель)

В программе

Б. ТЕРЕНТЬЕВ — Симфония
(в Риге исполняется впервые)

К. СЕН-САНС — Концерт для виолончели
с оркестром

М. РАВЕЛЬ — Вальс

Билеты продаются в кассах Филармонии

После третьего звонка вход в зал прекращается

Тип. «Cīņa» 1985. 3828 R 1900

27. Concert with the Latvian National Symphony Orchestra, Riga, October 10, 1985.

he informed me that they were unavailable in music stores, so he would present them to me as a gift if we could meet in Moscow. Both of us were scheduled to return to Moscow, so we agreed to meet at a certain café: it was inadvisable for me to visit his apartment. We met at the appointed hour, and he handed me the scores as furtively and warily as if he were turning over military secrets to a foreign spy.

He told me that composers like himself had mixed feelings of satisfaction and bitterness. There was a sense of satisfaction because when their works were played, which was seldom, the concert halls were com-pletely filled—at least in Moscow and in Leningrad—and the audience expressed its admiration and affection. However, there was also bitter-ness because they had attained success despite the opposition of the of-ficial agencies and the Soviet Composers' Union, whose main function was purportedly to support its members and protect their interests. But it was, in addition, mainly an instrument of control and repression. He added that he knew of several Western musical organizations that had attempted to commission a series of works. This type of request was handled by the Composers' Union, but whether from professional jeal-ousy or on orders from above, the letters commissioning these works had been systematically "mislaid." Among the pieces he gave me was his marvelous Sonata for Cello and Piano.

This repressive political system was to undergo a radical change with Gorbachev and the implementation of glasnost. Schnittke lived in Ham-burg from 1990 to his death in 1998.

A new tour in 1985 included recitals in Moscow, Tallinn and Pärnu (Estonia), Vilnius and Kaunas (Lithuania), as well as a performance with the Latvian National Symphony Orchestra in Riga. In 1985 Gorbachev rose to power as the new leader of the Soviet Union. Everywhere we saw signs of optimism; under Gorbachev there was hope. The consensus seemed to be that he was a modern leader who would be able to carry out profound reforms and bring great progress to the country. However, in each successive tour of the Soviet Union we could feel the people's increasing disenchantment and frustration.

The program for our recitals included Max Bruch's *Kol Nidrei* for cello and piano. I had been warned by a Russian Jewish friend from New York that Gosconcert—the official Soviet concert agency in charge of organizing my tour—might object to *Kol Nidrei* because of its religious connotations. (*Kol nidrei*, which means "all vows" in Aramaic, is the first prayer on the evening of Yom Kippur.) My pianist, Vadim Prokhorov, spent a long time before locating an old score buried in the Moscow Conservatory archives. Since there was no objection whatsoever, our programs included *Kol Nidrei* after all. However, this is the way they were printed:

Kol Nidrei (old Hebrew folk song)	Max Bruch
Sonata in A Major	Luigi Boccherini
Suite in E-flat Major	J. S. Bach
Sonata	Prokofiev

Kol Nidrei is, of course, much more than a "Hebrew folk song," but that description annulled its religious connotation, thus making it perfectly acceptable.

After our concert at the Philharmonic Hall in Vilnius, an elderly man came by to see us, saying he had enjoyed the music and handing me an envelope that he asked me not to open there. The note read: "Thanks for the concert. Special thanks for having played the Kol Nidrei!" I have kept it to this day. Such a moving note seemed to be the best possible justification for including Bruch's piece in our Soviet tour.

Our Moscow recital took place at the Glinka Museum. After a rehearsal, we stayed behind to confer with Anatoly Panyushkin and Vladimir Makarov, director and assistant director of the library, respectively, who knew of my project to write a long commentary on Shostakovich. They kindly showed me the available documents, which turned out to be fewer than those already in my own library.

We left the Glinka Library and decided to go for a stroll. Near Fadeev Street, we came upon a long line of people, a common sight in Moscow and in the USSR in general. People stood in line for a variety of reasons, ranging from a certain number of fresh fish to be sold on the street at bargain prices to products that had been marked down to meet a monthly sales quota. Whenever you spotted a line, it was a good idea to show up as quickly as possible, make sure you get in line, and then find out what was being sold. By following this simple rule, María Isabel once purchased several cans of caviar at rock-bottom prices in Leningrad's Hotel Europa. The line that caught our eye near Fadeev Street happened to be in front of a wine and liquor store; police were posted at the entrance to prevent any possible disturbances.

MY LAST CONCERT TOUR OF THE SOVIET UNION: 1991

The text for this section comes from my book *From the USSR to Russia*, written in 1991, just after my last tour of the Soviet Union.

*O*n October 15, 1991, six weeks after the unsuccessful coup against Gorbachev, María Isabel, the cello and I arrived in Moscow for a concert tour consisting of eight concerts (six recitals with pianist Victor Yampolsky plus two orchestral concerts) throughout a considerable part of the huge territories belonging to what was still the Soviet Union. The itinerary was the following: Moscow—Kurgan (southwestern Siberia)—Chelyabinsk—Ekaterinburg—Tbilisi (Georgia)—Kiev (Ukraine)—Moscow.

Shortly after our arrival in Moscow, we attended a sumptuous dinner party in our honor, hosted by the Mexican Ambassador Carlos Tello at the embassy residence. The guests were A. Panyushkin, Director of Moscow's Glinka Museum, the site selected for my last concert; the Director of Moscow's Tchaikovsky Conservatory Concert Hall, Volodia Sajarov, my friend of twenty-nine years, and his wife Tatiana; and the chief Latin American specialist from the USSR's Ministry of Culture, Ovsep S. Manasarian, who speaks perfect Spanish. The conversation turned out to be extremely enlightening in regard to the complete transformation of the Soviet Union, with candid comments on its economic and political crisis. Volodia Sajarov deplored the Tchaikovsky Conservatory's decline in academic excellence as a result of the death or emigration of its most eminent professors. Manasarian, half-jokingly remarked that had Gorbachev been a member of the United States' CIA, his goals would not have been much different. "The old Warsaw Pact has been dissolved. The Socialist nations in Eastern Europe, formerly under Soviet control, are turning into capitalist countries. The German Democratic Republic has been absorbed by the Federal Republic. And now, even the Soviet republics are proclaiming their autonomy and threatening to break away from the Soviet Union. The USSR is disintegrating, both politically and economically."

A CONCERT IN EKATERINBURG   Ekaterinburg is one of the many Russian cities that have recovered their prerevolutionary names. Until fairly recently, it was known as Sverdlovsk, in honor of the Bolshevik leader, Jakov Sverdlov.

I played a recital at the Philharmonic Hall with pianist Viktor Yampolsky. Practically in front of Philharmonic Hall there is a vacant lot where we spent a considerable amount of time, since it was the site of an event of historic importance: the assassination of Tsar Nicholas II, his family, and their retinue in 1918, the final chapter in the history of the tsars and a prelude to the terror unleashed the following year in Russia, the "Red Terror," which reached its climax under Stalin.[9]

The bare facts of the massacre have been public knowledge since the twenties, when Nicholas Sokolov, the chairman of the investigating committee appointed by Admiral Alexander Kolchak, published his report in Paris. However, new materials have recently come to light. In 1989, the magazine *Ogonëk* published the memoirs of Yacov M. Yurovsky, who was in charge of the execution.[10] This, briefly, is what occurred.

In early 1918, on orders from Lenin and Sverdlov, Nicholas II—who

28. *House of Ipatiev in Ekaterinburg, where the murder of Tsar Nicholas II and his family took place.*

by then was known as Nikolai Romanov—and his family were sent to Ekaterinburg, where they occupied the home of Nikolai Ipatiev (Fig. 28). Ipatiev, a local engineer, had been ordered by the Bolsheviks to vacate his house, which in fact, became a prison.

Along with Nicholas were his wife Alexandra; their four daughters; their fourteen-year-old son, the tsarevitch, who suffered from hemophilia; their family physician, Dr. Botkin; and other members of their retinue. They spent that spring in relative calm, although they had to put up with insults and thievery from the armed military guards who watched them day and night.

According to Richard Pipes, there is indisputable proof that Lenin decided on the execution of the Romanovs around May or June 1918 and ordered the secret police, then known as the Cheka, to carry out the plan.[11]

On July 4, 1918, the regular patrol was replaced. The new commander of the Cheka special force was a sinister character named Yakov Mikhailovich Yurovsky, a cruel, vindictive man, filled with hate.

At 1:30 in the morning on July 17, Yurovsky awakened Dr. Botkin and ordered him to rouse the entire family, claiming that, for security reasons, it was necessary to move them all to the cellar. At two, Yurovsky went down the cellar steps, followed by the eleven prisoners: Nicholas, carrying his son, Alexis, in his arms; his wife, Alexandra; their daughters Maria, Tatiana, Olga, and Anastasia; Dr. Botkin; Demidova, the lady-in-waiting; Trupp, the valet; Kharitonov, the cook; in addition to a group of guards. Once they were all gathered together, Yurovsky suddenly announced that in view of the fact that Nicholas's supporters were still fighting against the Bolsheviks, they had to be killed. Alexandra and

29. Site of the former Ipatiev house, 1991.

some of her daughters barely had time to make the sign of the cross. Yurovsky himself shot the former tsar. Although each guard aimed directly at a victim's hearts, six of them—moaning and whimpering—still survived: Alexis, three of his sisters, Demidova, and Dr. Botkin. Yurovsky dealt two coups de grace to Alexis, and the rest of the guards dispatched the survivors, including Jemmy, Anastasia's pet dog. The fact that the girls had concealed their jewels in their corsets had prevented the guards' bayonets from penetrating the victims' bodies.

The bloody corpses were taken to a shallow abandoned gold mine. In one of their most despicable acts, the guards stripped the tsarina and the girls before hurling them into the mine. The next day, Yurovsky returned with his men, concerned that it wasn't deep enough. They then dug up the remains and transported them to a nearby site, where they were doused with sulfuric acid and burned. Finally, they were buried a second time so they would be lost forever. The site sank into oblivion until 1989, when a group of scientists managed to locate it.

On the now empty lot once occupied by these premises, the perimeter and layout of the old building is marked with bricks, one of them bearing a commemorative tablet indicating the precise site of the massacre. A wooden Orthodox cross, eight feet high, has been erected nearby. A plastic bucket hangs from the cross where, as we observed when we visited this site, passersby occasionally place floral offerings (Fig. 29).

In 1977, Brezhnev, concerned about the increasing number of visitors to Ipatiev's house—by then transformed into a museum and club—ordered the secretary general of the Communist Party in Sverdlosvk to demolish the site. This man happened to be Boris Yeltsin. Although apparently he disagreed with these instructions, Yeltsin nevertheless complied, and that is why there is no trace of the Romanovs' final home.

EKATERINBURG-TBILISI: A RATHER DISORDERLY FLIGHT

The alarm clock rang at three in the morning, since the flight was scheduled to leave at 5:30. Judging by its size and the number of planes we saw, the Ekaterinburg airport must have been one of the major crossroads for Soviet airlines. However, at four in the morning it was a depressing sight indeed. Thousands of sleeping passengers were crammed together as if they were in jail. We were led to the waiting room for official passengers, and then, completely in the dark, we made our way through a distance of 500 yards, where we finally boarded the still-empty plane. The two airline hostesses and one flight attendant were engaged in lively conversation. The background music was turned up as loud as

30. Concert with the Georgian State Symphony Orchestra, Tbilisi, October 25, 1991.

possible, and they were obviously enjoying themselves. Standing under a brightly lit NO SMOKING sign, the three of them were puffing away like chimneys. Yulia (our escort from Gosconcert), María Isabel, pianist Victor Yampolsky, the cello, and I were still the only passengers aboard. The captain then made his appearance and informed us that we were the first foreigners to board a plane here, since until very recently Ekaterinburg had been forbidden to international travelers.

All of a sudden, the plane was completely full. The passengers, mostly Georgians and Azerbaijanis, were all carrying cumbersome packages that they brought into the cabin without the slightest objection from the flight attendants. Since the flight was oversold, there were still some fifteen passengers waiting on the steps and holding their tickets, but lacking assigned seats. Since they paid no attention to the flight attendants and refused to leave, the captain intervened, but his attempts to control the situation were futile. The problem was resolved when the captain and the flight attendants totally capitulated. Finally allowed onboard, the newcomers stood toward the rear of the aircraft. Those who had friends among the seated passengers squeezed in between their seats. The row in front of ours was occupied by five passengers wedged into three seats. They had lifted the armrests and, naturally, had not fastened their seat belts.

The flight lasted two hours, and during that time the flight attendants never once appeared to check on the passengers, much less to offer us at least a glass of water. Fifteen minutes before landing, as we were flying over the spectacular mountain peaks of the Caucasus and the plane was obviously descending, some passengers headed for the exits, since they wanted to be the first to leave. When we finally landed, at least fifteen people carrying their bulky packages were crowding around the door.

Our concerts in Tbilisi were the first held in that city after several weeks of disturbances and shootings in the principal streets of what had once been a beautiful city. It was a great pleasure to play with the Georgia State Symphony Orchestra and its excellent conductor, Jansung Kakhidze. The program consisted of Dvořák's Cello Concerto and Shostakovich's Tenth Symphony (Fig. 30).

The composer Sulkhan Tsintsadze and his wife invited us to their home for a delicious typical Georgian dinner, served with the local wines. Although Tsintsadze has received countless honors—Artist of the People of the USSR (when the USSR was coming to an end), the Stalin Prize, etc.—he claims they are now meaningless. After dinner, Tsintsadze presented me with the scores of his delightful Twenty-four Preludes for Cello and Piano and his Tenth String Quartet.

NOVEMBER 2, 1991: LAST CONTACT WITH THE SOVIET UNION

At six in the evening we took off for Frankfurt and New York. To sum up the many diverse impressions accumulated by the end of the tour, I must highlight the following principal aspects:

a) The USSR has undergone a radical transformation during the Gorbachev years. As we had first noticed in 1988, the fear that for seventy years has oppressed the Soviets has disappeared. Glasnost, openness, and transparency prevail. An incipient sense of freedom is in the air.

b) Unfortunately, this significant achievement has not been accompanied by improvements in the basic material necessities—quite the contrary. The standard of living has been gradually deteriorating since 1985, when perestroika was launched. Although indispensable, it was neither well conceived nor properly implemented. The economic reforms are distinguished for their inconsistency and volatility; they have been timid, contradictory, insufficient, and ill timed.

c) During our stay, we felt that we were in a country immersed in a severe crisis, on the verge of unforeseen dangers.

d) Every day, to our astonishment, we witnessed the disintegration of what had once been the Soviet Union and its institutions. We were also aware of the widespread brain drain that adversely affects every profession.

e) In the face of such startling, radical changes, the country and its people are totally bewildered. The hope and optimism we perceived toward the beginning of the Gorbachev era has vanished, now replaced by anxiety and pessimism. Gorbachev, so popular outside of the USSR, is constantly criticized in his own country.

f) One of the nation's greatest obstacles is the rampant outbreak of nationalism, which, transformed into irrational, primitive sentiments, threatens to damage relationships among the different ethnic groups, not only within the USSR, but also in each of its republics, creating potential targets for explosive situations.

In my previous visits to the USSR, with the exception of the one in 1988, I always experienced a great sense of relief at finally leaving such a stifling, oppressive system. This time, however, our emotions were ambivalent and completely different. We were distressed at the profound crisis afflicting the country and its inhabitants, alarmed at the very thought that should this crisis persist, totalitarianism may once again emerge, and annihilate the freedoms so recently and painfully acquired. However, we were also encouraged by the hope that the Russian people—who, throughout its history, have proved their capacity for sacrifice, struggle, and heroic feats—and the rest of the peoples in the USSR will consolidate

31. LEFT TO RIGHT: *Irina Shostakovich (widow of the composer), Carlos Prieto, and daughter Zoya Shostakovich, in Dmitry Shostakovich's apartment. Moscow, 1993.*

their freedom and ultimately find the path toward a more auspicious future.

Thus I concluded my last visit to the Soviet Union. Barely a few weeks later, on Christmas Day 1991, Gorbachev submitted his resignation and the Union of Soviet Socialist Republics officially ceased to exist. The red flag with the hammer and sickle, hoisted by Lenin in 1923, was lowered throughout the entire territory. That same day, Boris Yeltsin, president of Russia, occupied the offices formerly belonging to Mikhail Gorbachev, president of the USSR. Ever since, the red, white, and blue Russian flag has waved over the Kremlin.

1993: WITH IRINA AND ZOYA SHOSTAKOVICH

In 1993, I returned for a brief visit to Moscow to see Irina and Zoya Shostakovich, the composer's widow and daughter, at their Moscow apartment (Fig. 31). Since at that time I was writing a note on Shostakovich for my book *From the USSR to Russia*, Irina kindly offered to discuss it with me. That particular note, entitled "Dmitry Shostakovich: The Tragedy of an Artist under Communism" became a complete chapter of my book.

It was a moving experience to find myself in the same apartment where Shostakovich had lived for so many years, filled with his personal possessions. A bust of Beethoven caught my eye, immediately remind-ing me of the last work Shostakovich composed, a few weeks before his death in 1975: his Sonata for Viola and Piano, op. 147. Shostakovich's health had been perceptibly declining since 1973. Once, he mentioned that it would be impossible to live without composing, and, indeed, he continued working to the very end. He had composed the sonata in May and June of 1975, and in July he returned to the hospital, but kept on working and correcting the sheets submitted by the copyist. A few days later, on August 9, 1975, Shostakovich died.

The Sonata for Viola and Piano is an extraordinary work, both for its depth and its beauty. It consists of three movements: Moderato, Al-legretto, and Adagio. A calm, introspective mood prevails throughout the three movements, and a motif in the final Adagio is reminiscent of Beethoven's *Moonlight* Sonata, a tribute that the dying Russian composer paid to his illustrious predecessor. The piece concludes with a luminous though poignant beauty: the swan song of a great artist departing from his turbulent world.

2003: RETURN TO A NEW RUSSIA—ORENBURG, ST. PETERSBURG, MOSCOW

In October 2003 I returned to Russia on a new and multifaceted concert tour: two recitals and two lectures in Orenburg, two concerts in St. Petersburg—including the world premiere of the *Concerto da chiesa* for cello and strings by Spanish composer José Luis Turina at the Her-mitage Theater and at the Great Hall of the Philharmonic Theater—and a recital at the Moscow Conservatory with pianist Gennady Dzubenko.

I was greatly curious to see what changes had taken place since the momentous collapse, in 1991, of the Union of Soviet Socialist Republics. Indeed, I found amazing changes in the country. Though there was re-markable progress in some areas, in other areas I observed an alarming regression.

The last time I performed in Moscow, the city had been the capital of the Soviet Union. Now I was returning to the capital of the Russian Federation. Moscow was no longer the capital of the world's second-most powerful nation, but of a country whose economy—according to its gross national product—ranked tenth in the world. However, the Russian economy has been growing at an impressive rate over the past six years (1998–2003).

Our first activities took place in Orenburg, the capital of the province of the same name. Igor Khramov, chairman of the Eurasia Society, did an excellent job of organizing our stay. Incidentally, the name Eurasia is most appropriate, since Orenburg lies on the dividing line between Europe and Asia. Our Orenburg Airlines plane left Moscow's Domodedovo International Airport at nine at night, and after a two-hour flight we landed in Orenburg, where, because of the time difference, it was one in the morning.

Igor Khramov and Roustam Galimov met us at the airport to take us to our hotel, or so we thought. It was quite a surprise when we realized that our room, a most spacious suite, had been reserved at the Fyodorov Eye Clinic, which afforded the best accommodations in town. Our luggage was not carried by bellboys, but by two male nurses all dressed up in their green hospital gowns. Dr. Fyodorov, by the way, was an eminent surgeon who revolutionized eye surgery through the use of laser techniques.

The next day we were warmly received at a private home owned by the Goncharuk family, though it also serves as the Leopold and Mstislav Rostropovich Home and Museum. Mstislav himself lived here during part of World War II, from 1941 to 1943, while his father, Leopold Rostropovich, also a cellist, lived and died in this house.

In the afternoon I gave a talk and performed in a concert in the concert hall of Orenburg State University. The talk, titled "The Adventures of a Cello," centered on the story of my cello, as told in Chapter 3 of this book.

Our next activities were scheduled for St. Petersburg, which was still called Leningrad when I last performed there. The city, founded in 1703, was celebrating its 300th anniversary. I had been invited to participate in a festival of Spanish music and to play the world premiere of a new work by José Luis Turina, one of Spain's most talented composers: I would be playing his *Concerto da chiesa* for cello and strings with the State Hermitage Orchestra, conducted by Alexis Soriano. Our rehearsals took place in a splendid building on Moika 45, on the banks of the Moika, one of St. Petersburg's many rivers; its name appears in countless literary works by Dostoyevsky and other Russian writers. *Splendid* was the word that came to my mind when I saw the outside of the building. On the occasion of the city's 300th anniversary, its façade had been restored, like that of many buildings, although the renovation of its interior was barely underway.

The world premiere was held at the Hermitage Theater, and two days later the concert was repeated at the Great Hall of the Shostakovich Phil-harmonic. To play in this wonderful hall, so rich in musical history, was, for the Piatti and me, the supreme highlight of our 2003 Russian tour.

The last concert of our tour was at the Moscow Conservatory with pianist Gennady Dzubenko. The program included the Shostakovich Cello Sonata—which of course, I had to play on my return to Rus-sia—the Kodály Cello Sonata, and, after the intermission, the Russian premieres of works by Mexican composers Joaquín Gutiérrez Heras and Mario Lavista, plus encores by Astor Piazzolla.

The Tchaikovsky Conservatory showed evidence of the damage caused by a recent fire. However, far more serious than the fire itself was the fact that the conservatory had not yet regained the artistic excellence it had attained during the pre-Gorbachev era. Many of its legendary teachers had either passed away or moved abroad, lured by more attrac-tive opportunities and the freedom of movement granted by Russia's new, more tolerant policies. However, some outstanding teachers have returned, at least temporarily. Furthermore, other high-caliber conser-vatories have sprung up in cities like Novosibirsk, capital of Siberia and birthplace of such outstanding violinists as Maxim Vengerov and Vadim Repin.

OBSERVATIONS ON SOME OF THE RECENT CHANGES

Since time and space demand brevity, my summary will therefore touch only on five points: Nicholas II, Moscow's Cathedral of Christ the Savior, the remarkable improvement in the availability of goods and services, the relative freedom of the press and the media in general, and the increasing inequality in income distribution.

THE FATE OF TSAR NICHOLAS II'S REMAINS   Few phenomena so vividly illustrate the magnitude of these changes as the episode involv-ing the remains of the last tsar and his family.

The reader may recall my 1991 visit to Ekaterinburg and my account of the assassination of the tsar, his family, and his retinue.

When Boris Yeltsin became president of Russia, he decided that the remains of nine bodies discovered several years earlier in a wood near Ekaterinburg should be exhumed. They were subjected to DNA testing and other forensic tests, as scientists compared DNA from the skeletons to samples taken from the body of Nicholas II's younger brother Georgy Alexandrovich Romanov, who was buried in St. Peter and Paul Cathedral, situated inside the St. Peter and Paul Fortress in St. Petersburg. The remains of Tsarina Alexandra were compared to blood samples from her closest relative, her grandnephew Prince Philip, Duke of Edinburgh. Finally, after completing all these exhaustive tests, scientists in Russia, Britain, and the United States confirmed the identities of the last tsar and his family.

On July 17, 1998, exactly eighty years after the royal household was killed in the cellar of the Ipatiev house in Ekaterinburg, President Yeltsin ordered that the remains of the last tsar, his family, Dr. Botkin, and the three servants be laid to rest in St. Peter and Paul Cathedral, the traditional burial place for all the Romanov tsars since Peter I, the founder of St. Petersburg.

When I saw Nicholas II's tomb in the cathedral, my first reaction was of disbelief and amazement at such an inconceivable event. I could not help recalling my teacher of Marxism-Leninism at the University of Moscow and how she reacted with horror at the mere mention of the tsar's name. It also occurred to me that if Vladimir Ilyich Lenin were miraculously returned to life upon arising from his grave in the mausoleum by the Kremlin, he would immediately die again at the news of Nicholas II's reburial at the St. Peter and Paul Cathedral in St. Petersburg.

THE DEATH AND RESURRECTION OF THE CATHEDRAL OF CHRIST THE SAVIOR IN MOSCOW   Moscow has undergone numerous modifications throughout its long history. During the Soviet era, it was subjected to countless architectural and urban atrocities. Thousands of monuments and buildings of indisputable architectural merit were demolished, along with entire districts filled with artistic treasures, and approximately 1,000 churches disappeared. Despite opposition from a few extremely courageous groups and individuals, the picturesque medieval district of Zaradye, on the banks of the Moskva River, near the Kremlin and Red Square, was completely destroyed. Finally, after a series of unfinished constructions were abandoned, the enormous Hotel Rossia—a monument to bad taste—was erected on the ruins of the Zaradye district.

Among the thousands of buildings destroyed by Stalin was the Cathedral of Christ the Savior, originally erected in commemoration of the Russians' victory over Napoleon's French army. Its demolition entailed a long and complicated process with a twofold purpose: first, to eradicate one of Moscow's principal churches, whose worshippers were being poisoned by religion, the "opium of the people," and, second, to allow for the construction of the largest building ever conceived during the Soviet era, the Palace of the Soviets: 1,375 feet high (taller than the Empire State Building), and topped by a 325-foot statue of Lenin (over twice as tall as the Statue of Liberty). The very fact that the Palace of the Soviets was to be built precisely on the ruins of the Cathedral of Christ the Savior would symbolize the triumph of Communism over religion.

The construction work on this building, suspended during World War II, was subsequently abandoned. In the 1960s the building's foundations were converted into a gigantic swimming pool with a capacity for 2,000 people. Soon after President Yeltsin took office, it was decided that the Cathedral of Christ the Savior would be reconstructed as an identical, detailed copy of the original church. Although the government provided the necessary funds, there were also substantial public contributions, particularly two fund-raising concerts organized and conducted by Mstislav Rostropovich, at $1,000 a ticket. Construction work began in early 1995, and the new cathedral was completed and consecrated in September 1997 as part of the celebrations of Moscow's 850th anniversary.

If the construction of the Palace of Soviets over the ruins of the Cathedral of Christ the Savior was meant to symbolize the triumph of Communism over religion, the reconstruction of the cathedral symbolizes the deathblow to Communist ideology and Russia's return to its profound ancient roots.

THE LAND OF ENDLESS LINES COMES TO AN END: IMPROVEMENTS IN THE DISTRIBUTION OF BASIC PRODUCTS   Shortly after we landed at Sheremetyevo 2, we immediately noticed certain changes. The first was the heavy traffic on Leningradsky Avenue en route to Moscow, with a surprisingly large number of Mercedes, BMWs, Peugeots, and other Western-made vehicles. The slow traffic flow—two hours to our destination in downtown Moscow—allowed us to observe the proliferation of huge shopping centers, shops, department stores, dachas, brandnew apartment buildings, etc.

I recalled the rule from my previous visits that if you happened to spot people waiting in line, one must immediately join it before finding out what was being sold. Yet the endless lines have disappeared. The dreary stores whose shop windows displayed a handful of mediocre products and whose employees were often rude and short-tempered have given way to a remarkable variety of establishments selling every conceivable kind of product, similar to those found in First World countries, but at prices that often seem unaffordable to the average Russian.

I also remember the exasperating Soviet restaurants: waiting half an hour for a table, even if the restaurant was empty, waiting another half hour to catch the waiter's eye, and then ordering the few dishes available from an extensive menu. Today Russian cities are filled with small bistros and cafés where you can eat quite well, not to mention the more luxurious restaurants frequented by foreign tourists, successful entrepreneurs, and Russian oligarchs.

FREEDOM OF THE PRESS   While reading various newspapers every day, I realized that there was now freedom of the press, which, though not complete, would have been unthinkable during the Soviet era. Bookstores sold all kinds of books that were formerly banned. It was also evident in the different hotels we stayed in, at least in Moscow and St. Petersburg, since either through cable or satellite they received a number of foreign channels, such as the BBC, France's TV 5, and Televisión Española, as well as numerous broadcasts from the United States, Germany, etc. Russian TV, on the other hand, does not appear to enjoy or exercise this freedom. The two principal channels are government-owned, and the major newscasts, like *Viesti* on the Rosiya (Russia) channel and *Vremya* (Channel 1), are always progovernment.

INCREASING INEQUALITY IN INCOME DISTRIBUTION   During my approximately one-month stay in Russia, I spoke with a number of people involved in a wide variety of activities: musicians, writers, university leaders, taxi drivers, tourist guides, etc. Most people did not long for the Soviet regime, although they missed the social safety nets that it had provided. The economic situation had improved: gone were the product shortages that had exasperated Soviet consumers and wasted hours of their day. The possibility of affordable housing had also increased: there were fewer cases of two or three families having to share one tiny apartment. Unemployment had decreased over the past six years; young people felt they had more promising prospects before them; travel abroad was no longer out of the question, except for financial reasons; freedom and at least a modest progress seemed evident, especially in the largest cities.

However, conditions were far from ideal. The standard of living had declined for a great many people, especially the elderly. Many retired people, their pensions undercut by inflation, no longer had recourse to the social safety net available to them under the Soviet government, and now lived in abject poverty. Life expectancy actually decreased—unheard of in an industrialized Western nation—to 63.9 years. State support for the arts and education has decreased, resulting in growing inequalities between the haves and the have-nots. Many Russians or Russian-speaking people from other parts of the Soviet empire have immigrated to Russia, especially from the former Central Asian Soviet republics, which suffer from deteriorating economies as well as growing religious intolerance.

At the same time, however, there is an emerging class of so-called oligarchs, whose extraordinary fortunes were not always earned. Many of them are former government officials who took advantage of their high-ranking positions to make handsome profits during the wave of privatizations.

I cannot end these remarks about Russia without describing a remarkable metamorphosis we witnessed in Moscow.

Opposite the Cathedral of Christ the Savior, on the Moskva River, there is a huge bronze sculpture of Tsar Peter I on a caravel. Installed in 1996, it was designed by the famous Georgian sculptor Zurab Tsereteli. The sight of Peter I, founder of St. Petersburg, on a ship of that type is ludicrous indeed, but the reason becomes clearer when we learn that the statue was supposed to represent Christopher Columbus. Tsereteli tried to sell it during the quincentennial of the discovery of America, 1992. The prospective buyers in Spain, Latin America, and the United States were not interested. Without further ado, and all of a sudden, Christopher Columbus was transformed into Peter I!

CONCERTS IN IRELAND: SEARCHING FOR NEW LEADS ON THE PIATTI, AND A WORLD PREMIERE

I have visited Ireland four times. This country instantly captivated me with its beauty, its history, and its unique personality, so different from that of England, despite the countries' historical and geographical links.

When I was first invited to give several concerts in Ireland, I accepted without hesitation. Not only would I be visiting a fascinating new country, but with a little luck, the trip would allow me to follow up on some leads on the Piatti's "biography," since it had been in Ireland from 1818 to 1853.

RECITALS IN 1997

My visit to Ireland in October 1997 was short but fruitful. On the 17th I taught a master class and gave a miniconcert at the Royal Irish Academy of Music in Dublin. On the 18th I had a recital in Cork with Edison Quintana at the piano, at University College Cork's Aula Maxima (Great Hall), and on the 20th we performed again in Dublin, at the National Concert Hall's John Field Room.

Daniel Dultzin, who was then the Mexican ambassador, is a distinguished diplomat and cellist, extremely knowledgeable about the Irish musical world. He put me in touch with three people who proved invaluable to my inquiries about the Piatti: renowned pianist John O'Conor (director of the Royal Irish Academy of Music), historian Harry McDowell, and musicologist Bara Boydell. Thanks to them I was able to discover several additional facts about the Piatti's life in Ireland, particularly about Samuel J. Pigott, who, as I mentioned in Chapter 3, owned the cello between 1821 and 1853. While in Dublin, we visited the McCullough Pigott music store, founded by Samuel J. Pigott.

The Piatti's arrival in Ireland did not go by unnoticed. The program notes for my concerts made special mention of the cello's return after 144 years. Mr. Simon Taylor, head of musical programming for RTE (Radio Telefís Éireann, or Radio and Television of Ireland), scheduled a long interview with me. The main subject of our radio talk was the "biography" of the Irish Stradivari, whose voice was also heard, since some of my recordings were played during the interview.

In Dublin, at the end of my last concert in Ireland, I addressed the audience. "These concerts mark the return of the 'Irish Stradivari' after an absence of 144 years, to the country where it spent 35 years. For the past two decades it has lived in Mexico and has premiered approximately sixty musical works. I hope to return to Ireland some day to play the premiere of a work especially written for this cello by a great Irish composer."

BACK TO IRELAND WITH THE PRIETO QUARTET

Four months later, when I returned to Ireland with the Prieto Quartet, I was delighted to learn that the Arts Council had agreed to commission a concerto for cello and orchestra from the illustrious Irish composer John Kinsella. Ambassador Daniel Dultzin hosted a dinner party for John Kinsella at the Mexican Embassy so we could exchange views on the subject. Kinsella's fourth symphony, entitled *The Four Provinces*, is a musical description of each of the four Irish provinces: Munster,

Connacht, Ulster, and Leinster. Consequently, it occurred to me that this cello piece might be inspired by the six episodes in the Piatti's history: its birth in Italy in the time of Vivaldi and Bach, its years in Cádiz and the premiere of Haydn's *Seven Last Words of Christ*, its thirty-five years in Ireland, its thirty-seven years in the possession of Alfredo Piatti, its seventy-two years with the Mendelssohns in Berlin and New York, and, finally, its twenty years in Mexico. He found the idea interesting but said he needed to analyze the idea further. We had time. Kinsella was then composing his eighth symphony, after which he would begin the cello concerto. The new work, tentatively called *Episodes for a Cello and Orchestra*, was to be concluded by the year 2000, with a premiere date slated for sometime in 2002.

A NEW TOUR IN 2000

I returned to Ireland in March 2000 with a different program: a Bach suite, Kodály's Sonata for Cello, Samuel Zyman's Suite for Two Cellos, which I performed at its Irish premiere with cellist Bill Butt, and which received an excellent response from the audience. We played in Cork, Thomastown, and Dublin. The Dublin concert, held at the Hugh Lane Gallery, was attended by composer John Kinsella.

I was thrilled at the news that the Arts Council had officially commissioned the concerto. Since John had promised to send me the score by the end of the year, March 15, 2002, was the date set for its world premiere in Dublin.

MARCH 2002:
THE WORLD PREMIERE OF KINSELLA'S CELLO CONCERTO

I arrived in Dublin during the second week of March. First I had a long meeting with the composer. It is always a privilege to discuss a performance with the composer himself, since he is best able to clarify his ideas for phrasing, dynamics, and tempos. I then played the concerto through and received his "blessing" for my interpretation, especially regarding the cadenza, where I suggested some very minor changes.

Here is what the composer wrote about his cello concerto:

Early in February 1998 Eve O'Kelly, Director of the Contemporary Music Centre, telephoned me to enquire if I would be willing to discuss the possibility of composing a concerto for the Mexican cellist, Carlos Prieto. The idea came from Carlos, through the then Mexican Ambassador to Ireland, Daniel Dultzin.

I was aware from his previous visit to Ireland and his numerous recordings that Carlos Prieto had premiered a great number of new concertos and the possibility of writing one for him was tantalising. He also played on a famous Stradivarius instrument which had a colourful history, part of which was spent in Ireland in the possession of three owners during the nineteenth century, the last being Samuel Pigott of Samuel Pigott & Co., the famous Dublin music retailers. The combination of Carlos Prieto's superb playing and the unique history of the Stradivarius cello meant that I simply had to take up the challenge. The Prieto String Quartet played in Dublin on 20 February 1998 and that was the opportunity to meet and talk about the project. Various ideas referring to the history of the cello, not least its use in the first performance of Haydn's *Seven Last Words of Our Savior on The Cross* in Cádiz, were discussed as possible starting points for the new work . . .

When I began working on the score I tried many combinations of ideas based on the historical concept, which were very attractive in themselves, but I could not get them to work. Finally I decided on a display piece for Carlos and for the Stradivarius and together we are simply adding another Mexican/Irish episode to the history of the Red Cello rather than reviewing it.

The Concerto was completed just after Christmas 2000. It is scored for double wind, two horns, two trumpets, timpani and strings and is about 26 minutes in duration. There are two movements linked by a lengthy cadenza, the second of these being an *Allegro con Brio rondo*.[12]

We played the world premiere of the concerto on March 15 at the National Concert Hall, with the National Symphony Orchestra conducted by Robert Houlihan (Fig. 32). The concert was called the St. Patrick's Weekend Concert, since it took place two days before St. Patrick's Day. All the works performed that evening were by Irish composers (Frederick May, John Kinsella, Joan Trimble, and Gerard Victory).

A few months later I played Kinsella's concerto in Mexico with one of Mexico's finest orchestras, the Xalapa Symphony Orchestra, conducted by my son Carlos Miguel Prieto (Fig. 33); immediately afterward we recorded it for Urtext Digital Classics, on a CD that came out in December 2003.

32. World Premiere of John Kinsella's cello concerto, with the National Irish Orchestra and conductor Robert Houlihan. Dublin, 2002. Photo courtesy of Fennell Photography.

33. With my son, conductor Carlos Miguel Prieto, and the Xalapa Symphony Orchestra, 2002.

AN ENCOUNTER WITH HENRI DUTILLEUX
AND HIS CELLO CONCERTO

In May 1995 I played Dutilleux's Concerto for Cello and Orchestra with conductor Sergio Cárdenas at the International Forum of New
Music, which was founded in Mexico by composer Manuel Enríquez.

From the very first time I heard it, in a version by Mstislav Rostropovich, to whom it is dedicated, I fell in love with its mysterious, evocative
sonority and the masterly treatment of the cello and the orchestra.

Dutilleux is an individualistic, independent composer, who does
not belong to any particular aesthetic school or tendency, and who has
always remained faithful to his personal concepts of beauty and refinement. His art, distinguished for its perfection, clarity, and freedom of
form, as well as for the beauty of its sonorous weave, is an heir to the
tradition created by Debussy, Ravel, and Roussel.

Since Dutilleux is open to every form of artistic expression, it is not
unusual for some of his works to be inspired by nonmusical subjects. In
fact, his Concerto for Cello reflects the echoes of Charles Baudelaire's
poetry.

The concerto is entitled *Tout un monde lointain* (*A Whole Distant
World*). When the project was being conceived, Dutilleux was avidly
rereading Baudelaire's poetry, so each movement in the piece is inspired
by one of the poems from *Les Fleurs du Mal*. (The phrase "Tout un
monde lointain" comes from the poem "La Chevelure.") "The music is
not about illustrating this or that poem, but rather about awakening the
most secret echoes from Baudelaire's work through the music," Dutilleux explained.

The idea of writing a concerto for cello and orchestra had been suggested to the composer by Igor Markevitch during the 1960s. After a
long gestation period, the work was first introduced to the public at the
Aix-en-Provence Festival on July 25, 1970, with Mstislav Rostropovich as
the soloist.

Dutilleux had originally expected to attend his concerto's premiere in
Mexico City, but he cancelled his trip at the last minute in order to finish
a work commissioned by the Boston Symphony Orchestra, scheduled
to be performed at the Tanglewood Festival in July. Since he could not
come to Mexico, he invited me to visit him in Tanglewood, where we
spent several memorable days together, along with my wife María Isabel
and my children, Carlos Miguel and Isabel (Fig. 34).

That year the Tanglewood Festival was dedicated to Dutilleux, who

34. With French composer Henri Dutilleux. Tanglewood, Lenox, Massachusetts, 1995.

was the composer in residence. Several of his principal works were performed, except for the piece commissioned by the Boston Symphony, since the composer had not managed to finish it in time. Because Dutilleux is an extremely meticulous composer who demands utter perfection, he works intensely and deliberately. He himself admits that he is no good when composing under pressure of a deadline.

He was staying at a veritable mansion ten miles from Tanglewood. He had laid out the unfinished score on a large table, and worked on it several hours a day when his duties left him some spare time. Though averse to publicity, he accepts it as a necessary evil and grudgingly agrees to occasional press and television interviews. At that particular time he felt rather uneasy about a long interview scheduled with the BBC because it would take valuable time away from composing.

At the age of seventy-nine, he still drove his car around Tanglewood without eyeglasses and with an infallible sense of direction. Although he worked hard, he also knew how to enjoy life. One day he invited me to lunch at a famous Vietnamese restaurant, where we sampled some excellent French wine that he had carefully selected to complement the exotic dishes and our lively conversation.

He promised me that he would compose a work for cello and piano, and even contemplated a prelude for cello and piano. I was, of course, very grateful for this, although I knew that as soon as he completed the work commissioned by the Boston Symphony, he had to begin working on still another piece for the Berlin Philharmonic, as well as to compose a new string quartet for the Juilliard Quartet. Fully aware of his perfectionism, I have my doubts that he will compose the prelude any time in the near future.

ONCE AGAIN THE SIX BACH SUITES IN NEW YORK, BOSTON, AND MADRID

Certain musical compositions are extremely pleasing to the ear. However, after you play them several times, you realize that with every new execution, there is no more substance left. It doesn't take long to reach their essence. Other works, on the other hand, need time; they mature gradually in the minds of the interpreter and the listener. Each new encounter allows us to delve more deeply into them and to discover marvelous new facets. This is precisely what occurs with Bach's music, whose infinite depth, beauty, and rich texture know no bounds.

Several years after Bach's tercentennial, armed with new ideas and a new focus, I once again undertook the complete cycle of his suites for cello. In 1996, I played them in Alice Tully Hall at New York's Lincoln Center, in 1997 at the Boston Conservatory, and in 1998 at the Juan March Foundation in Madrid as part of a cello music cycle that also included Kodály's Sonata and suites by Britten and Reger.

Minutes before my concert in New York, while I was alone in the Alice Tully dressing room impatiently waiting for my cue, I was handed an urgent telegram bearing the following message:

Dear Carlos,
Wishing you a glorious journey through the suites tonight.
Our love to you and Isabel.
Jill and Yo-Yo Ma

I was deeply touched at this generous and uncommon gesture of companionship and friendship.

A CONFERENCE-CONCERT WITH CARLOS FUENTES IN GENEVA

One of the most unusual and interesting recitals I have ever played took place in May 1994 in Geneva. It formed part of a conference entitled "Dialogues with Great Latin-American Writers," jointly organized by the Simón I. Patiño Foundation and the University of Geneva. The guest author was Carlos Fuentes, who, together with the foundation, thought of rounding out the event with an art exhibit and a concert (Fig. 35).

The evening began with a dialogue between Carlos Fuentes and Luis Iñigo Madrigal, a professor at the University of Geneva; the talk centered on Fuentes's work and Latin American literature in general. As usual, Fuentes's erudition, sharp wit, and eloquence thoroughly captivated his audience, which jammed the auditorium and also occupied a huge outdoor area with a gigantic television screen. The first part of the program concluded with a barrage of questions from the audience and Fuentes's dazzling responses. It was followed by an exhibit of José Luis Cuevas's works and ended with a concert, preceded by an introduction I had prepared beforehand. I played a Bach suite and then, with pianist Doris Stevenson, several Latin American works.

35. With Mexican writer Carlos Fuentes in Geneva, 1994.

BACH, GARCÍA MÁRQUEZ, AND THE CELLO

Throughout its almost 290 years of existence, the Piatti has encountered countless distinguished personalities from the music world. However, as far as I know, only one recipient of the Nobel Prize for Literature has actually held it: Gabriel García Márquez. This great writer enjoys music enormously. Not only does he spend hours listening to it, but his range of musical interests is astonishing. One day we were chatting with Ramón Xirau, who remarked that he was so fond of music that he could not write poetry without listening to it. García Márquez replied that in his particular case, his attention becomes so concentrated on the music that he would be unable to write a single line. For García Márquez the *summum bonum* of music is found in Bach's Six Suites for cello. If he were stranded on a desert island and allowed only one piece of music, he would definitely choose the first suite. The cello is his favorite instrument because of its warm tone, the closest instrument to the human voice.

36. With Gabriel García Márquez and the Piatti in Mexico, 2000.

After years of listening to music—quartets, concerts, operas, and sonatas—rather haphazardly, like most people, he decided to adopt a method for expanding his musical horizons. As could be expected from such a pioneering writer, his method turned out to be original. "At first, I thought of listening to music in alphabetical order, by composers," he reported. "But I soon discarded this procedure, since *B* for 'Bach,' an inexhaustible composer, would take up half my lifetime." He then decided to make his way through each instrument's repertoire in chronological order, beginning with the violin: Bach, Mozart, Beethoven, Brahms (whose concerto he believes reigns supreme over all violin concertos), and so on until Bartók. Next he continued with the cello, which, as I mentioned earlier, was his favorite instrument. For some time now, he has been interested in the double bass and its concertos: von Dittersdorf, Bottessini, Koussevitzky.

One night, when I happened to mention my plan for writing this book, primarily centered on the "biography" of the Piatti, García Márquez immediately expressed a desire to "meet" this instrument. As a result, in a historic encounter, one of the greatest writers in the Spanish language held the Piatti in his hands and touched its strings (Fig. 36). Never in its long history has the Piatti been played by such a novice or by a more brilliant interpreter.

TEXAS: SEPTEMBER 2003

In September 2003 I returned to Texas for a series of recitals and lectures on "The Adventures of a Cello," that is, one of the subjects of this book.

I was extremely impressed by the University of Texas at Austin. I had of course, often heard of this institution's excellent reputation, but my visit made me much more aware of its importance and its remarkable achievements. It is, moreover, the leading center for Mexican studies after the National Autonomous University of Mexico, and its prestigious Benson Latin American Collection is famous the world over. It was a most gratifying experience to give a lecture and play a concert at Bates Recital Hall and to help reinforce the working relationship between the University of Texas School of Music and the Las Rosas Conservatory in Morelia, Mexico, a relationship I will discuss in the next chapter.

My Texas tour also included Texas Christian University in Fort Worth, where I gave a similar lecture on "The Adventures of a Cello" and then played parts of a Bach suite, as well as the Kodály Sonata and Zyman's

Suite for Two Cellos. As my partner in this performance I was delighted to have the brilliant young cellist Jesús Castro-Balbi, who had won first prize in the inaugural Carlos Prieto Latin American Competition, held in 2000 at the Las Rosas Conservatory. In 2002, I recorded Zyman's Suite with him. Jesús is now a professor at the renowned TCU School of Music, which also has a close bond with Latin America through its excellent faculty and the aforementioned Las Rosas Conservatory.

CARLOS MIGUEL PRIETO

My son, Carlos Miguel Prieto, has had a singular career. As I mentioned elsewhere, he started taking violin lessons at an early age. He had exceptional teachers in Mexico and the United States. As a young child he exhibited an extraordinary aptitude for music and for playing the violin; he also has the rare gift of perfect pitch, that is, the capacity to immediately identify any musical note.

Although Carlos Miguel studied engineering at Princeton University and earned a master of business administration from Harvard, he never abandoned the violin: he played the violin in the Princeton University Orchestra and took innumerable music courses. Upon his return to Mexico, there was every indication that Carlos Miguel would be embarking on a promising career as a businessman.

However, his heart was not in business. As a child he had caught the incurable music bug, and at a certain point in his life, early in 1995, his vocation and his irrepressible need to cultivate and expand his musical knowledge led him to renounce the business world. My wife and I supported his decision—which reminded me of my own from many years before—but we still felt deep apprehension about the uncertainty of a music career, fraught as it is with so many difficulties and obstacles.

On October 25, 1995, I attended his first rehearsal. He was conducting Mendelssohn's String Symphony no. 9 in C. Any doubts I might have had about his decision vanished on the spot. What I had seen convinced me of his talent and potential.

I had spent many years playing with Carlos Miguel in the Prieto Quartet, but after he became a full-time musician, our relationship entered an entirely new phase. In December 1996 I performed for the first time with Carlos Miguel as conductor: Haydn's Cello Concerto in C Major. Since then I have played thirteen cello concertos with him and recorded three CDs of new cello concertos.

In less than ten years, his career as a conductor has progressed most spectacularly: associate conductor of the Mexico City Philharmonic Orchestra and the San Antonio Symphony Orchestra, currently principal conductor of the Xalapa Symphony Orchestra in Mexico, the Huntsville Symphony Orchestra in Alabama, the Louisiana Philharmonic Orchestra in New Orleans, and the Youth Orchestra of the Americas, and associate conductor of the Houston Symphony Orchestra. He is a frequent guest conductor for numerous orchestras.

It would take a more eloquent writer than I to adequately describe my emotions while watching his career flourish and, even more, when performing in concerts with him as conductor.

SOME ANECDOTES OF TRAVELS WITH THE PIATTI

Chelo Prieto is neither my wife nor my daughter. This is the name used by my Piatti when traveling. Although the cello is a marvelous instrument, on concert tours it becomes an extremely cumbersome artifact, especially on airplanes. It cannot be registered with the rest of the baggage because of the very high probability that it will arrive at its destination in smithereens. Unlike a violin, it cannot be stored in the cabin free of charge, because it doesn't fit under the seat or in the overhead compartments. Therefore, the cello must travel like any other passenger, in its own seat. IATA (International Air Transport Association) regulations stipulate that the cello pays full price and sit next to its owner in an adjoining window seat, which must not be an emergency exit. Since the instrument doesn't eat, suffer from airsickness, and or ever need to get up and stretch its legs, the least one could expect is that it could travel at half fare, like children, but the IATA sets the rules, and the rule is that the cello pays full fare.

Despite these clear-cut regulations, ticket agents at many airlines are totally at a loss when someone tries to purchase a ticket for a cello. They frantically consult their manuals, call their supervisors, and lose considerable time in the process. One day my wife suggested we give a name to the cello. We christened her Chelo Prieto, or Cello Prieto, without specifying whether she was a Miss, a Mrs., or a musical instrument. This simple decision eliminated all the previous wastes of time. An added advantage was that Chelo Prieto, or Miss Chelo Prieto, started gaining frequent flyer miles on several airlines. (I must confess that to take advantage of that extra mileage I have occasionally had to forge Miss Prieto's signature.)

A MISSING PASSENGER IN THE SOVIET UNION

In 1985 I embarked on a concert tour that included Moscow, Pärnu and Tallinn (Estonia), Kaunas and Vilnius (Lithuania), and Riga (Latvia.)

On October 6, we flew from Tallinn to Vilnius on an Antonov AN-24. We had a stopover in Riga. Although we were passengers in transit, we had to present our passports once again in the terminal. We were about to board the bus en route to the aircraft when it was discovered that a passenger in our party had disappeared at the Riga airport, and to top it off, it was a foreigner! The flight attendants were scurrying back and forth in a frenzy. I approached them and offered my help in locating the missing passenger. They looked at me skeptically, almost indignantly. However, their expressions changed when I told them, "I think I know where your missing passenger is. It is already occupying its own seat on the plane, seat belt fastened and ready to go. It is my cello!"

Indeed, Miss Chelo Prieto was the foreign passenger who had caused the commotion. Because it travels like any passenger, with its own ticket and seat, the passenger count on the bus was one short of the number of tickets on the passenger list. Once the mystery was solved, our flight took off, and an hour later we landed in Vilnius.

A MEAL FOR MISS CHELO PRIETO ON AEROFLOT

In 1988 I toured the USSR once again, accompanied by my wife and my daughter, Isabel. On Sunday, October 2, we boarded a comfortable 350-seat Ilyushin—the largest in the Soviet fleet—and in four hours covered the 2,500 miles between Moscow and Alma-Ata, the capital of Kazakhstan. We were served a meal that can only be described as meager and unappetizing. The main dish looked like the leg of an exceedingly small bird. It was, in fact, the scrawny leg of an extremely undernourished chicken. We received another surprise when the flight attendant arrived with an additional ration—another skimpy chicken leg—for Miss Chelo, which, as always, was traveling in the adjoining seat. In addition to being puny, it was practically raw. We thanked the flight attendant and told her that Miss Chelo was not hungry.

A DISAPPOINTMENT IN LA JOLLA

After a concert in La Jolla, California, I was approached by two attractive young ladies, who were very interested in seeing the cello up close. "It's beautiful. It must be brand-new. How long have you had it?"

They asked. I replied that I had owned it for about fifteen years. The disappointment in their faces was quite evident, even more so when they learned that it really wasn't that new after all. "So your cello is secondhand?" "Not even that," I explained. "I think it must be more or less tenth-hand." At that the two girls left at once, feeling sorry for me because I had to settle for a "tenth-hand cello."

AT HARTSFIELD ATLANTA INTERNATIONAL AIRPORT

Shortly after the tragedy of September 11, 2001, I landed in Atlanta. Both the cello and its case were subjected to a thorough inspection. I always store extra strings in the case, but this time, for some mysterious reason, the inspector regarded only the G string as dangerous, since it might serve as a strangling device, and requested that I remove it. A supervisor who arrived at the scene then decided that all strings were equally dangerous but that it would be a complicated, time-consuming procedure to open the cello case and remove the strings once aboard the aircraft. Thus he finally ruled that cello strings could be allowed to travel as long as they remained inside the case.

I was stunned by yet another question: "Is this instrument new, or has it been used?" I replied that it was indeed old. He looked at it and concluded: "You're right. It looks used. You can go." I went on my way without bothering to find out what would have happened with a new cello.

AT MADRID BARAJAS AIRPORT

A short time ago I landed at Madrid's airport with María Isabel and Chelo Prieto. We carried our luggage to a taxi. As soon as the taxi driver spotted the cello case, he exclaimed, "That thing has to go on the luggage rack!" I explained that it was an extremely delicate instrument that had to be placed inside the taxi, especially since it was raining. "You're crazy!" he said politely. "You'd think it was an 'Estradivarius'!" To avoid further discussions, we decided to take the next taxi.

AT CHECKPOINT CHARLIE

When I was a member of Trío México, we went on a concert tour of the Federal Republic of Germany and East Berlin, which we had to enter through Checkpoint Charlie. Never in its life has the Piatti been subjected to such a meticulous inspection. The East German police, who were especially interested in finding out whether I was smuggling any forbidden articles, first inserted—quite carefully, I must confess—a dentist-type mirror through the f-holes. When they found nothing, they tried to unscrew the neck of the cello. I promptly grabbed the cello and was able to convince them that the neck was not unscrewable, not hollow, and not stuffed with anything. And this took place in the Germany of Bach!

A VERY LONG CELLO CONCERTO

I arrived in a Mexican city, which shall remain nameless, to play Dvořák's Cello Concerto. Before the concert, I had to attend the customary press conference. A young, somewhat shy reporter approached me and asked, "And you, sir, what will you sing tomorrow?"

"Nothing," I answered.

"What? Why?" she asked again, mystified.

"Because I actually sing very badly." I answered.

"Then what are you going to do?" she asked incredulously.

"I am going to play the Dvořák Cello Concerto."

"Nothing more?"

"Well, nothing more or nothing less, as you wish. Dvořák's concerto is one of the longest," I answered. This reply left the young reporter satisfied.

The following day, the newspaper's cultural section displayed the following headline: "Today Carlos Prieto will pay the longest concerto ever written for the cello." So far, I have yet to find either my name or Dvořák's in the *Guinness Book of World Records*.

THE NEW YORK–BOSTON SHUTTLE

In November 1999 I flew from New York to Boston. I had reserved the usual seats for Chelo Prieto and myself. The gate agent asked for some identification of Miss Chelo Prieto, and smiled when she saw it was a cello. "How old is she?" she asked. "This year," I said "exactly 279 years old." Her reply was immediate: "OK, then we will give her the senior-citizen discount!"

CHAPTER 6

∫ My Relationship with the Music and the Musicians of Latin America, Spain, and Portugal

MY INTEREST IN THE MUSIC OF IBERO-AMERICA

In 1980 I became seriously involved with Ibero-American works for cello. By "Ibero-American" I refer to the music from Latin America, Spain, and Portugal. I say "involved" because it was a question not only of learning the existing cello repertoire, but also of encouraging composers to write works for the cello, or, in other words, promoting the enrichment of the cello repertoire in those regions.

In light of the meager repertoire of Mexican works, especially those written for cello and orchestra, since 1980 I have tried to interest the most outstanding composers in Mexico, and later in Spain and the aforementioned countries, to write works for solo cello, cello and piano, and cello and orchestra. Naturally, I have also been extremely interested in discovering any unknown, forgotten, or lost works for cello written by composers in these countries.

Why consider this music as a whole? My answer is simple. Although our countries are separated by vast differences, we are connected by the indestructible link of a magnificent cultural heritage. This heritage is the sum of the contributions of European cultures, mainly from Iberia, and through them, of Roman, Greek, Moorish, and Jewish influences, as well as those of our indigenous civilizations—from Chichén Itzá and Copán to Machu Picchu—and Africa as well. To approach the art and culture of our countries in an isolated or individual manner is tantamount to depriving ourselves of a significant part of its richness. The language of Rubén Darío (from Nicaragua) is the same as that of Federico García Lorca (Spain), Alfonso Reyes (Mexico), Jorge Luis Borges (Argentina), José Ortega y Gasset (Spain), Pablo Neruda (Chile), Rafael Alberti (Spain), Octavio Paz (Mexico), Juan Rulfo (Mexico), Carlos

Fuentes (Mexico), Gabriel García Márquez (Colombia), Mario Vargas Llosa (Peru), and Julio Cortázar (Argentina), to mention only a few.

No Mexican, Peruvian, or Spaniard can ever begin to understand his or her country without at least a slight knowledge about the other Ibero-American countries on both sides of the Atlantic.

We Spanish- and Portuguese-speaking peoples have the obligation to extol and promote our cultural heritage—in my case, through music, especially in these times, as I wrote in the introduction, when most of the First World nations view our countries through a distorted mirror, filled with misconceptions and oversimplifications.

Music has enabled me to travel throughout a considerable part of this vast world, both on the Iberian Peninsula and throughout Latin America. I have never felt I was in foreign lands, but rather in countries that are endearingly close to me, and I have always been welcomed as a native rather than a stranger. I have often played in Spain and on numerous occasions in Portugal, Argentina, Uruguay, Chile, Brazil, Peru, Bolivia, Ecuador, Colombia and Venezuela. I have played in the Central American countries and in Cuba. Naturally, I have also traveled extensively throughout Mexico, playing in every single state of my country. Finally, my journeys through these countries have also encompassed the Spanish-speaking regions of the United States, those with a predominantly Hispanic culture. In many of my travels, I have been accompanied by Edison Quintana, with whom I formed a duo almost twenty years ago. A superb Uruguayan pianist, now a Mexican citizen, he shares my enthusiasm for Ibero-American music.

Since 1980 I have premiered some seventy new works, many of them dedicated to me, and other compositions that, though not so new, had been, for several reasons, either unknown or lost. I have recorded many of them on compact discs in Mexico, Europe, and the United States. The list of these works is detailed below in chronological order by date of performance. An asterisk marks those compositions that were dedicated to me.

WORKS PREMIERED, 1981–2003

TABLE 3

Composer	Work, date of composition	Site and date of premiere
Blas Galindo (Mexico)	Sonata for Solo Cello*, 1981	Mexico, Sweden, 1981

Composer	Work, date of composition	Site and date of premiere
Ricardo Castro (Mexico)	Cello Concerto, c. 1890	Mexico (repremiered), 1981; U.S., Berlin (recording), 1985
Joaquín Rodrigo (Spain)	*Como una fantasia**, solo cello, 1981	Mexico, Madrid, 1981
Raúl Ladrón de Guevara (Mexico)	*Movimiento concertante**, cello and piano, 1981	Mexico, 1982; Bologna, 1983
Mario Kuri-Aldana (Mexico)	Concerto *Tarahumara**, 1981	Mexico, 1982
Lourdino Barreto (India)	Piece for Cello and Orchestra, 1985	Goa (India), 1985
Manuel Enríquez (Mexico)	Cello Concerto*, 1985	Mexico, 1987
Blas Galindo (Mexico)	Cello Concerto*, 1985	Mexico, 1987
Carlos Chávez (Mexico)	Cello Concerto, unfinished	Mexico, 1987
Carlos Chávez (Mexico)	Madrigal for Cello and Piano, 1921	U.S., Mexico, 1988
Federico Ibarra (Mexico)	Cello Concerto*, 1988	Mexico, 1989; U.S., 1990; London, 1993; Russia, 2005
Manuel de Elías (Mexico)	Cello Concerto*, 1988	Mexico, 1989
Emmanuel Arias (Mexico)	Cello Concerto*, 1989	Mexico, 1989
Celso Garrido-Lecca (Peru)	Cello Concerto*, 1988	Mexico, 1990; Madrid, 2001; Caracas, 2003
Celso Garrido-Lecca (Peru)	Sonata-Fantasia for Cello and Piano, 1988	Mexico, 1990; Lima, 1991
Miguel Bernal Jiménez (Mexico)	Three Tarascan Dances*, cello and piano	Mexico, 1990; New York, 1991
Samuel Zyman (Mexico)	Cello Concerto*, 1990	New York, Mexico, 1990; Buenos Aires, 1991; Seville, 1992
José Rolón (Mexico)	Song for cello and piano	Mexico, 1990
Eduardo Hernández Moncada (Mexico)	Piece for Cello and Piano*, 1981	Mexico, 1990
Alfonso de Elías (Mexico)	Three pieces, cello and piano	Los Angeles, 1991; Mexico, 1992

Composer	Work, date of composition	Site and date of premiere
Silvestre Revueltas & Manuel Enríquez (both Mexico)	Three Pieces for Cello and Piano*, (orig. 1933 for violin and piano; transcr. 1991)	Los Angeles, 1991; Brussels, 1993; New York, 1995; Paris, Madrid, Washington, 1998
Manuel Enríquez (Mexico)	Fantasia for Cello and Piano*, 1992	Mexico, 1992; Spokane, Los Angeles, 1993
Federico Ibarra (Mexico)	Sonata for Cello and Piano*, 1992	Houston, 1992; Mexico, Brussels, 1993; Madrid, 1996; New York, Washington, 1998
Max Lifchitz (Mexico)	Voces de la noche*, cello and orchestra, 1993	Mexico, 1993
David Hush (England)	Partita*, solo cello, 1990	Mexico, 1993
Jorge Córdoba (Mexico)	Contra el tiempo*, cello and piano, 1992	Mexico, 1993
Ramón Montes de Oca (Mexico)	Elegy*, cello and piano, 1993	Mexico, 1994
Robert X. Rodríguez (U.S.)	Máscaras*, cello and orch., 1993–1994	Guanajuato, 1994
Samuel Adler (U.S.)	Emuah, cello and orch., 1994	Flint (MI), 1994
Federico Álvarez del Toro (Mexico)	El constructor de los sueños, cello, harp, and voices, 1994	Mexico, 1994
Astor Piazzolla–E. Quintana (Argentina)	Adiós Nonino, cello and piano	Mexico, 1994
Joaquín Gutiérrez Heras (Mexico)	Canción en el puerto*, cello and piano, 1994	Mexico, 1995; New York, 1998; Johannesburg, 1999; Moscow, 2003
Mario Lavista (Mexico)	Tres danzas seculares*, cello and piano, 1994	Mexico, 1995; Madrid, 1996; Paris, Dublin, 1997; New York, Washington, 1998; Moscow, 2003
Arturo Salinas (Mexico)	Netík 1, cello and piano, 1995	Mexico, 1995
Samuel Zyman (Mexico)	Fantasia for Cello and Piano*, 1994	New York, Mexico, 1995; Madrid, 1996

Composer	Work, date of composition	Site and date of premiere
Tomás Marco (Spain)	*Primer espejo de Falla**, cello and piano, 1994	Mexico, 1995; Madrid, 1996; New York, 1998
Manuel Castillo (Spain)	*Alborada**, cello and piano, 1994	Mexico, 1995; Spain, 1996
Leo Brouwer (Cuba)	Sonata, solo cello, 1960	Madrid, 1996
Robert X. Rodríguez (U.S.)	*Lull-a-Bear**, cello and piano, 1994	Mexico, 1995
George Shearing (U.S.); arr. Roberto Aymes (Mexico)	*To Antonio Carlos Jobim*, cello and piano, 1995	Mexico, 1995
José Antonio Alcaraz (Mexico)	*Otros cellos, otros ámbitos**, cello, narrator, and piano, 1996	Mexico, 1996
Roberto Aymes (Mexico)	*El señor de Ipanema**, 1995	Mexico, 1996
Celso Garrido-Lecca (Peru)	*Soliloquio II**, solo cello, 1996	Mexico, 1997; Lima, 1999
Marcela Rodríguez (Mexico)	Cello Concerto*, 1994	Guanajuato, 1997
Ricardo Lorenz (Venezuela)	*Cecilia en azul y verde**, cello and piano, 1998	Caracas, 1998; Mexico, 1999
Carlos Fariñas (Cuba)	Cello Concerto*, 1995–1996	Xalapa, 1998
Juan Orrego-Salas (Chile)	*Espacios**, cello and piano, 1998	Santiago, Mexico, Washington, Pretoria, 1999
Gustavo Becerra-Schmidt (Chile)	Sonata No. 5*, cello and piano, 1997	Mexico, Santiago, 1999
Blas Emilio de Atehortúa (Colombia)	*Romanza*, cello and piano	Bogotá, 1999
Samuel Zyman (Mexico)	Suite for Two Cellos*, 1999	Mexico, 1999; Ireland, 2000; U.S., 2003
Roberto Sierra (Puerto Rico)	*Cuatro versos**, cello concerto, 1999	Mexico, Caracas, 2000
Arturo Márquez (Mexico)	*Espejos en la arena**, cello concerto, 1999–2000	Mexico, Caracas, 2000; U.S., 2004
Xavier Montsalvatge (Spain)	*Invención a la italiana**, cello and piano, 2000	Mexico, 2000

Composer	Work, date of composition	Site and date of premiere
Alberto Villalpando (Bolivia)	Sonatita de piel morena*, cello and piano, 1999	Mexico, 2000
Claudia Calderón (Colombia)	La revuelta circular*, cello and piano, 2000	Mexico, 2000; New York, 2001
Eugenio Toussaint (Mexico)	Pour les enfants*, cello and piano, 2000	Mexico, 2000
Tomás Marco (Spain)	Partita Piatti*, solo cello, 1999	Mexico, U.S., Germany, 2001; Portugal, Spain, 2002
Alberto Andrés Heller (Brazil)	14 bis*, violin, cello, and orch., 2002	Florianópolis (Brazil), 2002
John Kinsella (Ireland)	Cello Concerto*, 2001	Dublin, 2002; Xalapa, Veracruz, 2002
Eugenio Toussaint (Mexico)	Cello Concerto no. 2*, 1999	Caracas, Mexico, 2003
Marlos Nobre (Brazil)	Partita latina*, cello and piano, 2003	Puebla, Guadalajara, 2003; Guanajuato, 2004
María Teresa Prieto (Spain-Mexico)	Adagio and Fugue for Cello and Orch.*, 1948	Oviedo (Spanish premiere), 2003
José Luis Turina (Spain)	Concerto da chiesa*, cello and strings, 1998	St. Petersburg (Russia), 2003
Tomás Marco (Spain)	Laberinto marino*, cello and strings, 2002	Morelia, Guanajuato, 2003
Luis Herrera de la Fuente (Mexico)	Sonatina*, solo cello, 2002	Mexico, 2004
Tomás Marco (Spain)	Ensueño y resplandor del Quijote*, violin, cello, and orch., 2004	Spain, 2004; South Africa, 2005
Joaquín Gutiérrez Heras (Mexico)	Fantasía Concertante*, cello and orch., 2005	U.S., 2005; Caracas and Mexico, 2006
Don Grantham (U.S.)	Son of Cimetière*, cello and piano, 2006	U.S., 2006

It would be pointless to give a detailed account of all these premieres. In this chapter, I will concentrate on the most interesting concerts and on those composers and works that are particularly relevant to this book.

MEXICO: FIRST WORKS FOR THE CELLO

So far, I have not found any musical compositions for the cello—
either with the piano, with the orchestra, or solo—composed prior to
the late nineteenth century. However, it is evident that there were cellists
in Mexico in the early eighteenth century. The first Mexican score that I
have found that includes cellos is *Lamentaciones* by Manuel de Sumaya
(1678–1755).[1] Sumaya, the most important composer in New Spain and
one of the most gifted in the New World, wrote several works that required cellos. In 1711 he premiered his opera, *La partenope*, at the palace
of the viceroy, the Duke of Linares. He was appointed maestro de capilla
of the Metropolitan Cathedral in Mexico City in 1715, and reinforced
the stringed-instrument section of the cathedral's orchestra in 1734. Two
years later he hired violinists, violists, and additional cellists, as well as
other instrumentalists.[2]

Just as eminent composers, organists, and violinists from Spain and
Italy came to Mexico, there is no doubt that cellists must also have arrived there. Most likely they became the teachers of the first cellists born
in New Spain.

The original version of Haydn's *Seven Last Words*—which includes
a cello role—was performed in Mexico in the late eighteenth or early
nineteenth century. The cathedral's archives preserve some orchestra
parts from the first edition of the *Sette Sonate con una introduzione, ed
al fine un Terremoto* (that is, the *Seven Last Words*). The parts are incomplete, which suggests that they were used for a concert. Haydn's obituary,
published on April 2, 1810, in the *Diario de México*, places the *Seven Last
Words* among his principal works.[3]

There are several valuable musical archives in Mexico, mainly in its ca-
thedrals. Since not all of them have been sufficiently researched, I have not
lost hope that some composition for cello might still turn up some day.
However, the works in these archives are mainly religious compositions.

The fact remains that, as far as we know, the oldest Mexican concerto
for cello and orchestra is Ricardo Castro's, probably composed toward
the end of the nineteenth century.

RICARDO CASTRO

Ricardo Castro (1864–1906) was born in the city of Durango, Mexico. He studied piano and composition at the National Conservatory of
Music, and in 1883 he represented Mexico at the celebrations in Venezuela for the centennial of Simón Bolívar's birth, as well as at a world's fair

in New Orleans in 1885. He met with such success that he was invited to play in Washington, New York, Philadelphia, and Chicago. It was Castro who introduced numerous chamber-music pieces in Mexico and also helped create the Mexican Philharmonic Society. Between 1883 and 1887 he composed two symphonies.

His cello concerto, composed during the late nineteenth century, was premiered on April 6, 1903, in Paris's Salle Erard, with Marix Loevensohn as soloist.[4] Incredible as it may seem, the concert was not performed in Mexico until seventy-eight years after its Paris debut. On July 11 and 12, 1981, I took great satisfaction in premiering this work at the Sala Neza-hualcóyotl with the Minería Orchestra conducted by Jorge Velazco.[5] We performed it again on three other occasions in 1985, and as I mentioned in an earlier chapter, that June we recorded it in Berlin.

This work reflects the influence of several European composers, although some of his themes are undoubtedly Mexican. Probably the most important Mexican composer of the nineteenth century, Castro was also the country's first symphonist and a precursor of musical nationalism. His opera *Atzimba* was the first Mexican opera written in Spanish, and his *Aires nacionales mexicanos*—a caprice for piano—is based on popular songs.

MANUEL PONCE

Manuel M. Ponce died in 1948, when I was eleven years old. The image of Don Manuel and his wife, Clema, is still engraved on my memory. The Ponces were friends of my parents, and for a time, my aunt María Teresa Prieto often consulted with Don Manuel on the finer points of composition.

In 1943 he composed a trio for violin, viola, and cello in which there were two versions of the cello part; one was a simplified version of the original. The manuscript bears the following dedication:

For Cécile, Carlos and Carlitos Prieto (a six year old cellist who surely will soon be able to play the more difficult cello part).
Cordially,
Manuel M. Ponce
Mexico, Nov. 4th, 1943

And indeed, I played the easier part, but soon I was able to play the other. In addition to the string trio, Ponce also dedicated a duo for violin and viola to my parents, who played those instruments in the family quartet. Ponce composed two works for cello and piano, a sonata, written in Cuba in 1915–1917 and inspired by rhythmic Cuban motifs, and three preludes, written in 1931–1932 while he was in France.

CARLOS CHÁVEZ

I had known Carlos Chávez since my childhood. I can distinctly remember listening with my parents and my brother to the National Symphony Orchestra concerts he conducted at the Palace of Fine Arts, the very first symphonic concerts I ever attended.

Many years later, I saw Carlos Chávez again, under radically different circumstances. In 1958–1959, when I was a student at MIT and living in Boston, Harvard University invited him to present the Charles Eliot Norton lectures. Only the most distinguished figures in the world of literature and the arts receive this honor, and only three musicians preceded Chávez: Igor Stravinsky, Paul Hindemith and Aaron Copland. The auditorium was always jam-packed, but I did not miss a single one of his superb lectures.

After my musical metamorphosis in 1975–1978, my interest in Chávez increased considerably. Soon, my repertoire included his Sonatina for Cello and Piano, written in 1924, which I have often played in recitals both in Mexico and abroad.

In late 1986 I heard the rumor that shortly before his death Carlos Chávez had started working on a concerto for cello and orchestra. The news interested me a great deal, since Chávez is one of the most important names in Latin American music. After a fruitless search for the manuscript in the New York Public Library, where most of his scores are kept, I then traveled to Mexico and visited his daughter, Anita Chávez, who had kept some of her father's manuscripts. Anita took out several of his personal files, and all of a sudden, to our great surprise, the concerto turned up. I was absolutely ecstatic when I discovered that the work comprised a great many pages. Conceived on a grand scale, it consisted of four movements: Allegro, Lento, Scherzo, and Presto. The Mexican Academy of Arts had commissioned the piece in 1975, but Chávez never completed it. However, since the first movement, filled with dramatic intensity, had been completed, I immediately contemplated the possibility of playing it.

The world premiere, commemorating the eighty-eighth anniversary of Carlos Chávez's birth, took place on June 13, 1987, in Mexico City's

Sala Nezahualcóyotl with Eduardo Diazmuñoz conducting the State of Mexico Symphony Orchestra and me as soloist.

Shortly after, Anita sent me yet another of her father's heretofore undiscovered manuscripts: a madrigal for cello and piano, written in 1921, when still a young man. I premiered this piece with pianist Doris Stevenson on January 31, 1988, at the Sheldon Concert Hall in St. Louis, Missouri.

I recorded the sonatina and the madrigal on two occasions, and in 1998 I also recorded the concerto, which means that Chávez's complete works for cello are now available. This, briefly, is the story of the unfinished concerto.[6]

On March 7, 1972, Carlos Chávez was commissioned by the Academy of Arts to compose an orchestral work of an undefined nature. Time passed, and in 1975 he informed the academy that he had completed more than half of the composition, a cello concerto. Soon after, however, he was diagnosed with an illness that required major surgery. In 1976 the work was delayed once again, since Per Brevig, the principal trombone player in the house orchestra of New York's Metropolitan Opera, had commissioned Chávez to write a trombone concerto. In January 1977 Chávez, who had undergone a second operation, managed to complete the trombone concerto, despite his ill health. During the last few months of his life, Chávez devoted himself to two projects: the cello concerto and the reorchestration of his opera *The Visitors*. However, he died in August 1978, leaving both projects unfinished.

MARÍA TERESA PRIETO

The composer María Teresa Prieto—my aunt on my father's side— was born in Spain and immigrated to Mexico in 1939. Since her musical repertoire was composed in Mexico, we can include her in the list of Mexican composers. She studied in Oviedo, her native city, with Saturnino del Fresno and in Madrid with Benito García de la Parra. In Mexico her teachers included Manuel M. Ponce, Carlos Chávez, and Rodolfo Halffter, and in the United States she studied with Darius Milhaud. Her considerable symphonic output was played by the National Symphonic Orchestra under the direction of such renowned conductors as Carlos Chávez, Erich Kleiber, Luis Herrera de la Fuente, and Emil Khachaturian. Her symphonic poem *Chichén-Itzá* was performed in Madrid by the National Orchestra, conducted by Ataúlfo Argenta.

In addition, she composed several quartets, one of which—the *Cuarteto Modal*, from 1958—was awarded the Samuel Rios Prize in Spain.

In 1948 she wrote Adagio and Fugue for Cello and Orchestra, which was first performed that same year with Imre Hartman, Carlos Chávez, and National Symphony Orchestra at the Palace of Fine Arts, where it was played again, in 1960, by cellist Maurice Eisenberg. María Teresa Prieto also composed a sonata for cello and orchestra, which, like her Adagio and Fugue, also exists in a piano version written by the composer herself.

FIRST CONCERTS IN SPAIN—ASTURIAS AND MADRID— AND THE GRANADA FESTIVAL

I have given innumerable concerts in Spain. Here I will only refer to some of my first concerts in that country.

For several reasons I must begin with Asturias, which is not only where I gave my first concerts in Spain, but also my first concerts as a soloist outside of Mexico. In 1979 I played Dvořák's Cello Concerto with the National Orchestra of Spain, conducted by Antoni Ross Marbá, in Oviedo's beautiful Campoamor Theatre, and then at the Universidad Laboral in Gijón. It seemed symbolic that my first concerts in Spain took place in Asturias, where my father was born, where he met my mother, and where the Prieto Quartet originated.

The following year, in October 1980, I returned to Asturias. I played Schumann's Cello Concerto in A Minor in Oviedo, Gijón, and Avilés with the Chamber Orchestra of Asturias, which was led by the talented young conductor Víctor Pablo Pérez. Also in October of that year I made my debut in Madrid with Shostakovich's Cello Concerto no. 1 at the historic Teatro Real with the Spanish Radio and Television Orchestra, conducted by Odón Alonso, marking this orchestra's 1,000th performance.

Never have I played in such spectacular surroundings as in July 1987 during the 35th Granada International Festival of Music and Dance, on the open-air Patio de los Arrayanes of the Alhambra, the most beautifully preserved and oldest of all extant Moorish palaces. The recital, with pianist Ángel Soler, began at nightfall, and was considerably enriched by unexpected echoes from the occasional chirping swallows and croaking frogs.

My dressing room at the Alhambra happened to be the *Cuarto Dorado* (Gold Room), no less, whose multicolored tiles were decorated with filigree trimmings. It overlooked the Patio del Mexuar, where the kings of Granada received their subjects a little over 500 years ago: more like a scene straight out of *The Arabian Nights* than a dressing room.

JOAQUÍN RODRIGO

In 1980, Spanish composer Joaquín Rodrigo wrote a piece for solo cello entitled *Como una fantasía*, which he graciously dedicated to me; he also let me choose the time and place for its world premiere.

The concert, a tribute to Rodrigo, was scheduled for March 19, 1980, at the Sala Nezahualcóyotl, with the participation of violinist Agustín León Ara (Rodrigo's son-in-law), guitarist Alfonso Moreno, and the State of Mexico Symphony Orchestra, conducted by Enrique Bátiz.

Joaquín Rodrigo and his wife, Vicky, who had reserved a room at the María Isabel Hotel, arrived in Mexico on March 10; their daughter, Cecilia, and Agustín León Ara stayed at our home. Our first rehearsal was on March 17. I had barely returned home when Cecilia called her parents to see how they had spent the afternoon. The hotel operator answered and, sobbing uncontrollably, informed her that most of the guests had been evacuated because of a dreadful fire at the hotel. We were all devastated, especially Cecilia. Had her parents—both in their eighties, one of them blind—managed to escape?

We immediately rushed to the hotel. Despite Cecilia's pleas, the police prevented us from going through. Nonetheless, since in Mexico any official-looking credential produces a magical effect, I had only to flash my card identifying me as honorary consul for Norway for them to let me by. I approached the hotel entrance, but it was impossible to obtain any information, and at considerable risk, I entered the hotel. I had to avoid being pelted by the pieces of shattered glass from the upper stories, and the ground floor was flooded. No one had any reliable information.

Finally, we learned that two chambermaids had led Rodrigo and his wife to a safe place in another wing of the hotel. My wife, María Isabel, was able to contact them and invited them to stay with us, and they readily accepted. They looked like shipwreck survivors: they had only the clothes they were wearing, but were extremely relieved at having been found.

On March 19 the tribute concert took place at the Sala Nezahualcóyotl with the following program:

Concierto de estio for violin and orchestra
Agustín León Ara, violin
Concierto galante for cello and orchestra (Mexican premiere)
Carlos Prieto, cello

Como una fantasía (world premiere)   Carlos Prieto, cello
Concierto de Aranjuez for guitar and orchestra
                                    Alfonso Moreno, guitar
Symphony Orchestra of the State of Mexico
                                    Enrique Bátiz, conductor

BLAS GALINDO

In early 1982 I received an unexpected telephone call. It was Blas Galindo, informing me that he had recently completed the composition of a sonata for solo cello that he was dedicating to me (Fig. 37). I thanked him for the honor, and a few days later I received the manuscript. I played the first performance of his sonata in September 1982 in Mexico City at a concert sponsored by the Academy of Arts at the Palace of Fine Arts' Sala Ponce. That same year I played it again in Norway and Sweden.

In 1984 Galindo began composing a cello concerto. He sent me the score in 1985, and the premiere took place on June 26 and 27, 1987, in the Palace of Fine Arts; the National Symphony Orchestra was conducted by Francisco Savín.

The case of Blas Galindo is unique in Mexican music. Of humble

37. With Mexican composer Blas Galindo in Mexico, 1987.

origins, he was born in 1910 in the town of San Gabriel (today known as Venustiano Carranza) in Jalisco, and became one of Mexico's most remarkable composers through sheer talent, hard work, and tenacity. In 1957 Blas Galindo was awarded the José Ángel Llamas Prize at the Inter-American Music Competition, which took place in Caracas, and in 1964 President Adolfo López Mateos presented him with Mexico's prestigious National Arts and Science Award. Among his best-known works are his *Sones de mariachi*, written in 1941, two concertos for piano, one for violin, three symphonies, and numerous choral and chamber works.

In 1941 and 1942 he received a grant from the Rockefeller Foundation to study composition with Aaron Copland at the Berkshire Music Center, in Lenox, Massachusetts. In 1947 he was appointed director of the National Conservatory of Music, where he remained until 1961.

In addition to the sonata for solo cello and the cello concerto, he composed several additional cello works, as can be seen in Appendix 2. Among the most noteworthy is the Sonata for Cello and Piano (1948), commissioned by the Koussevitsky Foundation. Cellist Leonard Rose and pianist Leonid Hambro premiered it in 1953 at the Library of Congress.

THREE CONCERT TOURS OF COLOMBIA

My first concert in Colombia—a country I am very fond of—took place in 1983 at a stately colonial mansion in Tunja. Later, in Bogotá, I played during the rededication of the magnificent, recently restored colonial church of Santa Clara, and also gave a concert at the Jorge Eliécer Gaitán Municipal Theater, as part of a series called "Musical Matinees" that was presented by the renowned Colombian musicologist Otto de Greiff.

I returned to Colombia in 1985, and since it was the tercentenary of Bach's birth, my recitals were dedicated to his suites for solo cello. I played them in the concert hall of the Luis Angel Arango Library in Bogotá, in Medellín, and in Barranquilla. The Luis Ángel Arango Library is of vital importance to Bogotá's intellectual and artistic life. The concert hall's ovoid ceiling is covered with precious woods from Colombian Amazonia, and its acoustics are extraordinary, ideal for the Bach suites.

I returned to Colombia two years later, in April 1987, this time accompanied by pianist Doris Stevenson, with whom I had often performed in the United States. In addition to a recital at the Luis Ángel Arango Library in Bogotá, we also played in Bucaramanga and in Cúcuta.

In addition to these recitals, on April 10th I played Dvořák's Cello Concerto with the National Symphony Orchestra of Colombia, conducted by Ernesto Díaz, at the Teatro Colón. Since our concert was programmed for 6:30 p.m., I arrived in the dressing room at 6:15 to warm up. A few minutes later, the conductor and the manager of the theater came into my dressing room, appearing quite anxious. They then asked me if I wouldn't mind delaying the first part of the concert. Since this is a usual practice for allowing latecomers to find their seats, I replied that of course I didn't mind if the concert started five to ten minutes late. "Oh no, we are talking about a delay of forty-five or fifty minutes!" they replied, explaining that the procession in honor of Our Lady of Sorrows would be passing right in front of the theater, accompanied by an extremely loud brass band that would interfere with the concert. The negotiations between the theater's management and the procession's coordinators had fallen through when the latter had refused to change the time of the procession.

Beginning one hour later than scheduled, the concert opened with Berlioz's *Roman Carnival Overture*. When the overture was over, I went onstage with the Piatti, and soon the orchestra began to play the first chords of Dvořák's concerto, which begins with a long orchestral tutti, followed by a horn solo. Then the orchestra fades to pianissimo to prepare for the dramatic entrance of the cello. I was just about to raise my bow to play my first note, when suddenly there came the earsplitting sounds of trumpets and drums. It was the Our Lady of Sorrows procession. I paused with my bow frozen in midair. Conductor Díaz stood stock-still and the orchestra stopped playing as the deafening sounds of the procession approached the theater. Ten minutes later the last echoes of the procession faded away, and once again we began the Dvořák Concerto, which this time proceeded without a hitch.

MANUEL ENRÍQUEZ (1926–1994)

Manuel Enríquez, born in Jalisco in 1926, was a multifaceted musician who studied in Mexico, the United States, and Europe. Composer, violinist, administrator, and active promoter of contemporary music, he was the founder and, until his death, director of the International Forum of New Music, an annual event, now bearing his name, held in Mexico City.

Our musical relationship began in 1980, when he invited me to participate in the Second International Forum of New Music. I played the

38. With Mexican composer Manuel Enríquez and pianist Doris Stevenson, after a recital with Stevenson in Los Angeles, 1991.

Mexican premiere of Witold Lutoslawski's brilliant Cello Concerto with
the National Symphony Orchestra of Mexico, led by Polish conductor
Antoni Wit.

Soon after, I added to my repertoire two of Enríquez's chamber
works: the 1961 Sonatina for Cello, and the Four Pieces for Cello and
Piano, dated 1962. One day he mentioned that he had just finished a
cello concerto, dedicated to me. We immediately started making plans
for its premiere, which took place on October 3 and 5, 1986, at the Palace
of Fine Arts, with the National Symphony Orchestra of Mexico conducted by Francisco Savín. After that, I played Enríquez's concerto several times with conductors Joel Thome, Manuel de Elías, and José Guadalupe Flores, and in 1993, in the presence of the composer, I recorded
it with the Philharmonic Orchestra of Querétaro, conducted by Sergio
Cárdenas.

There were other works that Enríquez dedicated to me. The first was
his transcription of Miguel Bernal Jiménez's *Tres danzas tarascas*, originally composed for violin and piano. A short time later, I premiered the
piece with Edison Quintana; we also recorded it and have played it in
many countries.

In 1991 I met with Enríquez to discuss a series of concerts that were
to feature Mexican music and be performed in Los Angeles and other
cities in California in conjunction with the impressive exhibition Mexico: A Work of Art. In passing, I mentioned that it seemed a shame that
Silvestre Revueltas, in my opinion Mexico's greatest composer, had never
written anything for the cello. When we parted, Enríquez suddenly announced, "I'm going to write a fantasia for cello and piano, for you and
Edison Quintana, in which both instruments stand out. I will also send
you a piece by Revueltas." I greatly appreciated the prospect of his fantasia but was rather bewildered about Revueltas's unknown composition.
Had Enríquez discovered a cello piece by Revueltas? He wasn't saying.

Three weeks later, Enríquez sent me the *Fantasía* and Revueltas's
work: *Three Pieces for Cello and Piano*. Actually, it was Enríquez's transcription of a composition originally written for violin and piano, which
he had worked on for the past few weeks. It is a superb transcription; we
premiered in California, and I have often played it since (Fig. 38). The
cello repertoire has thus been enriched not only by Manuel Enríquez's
remarkable works but also by his excellent transcriptions, making it possible for cellists to perform works by Revueltas and Bernal Jiménez.

TRAVELS AND CONCERTS IN ARGENTINA WITH A PRELUDE IN URUGUAY

The first stop in a long tour that Edison Quintana and I made in 1991 throughout South America was in Uruguay. Our concert in Montevideo took place in the National Library's Vaz Ferreira Concert Hall.

While in Argentina we played in Rosario, Buenos Aires, and La Plata. I also gave a concert in Buenos Aires with the National Symphony Orchestra, conducted by Eduardo Diazmuñoz.

I played the Argentinean premiere of Samuel Zyman's cello concerto and Tchaikovsky's *Pezzo capriccioso* with the National Symphony at the Belgrano Auditorium. The Zyman concert—the main item on the program—was enthusiastically received. Napoleón Cabrera praised the work in *Clarín*, noting that not only "was it the first piece by Zyman ever performed in our country, but also the first example of its genre—cello and orchestra—written by a living Latin American to be heard here. It is to this extent that we Latin Americans are unfamiliar with one another's music."[7]

In 1994 Edison and I returned to Argentina. In Buenos Aires, I played Max Bruch's *Kol Nidrei* and Haydn's Cello Concerto in C Major with the Mayo Chamber Orchestra, conducted by Fernando Lozano. Edison and I also played in Buenos Aires' Teatro de la Ópera, for a second time in Rosario, and in several cities that were new to us. Thus we had a chance to discover a considerable part of Argentina's vast territory: Bahía Blanca in the pampas; Neuquén in Patagonia, near the Andes and Chile; and Tucumán in the North.

Our recital program included, among others, a Mexican piece by Ponce and an Argentinean work, *Le grand tango* by Astor Piazzolla. We decided to play Piazzolla's tango because it is an excellent piece, though we were rather reluctant because we assumed it had been played repeatedly in its country of origin. Much to our surprise, we discovered that, in fact, in several cities on our itinerary it turned out to be its premiere performance.

THE TANGO

I cannot conclude this section on my concerts in Argentina without discussing Astor Piazzolla and the fascinating phenomenon known as the tango.

The tango as we know it emerged toward the end of the nineteenth century in Porteño cafés and brothels. (Porteño, by the way, is the name for the inhabitants of Buenos Aires.) The tango's history from its origins to the present day has been fully documented.[8] However, before delving into its history, it may be worthwhile to briefly examine its somewhat nebulous "prehistory." Certain rather simplistic theories claim that the tango originated in Spain during the early nineteenth century and that its name is derived from the Latin word *tangere*, which means "to play" or "to touch." It seems more likely that the term *tango* actually comes from Africa, either from the onomatopoeic *tambó* and *tangó* (from *tambor*, "drum") or from *tango*, meaning an "enclosed place" in several languages of western Africa. The place where slaves were confined was called *tango* by the slave traders.[9]

A Cuban publication dated 1836 defines "tango" as the "gathering of the newly arrived blacks where they dance to the beat of drums or tambours." The word 'tango' was introduced in the American continent by the Creole African-Portuguese via Saint Thomas and reached Spain through Cuba."[10] By the early nineteenth century, the word *tango* was already commonly used in Buenos Aires to describe the houses where blacks held their dances.

In Cuba, contra dances and habaneras of Spanish origin adopted certain African elements and, thus modified, returned to Andalusia as tangos and to Cádiz, as tanguillos. The 1852 edition of the *Dictionary of the Spanish Language* published by the Spanish Royal Academy defines *tango* as a "gypsy dance"; in Madrid the tango was incorporated into the zarzuelas (Spanish operettas), and it soon caught on in Buenos Aires' theaters.

As Horacio Salas observes,

> By the end of the [nineteenth] century the differences between the tangos from Andalusia and the Argentinean tangos tended to disappear, so themes of Spanish origin remained as mere precursors. The innumerable habaneras and the rhyming *tanguitos* were Spain's major contributions to the tango. On the other hand, it was another large group of immigrants—the Italians—who provided the very first interpreters of the tango and who, in turn, ultimately endowed the tango with the melancholic, nostalgic flavor, so characteristic of the music from the Río de la Plata.[11]

In this particular region, musical groups consisting of a flute, violin, and guitar soon began playing tangos at popular festivals and other social gatherings, and subsequently in cafés and brothels.

During the last few decades of the nineteenth century, a new instrument appeared on the scene: the bandoneon, a large concertina-like instrument. Invented in Hamburg by Heinrich Band, who mass-produced the AA (the mark of instrument maker Alfred Arnold) bandoneons, they became widely popular around 1864. Between 1890 and 1900, the bandoneon gradually replaced the flute in the tango groups. The flute's sweet and playful sound imbues the music with a joyful, lighthearted quality, whereas the bandoneon's deeply melancholic tone completely transformed the very nature of the tango. Perhaps it was actually the other way around: the bandoneon was better suited than the flute, precisely because it expressed the despondency and nostalgia associated with the tango.

During the late nineteenth and early twentieth century there was massive European immigration to Argentina—mostly from Italy, and to a lesser degree from Spain. Many who came were young men wanting to "make it in America." Although some were successful, most barely managed to get by, and longed for their native countries and their families. Hence, the importance of the brothels, which became a kind of a social club where, in addition to engaging in their main activity, prostitutes danced with their clients. This is also partly explains the plaintive, disenchanted tone of the tango.

The most luxurious brothels introduced a new instrument into the tango groups: the piano, either vertical or grand, depending on the establishment's finances. Sebastián Tallón's *El tango en su etapa de música prohibida* (The Tango in Its Phase as Banned Music) describes two such establishments: Laura's and María la Vasca's. "Their select clientele included dilettantes, actors, playwrights, businessmen, gentlemen, and all those who needed to conceal their affairs."[12] Many years passed before the tango was accepted by the middle and working classes, who regarded it as the epitome of moral turpitude.

During the second decade of the twentieth century, dancing the tango became all the rage in Paris. At that time, Argentina and other Latin American countries considered France the cultural capital of the world, the trendsetter for taste, fashion, and literary and artistic styles. Before long, the tango craze extended to other European countries and to the United States, unleashing the most heated debates. In 1914 the bishop of Paris proclaimed, "We condemn the dance of a foreign origin known as the tango, whose lascivious nature is an affront to morality."[13] In Boston Cardinal O'Connell denounced, "If this tango dance is the new woman, may God protect us from the advances of this abnormal creature." That same year, during a Bible conference in Atlanta, Georgia, Dr. Campbell Morgan declared that the "tango is the regression of man to ape and confirms Darwin's theory."[14]

Many Argentineans were disturbed that Europeans identified their country with such a "primitive and sensual" dance. In 1914, the Argentinean ambassador to France, Enrique Rodríquez Larreta, declared, "In Buenos Aires, the tango is a dance exclusively associated with houses of ill repute and the most disreputable bars. It is never danced in respectable places or among well-bred people. To Argentineans, tango music evokes the most distasteful images."[15]

Nevertheless, driven by its amazing popularity in Europe, the tango continued its relentless march back to the land that witnessed its birth, which, by the way, was not restricted to Argentina, since Uruguay also played a central role in the evolution of the tango. One of the first tangos to achieve worldwide popularity was "La cumparsita," by Uruguayan Gerardo Mattos Rodríguez, popularized by Roberto Firpo, one of the greatest tango personalities of the second and third decades of the twentieth century.

It was Roberto Firpo who transformed the piano into the tango's principal instrument. Firpo had formed a trio with piano, violin, and bandoneon, and some time later, it became a sextet when he added a second violin, a double bass, and the long-neglected flute. Firpo no longer played in "houses of ill repute" but rather in the newly established nightclubs. Even the attire had changed, since the men were required to wear tuxedos, complete with pleated front and bow tie.

Toward the end of the nineteenth century, a man who in time would become a living legend was born: Carlos Gardel. As in the case of most legends, even the place and date of his birth remain enveloped in mystery. On one hand, his personal documents indicate that he was Uruguayan, born in Tacuarembó in 1887, facts that Gardel himself confirmed in conversations with his friends.[16] On the other hand, a handwritten testament, discovered after his death—and considered false by several sources—cites his birth in Toulouse, France, in 1890; according to still other documents, he was born in 1883.

In any case, Gardel, nicknamed "Francesito" (little Frenchman), grew up in a suburb of Buenos Aires. Whether French, Argentinean, or Uruguayan, Gardel blended into his surroundings and soon made a name for himself as a singer of popular Argentinean songs. Although the tango was originally introduced as a dance, Gardel, among others, played a vital role in its evolution by transforming it into song—and thus the legend was born. He made hundreds of recordings; he was an overnight sensation in Paris when he appeared with Josephine Baker—one of the greatest stars of the time; and he starred in countless Argentinean and French films.

Gardel's international success was due not only to his voice and personality, but also to his collaboration with Alfredo Le Pera, the lyricist for many of his hits. Since Le Pera managed to write lyrics in standard Spanish without losing any Porteño flavor, their songs—such as the memorable tangos "Volver," "Soledad," and "Mi Buenos Aires querido"—were perfectly understandable throughout Latin America. Le Pera's lyrics were devoid of all *lunfardismos*, that is, expressions generally derived from Italian dialects and originally used by the Porteño underworld.

Gardel's death in 1935 was as mysterious as his birth. Officially, he died in a tragic airplane accident in Medellín, Colombia, but there were allegations that he had not actually died, but had been so horribly disfigured in the crash that he went into hiding. After his death, Gardel joined Hipólito Yrigoyen, Juan Domingo Perón, and Eva Perón in the pantheon of twentieth-century Argentinean legends. However, as Salas points out, only Gardel was accepted by all social strata and only Gardel was exempt from controversy and subsequent accusations.

Aníbal Troilo, "El Gordo," another legendary figure of the tango, was born in 1914, and formed his own orchestra in 1937, after performing with the most renowned tango personalities. Troilo was outstanding as a bandoneon player, as a conductor, and as the composer of the most popular tangos of the 1940s. In addition, he had a remarkable instinct for selecting his musicians, particularly singers like Edmundo Rivero and Roberto Goyeneche, bandoneon player and composer Astor Piazzolla, and cellist José Bragato, who would become Piazzolla's collaborator.

ASTOR PIAZZOLLA

For many reasons, the case of Piazzolla is unique in the history of tango and of music in general. He was born in Mar del Plata in 1921, and at the age of four, immigrated to New York with his family. On his sixth birthday, his father, a barber, presented him with a bandoneon, although he did not like the instrument: it was strange-looking, and one could not actually see the keys while playing it. However, when he turned eleven Astor discovered music. The Hungarian pianist Bela Wilda happened to be living in the same apartment building. One day Astor heard Wilda playing Bach, an experience he would remember for the rest of his life. Bela Wilda then became his first teacher, teaching him to play Bach pieces by adapting them to the bandoneon. Astor was regarded as a child prodigy in what was then the small Latin American community in New York, playing all kinds of Spanish and Mexican popular music, classical music, and jazz, which greatly attracted him at the time. There wasn't a single tango in his repertoire!

However, one day when Carlos Gardel was passing through New York, he met the thirteen-year-old Astor and invited him to be an accompanist on several of his performances, so Astor had to learn some tangos as quickly as possible. Years later Piazzolla reminisced about that meeting:

> My contact with Gardel was very brief. My greatest satisfaction was to appear with him in the film *El día que me quieras* as the newsboy and occasionally to accompany him on the bandoneon, which I was barely learning to play. To understand and love Gardel, one had to spend time in Buenos Aires, especially the market area, and I was only a thirteen-year-old kid living in New York who couldn't even play the tango on my bandoneon very well at all. Therefore, when he heard me for the first time, Gardel said, "Hey kid, you play the bandoneon like a Galician." Looking back on it, I would've loved to accompany Gardel as a grown man who loved the tango, but my fingers would've probably dropped from the bandoneon in awe, because he was the greatest.[17]

In 1937, when he was sixteen, Astor returned to Argentina with his parents. He started out by playing tangos in Mar del Plata, but realizing that he lacked the proper training, he left to study music in Buenos Aires. He composed a piano concerto that he dared to show to Artur Rubinstein. The pianist advised him to study with a good teacher. Alberto Ginastera agreed to teach Piazzolla, and did so for five years.

At the same time, Piazzolla attempted to join the orchestra led by his idol, Aníbal Troilo. Although the orchestra was filled, Troilo gave him a chance when he heard that Piazzolla knew his repertoire by heart: "So, you're the kid who knows my whole repertoire? Well then, come up here and play."[18] So Astor went up there and played. Troilo hired him on the spot.

Following Ginastera's advice, Piazzolla submitted his symphony in three movements, *Sinfonía de Buenos Aires*, to the Fabian Sevitsky Competition and ended up winning first place. One of the prizes was a public performance of the symphony, conducted by Sevitsky, and another was a scholarship for a year's study in Paris with the legendary Nadia Boulanger. In 1954, Piazzolla and his wife, Dedé, moved to Paris, where Astor studied harmony, analysis, and, above all, counterpoint. Boulanger believed that Piazzolla's works were well written but devoid of a genuine spirit. Astor had never dared mention his past involvement with the tango:

> I thought to myself, if I tell her the truth, she'll throw me out the window. Nadia had not only been a classmate of Ravel's, but had also taught Igor Markevitch, Aaron Copland, Leonard Bernstein, Robert Casadesus, and Jean Françaix. Even back then she was considered the finest teacher in the whole world, and I was a mere tango player. . . . I had to level with her, and confessed that I earned my living making arrangements for tango orchestras, and that I had played with Aníbal Troilo and then with my own orchestra, and that, tired of it all, I believed that my future was in classical music. Nadia looked me straight in the eye and asked me to play one of my tangos. . . . And then I began with "Triunfal." I don't think I even got halfway through before Nadia stopped me, took my hands . . . and said, "Astor, this is absolutely beautiful, I really like it very much. This is the real Piazzolla, and don't ever abandon him." This turned out to be the greatest revelation of my life.[19]

On his return to Buenos Aires, Piazzolla ultimately devoted himself to composing and conducting tangos and renovating the genre itself. He formed the Octeto Buenos Aires and later the celebrated Astor Piazzolla Quinteto, with pianist Jaime Gosis, violinist Simon Bajour—a former student of David Oistrakh's—Horacio Malvicino on the electric guitar, and Kicho Díaz on the double bass. He always chose outstanding musicians like pianists Gerardo Gandini (a classical pianist and an excellent composer) and Pablo Ziegler and cellist José Bragato. In 1968, with Uruguayan poet Horacio Ferrer, he composed a short opera, *María de Buenos Aires*, as well as several tangos that became famous, such as "Balada para un loco."

The Argentinean public and the tango connoisseurs alike regarded Piazzolla with a mixture of admiration and incomprehension. Many even went so far as to deny that his pieces were genuine tangos at all. Once, at the end of a Piazzolla concert in San Pedro in the province of Buenos Aires, someone in the audience stood up and asked, "Maestro, now that you have finished the concert, why don't you play a tango?" He often had to put up with this type of remark, which infuriated him to no end. Years later during an interview, he remarked, "I revolutionized the tango, it's true. I broke with the traditional models, which is why they attacked me and I had to defend myself, sometimes with words that went too far. However, what no one can deny are my roots; the tango is branded on my very soul, and I am proud of it."[20]

I had looked forward to meeting Piazzolla in 1991, either in Buenos Aires or in Punta del Este (Uruguay), during one of our tours. However, it was not meant to be, because in August 1990 he suffered a stroke, and died in 1992.

In 1994 our recital at Buenos Aires' Teatro de la Ópera featured Piazzolla's *Le grand tango*. Several prominent cellists attended the performance, including Christine Walewska and José Bragato, who presented me with several of Piazzolla's works, including the Milonga in D Major (for cello and piano) and *La muerte del angel*, a piece for string quartet.

The history of *Le grand tango* for cello and piano epitomizes the fact that Piazzolla's music was misunderstood for many years.[21] Classical musicians, who knew nothing of his training, regarded him as a "common tango player," and tango enthusiasts considered him a traitor to traditional tango.

In 1982 Efraín Paesky, secretary general of the Inter-American Music Council, commissioned a tango for cello and piano from Piazzolla, to be played by Rostropovich, to whom it is dedicated. Although Rostropovich played the piece, he was rather unimpressed by it and set it aside. It was precisely this circumstance that enabled Edison Quintana and me to make the first widely released recording of *Le grand tango* and to premiere it in numerous cities. It has always been well received, though with occasional differences of opinion. I remember one recent concert in Mexico City. Some German friends came by to see me after the concert and said, "We liked your concert, but playing a tango is outrageous!"

Since Rostropovich considered the cello part not brilliant enough, he came up with a revised version of the piece that he has played ever since. Sometime later, Rostropovich commissioned a piece for cello, bandoneon, and orchestra from Piazzolla, and planned to premiere it with the Berlin Philharmonic. Unfortunately, the death of the composer thwarted the project.

Le grand tango owes its French name to the fact that Piazzolla, with the help of Efraín Paesky, had the piece immediately published in Paris. The original title of the piece was *Tangazo*, which means "great tango," but since the French publisher objected to the rather vulgar name, it was published with the more genteel title of *Le grand tango*!

The Argentinean pianist Martha Argerich belonged to the legion of musicians who were skeptical about Piazzolla's merits. Piazzolla had thought of composing a piano sonata and dedicating it to her so that she would premiere it. Efraín Paesky acted as the liaison between the two musicians, but was flatly rejected: "What? Me play Piazzolla?"[22]

Piazzolla's image has undergone an extraordinary transformation. Today his music has transcended the confines of the Río de la Plata and the traditional tango; such eminent musicians as Gidon Kremer, Yo-Yo Ma, and Daniel Barenboim have recorded his music and often include it in their programs. However, the most amazing phenomenon of all is the tango's incredible journey from the brothels of Buenos Aires a century ago to the great concert halls of today.

BRAZIL: FROM SÃO PAULO TO MANAUS AND THE AMAZON, 1991

I have had extensive contact with this fascinating country. My first visits took place on business trips during the 1960s, and then in 1965 I returned with María Isabel on our honeymoon. I had studied Portuguese, understood it very well, and had a good command of the spoken language, or so I thought.

In 1991 I returned as a musician, with pianist Edison Quintana, eager to find out more about the country and its fascinating, widely diverse types of music. We played in São Paulo, Belo Horizonte, Ouro Preto, Brasília, and Manaus.

Our first concert took place at the Municipal Theater in the huge city of São Paulo, Brazil's industrial, financial, and commercial center. The contrast between São Paulo and Ouro Preto, where we gave our second concert, could not have been greater. Ouro Preto, a veritable colonial jewel located in the state of Minas Gerais, was declared a World Heritage Site by UNESCO. A typical mining town, it boasts the finest baroque "mining" architecture, the result of the prosperity generated by its gold mines. The small municipal theater (originally an opera house) where we played is a historic monument and the oldest functioning theater in the Americas.[23]

BRASÍLIA

The next place we visited was Brasília, one of the few cities in the world specifically planned and built as a capital. I am well acquainted with two of the most famous: Washington, D.C. and St. Petersburg, the latter built by Peter the Great as a "Window to the West," which, as we saw in the preceding chapter, celebrated its 300th anniversary in 2003. However, Brasília is the only such city that I have actually seen before its birth, since my first visit took place in 1960, two years before it became the capital.

Our concert took place in one of the buildings designed by the famous architect Oscar Niemeyer: the Claudio Santoro National Theater, named after one of Brazil's outstanding composers, Claudio Santoro (1919–1989).

MANAUS AND THE AMAZON

On Saturday, June 1, we flew from Fortaleza to Manaus, with stopovers in Belém, the Amazon delta, and Santarem. As we flew over Belém and Santarem, we could see the Amazon. Its sheer size boggles the imagination: the Amazon and its tributaries carry one-fifth of the world's fresh water. Its volume alone makes it the largest river in the world, ten times bigger than the Mississippi. We followed the river's course as we flew from Santarem to Manaus.

Manaus is located on the banks of the Negro River, very close to its confluence with the Amazon, 930 miles from the ocean. It is an extraordinary place, dominated by the proximity of the two immense rivers and its exuberant vegetation. Because of the oppressive temperature and humidity, everything seems to move in slow motion.

We had no sooner arrived at the hotel than we made telephone arrangements with Captain Francisco de Linhares da Silva, the owner of a small boat—*barquinho*—to take us early the next day on a trip to the Negro River and up the Amazon. It was one thing to see the two enormous rivers from the air, and another to see them on a boat. It seemed a shame to be there and not have contact with the rivers and their natural environment.

The next day, Edison and I met Linhares at the dock early in the morning. Edison Quintana is not exactly a nature lover, generally preferring to spend his time devouring one novel after another. He felt rather uneasy in our rickety barquinho, but Linhares assured him that all would be well. However, we had barely gotten halfway down the river when there was a sudden downpour. The awning turned out to be totally useless. In a few seconds we were all as drenched as if we actually had fallen into the Negro River. Edison demanded that we return immediately, crying out to Linhares, "Turn back, and turn back!" The captain and I, who were more optimistic, assured him that the storm would be over as suddenly as it had started. And, in fact, that was exactly what happened. The sun shone once again, and we soon dried off. It was at that precise moment, in midriver, that we ran out of gas. "Don't worry. There are gas stations nearby, and the current will take us to one shortly." the captain assured us. "Shortly," however, turned out to be about half an hour. Finally, at an exasperatingly slow pace, we managed to approach a boat anchored right in the middle of the river. It was the gasoline station, decorated with numerous birdcages filled with parrots and other multicolored birds; several monkeys were scampering about.

At last we arrived at what seemed to be the other side of the river, although the riverbanks were not exactly terra firma, being made up of islets, swamps covered with vegetation, and *igarapés* ("canoe paths"), aquatic paths hidden between the dense foliage. We ventured into a group of igarapés, some wider than others, and stopped for a while. We got out of the boat and, guided by Linhares, walked a short way on some planks laid out over the swampy terrain. Finally we arrived at a couple of shacks where the Manaos Indians sold their wares. However, what I really wanted to see were the Amazon's famous anacondas. Actually, we were able to see many, although they weren't really in the wild. The Indians kept them in huge wooden boxes, and for a small tip, five or six boys would take out the gigantic sucuris, anacondas that live in water, and then some jiboyas of a similar size, but that are primarily land creatures.

We returned to the boat and continued on our way toward the Amazon, which at this point was separated from the Negro by a few hundred meters of islets, swamplands, and igarapés. Linhares guided the boat with considerable expertise; whenever an igarapé became too narrow, like a watery dead end, he always managed to find others that were wider, always surrounded by impressive vegetation and huge trees. All of a sudden, the swampy lands ended, and we found ourselves on another river, the Solimões, as the Amazon is called before it converges with the Negro. The waters of the Solimões were of a muddy color, and the Negro's were true to its name: very dark from the black tannin it drags along. We sailed through a long stretch of the Solimões until we reached its confluence with the Negro. The rivers are of such different densities that they do not mingle for many kilometers, and one can clearly detect the dividing line between them.

Once our excursion was over, we returned to Manaus, dry and sunburned, just in time to eat and rest awhile before our rehearsal.

Built in 1896, the Amazonas Theater, a replica of Milan's La Scala, is an amazing sight. The building of such a monumental theater right in the middle of the Amazon jungle was financed by an extraordinary rubber bonanza. Other majestic buildings in Manaus also date from this particular period, such as the cathedral and the Alfândega (customshouse), which was built in England, disassembled, then transported to Brazil in pieces.

For over two decades large boats traveled the length of the Amazon, bringing famous singers and actors, such as Enrico Caruso, Sarah Bernhardt, and Jenny Lind, along with the cumbersome equipment required for the lavish operatic spectacles, to the Amazonas Theater. Around 1920 the rubber bonanza came to an end, plunging Manaus into a severe crisis, and the Amazonas Theater was virtually abandoned, ravaged by humidity, insects, and tropical animals.

Between 1987 and 1990, after Manaus had reemerged as an inland industrial center, the Amazonas Theater was completely renovated. That afternoon at rehearsal, we were warmly welcomed by the theater's director, Gerson Albano, who gave us a tour of the premises, along with a description of the theater's fascinating history. He explained—as we had seen and experienced for ourselves—that the theater's principal enemy was the dreadful humidity that seeps through, rotting the wood and fabrics. The dank humid smell was everywhere. In fact, since my arrival in Manaus, I had kept the Piatti in its case along with a package of moisture-absorbing salt.

The concert went quite well, and the audience was receptive, although less knowledgeable about and not as accustomed to chamber music as concertgoers in other Brazilian cities. Consequently, Edison and I had decided to simplify the program, making it more accessible. Since the programs had already been printed, director Albano offered to announce the changes, but I preferred doing it myself. I prepared a few notes in Portuguese and practiced them a few times with Albano, who corrected my diction and assured me that my Portuguese sounded perfect. After the concert, a number of people stopped by our dressing room. Two ladies congratulated me on the concert and, especially, my announcements, "spoken in such clear, pure Spanish that we were able to understand them perfectly." It was a little lesson in humility for those of us who think we have mastered Portuguese but actually speak "*portuñol*," a hybrid of Portuguese and Spanish. I would never forget that lesson.

That visit to Brazil only served to rekindle my enthusiasm for the country and its people. I left Brazil with the firm determination to return and explore it further, especially its language, music, and culture in general. As I will later recount, I have been fortunate enough to accomplish most of these goals.

CHÔRO BY MOZART CAMARGO GUARNIERI AND THE XALAPA SYMPHONY ORCHESTRA

Mozart Camargo Guarnieri, one of Brazil's most outstanding composers, as well as a remarkable teacher and conductor, was born in 1907 in Tietê, in the state of São Paulo, and died in São Paulo in 1993. An extraordinarily prolific composer, he wrote over 700 works, including three sonatas for cello and piano and the Chôro for Cello and Orchestra, dedicated to the famed Brazilian cellist Aldo Parisot, now a professor at both Juilliard and Yale. (Chôro is a type of Brazilian dance music.)

I played the Mexican premiere of the Chôro on November 25, 1995, with the Xalapa Symphony Orchestra, conducted by Manfred Neuman. In August 1998 I recorded it for Urtext Digital Classics with my son, Carlos Miguel, as conductor. It is a beautiful piece of music, with three contrasting movements (*Decidido e apaixonado, Calmo e triste, Com alegría*) that vividly convey the rhythmic melodious motifs of Brazil's popular music.

CELSO GARRIDO-LECCA AND PERU IN THE TIME OF CHOLERA

We arrived in Peru on July 12, 1991, during what turned out to be a badly timed concert tour. Both a cholera epidemic and terrorist attacks by Sendero Luminoso (Shining Path) were in full swing. Since the delicious *cebiche* and seafood were, of course, forbidden, all of Lima's traditional *cebicherías* were closed.

We were driven from the airport to the César Hotel in the residential neighborhood of Miraflores, a prudent distance from downtown Lima, which at this time was suffering the consequences of terrorism and street violence.

The tour's organizers had scheduled a recital for cello and piano and two concertos with the Prolírica Orchestra, which had been chosen because its headquarters were located at the Santa Úrsula Auditorium in the San Isidro district, whereas the National Symphony Orchestra's concerts were held at the National Theatre, precisely in the center of town.

At the Santa Úrsula Auditorium, I played the Dvořák Concerto with the Prolírica Orchestra, conducted by José de Santos. In our recital, Edi-

39. *With Peruvian composer Celso Garrido-Lecca and pianist Edison Quintana at Las Rosas Conservatory in Morelia, Mexico, 1990.*

son Quintana and I had the satisfaction of playing the Sonata-Fantasia for Cello and Piano by Garrido-Lecca in the presence of the composer himself. The work was well received by the public and critics alike.

CELSO GARRIDO-LECCA: A GREAT PERUVIAN COMPOSER

Composer Celso Garrido-Lecca was born in Piura, Peru, in 1926. After studying at Lima's National Conservatory of Music, he continued his musical studies in Santiago, Chile, in 1951. Between 1965 and 1973 he was head of the University of Chile's Department of Composition. Upon his return to Lima, he was appointed director of the National School of Music. The recipient of numerous international awards, his body of work includes chamber and choral works as well as symphonies.

I met Celso Garrido-Lecca in 1990, when he came to Mexico for the First Latin American Music Forum held in Morelia, as part of the Second International Music Festival (Fig. 39). On that occasion I had the double privilege of receiving the cello concerto that he dedicated to me and of premiering it in Morelia on August 1 with the Festival Orchestra and Brazilian conductor Henrique Morelenbaum.

During the early 1990s, Garrido-Lecca had earned his well-deserved fame as one of Latin America's most eminent composers. He is also one of the most illustrious names in Peruvian culture, along with his equally distinguished compatriots, Mario Vargas Llosa in literature and Fernando de Szyszlo in painting.

In 1992, because of a series of unforeseen circumstances, he became even more famous, his photograph appearing on the covers of countless international publications. It so happened that one afternoon the composer went to visit his niece, twenty-six-year-old Maritza Garrido-Lecca, a well-known ballet dancer, in Lima. She and her boyfriend shared a house whose first floor had been converted into a children's ballet school. Celso stayed until quite late, enjoying a delightful conversation with Maritza and her friend. At about midnight, when he decided to leave, the young couple saw him to the door. They had barely opened the door when a swarm of policemen forced their way inside, hurling Celso and his hosts on the floor and then handcuffing them. At the same time, another group of policemen entered through the rear of the building and captured a group of "guests" who were hiding in Maritza's house and who offered no resistance. At first Celso Garrido-Lecca thought the agents might belong to the narcotics squad, but soon discarded this idea when he heard them shout, "We got him! We got him!" The agents, members of the antiterrorism division known as Dirección Nacional Contra el Terrorismo (Dinconte), had just succeeded in capturing the most wanted man in Peru, Abimael Guzmán, better known as "Comandante Gonzalo," leader of the sinister Maoist movement known as Sendero Luminoso, along with several of his followers.

Everyone captured at the house that night was taken to a special prison, and once they were officially charged, the entire group was paraded before the press. Guzmán and some of his collaborators raised their arms and shouted revolutionary slogans. Celso watched in utter stupefaction as his niece, the delicate ballerina, vehemently shouted praise for Comandante Gonzalo and Sendero Luminoso, and insults at the police. It turned out that Maritza, a fanatic supporter and active member of Sendero Luminoso, had offered her house as a hideout for Guzmán and several of his companions. Who would have ever imagined that a children's ballet school also served as temporary headquarters for Sendero Luminoso?

Garrido-Lecca spent two weeks in prison, confined to a cubicle barely measuring four by five feet. Although he was not mistreated, a cubicle of that size is no bed of roses. Ever since his arrest, he had been informed that there was no doubt about his innocence, but because of a mandatory fifteen-day investigation period, he could not be released before then. Once the time limit was over, the head of Dinconte himself went to the prison and personally set him free, thus making it perfectly clear that Garrido-Lecca had never belonged to Sendero Luminoso or any subversive movement and that his presence at his niece's house during the raid had been due to an unfortunate coincidence. Abimael Guzmán, Maritza Garrido-Lecca, and many others are still behind bars, sentenced to spend the rest of their lives in jail.[24]

*I*n 2001, Celso Garrido-Lecca was awarded the Tomás Luis de Victoria Prize, the highest lifetime achievement award granted to a composer from Latin America, Spain, or Portugal. The presentation took place in Madrid's National Auditorium on June 8, 2001, during a gala concert devoted entirely to his works. I had the great pleasure of participating in this concert, giving the Spanish premiere of his Cello Concerto with the National Orchestra of Spain conducted by Pedro Ignacio Calderón.

In May 2002 in Mexico I played and recorded Garrido-Lecca's concerto with the Xalapa Symphony Orchestra conducted by my son, Carlos Miguel Prieto, and in February 2003, I played it again in Caracas, with the Simón Bolívar Symphony Orchestra, conducted by Eduardo Marturet.

PORTUGAL: THE GULBENKIAN FOUNDATION, MIGUEL GRAÇA MOURA, THE METROPOLITAN ORCHESTRA OF LISBON, AND THE CELLO CONCERTO BY GYÖRGY LIGETI

Two of my first concerts in Portugal in 1984 were by invitation of the Gulbenkian Foundation, an institution that plays a vital role in Portugal's cultural life. I was accompanied by my Catalan friend, pianist Ángel Soler, with whom I played two recitals. The first concert, on January 9, was held at the Gulbenkian Foundation's auditorium in Lisbon, and the second, on the following day, took place at the Arab Room of the Bolsa Palace in Oporto.

When I returned to Portugal ten years later, in November 1994, I played Saint-Saëns's Cello Concerto in A Minor with the Lisbon Metropolitan Orchestra, under guest conductor Jean-Marc Burfin.

In April 1996, with the same orchestra, I played the Portuguese premiere of the cello concerto by György Ligeti. The program, conducted by Miguel Graça Moura, also included Schumann's Concerto for Cello. Schumann's passionate Romanticism presented a dramatic contrast to Ligeti's unclassifiable modernism. Graça Moura had the excellent idea of preparing the audience for the experience of listening to such a "disconcerting" concert—so disconcerting, in fact, that, as we shall see, the piece begins with absolute silence.

LIGETI'S CONCERTO FOR CELLO

György Ligeti's multifaceted body of work is impossible to classify according to any established school. In his youth, Ligeti was such an avid follower of his compatriot Béla Bartók that his first string quartet is sometimes called "Bartók's Seventh Quartet." In November 1956, when Soviet tanks and troops invaded Budapest, Ligeti immigrated to Vienna and then to Cologne. These sojourns were crucial to his musical development, since they exposed him to the music of Karlheinz Stockhausen, Pierre Boulez, and Bruno Maderna. However, Ligeti's works do not correspond to avant-garde or postmodernist movements. Although the composer makes no concessions to his listeners, his works elicit a considerable reaction from the audience. The Concerto for Cello, written in 1966, was premiered by Siegfried Palm and the Berlin Radio Symphony Orchestra in 1967.

Ligeti's concerto bears none of the characteristics associated with traditional concert pieces. It is not conceived to highlight the soloist, nor does it contain a spectacular display of virtuosity. As the composer points out, the solo cello and the orchestra do not form two separate units, contrasting and concurring; the cello is just one more instrument in the group: the most active member in an orchestra of soloists.

The concerto emerges from total silence on the note E, played by the cello in a medium register and marked at the beginning with eight *p*'s: *pppppppp*. In fact, the score points out that the first note should begin "inaudibly, as if it came from nothing." Gradually, the note becomes more audible—although remaining *ppp* (pianississimo)—and changes its tonal color. The orchestra then joins in with the same note, lasting for a minute and a half, until the new note, an F, appears. Little by little other notes are heard, all within the narrow range of one fourth (E–A), until, abruptly, the tonal space opens, stretching for a B-flat five octaves away. The movement reaches its conclusion when the cello rises to a series of very high natural harmonics beyond the temperate tuning, accompanied only by the lower notes of the double bass, at a distance of six octaves. This image of being "alone and lost" leads to seven measures of absolute silence, which conclude the first movement.

The musical seeds planted in the first movement then flourish in the second. The previously long notes become trills and torrents of notes that are either compressed or expanded in an extraordinarily intricate manner. The pianissimos of the first movement become sudden explosions of sound. The concerto concludes with a return to nothingness: a pianissimo tutti leads to the final section, an astonishing cadenza for cello solo with the indication "Cadenza of murmurs: sempre prestissimo, quasi perpetuum mobile." At the end of the cadenza one ceases to use the bow, but the fingers of the left hand continue to produce indeterminate sounds, murmurs that become less and less perceptible until they are transformed into total silence lasting approximately ten seconds. The piece concludes only after these ten seconds have elapsed.

The initial concert was held at the Salão Nobre in Lisbon on April 19, 1996, and was subsequently repeated at the Palácio de Ajuda, the Palácio Queluz, and the Belém Cultural Center.

ROBERT X. RODRÍGUEZ AND *MÁSCARAS*

As I mentioned at the beginning of this chapter, my exploration of Ibero-American music also includes works from various regions of the United States with a strong Hispanic culture. *Máscaras* by Robert X. Rodríguez, a distinguished American composer, is a perfect example of music that has emerged from this world. At present, Robert is a professor at the University of Texas at Dallas, and while Eduardo Mata headed the Dallas Symphony Orchestra, Robert was the orchestra's composer in residence. His Hispanic, and specifically Mexican, background is reflected not only in his surname, but also in much of his music.

In October 1992, I gave two concerts in San Antonio, Texas, with the San Antonio Symphony, conducted by Christopher Wilkins. The program included Richard Strauss's symphonic poem *Don Quixote* (for cello, viola, and orchestra) and the world premiere of Robert's new work, *Tango de tango*, in the presence of the composer himself.

Our meeting in San Antonio served as the inspiration for a unique concerto for cello and orchestra: *Máscaras*, which Robert began composing early in 1993. The world premiere of *Máscaras* took place on October 22, 1994, during the Twenty-second International Cervantes Festival in Guanajuato, with the participation of the Italian conductor Guido M. Guida and the Guanajuato Symphony Orchestra.

The richly decorated masks worn by popular dancers in Mexico are the inspiration for this work. Instead of the three traditional movements of a concerto, *Máscaras* consists of six short movements. The extremely diverse thematic motifs in this work are incorporated into *Máscaras* in the author's highly distinctive style, described by the magazine *Musical America* as "an atonality filled with lyricism."

FEDERICO IBARRA:
THE GENESIS OF A CONCERTO AND A SONATA

I met Federico Ibarra at a dinner party in Mexico City in 1988. Although the possibility of his composing a piece for cello came up during the conversation, it was left up in the air. A month later, on February 29, I visited him at his home to confirm my interest and specifically to commission a concerto for cello and orchestra. Ibarra accepted with pleasure and promised to start working on the piece during the second half of the year.

On April 26, 1989, I received a call from Ibarra. The concerto—in three movements—was practically finished, and he needed only a few more days to clean up the cello part. When I visited him the morning of Saturday the 29th, he presented me with a clean copy of the manuscript. I started studying it right away and was filled with such enthusiasm that

40. *Premiere of the cello concerto by Federico Ibarra, with the Royal Philharmonic Orchestra of London led by conductor Enrique A. Diemecke, 1993. Photograph by Keith Saunders, by permission of the Royal Philharmonic Orchestra.*

I couldn't put it down all weekend. By Monday morning I could already play the entire piece, and that same afternoon we played it together, Ibarra taking the piano part.

The premiere took place on October 20 of that same year with the Xalapa Symphony Orchestra and conductor José Guadalupe Flores, in the presence of its composer. The success of the piece was remarkable, particularly in view of the fact that it was a contemporary work. We had to repeat the finale, a dazzling Presto.

Ibarra's concerto has since become one of the pieces I perform most frequently. Its Mexico City premiere was on May 5, 1990, during the inaugural concert of the Twelfth International Forum of New Music. In 1991 I premiered it in the United States at a music festival in Pueblo, Colorado, and its European premiere took place in 1993 in London's Barbican Centre, with Enrique A. Diemecke conducting the Royal Philharmonic Orchestra (Fig. 40). I subsequently recorded it, and played it at the Europalia Festival in Brussels; in Hulst, the Netherlands; at the Dorothy Chandler Pavilion in Los Angeles, California; in Johannesburg and Sasolburg, South Africa; and in Oviedo, Spain, in September 2003. The initial success of its premiere in Xalapa has been a common experience with this concerto.

In view of this precedent, it seemed quite logical when, in mid-1991, I asked Ibarra to consider composing a sonata for cello and piano. One year later, on July 18, 1992, he finished the piece. As with the concerto, I studied it for a few days, and then on July 21, I had the pleasure of playing it with him at his home.

Soon afterwards I premiered it at New York's Hofstra University with pianist Doris Stevenson. In October I played it in Houston with Edison Quintana. Since then, Ibarra's sonata has been frequently featured in my concerts, and I have also recorded it twice.

TEN DAYS IN CUBA

When the Instituto Cubano de la Música (Cuban Institute of Music) invited me for a series of concerts in Cuba, I accepted immediately. For many years I had felt the desire to visit Cuba, one of the few Latin American countries where I had not performed. It is also one of the very few socialist countries to survive the collapse of the Soviet Union, so I was extremely interested in seeing how Cuba was faring after the umbilical cord joining it to the USSR had been cut. In addition, I have always admired the musical talent and creativity of the Cuban people.

On November 19, 1993, María Isabel, Edison Quintana, Chelo Prieto, and I arrived in Havana. The Ministry of Foreign Affairs lodged us in a palatial mansion at 120 146th Street, in Reparto Siboney, one of the most elegant residential areas of old bourgeois Havana. The house, which before the revolution had belonged to a sugar tycoon, is now the property of the Cuban government; it is used as one of the *casas de protocolo*, complimentary accommodations—meals included—placed at the disposal of official guests. And as if this were not enough, we were assigned a beautiful 1950s shiny black Mercedes, complete with chauffeur.

Our first concert took place in the great hall of the Casa de las Américas at three in the afternoon on November 20, the anniversary of the Mexican Revolution. When we returned to our residence for dinner, we were served by two very pleasant women, Berkis and Myriam, who soon became our friends. Except for lunch and dinner invitations, we had our meals "at home," and they were delicious: eggs and milk for breakfast, and lunch and dinner delivered by a central kitchen that served all the protocol houses: fish or steaks, seafood, rice and beans, fruits, vegetables, desserts, etc. We felt privileged, since, as I will describe further on, the majority of these products were totally unavailable to Cubans.

We stayed in Cuba for ten days. It was a period of intense activity: recitals and concerts; meetings with educators, composers, leaders in the music and art fields; master classes; numerous interviews with the press, radio, and television, etc. Wherever we went, we were welcomed with an incredible warmth and kindness that seems to be innate with the Cuban people. We were also able to do some sightseeing, and our conversations with the people were generally quite frank. They did not try to hide—they could not possibly have done so—the obvious seriousness of Cuba's situation.

A GENERAL IMPRESSION OF HAVANA

Despite the numerous rehearsals, concerts, and other previously scheduled activities, we still managed to see quite a bit of Havana. We toured the city, especially "old" Havana, either by car or on foot. Our visits included the former Capitanía General (Captaincy General), the seat of Spanish power until 1898; the cathedral; El Morro and La Cabaña, the fortifications built to protect Havana from pirate ships; the Teatro García Lorca; and the *Granma*, the yacht that transported Castro and his group of young rebels from Mexico to Cuba in 1959. We visited also visited two famous prerevolution landmarks, now almost exclusively destined for foreign visitors, since their prices are quoted in dollars: the Bodeguita del Medio, the restaurant that Hemingway made famous, and the Floridita, the bar known as the birthplace of the daiquiri.

Havana is a beautiful city whose wide avenues, oceanfront location, lovely parks, and buildings are most impressive—from afar. I had the curious sensation of being transported back thirty-four years to a place that seemed very familiar. New buildings are found almost exclusively in the surrounding areas. The city's skyline is virtually the same as it was in 1959. The "modern" buildings are conceived in a style that was fashionable during the 1950s, and the automobiles, mostly from the United States, date from around the same period. The fact that they are still in good working order attests to the Cubans' remarkable resourcefulness. The décor of places like the Floridita or the Bodeguita del Medio is reminiscent of the bars and restaurants in old Mexican movies. All of this considerably reinforces the impression that this city has remained frozen in time. However, when viewed from up close, the deplorable condition of the buildings—which, as I mentioned, look so beautiful from a distance—becomes immediately apparent.

THE ECONOMIC CRISIS AND THE *PERIODO ESPECIAL*

The disappearance of the Soviet Union was a major disaster for Cuba, unleashing what has become known as *periodo especial* (special period). The USSR had been purchasing Cuba's sugar—its primary product—at prices well above the world market price while selling oil to Cuba at subsidized prices. Once the USSR ceased to exist, this doubly preferential treatment ended abruptly. Today Cuba's sugar exports do not generate enough income to pay for the imported products it requires, especially oil. The fuel shortage and the lack of funds have severely affected the Cuban economy.

The Cuban government's efforts for bringing in more foreign currency include according priority to international tourism, previously scorned as a "corrupting influence." Naturally, the United States' trade embargo has further aggravated the crisis, providing the regime with an excuse for its disastrous economy.

Although the Castro regime boasted that it had eradicated prostitution, "the scourge of capitalist countries, that shameful exploitation of women," prostitution has resurfaced with uncontrollable force. On practically every main thoroughfare or tourist spot, young prostitutes, often very young girls, openly approach cars and pedestrians to offer their services in exchange for dollars, dinner invitations, or an evening at the Tropicana nightclub. Therefore, flocks of young foreign tourists fly to Cuba for weekends of incessant partying.

THE *PERIODO ESPECIAL*, MUSIC, AND THE CONGRESS OF THE CUBAN UNION OF WRITERS AND ARTISTS

Our stay coincided with the congress held by the Cuban Union of Writers and Artists (UNEAC), which discussed, among many other topics, the situation of literature, art, and music during the *periodo especial.*

It is common knowledge that two of the revolution's most remarkable achievements were in the areas of education and health, with the country enjoying the highest standards in all of Latin America. In Cuba, the medical training, scientific research, per capita number of doctors, and quality of medical treatment are all comparable to their counterparts in the First World. However, these successful public-health issues are currently confronting serious obstacles because of a shortage of medicines resulting from the lack of foreign currency.

The economic situation has also exerted a negative impact on musical activity. To begin with, free and advanced schooling at the conservatories in the USSR and other old socialist bloc countries was discontinued. Furthermore, after many years of prohibiting artists from emigrating, as also happened in the USSR, the Cuban government has instituted a new policy of allowing foreign countries to hire Cubans temporarily. Therefore, those leaving Cuba under these conditions are no longer labeled *gusanos* ("worms," the name for anti-Castro Cubans) and are free to return if they wish. As a result, a great number of excellent musicians and teachers have gone to other countries, mainly in Latin America. Although this brain drain is certainly a great loss to Cuba, these selective permits are used as an escape valve that may avert more serious problems.

A CONCERT IN THE NATIONAL MUSEUM AND THE SCHEDULING OF CONCERTS

In Cuba, concerts are scheduled according to the current economic situation. In addition to planned blackouts for saving fuel, there are also sudden, unexpected blackouts from power plant breakdowns. Concerts are therefore scheduled well before nightfall. For example, the Casa de las Américas concert began at three, and the recital at the museum started at five, right at the end of the workday.

Our concert at the Salón Europeo of the National Museum of Fine Arts was filled to capacity, mostly with young people. It was also attended by one of Cuban music's most outstanding music personalities, including composer Carlos Fariñas, who divides his time between Cuba and Germany.

A CONCERT WITH THE NATIONAL SYMPHONY ORCHESTRA AND A MEETING WITH CARLOS FARIÑAS

Our tour ended with a noon concert on Sunday, November 28, at the National Theatre. I played Dvořák's Cello Concerto with the National Symphony Orchestra of Cuba, conducted by Irina Rodríguez, a young conductor who had studied in the Soviet Union.

Carlos Fariñas dropped by during the intermission and invited me to his home for coffee. When I arrived that evening, Carlos and his wife, Ela, holding flashlights, were already waiting for me at the front door. "We weren't supposed to have a blackout today," Carlos said. "But there is a problem at the Matanzas plant, so here we are, left in the dark." However, the Fariñas were fully prepared. Since they spend part of their time in Germany, they had bought some rechargeable flashlights, intended for precisely this kind of emergency. Two flashlights placed over the piano, pointing at the ceiling, managed to light up the entire living room, imbuing it with a pleasant, homey atmosphere.

When the subject of Fariñas's composing a cello concerto came up during our conversation, he remarked that during Rostropovich's visit to Cuba in 1960, he too had asked Fariñas to write a concerto for cello but he had refused, and now deeply regretted it. This time, he didn't want to miss another opportunity, so he promised to start working on it as soon as possible.

We left Cuba the following day, filled with gratitude for the warm welcome we received from our hosts as well as from our old and new Cuban friends. However, we were also filled with a sense of dread. We had witnessed the difficult times Cuba was living through, and we realized that the future looked quite bleak.

SOME OBSERVATIONS ON CUBAN MUSIC AND MUSICIANS

The two great figures of early twentieth-century Cuban music and the first musicians to obtain international recognition were Amadeo Roldán (1900–1939), who was born in Paris and educated in Spain but always considered himself Cuban, and Alejandro García Caturla (1906–1940). Although they both received their musical training in Europe, they returned to Cuba in the 1920s and were the first to conduct an in-depth investigation of the African influence on Cuban music. In 1925 they, along with Alejo Carpentier, launched a movement to foster an appreciation of Afro-Cuban folklore, which until then had been regarded with disdain. According to Carpentier, the 1925 premiere of Roldán's *Obertura sobre temas cubanos* (Overture on Cuban Themes) constituted a definite turning point in Cuban music.[25]

During a visit to the Music Museum I came across the manuscript of a work for cello and piano by Roldán, *Canciones vuelta abajeras*, which, I believe, is the only piece he ever wrote for this instrument. Naturally I was extremely interested in it, so the museum's directors kindly sent me a copy. I did not, however, find any cello music composed by García Caturla.

Roldán and García Caturla died in their youth. An eminent Spanish composer and teacher, José Ardévol, filled the void created by Roldán and García Caturla's premature deaths. Among his most exceptional students were Harold Gramatges, born in 1918, and Julián Orbón, who, though born in Spain in 1925, moved to Cuba in 1940.

Gramatges was the recipient of the first Tomás Luis de Victoria Prize, instituted in Madrid for the "purpose of bestowing a lifetime achievement award to a composer born in Ibero-America for his contribution to the enrichment of the culture of our countries."[26] Orbón rose to fame in 1954 during the Latin American Music Festival in Caracas. The jury, comprised of Vicente Emilio Sojo, Heitor Villa-Lobos, Edgar Varèse, Erich Kleiber, and Adolfo Salazar, awarded him second place for his work *Tres versiones sinfónicas*.

In 1960, disillusioned with the tenor of the Cuban Revolution, Orbón moved to Mexico at the invitation of Carlos Chávez. Since then, Orbón's name has been anathema in Cuba, to such a degree that he is not mentioned in the newer editions of Alejo Carpentier's book *La música en Cuba*.

In Mexico, Orbón was both a teacher at the National Conservatory and Chávez's collaborator in his composition workshop. After three fruitful years in Mexico, Orbón immigrated to the United States.

I visited him in Miami in March 1991. Orbón was in delicate health, and although I tried several times to shorten my visit so as not to tire him, he insisted I stay and have coffee. When I departed, he told me, "Carlos, if my health permits, I promise to compose a partita for cello and orchestra for you."

Unfortunately, as it turned out, his health did not permit it, and Orbón died shortly after. I have always regretted not visiting him sooner. The cello repertoire would have been greatly enriched by his work.

However, it was Carlos Fariñas who ended up giving me a concerto for cello and orchestra. He had started the piece in Havana, finished it in Bochum, Germany, and sent it to me in early 1996. I premiered it in 1998 in Xalapa, Mexico, with the Xalapa Symphony Orchestra under the baton of my son, Carlos Miguel.

Leo Brouwer is one of the most important names in Cuban music. An outstanding guitarist, he is also a noted composer and conductor, and for a long time he was head of Cuba's National Symphony Orchestra. I met him in 1995 at the International Festival of Contemporary Music in Alicante, Spain, and in 1996 I played his Cello Sonata at a concert series devoted to Ibero-American cello music in Madrid. In November 1997, I had the pleasure of playing Shostakovich's Cello Concerto no. 1, with Leo conducting the Córdoba Orchestra, which he had founded.

Among the younger composers, I would mention my friend Guido López Gavilán, then chairman of a music festival in Havana, who invited us for coffee at his apartment and presented me with a copy of *Monólogo*, his work for solo cello. We also met his son Aldo, then thirteen years old, who greatly impressed us with his remarkable piano improvisations.

MARIO LAVISTA AND THE THREE SECULAR DANCES

Mario Lavista, born in Mexico City in 1943, is without a doubt one of the most notable composers in Latin America today. He studied in Mexico with Carlos Chávez, Héctor Quintanar, and Rodolfo Halffter; in Paris with Jean-Etienne Marie at the Schola Cantorum; and in Germany with Stockhausen. He has composed an opera (based on Carlos Fuentes's book *Aura*), chamber and orchestral music, film scores, etc. His works have been performed in concerts and festivals all over the world.

Over the past few years, Lavista has collaborated closely with several outstanding instrumentalists. This work has been fueled by his interest in exploring new technical and expressive possibilities offered by traditional instruments, though always adhering to musical logic and without contravening the nature of the instrument. His music is completely devoid of flamboyant devices, and he makes no concessions for the sake of success.

As time passed, my admiration for Lavista increased. In 1987 I tried to convince him to compose a new cello piece. As the years went by, my attempts to persuade him turned into a veritable persecution. However, in February 1994, while having dinner in New York, he suddenly remarked: "I've already begun the work, a kind of suite for cello and piano with alternate slow and extremely rapid movements. I expect to finish it in a few months." Sure enough, toward the middle of year he handed me a draft entitled *Tres danzas seculares*. The composer himself has described this piece as follows:

> *Tres danzas seculares* for cello and piano attempts to "make audible" three moments—which defy all description—of the courtship ritual of imaginary birds. It is a triptych with a slow movement, a conversation between the two instruments within a slow harmonic field, followed by a rapid movement, based on an ostinato on the note A, first heard on the cello and then on the piano, joined by a contrapuntal melody with an ever-changing and different ostinato metric. Finally, there is a slow-fast movement with an introduction of homophonic texture and a melody of harmonics for the cello, ending with a canon for three voices. Each line has its own independent metric structure, which never coincides with the other two, at times giving the impression that they are moving at entirely different velocities. The piece features an epigraph by the British naturalist Gerald Durrell: "Birds are the Elizabethan lovers of the animal world: they attire themselves in magnificent costumes, dance, and exhibit themselves." The work was written in 1994 and is dedicated to Carlos Prieto.[27]

Tres danzas seculares was precisely the work of Lavista's that I had hoped for. It is beautifully written and highly innovative in its timbres, form, variety, and poetry. It also poses formidable challenges for the musician and immediately captures the audience's attention. Edison Quintana and I premiered the piece in 1995 in Mexico, and that same year we recorded it in New York. Since then I have played it in many cities: Madrid, Paris, Dublin, Washington, Moscow, and Caracas.

MEXICO: FOUR CONCERTS AND SIX WORLD PREMIERES

In March 1995 a series of recitals took place at the National Museum, organized by the National Institute of Fine Arts with the collaboration of the Spanish embassy. The series was called "Ibero-American Music for Cello and World Music: Seven Ibero-American Premieres." Here I premiered the works dedicated to me over the past two years. The programs also included more traditional pieces so as not to drive away those who dread contemporary music. The pianist was Edison Quintana, who shares my passion for contemporary and Ibero-American music. The programs consisted of the following (with the asterisk indicating works dedicated to me):

Ibero-American Music for Cello and World Music:
Seven Ibero-American Premieres

Program No. 1, March 8, 1995
Suite no. 3 for Solo Cello   J. S. Bach
Sonata Concertante (Mexican premiere) Xavier Montsalvatge (Spain)
Lull-a-Bear* (World premiere)   Robert X. Rodríguez (USA)
Sonata for Cello and Piano* (1992)   Federico Ibarra (Mexico)

Program No. 2, March 15, 1995
Sonata for Cello and Piano (1961)   Rodolfo Halffter
                                                                    (Spain-Mexico)

Sonatina for Cello (1961)   Manuel Enríquez (Mexico)
Suite popular española   Manuel de Falla (Spain)
Netík 1 (1994) (world premiere)   Arturo Salinas (Mexico)
Pezzo capriccioso, op. 62 (1887)   Tchaikovsky
Le grand tango (1982)   Astor Piazzolla (Argentina)

Program No. 3, March 22, 1995
Sonata op. 40 (1934)   D. Shostakovich
Tres danzas seculares* (1994) (world premiere)
                                                                    Mario Lavista (Mexico)
Primer espejo de Falla* (1994) (world premiere)
                                                                    Tomás Marco (Spain)
Pampeana no. 2 (1950)   A. Ginastera (Argentina)

Program No. 4, March 29, 1995
Sonata-Fantasia for Cello and Piano*   C. Garrido-Lecca (Peru)
Fantasía* (1994) (Mexican premiere)   Samuel Zyman (Mexico)
Alborada* (1994) (world premiere)   Manuel Castillo (Spain)
Variations on a Rococo Theme, op. 33 (1876)
                                                                    Tchaikovsky

CONCERTS IN MADRID:
AN UNPRECEDENTED THREE-CONCERT CYCLE

In September and October 1996 I played a series of recitals in Madrid
that for me represented a culmination of my work supporting contemporary Ibero-American music up to that time.

The recitals were superbly organized by the Juan March Foundation,

41. With pianist Chiky Martin and Spanish composer Tomás Marco. Madrid, 1996.

an exemplary institution in the Spanish cultural and scientific worlds. At the piano was an excellent pianist from Madrid: Chiky Martin, with whom I had played before in Spain and Mexico (Fig. 41).

The series, called "Panorama of the Ibero-American Cello in the Twentieth Century," consisted of three recitals with the following programs:

Program No. 1, September 25, 1996
Sonata for Cello and Piano (1915–1917) (Spanish premiere)
Manuel Ponce (Mexico)
Sonata al estilo antiguo español (1925)   Gaspar Cassadó (Spain)
Tres danzas seculares (1994) (Spanish Premiere)
Mario Lavista (Mexico)
Primer espejo de Falla (1994) (Spanish Premiere)
Tomás Marco (Spain)
Pampeana no. 2 (1950)   A. Ginastera (Argentina)

Program No. 2, October 2, 1996
Sonata for Cello and Piano (1956)   Roberto Gerhard (Spain)
Alborada (1994) (Spanish premiere)   Manuel Castillo (Spain)
Sonatina for Cello (1961) (Spanish premiere)
Manuel Enríquez (Mexico)
Siciliana (1929)   Joaquín Rodrigo (Spain)
Sonata for Cello and Piano (1992) (Spanish premiere) –
F. Ibarra (Mexico)

Program No. 3, October 9, 1996
Cello Sonata (1960)   Leo Brouwer (Cuba)
Sonata for Cello and Piano (1961)   Rodolfo Halffter
(Spain-Mexico)

Suite popular española (1934)   Manuel de Falla (Spain)
Three Preludes (1933)   Manuel Ponce (Mexico)
Fantasía (1994) (Spanish Premiere)   Samuel Zyman (Mexico)
Le grand tango (1982)   A. Piazzolla (Argentina)

We played nineteen works in all, including three encores. Of the nineteen works, seven were by Mexican composers, seven by Spanish composers, three by Argentineans, one by a Brazilian, and one by a Cuban. The concerts were by no means intended to represent the entire spectrum of Ibero-American music. Brazil's rich musical contributions were represented only by an encore by Villa-Lobos. It was impossible to include composers from every country, since that would have required innumerable recitals, but a series of Ibero-American cello works like this had never before been presented in the Spanish capital. Broadcast on RNE (National Radio of Spain), the three recitals were warmly received by the public and critics alike.

ROBERTO SIERRA: FOUR VERSES FOR CELLO AND ORCHESTRA

Roberto Sierra is one of America's most interesting and exciting composers. He rose to fame in 1987 when his first major orchestral composition, *Júbilo*, was performed at Carnegie Hall by the Milwaukee Symphony Orchestra. His works have been performed by many of the major orchestras of the world.

In 1989 Roberto Sierra became composer in residence of the Milwaukee Symphony, and during the 2000–2001 season, he held the same position with the Philadelphia Orchestra. Sierra recently completed his first symphony, commissioned by the Saint Paul Chamber Orchestra, and is currently working on a double concerto commissioned by the Pittsburgh Symphony and the Philadelphia Orchestra. The idea for a cello concerto first came up during a conversation we had in July 1997. Two years later, he had completed the concerto, a splendid work entitled Four Verses for Cello and Orchestra. The premiere took place on June 2, 2000, at the International Forum of New Music, with the Mexico City Philharmonic Orchestra led by Carlos Miguel Prieto (Fig. 42).

42. *Carlos Prieto, Roberto Sierra, and Carlos Miguel Prieto, after the world premiere of Sierra's cello concerto on June 2, 2000, in Mexico.*

Here is how Roberto Sierra describes his cello concerto:

> Of all stringed instruments, the violoncello is perhaps the one with the widest range of expression. To my ears it has been always the poet of the string family. The four movements of the concerto form a symmetrical outline split in the middle by a cadenza. The first two movements explore introverted, intense, and meditative expression, while the last two are extroverted and virtuosic. I wanted to create this Apollonian-Dionysian dialectic to guide the musical material, which is based mainly on two tetrachords (both containing the possibility of yielding all the intervals of the chromatic spectrum). The central cadenza serves as a point of transition from the Apollonian to the Dionysian.
>
> Four Verses is dedicated to Carlos Prieto, in admiration of his achievements and in recognition of his being an inspirational motivator in the creation of the modern repertoire for the cello in Latin America.[28]

Shortly after the premiere, we recorded Four Verses, and on November 17, 2000, Carlos Miguel and I played it again, this time with the Simón Bolívar Orchestra in Caracas.

YO-YO MA AND SAMUEL ZYMAN: A STORY IN FIVE SCENES

FIRST SCENE: MEXICO, 1993

While in Mexico for several concerts, Yo-Yo Ma, his wife, Jill, and his children, Nicholas and Emily, were invited for lunch at our home. We were in the middle of playing some pieces for cellos when we were called to the table. Yo-Yo suggested we leave the two cellos alone, out of their cases, and see if any romantic sparks flew between them. His cello was the famed 1712 Davidov Stradivari (Fig. 43).

SECOND SCENE: CAMBRIDGE, MASSACHUSETTS, 1994

We saw Yo-Yo Ma a year later at a reception hosted by MIT in honor of composer John Harbison and Yo-Yo, who was about to premiere John's cello concerto, which had been jointly commissioned by MIT and the Boston and Chicago symphony orchestras. Yo-Yo asked me whether the meeting of the two Strads in Mexico had produced some "little Strads." When I responded in the negative, Yo-Yo rejoined, "That meeting should not lie fallow. It should at least result in a new cello piece. You

43. With Yo-Yo Ma in Mexico: two Stradivari cellos in duo, 1993.

have premiered many works by Latin American composers, and I have premiered many by American composers. How about commissioning a work for two cellos? Why don't you choose the type of work and the composer?"

THIRD SCENE: NEW YORK, 1998–1999

I got together with Samuel Zyman to explore his interest in composing a suite for two cellos, since I was not aware of the existence of any such work, much less by a Latin American composer. Needless to say, he was absolutely thrilled. He started composing the suite in 1999, sent me the first four movements on July 10, and had finished all six movements by August.

FOURTH SCENE: NEW YORK, JANUARY 2001

On January 30, 2001, Yo-Yo and Jill Ma invited us to dinner to celebrate an important event in María Isabel's life. Before dinner, Yo-Yo and I played the Zyman suite—"dedicated to Yo-Yo Ma and Carlos Prieto." Yo-Yo was so delighted with it that we repeated the entire suite and even played several movements three times!

44. Yo-Yo Ma and María Isabel, Carlos Prieto's wife, in Mexico in 1993.

45. Yo-Yo Ma and the Prieto String Quartet, Huntsville, Alabama, 2005. LEFT TO RIGHT: *Son Carlos Miguel Prieto (conductor and violinist), nephew Juan Luis Prieto Jr. (violinist), Yo-Yo Ma, Carlos Prieto, and brother Juan Luis Prieto (viola).*

FIFTH SCENE: MEXICO, IRELAND, AND THE UNITED STATES

Besides playing the suite with Yo-Yo, I had the opportunity to perform it quite a few times. In 1999, in Morelia, I premiered its preliminary four-movement version with Juan Hermida—winner of the first Carlos Prieto Cello Competition—and subsequently played the entire six-movement version in Mexico City and Puebla. I played it in Ireland in 2000 with cellist Bill Butt, and recorded it in New York with Jesús Castro-Balbi—whom I mentioned in the preceding chapter—in the presence of the composer, who made some minor but effective changes. Jesús and I performed it again in 2002 during the Fourteenth International Music Festival in Morelia and in September 2003 at Texas Christian University's Pepsico Recital Hall in Fort Worth.

The meeting of the two Strads in Mexico had not been in vain after all!

EUGENIO TOUSSAINT AND A NEW CELLO CONCERTO

The first seed for Toussaint's new concerto was planted on January 31, 1997, when Eugenio and I met to discuss my ideas for a new cello concerto. Born in Mexico City in 1954, Eugenio Toussaint started his music career as a self-taught jazz pianist and composer. He then studied in Mexico and the United States, becoming well known for his compositions and the groups he played with. I thought Toussaint's unusual background and unique style could result in something quite interesting for the cello, as indeed turned out to be the case.

In an interview with Juan Arturo Brennan, Toussaint had this to say about his new cello concerto:

> My first cello concerto was, in fact, my first symphonic work. . . . In this piece, it was my intention to depart from the language of jazz and come into closer contact with the world of "classical" music, so to speak. For the second cello concerto, however, I did the exact opposite; Carlos Prieto told me that he felt that in my first concerto "I had applied the brakes to my personal way of composing," and he wanted a piece more akin to my jazz style. Therefore, I composed a work that is much freer, and closer to my jazz roots. . . . The first movement, highly angular and syncopated, is written in 5/4 time, a time signature I like a great deal. . . . The solo part for the cello is

extremely colorful and dynamic, especially distinguished by the fact that the strong beats never fall where one expects. The second movement is a kind of homage to Wayne Shorter, the great saxophone player from Weather Report, a group that had considerable influence on my career. . . . The third movement, the jazziest of the three, is based on a rhythmic cell that I remember from a classic swing song, with a marked jazz spirit that might remind us of Gershwin or Bernstein. The general idea here is to imbue the orchestra with the spirit of jazz, but without a single improvised note. In other words, there are moments when one can distinctly feel the swing, although strictly speaking there is none. It is, without a doubt, the concerto's most difficult movement, due to the rhythmic interplay between soloist and orchestra.[29]

The world premiere took place not in Mexico, but in Caracas, on March 28, 2003, with the Simón Bolívar Orchestra conducted by Eduardo Marturet. I played the Mexican premiere on November 26 and 28 with the Philharmonic Orchestra of the National Autonomous University under its artistic director, Zuohuang Chen.

ARTURO MÁRQUEZ AND *MIRRORS IN THE SAND: FOUR DANCES FOR CELLO AND ORCHESTRA*

Arturo Márquez was born in Alamos, Sonora, Mexico in 1950. He studied music at the National Conservatory of Music in Mexico, at the composition workshop of Mexico's National Institute of Fine Arts, and at the California Institute of the Arts; he also had private lessons in Paris. His principal teachers have been Federico Ibarra and Morton Subotnick. He has received numerous grants and awards from the Mexican and French governments, as well as a Fulbright Scholarship. His music often incorporates popular musical elements, as in his *danzóns* for orchestra, which have become extremely popular, especially his *Danzón* no. 2.

Having premiered many rather abstract cello pieces, I thought it was time for a change. After listening to several of Márquez's pieces, one thing that struck me was the impression of continually hearing the cello in its most melodic, singing vein. I was also attracted by his often ironic style.

On April 24, 1998, Márquez and I had breakfast together, and I observed that since his style lent itself very naturally to the cello, he should compose a cello concerto. He readily accepted, and told me he would start working on it after March 1999, when he concluded his term as composer in residence for Mexico's National Symphony Orchestra.

He called me in June 2000, and we met at his home to hear a preliminary computer version of the concerto. On August 29 he gave me the score of the three movements and the cello part. With his approval, I made a few changes to the cello part to make it more idiomatic. Here is what the composer said in an interview with Mexican writer and music critic Juan Arturo Brennan:

> As a general concept, the work is exactly what is subtitle says: three dances for cello and orchestra. Structurally speaking, it is also conceived in that manner, but it is actually a concerto, in the sense that there is a formal disposition of the movements toward a common end, and the development is almost cyclical in character. Nevertheless, the development itself is not strictly thematic. The mirrors in the title are associated with very personal, autobiographical reflections. I am somehow returning to my homeland, a land of dry sand. The polka is a very sarcastic moment in the work, and it is also typical of northern Mexico. I believe the third movement will be most surprising for the listener. In the first movement, entitled *Son de tierra candente* (*Son* of the scorching earth), I work with elements I have been using since my Homage to Gismonti and other pieces based on the *son*, basically the *son* from Veracruz and central Mexico. [A *son* is a Latin American song with a lively, danceable beat.] In this case, because of the rhythm and my particular use of the solo instrument, the *Son de tierra candente* is more related to the *son* from the Huasteca region. The second movement, *Lluvia en la arena* (Rain on the sand), is a sort of *danza-danzón* that I've also used in some of my recent works. The surprise in the third movement, *Polka derecha-izquierda* (Right-left polka), is that I have never worked with a specifically northern genre such as the polka. Although the entire work is tonal, in the last movement I use considerable pantonality and some surprising elements in regard to tonality.[30]

The world premiere took place on October 21 and 22, 2000, with the Mexico City Philharmonic Orchestra, conducted by my son, Carlos Miguel Prieto. On November 9, Arturo gave me an additional movement, entitled *Cadenza de milonga*, based on another dance. It is a cadenza for solo cello to be played after the second movement. On November 17, 2000, I played the concerto with its new movement, in Caracas, with the Simón Bolívar Orchestra, conducted by Carlos Miguel Prieto.

I played the U.S. premiere of the concerto on February 21, 2004, with the excellent Michigan State University Orchestra, conducted by Raphael Jiménez.

AN EXTENDED BOOK AND CONCERT TOUR THROUGHOUT LATIN AMERICA AND SPAIN, MARCH–MAY 1999

From March to May, 1999, I had the extraordinary experience of touring many of the principal cities of the Spanish-speaking world, giving a series of recitals and orchestral concerts and promoting this book, *The Adventures of a Cello*, in the recently published Spanish edition. Within a two-month period, I played twenty-eight concerts and presented my book in Mexico, Spain, Venezuela, Colombia, Ecuador, Peru, Bolivia, Argentina, Uruguay, and Chile. The book presentation usually consisted of comments by one or more local personalities followed by a twenty-minute talk about my cello and its adventures. The second part of the event was a brief recital—with pianists Chiky Martin in Spain, and Edison Quintana in the other countries. The program generally included a work from the great European repertoire, a new Mexican piece, and the world premiere of a work by a great composer from the country we were visiting.

GUADALAJARA AND ÁLVARO MUTIS

The launching of this book took place at the Guadalajara International Book Fair. Among the presenters was Álvaro Mutis, the great Colombian writer, now living in Mexico, and author of this book's prologue (Fig. 46).

SPAIN: MADRID, OVIEDO, CÁDIZ

In Spain the book was presented in Madrid, Oviedo, Cádiz, and Barcelona. We played works by Bach, by Mexican composers Gutiérrez Heras and Mario Lavista, and the premiere of *Primer espejo de Falla* by Spanish composer Tomás Marco, who participated in the book presentations.

During our three-hour train ride from Madrid to Cádiz, Tomás

46. With Mexican composer Mario Lavista and Colombian writer Álvaro Mutis in Mexico City, 2002.

Marco took out a blank sheet of music paper, and while we were passing through Ciudad Real, he wrote the first notes of what would become his *Partita Piatti* for solo cello, which I have recorded in New York and played in Mexico, the United States (Bloomington, Indiana), Germany (Kronberg Cello Festival), Spain, and Brazil.

The book presentation turned out to be a major event in Cádiz, where my cello had lived for fifty-eight years. I took the cello out of its case and introduced it to the audience as the Cádiz Stradivari that had returned after an absence of 181 years. The audience greeted it with a standing ovation, as if welcoming a local hero!

BARCELONA AND XAVIER MONTSALVATGE

In Barcelona, the book presentation and the ensuing recital took place at the Círculo de Liceu, located in a historic area of the city. Although Xavier Montsalvatge and his wife, Elena, were unable to attend the event at the Liceu, they invited me over to their apartment for coffee the next day. A delightful couple, they combine old-fashioned courtesy with great personal charm. Montsalvatge, one of Catalonia's—and Spain's—most distinguished composers, has written several noteworthy cello works, including a Sonata Concertante for Cello and Piano and several shorter pieces.

When referring to my book and all the works I had premiered, he remarked that he had something in mind that could become a cello piece, but, unfortunately, his poor health would prevent him from even considering such a project.

The reader can imagine my surprise and joy when I received the following letter a few weeks later:

Barcelona, April 19, 2000
My dear friend:
. . . I have been thinking of a piece for cello and piano, and already have in mind an epicurean melodic line that I believe is attractive and has many possibilities for development. If my ideas and my strength do not fail me, I think I can finish it by early autumn.

This work, conceived especially for you, who also inspired it, would be yours, with exclusive rights to the premiere, and if you wish, I could extend this exclusive right to the interpretation and to the eventual recording of this piece for a specific period of time.

I would greatly appreciate hearing your decision, which, logically, I hope will be favorable, granting me the joy and the honor of your being the "discoverer," interpreter, and possible divulger of my most recent music.

This was the origin of his charming piece entitled *Invención a la italiana* for cello and piano, which I premiered in Mexico in September 2000 and recorded in New York in January 2001. Unfortunately, Xavier Montsalvatge passed away shortly after, in May 2002.

CHILE: JUAN ORREGO-SALAS AND GUSTAVO BECERRA-SCHMIDT

In Chile we played not one but two world premieres of Chilean compositions: *Espacios*, a rhapsody by Juan Orrego-Salas, and a new sonata by Gustavo Becerra Schmidt. Juan Orrego-Salas, composer, educator, and promoter, is one of Latin America's outstanding musical personalities. After a highly distinguished career in Chile, in 1961 he arrived in Bloomington to establish a Latin American music center and serve as professor of composition at the Indiana University School of Music. The Juan Orrego-Salas Scholarship Fund, which provides annual awards to composition students at the IU School of Music, was established in 1994 in honor of Professor Orrego-Salas's twenty-eight-year career there.

When Edison Quintana and I spent a day with Juan and his wife, Carmen, at their beautiful country home near Bloomington, I had the opportunity to play *Espacios* for the composer and hear his comments and suggestions. After the premiere in Chile (in Santiago and Viña del Mar), we played it in Mexico, in South Africa, and at Washington's Kennedy Center during a concert honoring the composer, who was present. A few months later I received a most touching gift from Orrego-Salas, his Fantasias for Cello and Orchestra, with a lovely dedication; I expect to premiere the work in 2005.

My contact with Gustavo Becerra-Schmidt, another eminent Chilean composer, was completely different, since it was entirely the result of the cybernetic age. We conducted an extensive e-mail correspondence before and after he composed his Cello Sonata, becoming friends in cyberspace, but we never actually met! His sonata consists of three movements: Rhapsody, Theme and Variations, and Rondo-Sonata. Its form is based on the classic three-movement sonata. However, its tonal structure is free, although it is determined by a twelve-tone chromaticism that even allows for the thematic treatment of Ibero- American elements, particularly Chilean ones. The overall effect is that of an arch, since its theme reemerges at the end of the third movement.

PERU AND AN EARTH-SHATTERING RECITAL IN LIMA

I presented the book and played in Lima and Trujillo, Peru's second-largest city. The new Peruvian composition I played was the *Soliloquio II* for cello by Celso Garrido-Lecca.

In addition, Edison Quintana and I gave a recital in the Peruvian capital. When we finished, the audience started to applaud and the theater to shake. It was, in fact, a powerful earthquake. I addressed the public, saying we appreciated their enthusiasm, but that it was somewhat exaggerated. All the spectators remained in their seats, except for one woman who, as she shouted, "Everybody keep calm!" rushed, panic-stricken, out of the concert hall.

BOLIVIA: ALBERTO VILLALPANDO AND AN UNEXPECTED HONOR

In our extensive concert tour through the world and music of Ibero-America, only composers from Bolivia and Ecuador had not been represented, and I had searched in vain for Bolivian cello works. After finishing our last, and very elevated, concert in La Paz (over 12,000 feet above sea level), Alberto Villalpando, Bolivia's most distinguished composer, assured me that the lack of music from his country would be remedied and that he would immediately compose a work for cello and piano to be sent to me in the "near future." And indeed, in late July 1999 I received an envelope from Bolivia containing the promised piece, *Sonatita de piel morena* for cello and piano. We premiered it Mexico a few months later, in 2000, and recorded it for Urtext Digital Classics shortly after.

During a solemn congenial ceremony in La Paz, the minister of culture, Dr. Ramón Rocha Monroy, presented me with an honorary title from the Bolivian government. I was about to express my gratitude for this noble gesture when Dr. Rocha Monroy announced that he also had another honor to bestow—on Chelo Prieto. The elegant parchment awarded to the Piatti features a color reproduction of the Bolivian national emblem crowned with a condor. The text reads as follows: "Chelo Prieto, ex-Piatti, created by D. Antonio Stradivari in the Year of Our Lord 1720, is hereby declared Illustrious Guest of Bolivian Culture." On behalf of Don Antonio Stradivari, Chelo Prieto, and myself, I thanked the minister for these distinguished honors.

VENEZUELA: CLAUDIA CALDERÓN, PAUL DESENNE, AND THE FINCA GALEÓNICA

The book presentation in Caracas, with the participation of Mexican ambassador Jesús Puente Leyva and Venezuelan cellist-composer Paul Desenne, and the subsequent recital took place at the Bank of the Republic's auditorium.

A few days later, Paul Desenne and his wife, Colombian composer and pianist Claudia Calderón, invited us to the Finca Galeónica, their weekend retreat in the mountains, two hours from Caracas. In the afternoon, Claudia sat at the piano and played the *música llanera* (music from the plains) she had collected throughout the "llano" regions of Colombia and Venezuela, somewhat as Bartók and Kodály had done, on a grand scale, with Central European folk music of Hungary, Bulgaria, and Rumania. Her piano versions were simply wonderful. So the idea came up of her composing a cello-and-piano piece based on the rhythms and motives of this type of music. This was the origin of the piece called *La revuelta circular*. The piece is extremely difficult, but a lot of fun to play if one can overcome its numerous obstacles. I played it and recorded it the following year.

The tour also included book presentations and concerts in Argentina (at the Teatro Colón), Uruguay, and Ecuador, and was later extended to Guatemala, but I will have to omit my impressions of events in those countries so as not to make this book impossibly long!

BOOK AND CONCERT TOURS IN BRAZIL (2001 AND 2002)

In 2001 and 2002 I had a similarly extraordinary experience, but this time it involved the Portuguese-speaking world. These particular tours were made possible by UniverCidade (Universidade da Cidade), a remarkable university in Rio de Janeiro, and by the Rio publishing firm of Top Books, which had the book translated into Portuguese by Brazilian writer Pedro Lyra.[31]

In 2001 and 2002 my Brazilian tours included concerts, master classes, and book presentations in Fortaleza, Brasília, São Paulo, Curitiba, Rio de Janeiro, Campinas, Florianopolis, Porto Alegre, and Belo Horizonte. Chelo Prieto and I flew many thousands of miles over this fascinating country, the fifth largest in the world.[32]

I will recount only a few of my Brazilian experiences. When I was informed about the forthcoming Portuguese translation of my book, I decided to study Portuguese in depth. I did so with the help of teachers from the Brazilian Cultural Center in Mexico, and I read as many books in Portuguese as my concert schedule allowed. I had not forgotten my embarrassing experience in Manaus in 1991, when my speech in Portuguese had been so easily understood "because I spoke such pure Castilian Spanish."

FORTALEZA

My first experience with the language took place in Fortaleza, capital of the northern state of Ceará, and it went better than expected. I gave the usual talk-recital at the University of Fortaleza (UNIFOR), and at least this time nobody thought I was speaking Spanish!

BRASÍLIA

The book and concert tour included the School of Music of Brasília, the Latin American Center of the University of Brasília, and the Itamaraty Palace. Without a doubt, the most impressive presentation during my visits to Brazil took place in the Sala Brasília of the magnificent Itamaraty Palace (headquarters of the Ministry of Foreign Relations). I was introduced by Celso Lafer, the minister of foreign relations, and by Marilú Seixas, an old friend and high-ranking official in the ministry. I gave my usual talk and then played two Bach suites.

The Itamaraty Palace is one of Brasília's crown jewels. It was designed by the legendary architect Oscar Niemeyer, who played a major role in creating Brasília itself.

RIO DE JANEIRO, UNIVERCIDADE, AND MARLOS NOBRE

From Brasília we flew to Rio de Janeiro, which, trite as it may sound, is truly one of the most spectacular cities in the world.

The book presentation and recital took place at the auditorium of UniverCidade, the institution in charge of translating and publishing my book. I am grateful to UniverCidade and to its chairman, Dr. Ronald Guimarães Levinsohn, not only for the translation but also for the excellent organization and extensive press and TV coverage of my tours.

Marlos Nobre, one of the most remarkable Brazilian composers of our day, and whom I had known for a long time, was one of the many musicians attending this event (Fig. 47). We had a *cafezinho* (Brazilian-style coffee) a few days later, and well aware of my eagerness to play new works from Brazil, he assured me he that would soon start working on a

47. With Brazilian composer Marlos Nobre. Río de Janeiro, 2002.

piece for cello and piano. And indeed, a few months later I received the *Partita latina* for cello and piano, a work that I subsequently premiered in Mexico and recorded in New York in 2003.

RIO DE JANEIRO: A CONCERT WITH THE ORQUESTRA DE CÁMARA DA GROTA DE SURUCUCU

An entirely different experience in Rio was a visit to one of its slums, the Favela São Francisco, where an exemplary social and musical experiment is taking place. It is here that Jonas Caldas, an ex-convict turned violin maker, has established a school where children are taught not only how to play stringed instruments but also how to make them. I listened to their concert in utter amazement, and when it was over, I asked if I could play something with them. They gladly agreed, and so I had the unforgettable experience of playing with the Orquestra de Cordas da Grota do Surucucu, which means the "String Orchestra of the Cave of the Bushmasters"; until quite recently, the cave where they play was full of these incredibly venomous snakes! It was quite a contrast with the Itamaraty Palace.

MY LONG INVOLVEMENT WITH VENEZUELA

My musical relation with Venezuela began in 1991, when I placed a series of recitals in Caracas.

1998: RICARDO LORENZ AND THE SIMÓN BOLÍVAR SYMPHONY ORCHESTRA

On May 8, 1998, I played with the Simón Bolívar Symphony Orchestra, conducted by my compatriot Eduardo Diazmuñoz at the Teresa Carreño Theatre. The program included the Venezuelan premiere of Federico Ibarra's Cello Concerto—the first Mexican cello concerto ever performed in Venezuela—and Tchaikovsky's Variations on a Rococo Theme. During this, my first appearance with this orchestra, I was able to corroborate conductor Eduardo Mata's opinion that it is one of the finest in Latin America. It is comprised of young Venezuelan musicians who play with remarkable technical and musical skill as well as exemplary devotion. It is the crown jewel of the National System of Youth and Children's Orchestras of Venezuela, which I will discuss later on.

RICARDO LORENZ AND CECILIA IN BLUE AND GREEN

On May 10, Edison Quintana and I played a recital at Quinta Anauco, a colonial mansion where Simón Bolívar once stayed, now a venue for Sunday chamber music concerts. As usual, the program included a combination of European and Latin American works: Shostakovich's and Kodály's sonatas during the first half of the program, and, after intermission, the world premiere of a work entitled *Cecilia en azul y verde* by the young Venezuelan composer Ricardo Lorenz, the Venezuelan premiere of Mario Lavista's *Tres danzas seculares*, and Astor Piazzolla's *Le grand tango*.

Lorenz's piece, its peculiar title, the unusual circumstances under which it was composed, and the premiere itself all warrant an explanation. As soon as we had settled on the dates for my concerts in Caracas, I decided to play a Venezuelan piece. I had often heard of Ricardo Lorenz, a young composer with a most promising international career.[33] He was in the process of completing his PhD studies in Chicago when I telephoned him in July 1997, asking if he had ever composed anything for the cello. He hadn't, although he was especially fond of this instrument.

We agreed that he would compose a piece and have it finished by February 1998, which would give me enough time to prepare it for a premiere in Caracas in May. Our subsequent contacts were not direct—since I was unable to go to Chicago and he couldn't come to Mexico—and we did not speak on the telephone, so our communication was all by e-mail. Before meeting personally, we had already become friends through the computer!

Ricardo began the composition in September 1997. In January 1998, Ricardo's mother died in Caracas, and he flew to Venezuela to spend some time with his family, so it was impossible for him to finish the work by the previously established date. His e-mail dated January 15 reads as follows:

> The work for cello and piano was going very well but has now taken a new, mystical turn. It turns out that I remained in Chicago over the Christmas holidays to work in peace on the composition that, curiously, I had decided to create as an homage to the happiest moments in my mother's life. I had brought it up during my last telephone conversations with her. From the symbolic point of view, it is perhaps one of my most significant works. I hope this will also be true from a musical point of view. I had hoped to finish the piece by the date I had promised. Having to go to Venezuela will undoubtedly set me back. If you need a title, I have one in mind, *Cecilia en azul y verde* (Cecilia in blue and green).

Early in April, one month before the scheduled date of the premiere, Ricardo faxed me the first pages so that Edison and I could begin reviewing it. We received the final version a few days before we flew to Caracas.

By coincidence, Sunday, May 10, the day of the premiere, happened to be Mother's Day. When Edison and I arrived at Quinta Anauco to get ready for the concert, the entire Lorenz family was waiting for us, except for Ricardo, who had to remain in Chicago (Fig. 48). I was immediately captivated by the family's sensitivity, graciousness, and charm. Ana Cecilia Lorenz, the composer's sister, gave me a flower and a card that read, "Maestro Prieto, Our Cecilia thanks you for this beautiful, most timely tribute with the gift of this humble rose, her favorite flower. Thank you. Lorenz family. Ana Cecilia Lorenz Abreu."

Alex Lorenz, her father, told me how moved they were at the prospect of listening to the piece composed by Ricardo in memory of their mother. He explained to me that the title was inspired by a photo of

48. With Venezuelan composer Ricardo Lorenz in Chicago, a little before the premiere of Cecilia en azul y verde *in Caracas, 1998.*

—Cecilia Abreu taken in the garden of her house against a blue and green background.

Cecilia en azul y verde was enthusiastically acclaimed by the public, and we recorded it two months later.

JOSÉ ANTONIO ABREU AND THE NATIONAL SYSTEM OF YOUTH AND CHILDREN'S ORCHESTRAS OF VENEZUELA

The year 1975 was a milestone in the history of Venezuelan music, since it was during this same year that a brilliant musician, economist, and entrepreneur, José Antonio Abreu, finally fulfilled his long-cherished dream of creating an orchestra for young people. The Youth Symphony Orchestra, now known as the Simón Bolívar Symphony Orchestra (OSSB), was not conceived as an isolated project, but rather as the seed of a vast movement called the Sistema Nacional de Orquestas Juveniles e Infantiles de Venezuela (National System of Youth and Children's Orchestras of Venezuela), which has created almost 100 orchestras, the University Institute of Music Studies, a scholarship system, violin-making workshops, etc. This system has completely transformed the country's musical perspective.

The OSSB has earned enthusiastic praise during its numerous concert tours throughout Europe, Latin America, and Japan. Eduardo Mata, the great Mexican conductor, was closely associated with the OSSB, which he conducted for several years prior to his tragic death in an airplane crash in 1995. Mata's contribution to the OSSB was fundamental to the level of excellence it has since attained. A few years before his death, Mata had also recorded a highly acclaimed series of Ibero-American music with this orchestra. Shortly after his death, a poignant tribute was held in his memory at the Teresa Carreño Theatre.

A key factor in the success of the National System of Youth and Children's Orchestras of Venezuela is that its creator and director, José Antonio Abreu, has remained in his post since 1975. Therefore, despite Venezuela's political and financial upheavals since 1967, the system has not been affected, largely because of the unflagging determination and the political and administrative expertise of Abreu and his collaborators. Venezuelan and Latin American music are therefore deeply indebted to them, since the success of the Venezuelan system has inspired several other Latin American countries to implement similar programs. Compared to other Latin American countries, Venezuela came to classical music late. Today, however, it has become one the most dynamic musical centers in the region.

CARACAS, 2000: WILLIAM MOLINA AND THE SIMÓN BOLÍVAR INTERNATIONAL CELLO FESTIVAL

William Molina is an outstanding cellist and teacher. An alumnus of the national system, he later studied at the Paris Conservatory, where he received a first prize. Upon his return to Venezuela, he became the first-chair cello of the Simón Bolívar Symphony Orchestra, and developed into one of Latin America's most important educators. The founder and director of the Latin American Cello Academy, he also coordinates the

Simón Bolívar International Cello Festival in Caracas. José Antonio Abreu and William Molina invited me and my son, conductor Carlos Miguel Prieto, to the 2000 cello festival. Our concert took place on November 17, 2000, with the OSSB, at the Teresa Carreño Theatre, with the following program:

Overture to *The Happy Slaves*   Arriaga (Spain)
Four Verses for Cello and Orchestra (Venezuelan premiere)
      Roberto Sierra (Puerto Rico)
Mirrors in the Sand for cello and orchestra (Venezuelan premiere)
      Arturo Márquez (Mexico)
Intermission
The Night of the Mayas   Silvestre Revueltas (Mexico)

Arturo Márquez was present at the concert, and as an encore, Carlos Miguel and the orchestra played Márquez's extremely popular *Danzón* no. 2 (Fig. 49). Among the cellists who participated in the festival were Arto Noras; Edgar Fischer, from Chile, with his wife, pianist María Iris Radrigán; Jesús Castro-Balbi and his wife, pianist Gloria Yi-Chen Lin; and others. Castro-Balbi was invited as the winner of the Carlos Prieto Cello Competition held in Mexico, which I will discuss later.

BACK IN CARACAS

In February 2003, I once again flew to Caracas, this time to participate in the concert entitled "Homage to the Latin American Cello Academy," directed by William Molina. Once again I played two concertos: the world premiere of the Cello Concerto by Eugenio Toussaint and the Venezuelan premiere of the Cello Concerto by Garrido-Lecca, both conducted by Venezuela's Eduardo Marturet.

At lunch with my friend José Antonio Abreu, I expressed my admiration and amazement regarding the results of the national system he created in 1975 and continues to head. I look forward to future collaborations with José Antonio Abreu, William Molina, and Venezuela's extremely talented group of young cellists.

2003: PREMIERES IN SPAIN, RUSSIA, AND MEXICO

In September in Oviedo, Spain, I played two Spanish premieres: the Adagio and Fugue for cello and orchestra composed in 1948 by my

*49. With Mexican composer Arturo Márquez, and Dr. José Antonio Abreu,
president of the National System of Youth and Children's Orchestras of Venezuela.
Caracas, 2000.*

aunt María Teresa Prieto, and the Cello Concerto of Mexican composer Federico Ibarra. The concert took place at the magnificent new Auditorio Príncipe Felipe.

I spent almost the entire month of October in Russia, where, as described in the previous chapter, I played the world premiere of José Luis Turina's Cello Concerto in St. Petersburg. I barely had time to return to Mexico in November to play another world premiere, that of Spanish composer Tomás Marco's *Laberinto marino* (*Marine Labyrinth*) for cello and strings at the International Music Festival in Morelia.

TOMÁS MARCO AND THE *MARINE LABYRINTH*

Early in 2003 while having dinner with Tomás and María Rosa Marco in Madrid, Tomás unexpectedly handed me an envelope, saying: "Here is a new work for you!" It was the *Marine Labyrinth*. With just one glance, I decided then and there to premiere it at the International Music Festival in Morelia in November, especially since that festival honors a particular country every year, and 2003 happened to be Spain's turn.

Here is what the composer wrote about it:

> This work for cello and string orchestra is the third in a series of compositions written at the encouragement of Mexican cellist Carlos Prieto, as a tribute of admiration and friendship. After *Primer espejo de Falla* for cello and piano and *Partita Piatti* for solo cello, I wanted to write a concert work of a very distinct and concrete nature, so I focused on writing for a smaller, tighter ensemble than the large orchestra required for my 1976 concerto for cello and orchestra. This new work is devised for the soloist, a string orchestra with three violin parts, two viola parts, two cello parts, and one double bass part.[34]

THE CONSERVATORIO DE LAS ROSAS
IN MORELIA, MEXICO

No nation on the continent has such a rich, long-established musical tradition as Mexico. In 1524, barely three years after the conquest, the Franciscan brother Pedro de Gante founded the first music school in the New World. Brother Pedro, who had arrived in 1523, along with two other Franciscan missionaries, went on to complete an impressive project. He learned Nahuatl and devoted himself not only to converting the Indians, but also to teaching them arts and crafts in Tlaxcala, Texcoco, and Mexico City. At the music school, the Indians learned plainsong and the craft of instrument making.

By 1735, when Antonio de Mendoza was appointed the first viceroy of New Spain—as Mexico was then called—Spain started sending a number of eminent composers and teachers to Mexico. Their teachings fell on fertile ground, since even in pre-Columbian times, musicians had enjoyed great prestige and were accorded a privileged status. This helps explain the extraordinary upsurge in music production in New Spain during the sixteenth, seventeenth, and eighteenth centuries, a flowering that was without parallel in the New World.

Founded in Morelia in 1743–1744 as a school for girls, the Colegio de Niñas de Santa Rosa de Santa María (now known as the Las Rosas Conservatory) is the oldest music school in Mexico and probably on the continent. The school has undergone innumerable crises, descriptions of which lie well beyond the scope of this book. However, it unquestionably occupies a very special place in the history of music in Mexico. Its main campus is located in one of the most beautiful and prominent eighteenth-century buildings in the city of Morelia, while the preschool, elementary school, and high school are located in a brand-new campus, inaugurated in 2001.

The conservatory owes a great deal to the vision and determination of Miguel Bernal Jiménez, one of Morelia's greatest composers. He studied at the Pontifical Institute of Sacred Music in Rome, obtaining his master's degree in organ and musical composition and his PhD in Gregorian chant.

My first contact with the Las Rosas Conservatory goes back to 1989 and 1990, when I participated in the second and third International Music Festivals in Morelia and the first Conferences of Latin American Composers. In 1995 I was appointed chairman of the conservatory's foundation, further reinforcing my relationship with this institution. Our goal is for the oldest conservatory in Latin America also to be regarded as its finest. The conservatory has established successful agreements with the University of Texas at Austin and with the Liceu Conservatory of Barcelona.

THE CARLOS PRIETO CELLO COMPETITIONS

The conservatory, the National Council for Culture and the Arts, and the Michoacán government sponsor a biennial cello competition that, despite my objections, bears my name. Instituted as a nationwide

50. The Carlos Prieto Latin American Cello Competition, Morelia, Mexico, 2000.
LEFT TO RIGHT: *Aldo Parisot (judge), William Molina (judge), Arturo Serna (special mention), Claudio Santos Mazzini (2nd place), Jesús Castro-Balbi (1st place), Carlos Prieto, Ilein Bermúdez (3rd place), Gilberto Munguía (judge), Edgar Fisher (judge), and José Luis Gálvez (judge).*

competition in 1998, it was so successful that in 2000 and 2002 it was expanded into a Latin American competition; in 2004 it became an Ibero-American competition, open to all young cellists born or residing in Latin America, Spain, or Portugal; and in 2006 it will be an international competition (Fig. 50).

Music competitions are often unfair. Our goal is to encourage and assist promising young cellists—not only the winners—and to foster the appreciation and performance of Ibero-American cello music. The winners so far have been Juan Hermida (1998), Jesús Castro-Balbi (Peru-United States; 2000), and Dmitri Atapine (Russia-Spain; 2004). (No first prize was awarded in 2002.)

FUTURE PLANS

NEW WORKS

Although I never abandon the traditional repertoire, I continue to encourage composers to write new cello works, which I continue to premiere. It is often a thankless task, since in the time required to study a single new composition, I could easily prepare several programs consisting of older pieces that have earned their rightful place in the repertoire, works whose exceptional quality distinguish them, like the tip of an iceberg, from the enormous mass of mediocre compositions that now are forgotten. By the same token, the passage of time will filter out many contemporary compositions. Consequently, I am sometimes accused of adopting a quixotic attitude, of fighting a losing battle, since a considerable part of my efforts will have been in vain. However, I am inspired by the relentless quest for the masterpieces of the future. If even a small fraction of these works manages to survive, I will be extremely satisfied.

At present, in addition to my scheduled concerts and international tours, I am preparing the world premiere of ten works that are either already in my possession or are being written.

RECORDS

Records are the great medium for the dissemination of music. To date I have recorded eighty works (from the complete Bach Suites for Solo Cello to sixty compositions by composers from Mexico, Latin America, and Spain), as can be seen in Appendix 3.

Part Three

A BRIEF HISTORY OF
MUSIC FOR CELLO FROM
THE TIME OF STRADIVARI
TO THE PRESENT

CHAPTER 7

The Seventeenth and Eighteenth Centuries

THE REPERTOIRE BEFORE 1700

For most of the seventeenth century, the cello was an accompanying instrument, playing the *basso continuo* for religious vocal and instrumental music or for songs and dances. A cello of that time was often adapted to hang from a musician's neck so it could be played either while standing or while walking in processions. With their powerful tone in the lower-pitched registers, these large cellos were perfectly suited to their designated task.

During the last decades of the seventeenth century, the cello's function gradually evolved into occasional solo parts. Among the earliest examples of this particular development we find Corelli's Twelve Trios for Two Violins and Cello, composed in 1683. We should also mention the group of composers who were members of the Accademia dei Filarmonici, founded in Bologna in 1675: Domenico Gabrielli (1651–1690,) Giovanni Battista degli Antoni (1660–1697) and Giuseppe Jacchini (1663–1727), whose works for the cello are remarkably fresh and original. Gabrielli and Jacchini were also highly respected cellists who composed a series of what were then called sonatas for cello and basso continuo.[1]

The oldest known works for cello solo are the following: *Ricercare* (1687) by Giovanni Battista degli Antoni, *Ricercari per violoncello solo, con un canone a due violoncelli e alcuni sonate per violoncello e basso continuo* (1689) by Domenico Gabrielli, and *Trattenimento musicale sopra il violoncello a' solo* (1691) by Domenico Galli. (A ricercare, from the Italian for "to seek," is a musical form common to the sixteenth and seventeenth centuries, rather like a fugue and meant as a technical exercise.)

EARLIEST SONATAS AND CONCERTOS FOR CELLO

By the year 1700, the importance of the cello had increased with the advent of such composers as Alessandro and Domenico Scarlatti, Nicola Porpora, Benedetto Marcello, and, above all, Antonio Vivaldi, whose six sonatas transported the sonata for cello and basso continuo to new heights. Vivaldi was also the first to write concertos for cello and orchestra, composing at least twenty-seven of these pieces.

Undoubtedly, Stradivari's new cello model, designed around 1707, responded to the cellists' need for more comfortable instruments, thus allowing them to play the higher notes with far greater virtuosity than before.

THE SUITES FOR SOLO CELLO BY J. S. BACH

The ricercari of Gabrielli and degli Antoni are perfectly structured works that demand considerable mastery of the cello. Nevertheless, they cannot be compared to the extraordinary legacy bequeathed by Bach in his Six Suites for Cello Solo, the first cardinal work in the history of the cello, which had never before been used for works of such musical richness and technical difficulty. The cello suites date from the period when Bach was Kapellmeister and musical director at Cöthen (1717–1723).

Prince Leopold von Anhalt-Cöthen (1694–1728), an avid music lover, not only played the violin, viola da gamba, and harpsichord, but also had an excellent orchestra comprised of eighteen musicians. During this period Bach composed the majority of his instrumental works and almost all his chamber music, including the three sonatas for gamba and harpsichord, the six suites for cello solo, the three partitas and three sonatas for solo violin, the orchestral suites, and the Brandenburg Concertos. The Cöthen orchestra, which incorporated both the cello and viola da gamba, included cellist Christian Bernhard Linike and gambist Christian Ferdinand Abel, who was also a noteworthy cellist. It is believed that Bach composed the gamba sonatas and cello suites for Abel.

Since the cello had not yet attained its tonal potential in the higher-pitched registers nor in cantabile ("singing manner"), Bach used a tenor instrument, the viola da gamba, for his three sonatas with harpsichord, as he did in several of his cantatas and the mournful passages in his two Passions. In 1756 Leopold Mozart, the father of the composer and a prominent violinist and teacher, wrote, "The viola da gamba differs from the cello in many aspects. It has six or even seven strings, while the

'bassel' (cello) has only four. They are tuned in a totally different manner; it has a more pleasurable sound and is used for higher registers than
those of the cello."[2]

In the suites for solo cello, Bach ventured into new territory for both
himself and music. It has been said that by composing his cello suites
Bach pursued a didactic objective, apart from the purely musical aspect,
as in the case of Two- and Three-Part Inventions and the first part of his
Well-Tempered Clavier. We know that Bach, most famous as an organist
and harpsichordist, was also an excellent violinist and violist. The partitas and sonatas are palpable proofs of his extraordinary command of the
violin, but there are no indications that he played the cello. It is possible,
therefore, that the somewhat didactic nature of the suites resulted from
Bach's desire to explore the potential of the cello, since its technique was
far less developed than that of the violin. Indeed, the technical difficulty
clearly increases from one suite to another.

In regard to these pieces, Adolfo Salazar observed the following:
"Bach's gigantic effort to encompass polyphonic voices in one single
instrument makes his sonatas, suites and partitas for solo violin and
cello—without a bass accompaniment—so difficult that we can barely
understand how they were even played at the time."[3]

The suite, a musical composition of French origin, is exactly what
the name indicates: a succession or series of movements, based on dance
forms in this case. Originally the Baroque suite consisted of four movements: allemande, courante, sarabande, and gigue. In his cello suites,
Bach added a prelude as a first movement and inserted a pair of *galant*
dances, or *galanteries*, between the sarabande and the gigue. All the suites
follow the same order: prelude, allemande, courante, sarabande, galan-
terie, gigue. The galant dances are two minuets in Suites 1 and 2, two
bourrées in Suites 3 and 4, and two gavottes in Suites 5 and 6. The freely
structured preludes are introductory movements, exemplars of Bach's incomparable improvisational skill. Each prelude endows the corresponding suite with its general character. The rest of the movements are based
on dances.

The allemande, obviously from Germany, was, in Bach's time, a dance
form with a fluid but reflective character, generally written in 4/4 time.

The courante was a dance of French origin, and the verb *courir* ("to
run") describes its rapid tempo. The courante has two versions: the Italian courante, in 3/4 time, and the French courante, somewhat slower
and with a more nervous rhythm, composed in 3/2 time.

The sarabande, of Spanish origin, was so widespread in New Spain that at one time it was even regarded as its birthplace. Fray Diego de Durán noted that before 1579 the sarabande, extremely popular in New Spain, was endowed with a "sinful sensuality."[4] As a result, it was banned by the Inquisition, not only in New Spain, but also throughout the entire Spanish Empire. By Bach's time, however, the dance had lost its obscene, lascivious connotation. All the sarabandes of the cello suites are slow, equivalent to the adagios of classical sonatas.

The galant movements originate from old French dances. The minuetto, or minuet, was meant to be danced gracefully, with small, dainty steps, as denoted by its etymology: *pas menu* ("small step"). The bourrée, whose name is derived from the verb *bourrir* (Old French for "to flap like wings"), is typical of the Auvergne region whereas the gavottes were dances performed by Gavots, inhabitants of the French Dauphiné region.

Finally, there is the gigue, probably derived from the Irish word *jig*. Both the dance and the term itself were transported from Ireland to England and then on to the continent.

Suite 1 in G Major is the least complicated, both musically and technically, and like Suite 2, predominately uses the cello's easiest tonal registers.

For Suite 3, in C Major, Bach expanded the dynamic range to take full advantage of the resonance produced by the lowest string, C, and by chords featuring predominantly open strings. From the very onset, the majestic prelude, its downward scales producing veritable cascades of sound, this suite is truly impressive indeed.

Suite 4, with its problematic tonality in E-flat major and abrupt bow jumps between the most distant strings—C and A—presents a whole new series of challenges.

Suite 5, in C minor, is the most dramatic and profound of the six; it requires an exceptional understanding of music and absolute technical command of the cello. The prelude starts off with a somber section, after which comes the only fugue to be found in the six suites, a truly extraordinary feat of polyphonic composition for a primarily monophonic instrument. The sarabande is one of the most solemn, sublime movements in all of Bach's work. This suite is written for a *discordato* cello, that is, a cello tuned in a different manner, since the A string must be moved down one tone, to G. The *scordatura* ("being out of tune") allows for the execution of certain chords and also gives the cello a darker tone, perfectly suited to the profound, dramatic quality of this particular suite.[5]

Bach originally conceived Suite 6 for a cello with five strings instead of usual four. According to a popular theory, Bach invented a large viola called *viola pomposa* for this particular suite. But I believe that he actually composed it for a *violoncello piccolo*, similar, in fact, to the smaller Stradivari model, except for its five strings. In this particular suite, Bach must have sensed that the cello had untapped potential. And indeed, cellists of the time used less than half the tonal range of the cello, since they did not yet use the so-called "thumb position," which allows for the playing of extremely high notes.

Bach's solution, therefore, was to add a fifth, and higher, string: an E, a fifth above the A. Besides the presence of a fifth string, Suite 6 differs from the previous suites in its technical demands: numerous double stops, chords, and extremely fast tempi. Its grandiose scale and joyful spirit make Suite 6 the perfect culmination of this extraordinary cycle.

There is no data available on the first performances of the suites. Most likely Bach composed them for the palace, without ever imagining that they would be performed elsewhere, much less in public. However, we know that after his death they were consigned to oblivion, like most of his works. The original manuscripts of the cello suites and the violin sonatas and partitas were lost. The first publication of the violin pieces (1802) and the cello works (1825) were based on rather slipshod copies made by Bach's second wife, Anna Magdalena.

In 1890, a sensational discovery took place: the original manuscript of the partitas and sonatas for violin was found in Munich. It turned out to be among Bach's most beautiful manuscripts, written with exceptional clarity. Johannes Brahms, an avid collector of autographed manuscripts, was so enthralled when he saw it that he was about to purchase it himself, although as he later stated in a letter, "It is impossible to set a price on a treasure such as this."[6]

The importance of this discovery lies in the fact that it immediately clarified the errors in Anna Magdalena's copy, and because Bach himself had very distinctly marked the bowing, we have a clearer idea of the author's intentions and the correct phrasing in each movement. Joseph Joachim, who was the first violinist to play these works in public, first saw the manuscript in 1892, after which he prepared a new, far more accurate edition, the first to be based on the original source.

On the other hand, the original manuscript for the cello suites has never been found, although two additional copies produced by two of Bach's pupils, Johann Peter Kellner and Wolfgang Westphal, were discovered in 1960. Comparing these different copies turns out to be a useful exercise in the never-ending search for the ideal interpretation of Bach's cello solo suites, an incomparable musical crown jewel of the cello repertoire.

FRANCISCELLO (1691–1739) AND THE DEVELOPMENT OF CELLO TECHNIQUE

Cellist Francesco Alborea—better known as Franciscello—is thought to have been the first to use thumb position, an invaluable contribution to the technique of cello playing. We know very little about Franciscello except that his contemporaries considered him "supernatural." Quantz, who heard him play with Alessandro Scarlatti, proclaimed him "incomparable" and "outstanding." Scarlatti himself claimed that "only an angel could play like Franciscello."[7]

Franciscello's technique was then adopted by Jean-Baptiste Stuck (1680–1755), also known as Batistin, who had gone to France as a member of Louis XIV's orchestra. Franciscello's basic principles, as well as his thumb-position technique were subsequently incorporated into a treatise written by Michel Corrette in 1741, entitled *Méthode théorique et pratique pour apprendre en peu de temps le violoncelle dans sa perfection* (Theoretical and Practical Method for Learning How to Play the Cello Perfectly within a Short Time).

GIUSEPPE TARTINI (1692–1770) AND CARL PHILIPP EMANUEL BACH (1714–1788)

Although not widely known, the two cello concertos by Tartini—one of the great eighteenth-century violinists and composers—and the three concertos by Carl Philipp Emanuel Bach, J. S. Bach's second-eldest son, are certainly well worth playing.

LUIGI BOCCHERINI (1743–1805), THE FIRST GREAT MODERN CELLO VIRTUOSO

Luigi Boccherini, the first great modern cello virtuoso and the only outstanding cellist who was also a distinguished composer, took full advantage of every improvement in instrumental technique made so far.[8]

He was born in 1743 in Lucca, a village near Florence; he first studied with his father, Leopoldo, a double bass player and cellist. When still very young, Boccherini dazzled audiences in Italy and Vienna with interpretations of his own cello works. He spent a year in Milan, where he created what was probably the first string quartet in history: Filippo Manfredi, first violin; Pietro Nardini, second violin; Giovanni Giuseppe Cambini, viola; and himself, cello.

In 1768, the same year Boccherini acquired a Stradivari cello, fame and fortune smiled upon him when, together with Manfredi, he presented a hugely successful series of concerts in Paris, and Parisian editors fiercely competed for the publication of his works. While in Paris, Boccherini and Manfredi became acquainted with the ambassador from Spain, Count de Fuentes, who painted a dazzling picture of the Spanish court.

Armed with the ambassador's effusive letters of recommendation, Boccherini and Manfredi traveled to Madrid in 1768. However, their idyllic image of the court was soon shattered. Its musical activity had declined considerably since 1759, after the death of Queen Bárbara de Braganza, who had been Scarlatti's pupil. But Boccherini's life took a favorable turn in 1770, when he was granted a position as cellist and composer in the orchestra of Prince Luis, the younger brother of Charles III.

The members of the orchestra included Boccherini's friend Manfredi and a family of musicians, the Fonts, with whom he immediately struck up a close friendship. Since the father and his three sons formed a string quartet, Boccherini had only to add his cello in order to create a new kind of musical ensemble: the two-cello quintet, for which he composed over one hundred pieces.

Boccherini was an extraordinarily prolific composer. He wrote ten concertos for cello and approximately thirty sonatas, all of which deserve far greater recognition. It is a curious paradox that his most famous concerto, the Concerto in B-flat Major, is not, in fact, all his own, since it was rewritten—with a great many alterations—by the German cellist Friedrich Grützmacher. Although the concerto's second movement, an adagio, is indeed Boccherini's, it comes from a different concerto, and Grützmacher substantially altered the two allegros, the first and third movements, as well.

FRANZ JOSEPH HAYDN (1732–1809)

As kapellmeister at Prince Esterházy's court from 1778 to 1790, Haydn usually conducted the orchestra either from his place as concertmaster or from the harpsichord, depending on the circumstance. Between 1761 and 1769 the cellist in the orchestra was Joseph Weigl, who was followed by Anton Kraft, one of the most prominent cellists of the period. For a time, Haydn taught composition to Kraft, and undoubtedly learned a great deal about the cello from both Weigl and Kraft, as can be clearly seen in his concertos in C major and D major, whose importance and beauty accord them a special place in the cello repertoire.

The Concerto in C Major is a curious case indeed. Although its existence was corroborated by Haydn himself in his catalogue of his works—the *Entwurf-Katalog* that he began in late 1765—the manuscript had since disappeared. Finally, in 1961, a copy was discovered in the Radenin Archives of the National Museum of Prague.[9] Since then, the concerto has immediately captivated audiences the world over. The Concerto in C Major, composed between 1762 and 1765, was probably written for Joseph Weigl.

The Concerto in D Major, dated 1783, was erroneously attributed to Anton Kraft. Today, however, there is no doubt that Haydn actually composed the piece, probably for Anton Kraft, who premiered it. On the other hand, some concertos for cello and orchestra originally attributed to Haydn have been called into question, since there is no documented evidence for verifying their authenticity.

WOLFGANG AMADEUS MOZART (1756–1791) AND HIS APPARENT DISDAIN FOR THE CELLO

Mozart's apparent disdain for the cello puzzles and disconcerts cellists, especially since he composed so many memorable pieces for other instruments. To imagine what he might have composed for the cello, we need only think of his violin concertos; the Sinfonia Concertante for violin, viola and orchestra; his duets for violin and viola; and the sonatas for violin and piano.

The cello's relative novelty as a solo instrument could not possibly have been the reason. Mozart, whose curiosity was always open to all musical creations, was undoubtedly familiar with Vivaldi's and Boccherini's concertos, as well those of Haydn, whom he greatly admired. He was also probably well acquainted with the art of such cello virtuosos, so celebrated in Vienna, as Anton Kraft and his son Nikolaus, and certainly with the work of his friend, Carl Philipp Emanuel Bach, who had written several highly commendable cello concertos. On the other hand, Mozart had probably not heard of Bach's cello suites, since by that time Bach's music, regarded as old-fashioned, was almost forgotten. Perhaps the real reason is due to no cellist ever having asked Mozart to write a concerto or a sonata, since at that time nobody composed except on commission.

King Frederick William II of Prussia, son of Frederick the Great and a competent amateur cellist in his own right, certainly deserves our deepest gratitude for commissioning numerous cello works from the principal composers of the time. Among these were Mozart's last three string quartets (the "Prussian" quartets), which were obviously dedicated to the king and which accord the cello a particularly significant role.

Mozart's famous Sinfonia Concertante for violin, viola, and orchestra was initially conceived with a solo cello part, as several manuscript drafts confirm, but Mozart finally decided to discard it. In 1782, he began work on an Andantino in B-Flat Major for Cello and Orchestra, abandoned it after writing only thirty-three bars.[10] We also know that Mozart composed a concerto for cello and orchestra, K. 206a, but unfortunately the manuscript was lost, and there is no information on whether it was ever performed during the composer's lifetime.[11]

THE END OF THE SONATA PERIOD FOR CELLO AND CONTINUO

The sonata for cello and continuo was a fundamental genre in the repertoire of this instrument. Practically all the sonatas written before Beethoven's time, including those by Vivaldi, Marcello, Scarlatti, and Boccherini belonged to this genre. The word *continuo* is used because the harpsichord has a continuous line of low notes in the harmony that are sometimes "figured," that is, beneath each note of the continuo, the composer wrote the harmonic complement by using numbers, for example, 5 or 6/4. This figured bass could be played, or "executed," in different ways, which required the harpsichordist to have considerable expertise in order to avoid errors of harmony.[12]

At present, since few musicians are able to master the figured bass, these sonatas are generally played in modern versions in which the figured part has been written for piano by various authors. Thus, for example, there are at least six different versions of the continuo part for Vivaldi's sonatas.

Boccherini's sonatas were composed for *violoncello solo e basso*. We do not know for certain what instrument was intended to play the basso. It could have been the harpsichord, the double bass, or even the violin, as illustrations of the time suggest. Today his sonatas tend to be played with harpsichord or piano accompaniment. What remains clear, however, is that the requirement for a solo cello is explicit, since these particular sonatas were especially meant to highlight the lyrical and virtuosic qualities of the cellist; thus, there is no justifiable reason for the elaborate piano versions written by some composers.

CHAPTER 8

From Beethoven to the End of the Nineteenth Century

The eighteenth and nineteenth centuries lacked figures of the personality and magnetism needed to raise the cello to the same prominence as the piano or violin. For example, no cellist was like Paganini, who astonished all of Europe with his virtuoso demonstrations of the violin's extraordinary potential. For the piano, we need recall only the glorious heights attained at the piano by Mozart and Beethoven or, years later, Chopin and Liszt. This explains why most nineteenth-century composers were more attracted to writing concertos, sonatas, and other works for the violin and for the piano, and why the repertoire for these instruments is so extensive.

This is also the reason for the limited repertoire of memorable cello compositions from the Romantic era. Neither Beethoven, nor Brahms, nor Tchaikovsky ever wrote a cello concerto, although Beethoven composed the Triple Concerto for Violin, Cello, Piano and Orchestra and Brahms wrote the Double Concerto for Violin, Cello, and Orchestra.

The basic repertoire for cello and piano comprises sonatas by Beethoven, Schubert, Mendelssohn, Brahms, Chopin, Grieg, Saint-Saëns, and Richard Strauss. Few nineteenth-century works for cello and orchestra have managed to stand the test of time and be incorporated into the standard repertoire. Most cellists would agree that the works that should be included are, among others, Beethoven's aforementioned Triple Concerto (1804), Schumann's Concerto (1850), the first concerto by Saint-Saëns (1873), Tchaikovsky's Rococo Variations (1876), Brahms's Double Concerto (1887), Lalo's Concerto (1887), Dvořák's Concerto (1895), and Richard Strauss's *Don Quixote* (1897).

LUDWIG VON BEETHOVEN (1770–1827)

We will examine Beethoven's work in detail, not only because his music marked a rupture with the past but also because it paved the way for the future evolution of the cello.

By Beethoven's time, the term *sonata* had acquired a different meaning, since it now applied to an entirely new musical form and genre, so much so that it is misleading to apply exactly the same term to sonatas by Vivaldi and by Beethoven. "Sonata form," invented by Haydn and other composers, was later developed by Mozart and Beethoven.[1] It defines the characteristics of the first movement of symphonies and of chamber works such as duets, trios, quartets, etc. The term *sonata* is also applied to a genre of unaccompanied works for instruments like the piano, or to duets (for violin and piano, for cello and piano, etc.,) whose first movement corresponds to sonata form.

To avoid confusion, we will therefore refer to the Baroque sonata, such as Vivaldi's, and to the new classical sonata. Since neither Haydn nor Mozart explored this genre for the cello, the first classical sonatas for cello and piano were those written by Beethoven.

The five sonatas can be assigned to the three periods commonly employed for classifying Beethoven's work: the first two are his op. 5; the third, op. 69, comes from his middle period; and the fourth and fifth, op. 102, from his last period. The two sonatas of op. 5 were composed in 1796 for French virtuoso Jean-Pierre Duport, who was at the service of Prussia's King Frederick William II, to whom they are dedicated. Both sonatas were premiered in Berlin in the presence of the king, with Duport at the cello and Beethoven at the piano. As could be expected from a composer who was an exceptional pianist, the piano part is brilliant and masterful; the sonatas composed at the same time by cellists Kraft, Bréval, and Duport were still characterized by the figured accompaniment for continuo, or, in other words, an accompaniment that, within certain limits, was subject to improvisation.

Three additional works reflect Beethoven's enthusiasm for the piano-cello combination: two series of variations on themes from Mozart's *Magic Flute* and the variations on the theme from Handel's *Judas Maccabaeus*. With this group of works, and especially with the sonatas, Beethoven established the combination of piano and cello as an authentic duo by elevating the piano from the role of mere accompanist to an equal partnership in the musical dialogue. This case is precisely the opposite of what occurred with the violin. Sonatas for violin and piano originated from the sonatas for harpsichord with violin obbligato, in which the violin part simply doubled up the right hand of the harpsichord and occasionally the left hand.

The third sonata, op. 69, dates from 1808, one of the most productive years of his life, when he composed the two piano trios of op. 70 and the Fifth and Sixth Symphonies. In his third sonata, Beethoven achieved an ideal balance between the piano and cello parts. It has often been said that this sonata is one of the best-written works for these two instruments. It is also, perhaps, the most frequently played of all cello sonatas. The easy, lighthearted flow of the piece might suggest that Beethoven composed it in during one of his rare moments of happiness. However, the following words appear on the manuscript: *Inter lacrimas et luctum* (Between tears and sadness).

In an undated letter, though it must have been around 1815, Beethoven sent the following message to his friend, the cellist Joseph Linke, "Dear Linke, be so good as to have breakfast with me early tomorrow morning, as early as you like, but not later than half past seven. Bring a cello bow with you, for I have something to discuss with you."[2] What Beethoven wanted to show him was the manuscript or advanced drafts of his last two sonatas for cello and piano, those of op. 102.

Both works belong to the same world of abstraction and extraordinary depth as his last piano sonatas and the last string quartets. The two sonatas received a hostile reaction from the public and critics alike—the fugue that concludes the fifth sonata was especially reviled—as occurred with the rest of his works from this particular period. The fugue in question had cost Beethoven a tremendous effort, attested to by the numerous drafts of the movement.

When analyzing and playing these sonatas, one must recall the type of pianos used at the time. The piano was undergoing constant modifications during Beethoven's life. He owned several different pianos, including an Anton Walter (Vienna, 1785), an Erard (France, 1803), a Broadwood (England, 1817), and a Graf (Vienna, 1825). Although each had a different tone, they had similar components: relatively lightweight wood, and fine strings that were not subject to strong tension. Modern pianos—no more than a century old—are equipped with a sturdy steel structure, specially designed to withstand the approximately thirty tons of combined tension produced by much thicker strings. The pianos of Beethoven's time were distinguished by their crystal-clear, transparent tone, rather than by the power characterizing modern pianos. I would venture to say that every present-day violinist or cellist who plays Beethoven's sonatas or trios has, at one time or another, asked the pianist to play less forte, so as not to "cover" the sound of the string instrument, especially the cello.

This type of problem certainly did not exist at that time, and in fact, the exact opposite may have been true. The very titles of the different sonatas clearly illustrate the evolution of the piano. The two sonatas of op. 5 are entitled *Deux grandes sonates pour le clavecin ou piano-forte avec un violoncelle obligé*, whereas the third, which no longer mentions the harpsichord, bears the following title on the cover: *Grande sonate pour pianoforte et violoncelle*. The last two are called *Sonates pour le piano et le violoncelle*.

Beethoven never considered the possibility of composing a concert for cello and orchestra, although he spent considerable time with several of the most distinguished cellists of his era, such as Jean-Louis Duport, Jean-Pierre Duport, Nikolaus Kraft, and Joseph Linke. In his youth, Beethoven played viola in a string quartet with Franz Ries, first violin; Andreas Romberg, second violin; and the great Bernhard Romberg, cello.

There may be several reasons why Beethoven did not compose a cello concerto. On one hand, cellists like the Duport brothers, Kraft, Romberg, and others played only their own cello concertos. According to one witness, when Beethoven's first Rasumovsky Quartet was initially rehearsed in Moscow, "Romberg seized the cello part and trampled it underfoot as a piece of unworthy mystification."[3] On the other hand, anyone interested in commissioning a cello concerto from Beethoven probably lacked the resources to do so. A good number of Beethoven's works were commissioned at high prices, such as the three quartets of op. 59, dedicated to Count Razumovsky; the three quartets, opp. 127, 130, and 132, dedicated to Prince Nikolai Galitsïn; the Mass in C, op. 86, commissioned by Prince Esterházy; the sonatas for piano, opp. 78 and 79, commissioned by the editor and musician Clementi (and dedicated to Countess Therese von Brunsvik), and several other works.

Beethoven's understanding of the cello's potential is clearly evident in his sonatas, trios, quartets, and above all in his Triple Concerto in A Major for Violin, Cello, Piano, and Orchestra (1804). The idea of a Triple Concerto did not just come to Beethoven like a bolt from the blue. There are long drafts of another triple concerto, which Beethoven abandoned before returning to this genre years later.

FRANZ SCHUBERT (1797–1828)

The sonata *Arpeggione* occupies a special place in the cello repertoire because it was composed in 1824 for an instrument called the *arpeggione*, invented by Johann Georg Stauffer the previous year. A cross between a guitar and a cello, the arpeggione had six strings, no corners (like a guitar), and frets on its fingerboard. Like the cello, it was played with a bow and held between the knees. However, the instrument was abandoned almost immediately, and Schubert's sonata remained in limbo. The ideal instrument to substitute for the arpeggione was the cello. The sonata is endowed with the typical Schubertian charm, and since the cello repertoire was relatively sparse, transcriptions were soon made for the cello, so the *Arpeggione* has survived as a cello and piano sonata.

FELIX MENDELSSOHN (1809–1847)

Mendelssohn composed four works for cello and piano: the *Variations concertantes*, op. 17 (1829); two sonatas, op. 45 (1838) and op. 58 (1843); and *Song without Words*, op. 109 (undated, possibly 1845). The *Variations concertantes*—one theme and eight variations—have only a limited appeal. Although the first sonata is a fine work, it is somewhat superficial, and the cello part is weak in relation to the piano part. The second sonata is far more interesting in every way. Consisting of four movements, Allegro assai vivace, Allegretto scherzando, Adagio, and Molto allegro vivace, it has a more dramatic, expressive character and better balance. The *Song without Words* is an exquisite composition, worthy of the finest pieces Mendelssohn ever composed for this genre.

FRÉDÉRIC CHOPIN (1810–1849)

Frédéric Chopin left us two works from entirely different periods: the Introduction and Polonaise Brillante, op. 3, (1830) and the Cello Sonata, op. 65 (1847), written for the French cellist Auguste Franchomme. In both works one can clearly appreciate the composer's essentially pianistic nature, since he assigned a dominant role to the piano; however, the Largo contains some of the most beautiful lyrical pages Chopin ever wrote.

ROBERT SCHUMANN (1810–1856)

Schumann was a cellist in his youth. The expressive qualities of the cello, encompassing both elegiac chant and an exhilarating, passionate musical discourse, are perfectly attuned to Schumann's Romanticism, exemplified in his Cello Concerto in A Minor, op. 129, one of the concertos with the most impressive thematic beauty in the entire repertoire. Schumann conceived this work as a "concert piece for cello with an accompanying orchestra," a perfect description indeed, since it is absolutely devoid of the "rivalry" between the soloist and the orchestra characteristic of other concertos. Schumann composed the concerto quickly. He began the first draft on October 10, 1850, and finished the complete score ten days later. However, the work remained unperformed for a number of years: it was premiered in June 1860 when the Oldenburg Chapel Orchestra in Leipzig and its principal cellist, Ludwig Ebert, played it for the first time, during an evening dedicated to the composer on what would have been his fiftieth birthday.[4]

It was a long time before the concerto was actually incorporated into the standard repertoire, since it was played for a second time only in 1867, when David Popper premiered it in Breslau (Wroclaw).[5] Schumann's only original work for cello and piano is the *Fünf Stücke im Volkston* (Five Pieces in the Popular Style), op. 102. However, several of his other works are included in the repertoire, such as his own transcriptions for cello and piano of two beautiful pieces: the Adagio and Allegro, op. 70, and the *Fantasiestücke*, op.73, originally written for horn and piano and for clarinet and piano, respectively.

CAMILLE SAINT-SAËNS (1835–1921)

Camille Saint-Saëns composed two sonatas for cello and piano, op. 32 (1873) and op. 123 (1905). The first has disappeared from the current repertoire, and even the second, although vastly more interesting, is rarely performed.

Of his two concertos for cello and orchestra, op. 33 (1873) and op. 119 (1902), the former has earned a privileged position as an indisputable favorite among audiences and cellists alike. Although it does not aspire to great musical depth, it is perfectly structured, and its orchestration is ideal for a cello concerto. The orchestra, comprising the usual number of musicians, is richer and more sonorous than that called for in Schumann's concerto, and yet never overpowers the cello. I learned from Mstislav Rostropovich that when Shostakovich first conceived his first cello concerto, he analyzed the principal scores of past concertos and came to the conclusion that no orchestration was as perfect as Saint-Saëns'.

Few pieces in the cello repertoire are as popular as "The Swan," a movement from the *Carnival of the Animals*, originally written for cello and two pianos.

PYOTR ILICH TCHAIKOVSKY (1840–1893)

Although at one time Tchaikovsky contemplated writing a cello concerto similar in length to his piano and violin concertos, he never actually got around to it. He composed only two works for cello and orchestra, but neither was conceived on the monumental scale of his two concertos: the enchanting, virtuosic Variations on a Rococo Theme, op. 33, and the *Pezzo capriccioso*, op. 62. He also made transcriptions for cello and orchestra of the Andante cantabile from the String Quartet no. 1, op. 11 and the Nocturne, op. 10, no. 1.

Tchaikovsky composed his Variations on a Rococo Theme in December 1876, a few months before he wrote his Fourth Symphony and the opera *Eugene Onegin*. The theme he selected—in true eighteenth-century style—as well as the seven virtuoso variations, divided by orchestral interludes and cadenzas, reflect his great admiration for Mozart. His passages of extreme virtuosity, exploiting all the technical possibilities of the solo instrument, alternate with elegant, joyful cantilenas. This piece was written for cellist Wilhelm Fitzenhagen, who convinced the composer to suppress one of the eight original variations and alter their order. However, several cellists prefer the original version, published a few years ago, to the "definitive" version.

The *Pezzo capriccioso*, written in 1887 and dedicated to Anatoly Brandukov, consists of two parts: a slow, dramatic introduction (andante) and a dazzling scherzo.

EDOUARD LALO (1823–1892)

The Concerto in D Minor by French composer Edouard Lalo was written in 1877. Its three movements, Allegro maestoso, Intermezzo, and Allegro vivace, are characterized by bright melodious themes and rhythms inspired by Spanish popular music. The transparent orchestration never covers the soloist, and the concerto has become established as one of the favorite of the Romantic repertoire, although never quite attaining the popularity of his *Symphonie espagnole* for violin and orchestra. Pablo Casals made his historic Paris debut in 1899 playing Lalo's Cello Concerto.

EDVARD GRIEG (1843–1907)

In 1882–1883, Grieg wrote his Cello Sonata in A Minor, consisting of three movements: Allegro agitato, Andante molto tranquillo, and Allegro molto e marcato. A fine piece that deserves to be played more often, it was premiered by cellist Friedrich Grützmacher and Grieg in Dresden in 1883. Pablo Casals subsequently played it several times with the composer at the piano.

JOHANNES BRAHMS (1833–1897)

Along with those by Beethoven, the two sonatas by Johannes Brahms—veritable masterpieces—are among the most frequently performed in recitals.

Brahms had been attracted to the cello since he was a young man. He composed a duet for cello and piano that he played in Hamburg once, but unfortunately he destroyed it during one of his bouts of self-deprecation.

In 1862 Brahms wrote three movements of what eventually became his Cello Sonata no. 1, but he did not actually complete the fugue for the finale until 1867. Prior to its publication, he eliminated an Adagio from the original four movements. One copy of the Adagio survived until the 1930s, when it ultimately joined the long list of lost works.

In its final version, the Cello Sonata no. 1 in E Minor, op. 38, consists of three movements. Concluded when Brahms was thirty-two, it was undoubtedly the most important cello sonata since Beethoven's death. It is also the first of the seven sonatas that Brahms wrote for various instruments and piano: three violin sonatas, two cello sonatas, and two clarinet sonatas.

The first movement is a splendid Allegro non troppo, characterized by the nobility of its themes, and the second—Allegretto quasi menuetto—is endowed with a melancholy grace. The finale is a three-voice fugue whose theme was inspired by Bach.[6] Its abrupt, tempestuous style evokes the fugue from Beethoven's last cello sonata.

Twenty years later Brahms composed his Cello Sonata no. 2 in F Major, op. 99 (1886), a colossal work dedicated to cellist Robert Hausmann. This sonata, comprising four movements, is far more complex and much longer than the first, as well as being distinguished by the richness of its thematic content, tortured development, and rich contrasts.

In 1975, cellists were presented with what seemed an extraordinary gift: Brahms's third sonata for cello. I am referring to the publication of his sonata for violin and piano op. 78, thought to have been transcribed for cello by the composer himself. Unfortunately, further research has established that the transcription was the work of Paul Klengel.[7] Not content with merely transcribing, Klengel changed the key from G major to D major and incorporated 200 additional modifications, some in the cello part and others in the piano part.[8]

In 1887, when Brahms composed his Double Concerto, there was not yet a prototype for a concerto that featured a violin and a cello. In fact, the few cello concertos existing at the time were seldom performed, including Schumann's, with whom Brahms sustained a long friendship. It is possible that Brahms's models were Bach's Double Concerto for two violins, Mozart's *Sinfonia concertante* for violin and viola, and Beethoven's Triple Concerto.

In a letter written in August 1887, Brahms wrote Clara Schumann that he had an "amusing idea" for his double concerto, adding:

If it is at all successful it might give us some fun. You can well imagine the sort of pranks one can play in such a case. But do not imagine too much! I ought to have handed on the idea to someone who knows the violin better than I do (Joachim has unfortunately given up composing). It is a very different matter writing for instruments whose nature and sound one only has a chance acquaintance with, or only hears in one's mind, from writing for an instrument that one knows as thoroughly as I know the piano. For in the latter case I know exactly what I write and why I write it as I do. But we will wait and see. Joachim and Hausmann want to try it.[9]

Brahms asked Joachim and Hausmann to meet him in Baden-Baden on September 21, 1887, so that they could examine the score together. They played it for the first time with Brahms at the piano. Joachim objected to the fact that it was not in true concerto style—it is virtually a symphony with two soloists—but Brahms was so pleased that two days later he scheduled a second reading of the score with the municipal orchestra that he himself conducted. On October 18, it was premiered in Cologne with the same soloists.

Its originality, depth, and beauty make the Double Concerto a truly extraordinary composition. The problem of achieving a balance between the cello and the violin was resolved by Brahms, who used the cello, often solo, to introduce the concerto's principal themes.

RICHARD STRAUSS (1864–1949)

Richard Strauss composed two works for cello: the Sonata in F Major, op. 6 (1883), and the symphonic poem *Don Quixote*, op. 35 (1897). The Sonata in F Major was written in his youth, when he was barely nineteen. Little in this piece suggests the future evolution of the composer. It is an attractive sonata, conceived in a traditional manner, often reminiscent of Mendelssohn and Brahms; the cello part reflects his thorough understanding of stringed instruments, a testament to his early training as a violinist.

Don Quixote, a symphonic poem for cello, viola, and orchestra, consists of an introduction followed by ten "fantastic variations" and a finale. It is a programmatic work, based on the novel *Don Quixote*: the cello representing Quixote and the viola taking the part of Sancho Panza. Each variation is based on a chapter of the book, and the music, which is extremely original and imaginative, closely adheres to Cervantes's text.

ANTONIN DVOŘÁK (1841–1904)

It is a little known fact that Dvořák composed his first cello concerto in 1865, in his youth. The work obviously did not satisfy him, since he neither orchestrated it nor gave it an opus number.[10]

For several years, Bohemian cellist Hanus Wihan, Dvořák's friend and classmate at the Prague Conservatory, tried to convince him to compose another concerto, but Dvořák only agreed to write him two short pieces for cello and piano, *Silent Woods*, op. 68, no. 5, and the Rondo, op. 94. Both were so successful that he subsequently created orchestral versions of them.

In March 1894, during his sojourn in the United States, Dvořák heard Victor Herbert, a U.S. cellist and composer of Irish origin, play his own Concerto no. 2 for Cello and Orchestra in Brooklyn. Favorably impressed with this work, Dvořák finally decided to listen to Wihan and compose a cello concerto. The result was the Cello Concerto in B Minor, op. 104, the last work that Dvořák composed during his three-year stint (1892–1895) in New York as the director of the National Conservatory.

He started working on the composition by the end of 1894. That winter, the composer felt an intense nostalgia for his family and homeland. Perhaps this is why, of all the works he composed in the United States, this concerto is the least influenced by American folk music. The second movement contains a quote from his *"Lasst mich allein"* ("Leave me alone"), the favorite song of his sister-in-law Josefina Cermáková, to whom the composer had been deeply attached since his youth; she was now gravely ill in Bohemia. Dvořák finished the third and last movement in New York in February 1895. The conclusion of this movement was, however, thoroughly revised upon his return to Bohemia, as a note in the new, definitive manuscript shows: "I finished the concerto in New York, but when I returned to Bohemia, I completely changed the conclusion, as it appears here."[11]

It is possible that the reason for this change was Dvořák's overwhelming grief over his sister-in-law's death in May 1895. He then replaced six bars of the triumphal crescendo leading into the final section with sixty-four bars of sad contemplative music in tribute to his sister-in-law's memory.

Dvořák dedicated the concerto to his friend the cellist Hanus Wihan. Wihan suggested a few changes, and Dvořák accepted all of them except for a great cadenza that ran totally contrary to his ideas. In a letter dated October 1895 to his publisher, Simrock, Dvořák states: "There is no *cadenza* ... the *finale* concludes with a gradual *diminuendo*, like a sigh, reminiscent of the first and second movements. The solo cello decreases to a *pianissimo*, only to increase once again, leading into several bars of an orchestral *tutti*, bringing the piece to a tempestuous conclusion."[12] It is quite probable that because of these differences between Wihan and Dvořák, it was English cellist Leo Stern who premiered the concerto in London on March 19, 1896, with the Philharmonic Society Orchestra conducted by Dvořák himself.

Dvořák's concerto for cello and orchestra is a masterpiece from beginning to end, and for many musicians it is the indisputable king of cello concertos. Brahms, a friend and admirer of Dvořáks, was familiar with the concerto, and in a letter to Simrock he described it as "a great and excellent work."[13] Brahms's opinions are well known, since he expressed them to the cellist Robert Hausmann: "Why on earth didn't I know that one could write a cello concerto such as this? If I had only known it, I would have written one long ago."[14] Sadly, this occurred when Brahms had practically stopped composing (he died a few months later). Thank goodness Dvořák heard Victor Herbert's concerto in time!

CHAPTER 9

The Twentieth and Twenty-first Centuries: The Cello Comes of Age

As we have seen, over the past few centuries the cello did not receive as much attention from composers as the violin and piano did. On the other hand, the twentieth century produced a veritable explosion of works for the cello. Significant improvements in the cello-playing technique and the advent of brilliant, charismatic cellists soon raised the cello to the same rank as the other main solo instruments and attracted the attention of numerous great composers. At the same time, many composers and cellists from countries not traditionally associated with the musical world appeared on the scene.

GREAT CELLISTS OF THE TWENTIETH AND TWENTY-FIRST CENTURIES

Never before have there been so many brilliant cellists—and from so many different countries—as there are today. Since any list I could possibly submit here would probably be woefully incomplete, I will briefly discuss only a few cellists who deserve special mention because of their impact on music and their relevance to this book.[1]

PABLO CASALS (1876–1973)

Naturally, the first cellist to be discussed here is Pablo Casals. His incomparable artistry and powerful personality transformed him into a public figure who, beginning in the early part of the century, succeeded in awakening unprecedented interest in the cello.

Casals was born in the small Catalan town of El Vendrell, and at the age of twelve was accepted at Barcelona's prestigious Municipal School of Music. He met Isaac Albéniz, who, impressed with Casals's obvious talent, gave him a letter of introduction for the Count de Morphy, secretary of Queen María Cristina, mother of and regent for the future King Alfonso XIII, who was then still a child.

Albéniz's letter gave Casals an entrée to the royal palace, and soon, in Casals's own words, Queen María Cristina became his "second mother." For over two years he remained in Madrid, where he pursued his music studies and attended concerts and exhibitions under the Count de Morphy's guidance.

The queen granted him a scholarship to continue his studies at the Brussels Conservatory. At the age of nineteen, his mother and siblings departed for Brussels, a journey involving considerable financial sacrifice. F. A. Gevaert, the director of the conservatory, introduced him to the cello teacher. The following incident, told in his own words, is highly illustrative of the character that distinguished Casals all his life.

The next day I appeared at the class. I was very nervous . . . I sat in the back of the class, listening to the students play. I must say I was not too greatly impressed, and I began to feel less nervous. When the class had finished, the professor . . . beckoned to me: "So," he said, "I gather you're the little Spaniard that the Director spoke to me about." I did not like his tone. I said yes, that I was the one.

"Well, little Spaniard," he said, "it seems you play the cello. Do you wish to play?"

I said I would be glad to.

"And what compositions do you play?"

I said I played quite a few.

He rattled off a number of works, asking me each time if I could play the one he named, and each time I said yes—because I could. Then he turned to the class and said, "Well now, isn't remarkable! It seems that our young Spaniard plays everything. He must be really quite amazing."

The students laughed. At first I had been upset by the professor's manner—this was, after all, my second day in a strange country—but by now I was angry with them and his ridicule of me. I didn't say anything.

"Perhaps," he said, "you will honor us by playing the *Souvenir de Spa*?" It was a flashy piece that was trotted out regularly in the Belgian school.

I said I would play it.

"I'm sure we'll hear something astonishing from this young man who plays everything," he said. "But what will you use for an instrument?"

There was more laughter from the students.

I was so furious I almost left then and there. But I thought, all right, whether he wants to hear me play or not, he'll hear me. I snatched a cello from the student nearest to me, and I began to play. The room fell silent. When I had finished, there wasn't a sound.

The professor stared at me. His face had a strange expression "Will you please come to my office?" he said. His tone was very different than before. We walked from the room together. The students sat without moving.

The professor closed the door to his office and sat down behind his desk. "Young man," he said, "I can tell you that you have a great talent. If you study here, and if you consent to be in my class, I can promise you that you will be awarded the First Prize of the conservatory."

I was almost too angry to speak. I told him "You were rude to me, sir. You ridiculed me in front of your pupils. I do not want to remain here one second longer."[2]

The next day, the Casals family immediately left for Paris. The young cellist wrote to the Count de Morphy, describing the incident. The count, who was extremely vexed, chastised Casals for his insubordination and presented him with an ultimatum: either return to Brussels or lose his scholarship. However, even then there was no power on earth that could make Casals change his mind once it was made up. The family remained in Paris, where they underwent considerable hardship.

On his return to Barcelona, his life began to improve. Josep García, his cello teacher at the Municipal Music School, had been appointed first cellist of the Liceu. Casals made peace with Count de Morphy and Queen María Cristina, who, after a concert at the Royal Place, presented him with a Gagliano cello.[3]

Another letter of recommendation from Count de Morphy introduced Casals to the famous French conductor Charles Lamoureux, who invited him on the spot. His legendary Paris debut in 1899—where he played the first movement of the Cello Concerto in D Minor by Edouard Lalo—was the first step in his glorious career as a world-famous cellist.

His life was profoundly altered by the Spanish Civil War. From the beginning of the conflict, his position was unequivocally in favor of the Republican forces. Soon after the end of the war, Casals settled in the small village of Prades in southern France. The advent of the Second World War further complicated his life, particularly after the establishment of the Vichy regime. His American friends sent him numerous invitations urging him to move to the United States, where he would be safe and also earn a fortune with his concerts. Casals refused. He felt it was his duty to remain with his fellow immigrants in exile and assist them in every possible way. "The artist is first a man and, as such, he must make common cause with his companions. The blood that has been shed and the tears from the victims of injustice are far more important to me than my music and all my cello recitals," Casals declared.[4]

When the war ended, Casals decided to end his exile and play in public once again, starting with several memorable concerts in England and Paris. Believing that the days of the Franco regime were numbered, he was certain that his exile was coming to an end. But Casals was deeply disillusioned by the tolerance shown by Western governments toward a totalitarian regime that had received support from the Nazis and the Italian Fascists. In 1946 Casals announced that he would not accept any invitations from any country "until Spain reestablished a regime that was respectful of fundamental liberties and popular will. I myself closed all doors. It was the most painful sacrifice an artist could ever impose upon himself."[5]

Then came 1950, the year commemorating the bicentennial of Bach's death. In light of Casals's refusal to abandon his self-imposed exile, a group of musicians—mostly from the United States, though headed by Russian violinist Alexander Schneider—proposed that they join Casals in Prades to celebrate the glory of Bach. Thus, in 1950 the most eminent musicians of the time helped establish the Prades Bach Festivals, which lasted—with only a few interruptions—until 1960.

Casals has been a legendary figure to me since I was eight or nine years old. His unique tone produced a profound impression on me from the very first time I ever heard him. I remember often listening to his recordings of Boccherini, Dvořák, and Bach's suites. Then, in 1950 I had the good fortune of meeting Casals. My father, who was a friend of his, arranged to visit him on January 1, 1950, which happened to be my thirteenth birthday. Don Pablo welcomed us most graciously in his modest house and conversed with my parents on a number of subjects, such as their many friends in common, mostly Spanish exiles in Mexico. When he learned that I was studying the cello, he asked me to play something for him. On an instrument he lent me, I played a Bach adagio that had been transcribed by Casals himself. He did not interrupt me, but as soon as I finished he said, "You have talent, young man, but I'm going to show you how this adagio should be played." Without removing his pipe from his mouth, he proceeded to show me, occasionally pausing to explain certain details that he believed were important. That visit with Casals has remained deeply etched in my memory.

In 1954 Casals said, "If some day there is a change in the circumstances that keep me in Prades, the first country I would like to visit is Mexico, as a tribute to their great loyalty toward democratic Spain."[6] In December 1955 and January 1956, Casals fulfilled his long-cherished dream of visiting Puerto Rico, his mother's birthplace, and fulfilled his promise to return to Mexico. Casals's visit to Mexico was extremely brief. For medical reasons, he traveled only to Veracruz, since Mexico City's high altitude could have proved detrimental to his health. There were no direct flights from Havana, the first stop on his trip, to Veracruz, since all of them stopped over in Mexico City first. Therefore, my father—a prominent industrialist, an excellent musician, and a patron of the arts and humanitarian causes—arranged for a private plane to transport Don Pablo from Havana to Veracruz. My father even flew to the Cuban capital with my mother and brother to accompany him on this trip. At that time I was studying for my exams at MIT, so I decided to forgo the historic opportunity to accompany my parents and Casals on this particular trip. Needless to say, today I deeply regret my excessive academic zeal.

Three years later, Casals returned to Mexico—to the city of Xalapa, where he attended the Pablo Casals Music Festival and the Second International Cello Competition. The competition took place from January 19 to January 31, 1959. The members of the judging panel, presided over by composer Blas Galindo, included cellists Pablo Casals, Gaspar Cassadó, Maurice Eisenberg, Rubén Montiel, André Navarra, Zara Nelsova, Adolfo Odnoposoff, Mstislav Rostropovich, Milos Sadlo, and Brazilian composer and cellist Heitor Villa-Lobos.[7]

In 1956 Casals married Marta Montañez, his Puerto Rican pupil, a woman of remarkable talent, intelligence, and charm; her devotion to Don Pablo was a constant source of comfort throughout his life. As a result, his relationship with Puerto Rico, his mother's birthplace, became even more intense. The newly married couple settled in San Juan, where they instituted the Pablo Casals Festivals, which, like the Prades Bach Festivals, attracted the world's musical elite. Casals died in Rio Piedras, Puerto Rico, in 1973.

Many of the major twentieth-century composers were characterized by their defiance of traditional musical concepts, whether by taking tonality and rhythm to the very limit or by venturing into the virtually unexplored areas of polytonality and atonality. Casals's taste in music, however, was well defined. For him music meant only tonal music, in which the melody plays a distinct, fundamental role. Therefore, he harshly criticized most of the leading composers of his time.

We can only regret the fact that Casals refrained from fostering and promoting the composition of cello works, a task that would have been easy for him to accomplish, either directly or through musical organizations that would have enthusiastically supported these projects.

EMANUEL FEUERMANN (1902–1942)

Feuermann was one of the greatest virtuosos of the twentieth century. He was born in Kolomea, Ukraine, in the bosom of a musical family, but from his early childhood he lived in Vienna.

Feuermann first studied with his father, and subsequently with, among others, the famous Julius Klengel. In 1929 he was appointed Hugo Becker's successor in Berlin's Akademische Hochschule für Musik (Academic University of Music), where he remained until 1934, when the alarming political situation in Germany drove him to immigrate to the United States.

Feuermann's technical perfection, exquisite tone, and elegant interpretations are truly legendary. The young Emanuel grew in the shadow of Pablo Casals, about whom he said, "No one who has heard him play can doubt that a new period for the cello began with him . . . He has been an example for younger cellists and he has demonstrated . . . that to listen to the cello can be an extraordinary artistic delight."[8]

However, Feuermann's refinement of the cello technique attained new and unprecedented heights. It is possible that the example of his eldest brother, who also played the violin, and his contact with a series of outstanding violin virtuosos convinced Feuermann that the cello could be played with the same purity and perfection as the violin, with the same impeccable technique, ease, and passion that Heifetz displayed on the violin. The hugely successful collaboration between the two artists, Feuerman and Heifetz, is reflected by the recordings they made together: Brahms's Double Concerto, with Eugene Ormandy and the Philadelphia Orchestra; Mozart's Divertimento, and Dohnányi's Serenade op. 10, both with William Primrose on the viola; and trios by Beethoven, Brahms, and Schubert, with Artur Rubinstein on the piano.

In the spring of 1938, Feuermann gave a series of four concerts at Carnegie Hall with the National Orchestral Association. The unprecedented program featured a sizeable part of the repertoire for cello and orchestra from the eighteenth century to 1932.

Feuermann's career flourished, and would have attained dazzling heights if a tragedy—an infection following a routine surgical procedure—had not ended his life in 1942, at the age of thirty-nine. If we bear in mind that Casals turned thirty-nine in 1916, the year of his earliest recordings (several now forgotten salon pieces) and that he lived another fifty-nine years, we can better appreciate the dreadful loss that the death of Emanuel Feuermann, one of the greatest figures in the history of the cello, meant to the world.

GREGOR PIATIGORSKY (1903–1976)

Piatigorsky was not only one of the great cellists of the twentieth century, but was also a highly charismatic figure. His personality, sense of humor, and joie de vivre were particularly appreciated in his adopted country, the United States, where he was most successful in promoting and popularizing the cello repertoire.

Born in 1903 in Ekaterinoslav, in southern Ukraine, he started studying the cello at the local conservatory at the age of seven. When the family moved to Moscow, "Grisha," who was barely nine, was awarded a scholarship to the Moscow Conservatory, where he studied with Professor Alfred von Glehn, a student of the famous Davidov. Despite his young age, Grisha found a job as a cellist to help with his family's financial problems. He performed in nightclubs—where he sat with his back to the audience to prevent him from looking at the scantily clad dancers—in cafés, and with second-rate bands that entertained patrons with all types of music.

He was fourteen when Lenin carried out his coup d'état in October 1917. Despite the turbulent times, Grisha always managed to find work. Before he turned fifteen he was offered the highly coveted position of first cello in the Bolshoi Theater Orchestra. He also joined a well-known string quartet, which, during that period of constant name changes, was renamed the Lenin Quartet. He had the opportunity to meet Lenin, who impressed him with his apparent unpretentiousness. "He spoke with a slight burr. There was nothing of the mighty revolutionist in his appearance. His manner of speaking was simple and mild. His jacket, his shoes were like those of a neighborhood tailor . . . He spoke in parables, not touching big topics. But whatever he said was profoundly human and was said with disarming simplicity."[9]

When Piatigorsky decided to emigrate in order to pursue his studies in either France or Germany, he had an interview with Anatoly Lunacharsky, the minister of education, who denied him the necessary permit. While on tour with the Bolshoi Ballet, Piatigorsky decided to defect in Volochisk, a village on the Polish border (now in the Ukraine). In the middle of the night, just as he was about to cross the bridge bordering the Zbruch River, he heard gunshots coming from both sides of the border. Piatigorsky waded into the shallow waters, holding his cello above his head, and managed to reach Poland.

In Berlin Piatigorsky studied with the famous Hugo Becker, and in Leipzig with the equally famous Julius Klengel. Word of Piatigorsky's increasing reputation as a musician had reached Wilhelm Furtwängler, conductor of the Berlin Philharmonic, who invited him to audition. Furtwängler was so impressed that he immediately offered Piatigorsky the position of principal cellist. It was around this time that Piatigorsky was introduced to the Mendelssohn family, especially Francesco, and to the Piatti. His heavy concert schedule as a soloist forced him to resign from the Berlin Philharmonic after four years.

In 1929 Piatigorsky embarked on his first—and highly successful—tour of the United States and recorded Schumann's concerto in London, thus consolidating his remarkable musical career. During the late 1930s, Piatigorsky, like many other European musicians, became an American citizen, and he moved to Los Angeles.

Piatigorsky's fascination with contemporary music generated a considerable number of commissions and world premieres, such as the concertos by William Walton, Mario Castelnuovo-Tedesco, Paul Hindemith, Vladimir Dukelsky, Ildebrando Pizzetti, as well as Bloch's *Schelomo*, among others.

His friendship with Prokofiev culminated in the Cello Concerto, op. 58. The cellist Lev Berezovsky premiered it in Moscow in November 1938, but according to Sviatoslav Richter, the premiere was "a complete failure."[10] When Piatigorsky premiered it in the United States, with the Boston Symphony Orchestra conducted by Sergey Koussevitsky, he wrote to the author, pointing out several of the weak spots in the piece and suggesting certain changes.

Although Igor Stravinsky did not compose any pieces for the cello, Piatigorsky persuaded him to adapt part of his orchestral suite *Pulcinella* for cello and piano. Piatigorsky himself collaborated with Stravinsky on the transcription, entitled *Suite italienne*. Prior to sending the finished manuscript to press, Stravinsky suggested they draw up a royalty contract and offering to share half of the royalty payments with Piatigorsky, who refused, since he felt that the percentage offered was much too generous. Stravinsky then explained his proposition in detail:

"I am not convinced you understand. May I repeat again: fifty-fifty, half for you, half for me. You see, it's like this: I am the composer of the music, of which we both are the transcribers. As composer I get ninety per cent, and as the arrangers we divide the remaining ten per cent into equal parts. In total, ninety five per cent for me, five per cent for you, which makes fifty-fifty." Chuckling, I signed the contract. Since then I have shied away from fifty-fifty deals, but I continue to love Stravinsky's music and to admire his arithmetic.[11]

In 1961 Heifetz and Piatigorsky founded the Heifetz-Piatigorsky Concerts, dedicated to chamber music. They frequently performed in Los Angeles and New York and made numerous recordings with such illustrious musicians as Artur Rubinstein, William Primrose, and Leonard Pennario, to name only a few. Piatigorsky was also devoted to academic activities, mainly in such prestigious institutions as the Curtis Institute of Music in Philadelphia, Boston University, the Tanglewood Festival, and the University of Southern California in Los Angeles.

MSTISLAV ROSTROPOVICH (B. 1927)

Rostropovich is a virtuoso with a supreme mastery of the instrument, a conductor, and a total musician, but driven by his enthusiasm for contemporary music, he has also promoted a remarkable number of works that have enriched the cello repertoire.

Mstislav Rostropovich was born in 1927 in Baku, the capital of what was then the Soviet Socialist Republic of Azerbaijan. His first teacher was his father, Leopold, a distinguished cellist, who in his youth had studied with Pablo Casals. When he was sixteen, young "Slava"—the nickname for "Mstislav"—enrolled in Semyon Kozolupov's class at the Moscow Conservatory.

In 1947, at the age of twenty, Slava had the audacity to play Prokofiev's Cello Concerto, op. 58, a piece that did not quite satisfy the composer and had been the target of unanimous criticism in the USSR (at its premiere, nine years earlier) for its so-called ideological bourgeois content. The composer was so delighted with Rostropovich's interpretation that he promised to rewrite the concerto, although he first composed his Sonata for Cello and Piano, op. 119. In 1949, when the sonata was completed, he invited Slava to his dacha in Nikolina Gora, near Moscow, so they could play and revise it together, thus marking the beginning of an intense though brief collaboration that was cut short by Prokofiev's death in 1953. Rostropovich spent two summers with Prokofiev and his wife, Mira, in Nikolina Gora, where they rewrote the concerto together. The new version, the Symphony-Concerto for Cello and Orchestra, op. 125, dedicated to Slava himself, was concluded in 1952. A truly magnificent work, it now forms part of the standard twentieth-century cello repertoire.

In 1955 Rostropovich married the great soprano Galina Vishnevskaya, whom he often accompanied, either on the piano or as conductor of the opera orchestra of the Bolshoi Theater. He had embarked on a conducting career in 1961 with the Nizhny Novgorod orchestra and then with the Bolshoi Ballet.

On August 2, 1959, Shostakovich presented him with an extraordinary gift: the recently completed Concerto in E-flat Major for Cello and Orchestra. Slava then withdrew to his house, where he studied it all the way through almost without a break. On August 6, he and pianist Alexander Dedyukhin set off for Shostakovich's dacha in Komarovo, near Leningrad, to play the concerto for the composer. When Shostakovich offered to bring him a music stand, Slava replied that it wasn't necessary since he had learned the piece by heart. "That's impossible, impossible!" Shostakovich exclaimed, but Rostropovich sat right down and played the entire concerto during what turned out to be a truly memorable session in the presence of the composer and the small group of friends he had invited to hear his composition performed for the first time.[12] It is certainly one of the most glorious cello concertos of the twentieth century.

In 1955, the Soviet government started allowing its most distinguished artists to travel to the West. Almost overnight, Rostropovich became an international celebrity. His passion for contemporary music had already borne fruit in his own country, and it proved to be an effective catalyst for the creation of new cello compositions. Benjamin Britten's five works for cello were all written for Rostropovich: the Sonata for Cello and Piano, the Symphony for Cello and Orchestra, and the three Suites for Solo Cello. Since I cannot possibly name every composer who wrote works for him, because the list would be much too long, I will only mention Witold Lutoslawski, Krzysztof Penderecki, Henri Dutilleux, Henri Sauguet, André Jolivet, Cristóbal Halffter, Lukas Foss, Leonard Bernstein, Alberto Ginastera, Olivier Messiaen, Alfred Schnittke, Pierre Boulez, and Luciano Berio.

In spring of 1968, when Rostropovich gave a concert in Kazan with the Moscow Symphony Orchestra, Aleksandr Solzhenitsyn and his wife, Natalia, were in the audience. The next day, the cellist, who had never met Solzhenitsyn, unexpectedly showed up at the writer's house, and introduced himself: "I am Rostropovich. I have come to embrace Solzhenitsyn."[13]

A short time later, he learned that Solzhenitsyn, who was living in Rozhdestvo at the time, had fallen ill. With his characteristic impulsiveness, Rostropovich immediately got in his car and drove to Rozhdestvo. When he realized that the writer, suffering from an acute case of sciatica, was cooped up in a cold damp cottage, Rostropovich promptly invit-

51. With Rostropovich in Mexico City, 1994, examining the score of Shostakovich's Cello Concerto No. 1.

52. Rostropovich and the Prieto Quartet, Mexico City, 1994. LEFT TO RIGHT:
*Carlos Miguel Prieto, Juan Luis Prieto, Mstislav Rostropovich, Carlos Prieto,
and Juan Luis Prieto, Jr.*

ed the Solzhenitsyns to spend the winter at his property at Zhukovka,
where he had just built a small guesthouse. It was then that Rostropovich started having problems that at first seemed to be nothing more than
the usual bureaucratic red tape.

When Solzhenitsyn was awarded the Nobel Prize for Literature
in 1970 and the media unleashed a virulent campaign against him,
Rostropovich was reminded of the times when Stalin's henchmen had
attacked Shostakovich and Prokofiev and no one had dared to speak out
in their behalf.

Rostropovich sent a letter to the main Soviet newspapers in defense
of the writer. The reactions were not long in coming. Invitations to conduct the Bolshoi Opera were inexplicably withdrawn, and requests for
concert tours abroad and performances with the major orchestras dwin-
dled considerably, for no other reason than the usual lame excuses and
stumbling blocks.

Finally, Galina placed her own career in jeopardy by proposing that
she and Slava write a letter to Brezhnev and request permission to leave

the USSR. Brezhnev agreed, and in the spring of 1975, Slava, Galina, and their two daughters departed for what was officially described as a two-year trip "for artistic purposes."

In the West, Rostropovich continued his work as the driving force behind the creation of new works for cello and new orchestral pieces, since, though never abandoning the cello, he was devoting more time to conducting. In 1977, he was appointed musical director of the National Symphony Orchestra in Washington, where he remained until 1994.

In 1978, because of their "anti-Soviet activities," Galina Vishnevskaya and Mstislav Rostropovich—two artists who had garnered extraordinary prestige and glory for their country—were stripped of their Soviet citizenship by the Central Committee of the Communist Party.

In 1985, however, the situation began to change when Gorbachev came to power. Five years later in Moscow, Rostropovich and Galina received an enthusiastic welcome from the people and the Soviet government when Rostropovich returned for a concert tour as conductor and soloist with the National Symphony Orchestra.

In 1991, as soon as he heard of the coup that threatened to crush Gorbachev's reforms and remove Boris Yeltsin as president of the Russian Republic, Rostropovich took the first plane to Moscow. A photograph of Rostropovich standing in front of the Russian "White House," joining forces with the thousands of protestors opposing the coup by defying the Russian army's tanks, was published around the world. It was this gesture, along with his long struggle in defense of human rights in Russia, that subsequently earned him the State Prize of Russia.

I met Rostropovich in 1959 when he came to Mexico for the first Pablo Casals Music Festival and the Second International Cello Competition in Veracruz. We were introduced by Vladimir Wulfman and violinist Luz Vernova, friends we had in common, at his concert in Mexico City. At that time, Rostropovich was thirty-three and very slender, exuding the same energy he still does today. When Luz Vernova mentioned that I played the cello, Rostropovich invited me to his dressing room and took out his cello. "What movement from Bach's Suites would you like to hear?" he asked. "The gavotte from the sixth suite," I answered. He played this movement, as well as the gigue from the same suite. The session was cut short because he had a previous engagement at the Soviet Embassy. I drove him there myself, and after a few glasses of vodka, he caused a sensation by playing a piece on the piano. Rostropovich happens to be an excellent pianist, but what really brought down the house was that he played the piece from three different positions: sitting in front of the piano, sitting with his back to the piano, and, finally, lying under the piano.

In May 1994, we spent considerable time with Slava when he was in Mexico during the four concerts he played in the Palace of Fine Arts. After a Sunday concert, we invited him to a luncheon at our home with what was supposed to be a small group of friends and family. However, the group increased considerably as friends of Slava's started arriving at the last minute. Before Slava left, he wanted to meet the Piatti, and he played it for quite awhile. Neither his pulse nor intonation ever hinted at the not inconsiderable amounts of vodka and tequila he had imbibed (Figs. 51 and 52). Rostropovich's vitality and energy are boundless, as are his invaluable contributions to the cello and to the world of music itself.

YO-YO MA (B. 1955)

Yo-Yo Ma is an extraordinary and unique case of talent, personality, and charisma. His multifaceted activities have drawn unprecedented attention to the cello while enriching music in many ways and building bridges of understanding across cultures throughout the world.

Yo-Yo Ma was born in 1955 in Paris to Chinese parents; when he was four, he started studying the cello with his father. His family moved to New York in 1962, and after studying with János Scholz, Yo-Yo, barely seven, became Leonard Rose's pupil at Juilliard. While a teenager, he was already being compared to Casals.

Besides keeping a hectic concert schedule as a soloist with the principal orchestras of the world, Yo-Yo is also intensely devoted to chamber music, recording with colleagues and friends such as Isaac Stern, Jaime Laredo, Emanuel Ax, and others. With Emanuel Ax he has created one of the most extraordinary duos of our times, offering frequent recitals and recording the standard repertoire for cello and piano.

Contemporary music plays a fundamental role in Yo-Yo Ma's career. Over the past few years, he has premiered countless works for cello and orchestra. Most of these pieces, the result of his active collaboration with the composer, have been dedicated to him. He has premiered pieces for cello and orchestra composed by William Bolcom, Ezra Laderman, David Diamond, Peter Lieberson, Tod Machover, Stephen Albert, Leon Kirchner, John Harbison, Christopher Rouse, and Richard Danielpour, to name only a few.

Obviously, his interest is not restricted to works by American composers. In 1997, for example, he premiered a piece commissioned for him from Chinese composer Tan Dun, on the occasion of Hong Kong's reintegration with China. His exploration of music from the Silk Road region has resulted in a series of fascinating musical experiences.

Yo-Yo Ma's successful forays into other musical genres are borne out by his jazz recordings with Claude Bolling; *Hush*, with Bobby McFerrin; *Appalachia Waltz*, with Mark O'Connor and Edgar Meyer; and recordings of tangos and Brazilian music. He has immersed himself in Chinese music played on native instruments and in the music of the Kalahari bush people in Africa.

Yo-Yo Ma also devotes a great deal of time to master classes and informal contacts with young musicians, as well as to frequent television appearances, both in concerts and on educational programs.

I met Yo-Yo Ma in 1983 in New York during a tribute for our teacher, Leonard Rose. Since then, we have seen each other a number of times, and I am always impressed not only by his extraordinary musical talent, but also by his charm, intelligence, and kindness.

In 1993 we had the pleasure of having him as our houseguest in Mexico, along with his wife Jill and their small children, Nicholas and Emily. The children, eight and six years old, respectively, were every bit as delightful as their parents. María Isabel, my wife, who one day accompanied Jill, Nicholas, and Emily on the obligatory visit to the pyramids in Teotihuacan, was amazed at Nicholas's perceptive questions, although, given his parents, his precocity came as no surprise. Unlike many of my colleagues who are extremely knowledgeable about music but very little else outside their field, Yo-Yo is interested in a wide variety of subjects. He studied history at Harvard University, and since he was born in France and his parents are Chinese, speaks French and Mandarin, and is very familiar with Chinese culture. Although Yo-Yo, who lives with his wife and children in Cambridge, a few steps from Harvard, is a U.S. citizen, he is, in fact, a citizen of the world.

The day they toured Teotihuacan, the four Mas were invited to dinner at our house in San Angel. Yo-Yo arrived with his Stradivari, the famous 1712 Davidov, and I had the privilege of playing some duets with him. While we were at the table, we left the two Stradivari cellos alone in the music room, outside of their cases. Yo-Yo thought that perhaps they might fall in love and produce some "Stradivari babies." I described the outcome of the meeting of the two Strads in Chapter 5.

JACQUELINE DU PRÉ (1945–1987)

English-born Du Pré's meteoric career—and life—were cut short by multiple sclerosis. Her legendary recording of Elgar's Concerto catapulted her into musical stardom in 1965. Married to pianist and conductor Daniel Barenboim, they were among the most celebrated couples in the history of music.

GASPAR CASSADÓ (1897–1966)

In Chapter 3 I described the career of this brilliant Spanish cellist, composer, and teacher, who played the Piatti for some time. Further on, in the section devoted to twentieth-century cello works, readers will find comments on his work as a composer.

53. With cellists Leonard Rose, Raya Garbousova, and Mstislav Rostropovich at the University of Maryland, 1981.

54. After receiving the Chevalier du Violoncelle award, presented by the Eva Janzer Memorial Cello Center of Indiana University. With fellow cellists Janos Starker (LEFT) and Tsuyoshi Tsutsumi (RIGHT), Bloomington, 2001.

PIERRE FOURNIER (1906–1986)

Fournier, who studied at the Paris Conservatory, performed with the greatest conductors of his time—Furtwängler, Rafael Kubelik, and Herbert von Karajan, among others. In addition to his incomparable recordings of the principal works in the cello repertoire, he premiered Poulenc's Cello Sonata, Martinu's Cello Concerto no. 1, and other works dedicated to him. He participated in numerous trios with violinist Henryk Szeryng and pianist Artur Rubinstein, and taught at the École Normale de Musique (a training college for music teachers) and later at the Paris Conservatory. I knew him well, since he was my teacher in Geneva in 1978.

LEONARD ROSE (1918–1984)

Rose, born in Washington, D.C., was one of the most distinguished American cellists and teachers of the twentieth century (see Fig. 53). Principal cellist for orchestras in Cleveland and New York, as well as the NBC Orchestra, he subsequently devoted all his time to his career as a soloist and as a teacher at Juilliard, where he taught such celebrated musicians as Yo-Yo Ma, Lynn Harrell, and Stephen Kates. He was also a member of the Stern-Rose-Istomin Trio. I consider myself extremely fortunate to have studied with him in New York.

JANOS STARKER (B. 1924)

Starker, one of the great virtuosos of the twentieth century, studied music in his native Budapest. In 1948, he immigrated to the United States and became principal cellist of the Dallas Symphony Orchestra. Since 1958 he has devoted all his time to his twofold activities as an international soloist and a teacher. He has premiered numerous works dedicated to him; he has made over 150 recordings of the most varied cello repertoire; he is a faculty member at Indiana University's School of Music in Bloomington.

On October 20, 2001, Janos Starker, the IU School of Music, and the Eva Janzer Memorial Cello Center presented me with the Chevalier du Violoncelle award, an honor for which I am profoundly grateful (see Fig. 54).

ALDO PARISOT (B. 1920)

Brazilian-born Aldo Parisot has had an extremely brilliant career as a soloist and as a teacher, especially at Juilliard, Yale, and countless international festivals and seminars. Aldo Parisot is a permanent member of the judges panel for the Carlos Prieto Cello Competitions, described in Chapter 6. We owe him an enormous debt for his invaluable contributions.

PRINCIPAL WORKS FOR CELLO IN THE TWENTIETH CENTURY

Appendices 1 and 2 include charts listing the principal cello works of this period. The first chart comprises 337 works by 129 European, U.S., and Japanese composers. The second chart lists 425 works by 189 composers from Latin America, Spain, and Portugal; it is particularly extensive because, as far as I know, a list of cello works by composers from these regions has never before been published. –

On the following pages, I will refer to only a few of the fundamental works of the twentieth-century cello repertoire (the lists are in alphabetical order by country). It would be pointless for the charts in the appendices to include an exhaustive list of compositions, since the concept of what constitutes an "important" work is highly subjective and relative. For example, there may be certain works worth mentioning that I know nothing about, whereas some that appear on the list may not withstand the test of time, and soon be forgotten.[14]

EUROPE AND THE UNITED STATES

AUSTRIA   Anton Webern (1883–1945) was an active cellist while he was a student. In his youth he composed Two Pieces for Cello and Piano (1889), the Sonata for Cello and Piano (1914), and Three Small Pieces for Cello and Piano (1914), all distinguished for their conciseness and concentration. The Three Small Pieces consist of, respectively, only nine, thirteen, and twenty measures.

Arnold Schoenberg (1874–1951) was also a cellist in his youth. In 1914 he published an edition of the Concerto in G Minor for Cello by the Viennese composer Georg Matthias Monn (1717–1750); from 1932 to 1933 he made an arrangement for cello and orchestra of Monn's Concerto for Harpsichord in D Major.

BELGIUM   The great violinist Eugène Ysaÿe (1858–1931) was profoundly familiar with the cello, as can be seen in his Poem for Cello and Orchestra, op. 16, and in his Sonata for Solo Cello, op. 28 (1924).

CZECHOSLOVAKIA   A dominant figure of twentieth-century Czech music was Bohuslav Martinu (1890–1959), a prolific composer who left numerous works for the cello: two concertos for cello and orchestra, three sonatas for cello and piano, and a series of variations and minor works, of which the most outstanding is his Variations on a theme by Rossini.

Leoš Janáček (1854–1928) composed *Prohadka*, (Fairy Story) for cello and piano in 1910.

ENGLAND   For almost a century and half after Purcell and Handel, England had no composers comparable to those on the European continent. It was not until the end of the nineteenth century that Great Britain began to experience a remarkable musical renaissance. A wide range of British composers have enriched the cello repertoire with numerous works; so numerous, in fact, that here I will mention only four composers whose contributions have proved especially valuable: Delius, Elgar, Walton, and Britten.

Frederick Delius (1862–1934) composed several noteworthy works for the cello: Romance for Cello and Piano (1896), Double Concerto for Violin, Cello, and Orchestra (1916), Sonata for Cello and Piano (1917), Capriccio and Elegy for Cello and Orchestra (1925), and Concerto for Cello and Orchestra (1921).

The Concerto for Cello and Orchestra (1919) by Edward Elgar (1857–1934) is one of the last great Romantic concertos.

In 1956 William Walton (1902–1983) composed his cello concerto, which, as we have seen, was dedicated to Gregor Piatigorsky. It consists of three parts: a melodious Moderato, an Allegro appassionato—resembling a scherzo filled with rhythmic energy—and a Theme with Variations.

Another composer who bequeathed an invaluable legacy for the cello was Benjamin Britten (1913–1976). Inspired by his friendship with Rostropovich, he created five great, original, and imaginative works, all dedicated to the great Russian musician: Sonata for Cello and Piano, op. 65 (1961), the Symphony for Cello and Orchestra, op. 68 (1963), and Three Suites for Cello Solo, opp. 72 (1964), 80 (1968), and 87 (1971).

FINLAND   The best known figure in Finland's music world is Jean Sibelius (1865–1957). Whereas his violin concerto is one of the principal works of that genre, his compositions for the cello, such as his *Malinconia* for cello and piano (op. 20), are minor works.

His compatriot, Leif Segerstam (b. 1944,) a world-renowned composer and conductor, is also a pianist, violinist, and one of the most interesting figures in contemporary Scandinavian music. One of the most prolific composers of our time, he has written twenty-nine quartets, seven concertos for cello and orchestra, and twenty-four symphonies.

FRANCE   No reference to twentieth-century French compositions for cello would be complete without mentioning the magnificent sonata for cello and piano written in 1915 by Claude Debussy (1862–1918). That same year Debussy announced that he was composing a series of six instrumental sonatas entitled *Six sonates pour divers instruments composées par Claude Debussy, Musicien français*. He actually completed only three, including the cello sonata (1915). The sonata for cello is an original work in all respects: form, themes, sound, and innovative effects. Its three movements—Prologue (*lent*), Sérenade (*fantasque et léger*), and Finale (*animé, léger et nerveux*)—are so varied and create such diverse moods that it is hard to believe it lasts only ten minutes!

The two sonatas (1918 and 1922) by Gabriel Fauré (1845–1924) contain music of great beauty. They could be compared to two paintings rendered in pastel tones, completely devoid of harsh colors and flamboyant effects. These pieces, of indisputable musical merit, were not written to allow instrumentalists to display their virtuosity, and they are not performed as often as they deserve. However, some of his short pieces for cello and piano now occupy a solid position in the standard repertoire. I will mention them here, although they were composed at the end of the nineteenth century: *Elégie*, op. 24 (1883), *Papillon*, op. 77 (1898), and *Sicilienne*, op. 78, also from 1898.

Maurice Ravel (1875–1937) composed a wonderful Sonata for Violin and Cello (1920–1922). It was premiered in 1922 by violinist Hélène Jourdan-Morhange and Maurice Maréchal, an eminent cellist of the first half of the century.

Maréchal, in fact, premiered several noteworthy compositions from the French cello repertoire. André Caplet (1892–1925) composed a symphonic fresco for cello and orchestra, entitled *Épiphanie*, and the particularly demanding solo part was first played by Maurice Maréchal in 1922.

Arthur Honegger (1892–1955) composed a sonata for cello and piano and a concerto for cello and orchestra that he dedicated to Maréchal. The concerto, a modest work lasting fifteen minutes, calls for a small orchestra. Its mood is lighthearted, in the manner of a divertimento, with touches of jazz.

Darius Milhaud (1892–1974) was an extremely prolific composer. The most noteworthy of his cello works is the Concerto no. 1, op. 136, also dedicated to Maréchal. It is truly a fun piece to play, typical of its author. The concerto begins with a cadenza for solo cello, and the somber, solemn tone turns into a fox-trot as soon as the orchestra joins in. Its three movements (Nonchalant, Grave, Joyeux) barely last fourteen minutes.

The sonata by Francis Poulenc (1899–1963), completed in 1948, was dedicated to Pierre Fournier, who assisted him with the technical aspects of the cello part, since the composer was unfamiliar with the instrument. The four movements of this magnificent sonata are Allegro (tempo di marcia), Cavatine, Ballabile, and Finale.

The Concerto for Cello and Orchestra entitled *Tout un monde lointain . . .* (A Whole Distant World) by Henri Dutilleux (b. 1916) is, in my opinion, one of the great cello masterpieces of the late twentieth century (see Chapter 5 for a more detailed account of this work). As I mentioned earlier, during its long gestation process, Dutilleux happened to be immersed in Baudelaire's works. Each of its five movements is inspired by poems from *Les fleur du mal* (Flowers of Evil). The work was performed in public for the first time during the Aix-en-Provence Festival on July 25, 1970, with Mstislav Rostropovich as soloist.

GERMANY   Among the important twentieth-century cello works that I know of are the three suites for cello solo by Max Reger (1873–1916). Dated 1915, they were based on Bach's suites. Paul Hindemith (1895–1963) composed several works for the cello, such as his Sonata for Solo Cello, op. 25, no. 3 (1923), Concerto for Cello and Orchestra (1940), and Sonata for Cello and Piano (1948). Bernd Alois Zimmermann (1918–1970) made significant contributions to the cello repertoire with works for solo cello, cello and piano, and cello and orchestra, several of them dedicated to Siegfried Palm, a champion of contemporary music.

HUNGARY   During the first half of the twentieth century, Hungary's musical panorama was dominated by the figure of Béla Bartók (1881–1945). Unfortunately, Bartók's only work for cello and piano was not even originally conceived for the cello, since it is his own transcription of his First Rhapsody for Violin and Piano.

However, Zoltán Kodály (1882–1967), Bartók's companion and colleague, has left us several major works for the cello, such as the incomparable Sonata for Cello Solo, op. 8, a work that takes full advantage of the instrument's tonal and expressive potential; a Sonata for Cello and Piano, op. 4 (1909–1910), and a Duo for violin and cello, op. 7.

During the second half of the century, the predominant figure was György Ligeti (b. 1923), who immigrated in 1956 to Austria, and then to Germany. In Chapter 5, I describe his Concerto for Cello and Orchestra, composed in 1966.

ITALY   Ottorino Respighi (1879–1936) composed Adagio with Variations for cello and orchestra in 1920, a piece in the neoclassical style, now fully incorporated into the contemporary repertoire.

Alfredo Casella (1883–1947) wrote several works for the cello: two sonatas with piano, a concerto for cello and orchestra (1934–1935), and a triple concerto for violin, cello, piano, and orchestra. His Cello Sonata no. 1, op. 8 (1906), a clear, melodious work, is dedicated to Pablo Casals.

Luigi Dallapiccola (1904–1975) left us two compositions: *Ciaccona, intermezzo e adagio* (1945) for solo cello and *Dialoghi* (1959–1960) for cello and orchestra, both dedicated to Gaspar Cassadó.

More recently, Luciano Berio (1925–2003) composed *Il ritorno degli Snovidenia* (1976–1977) for cello and instrumental ensemble and *Les mots sont allés . . .* (1976–1978) for solo cello.

POLAND

Precisely during the period when artistic expression in countries in the orbit of the Soviet Union was stifled by the shackles of socialist realism, Poland was experiencing an extraordinary musical renaissance and turning into an important forum for contemporary music.

Witold Lutoslawski (1913–1994) composed a remarkable cello concerto (1970), mentioned in Chapter 6, and the *Sacher Variation* (1975) for solo cello.

Krzysztof Penderecki (b. 1933) is the author of two concertos for cello, the first (1972) dedicated to Siegfried Palm and the second (1982) to Yo-Yo Ma. He also composed a concerto for three cellos and orchestra and the *Capriccio per Siegfried Palm* (1968) for solo cello.

RUSSIA AND THE USSR

There are numerous cello compositions written by composers from Russia and from several nations that were once part of the USSR. During the second half of the twentieth century, they were, for the most part, inspired by Mstislav Rostropovich. As I pointed out earlier, we will only present a brief overview of the most important works.

Sergey Rachmaninov (1873–1943) composed his Sonata in G Minor for cello and piano, op. 19 (1901), immediately before beginning work on his second piano concerto. The sonata, filled with rich melodic content, is typical of the composer at the height of his creative power. Although its diverse themes are highly suited to the nature of the cello, the fact that the composer was a virtuoso pianist means that he occasionally allows the piano to dominate the work. Nevertheless, this sonata is one of the important cello pieces of the century and, certainly, one of the most beautiful.

Igor Stravinsky (1882–1971) was born in Russia but emigrated prior to the Russian Revolution. His only cello composition is the *Suite italienne* for cello and piano, a transcription he and Gregor Piatigorsky made of a ballet suite from *Pulcinella*.

Among the most outstanding cello works composed by Sergey Prokofiev (1891–1953) are his Sonata in C Major for cello and piano, op. 119 (1949), and his Symphony-Concerto, op. 125 (1950–1951), whose origins were discussed earlier. Both works were dedicated to Rostropovich.

Aram Khachaturian (1903–1978), an Armenian, studied the cello at the Gnessin Music Academy in Moscow. Apart from some juvenile works, his main compositions for the cello include a concerto for cello and orchestra (1946), the Concerto-Rhapsody for cello and orchestra (1963), and the Sonata-Fantasy for solo cello (1974).

Dmitry Kabalevsky (1904–1987) wrote several works for the cello, including two sonatas for cello and piano and two concertos for cello and orchestra. The first concerto (1948–1949), dedicated to youth, is a light and well-accomplished work.

Dmitry Shostakovich (1906–1975), a legendary—though highly controversial and complex—figure, is now viewed in a new light. His operas—once so disputed—symphonies, concertos, and countless chamber works are now an essential part of the standard music repertoire.

His three cello compositions have earned a well-deserved place among the principal cello works of the twentieth century: the Sonata for cello and piano, op. 40 (1964), and the Concertos no. 1, op. 107 (1959) and no. 2, op. 126 (1966).

Moishei Vainberg (1919–1996) was born in Poland as Mieczyslaw Weinberg, but is better known as Moishei Vainberg, since he spent most of his life in Russia, where he composed all his works. Highly regarded by Shostakovich, he is only now beginning to be recognized as an outstanding composer. He composed twenty-two symphonies, seventeen string quartets, seven operas, and numerous cello works, including four sonatas for solo cello, two sonatas for cello and piano, twenty-four preludes for solo cello, and two cello concertos.

Of the post-Shostakovich generation, there are three especially noteworthy composers: Edison Denisov, Sofia Gubaidulina, and Alfred Schnittke, who all took advantage of the new freedoms in Russia and chose to immigrate (Denisov to France, Gubaidulina and Schnittke to Germany).

Edison Denisov (1929–1996), a Siberian, composed many cello works: a sonata for cello and piano (1971), three pieces for cello and piano (1967), and a cello concerto (1972).

Sofia Gubaidulina was born in 1931 in Chistopol in the Tatar Republic of the Soviet Union and lived in Moscow until 1992. Since then, she has made her permanent home near Hamburg. She too has composed numerous cello works: two concertos, two pieces for cello and small ensembles, ten preludes for solo cello (1974), and various compositions for cello and piano.

Alfred Schnittke (1934–1998), a remarkable composer, is the author of two concertos for cello and orchestra; a triple concerto for violin, viola, cello, and orchestra; the Dialogue for cello and seven instruments; and two sonatas for cello and piano.

Sulkhan Tsintsadze (1925–1991) was, along with Giya Kancheli (b. 1935), perhaps the most celebrated composer in Soviet Georgia. Tsintsadze studied the cello during his years at the conservatory in Tbilisi. His numerous cello works include three cello concertos (1947, 1963, and 1974) and a collection of twenty-four preludes for cello and piano (1980). Kancheli composed *Simi* (Joyless thoughts) for cello and orchestra (1995).

SWITZERLAND

In the twentieth century, the two most outstanding composers from this country were Ernest Bloch and Frank Martin.

The most frequently played cello piece by Bloch (1880–1959) is *Schelomo: Hebraic Rhapsody for Cello and Orchestra* (1915–1916), one of his finest, most eloquent compositions. In this piece, the solo cello represents the feelings and passions of King Solomon (*Schelomo* in Hebrew.) Bloch composed a minor work for cello and orchestra entitled *A Voice in the Wilderness* (1936), as well as three suites for solo cello (1956, 1956, and 1957).

Frank Martin (1890–1974) wrote a concerto for cello and orchestra (1966), dedicated to Pierre Fournier, that is also worth mentioning.

Arthur Honegger was born in Switzerland, but since spent most of his life in France and is therefore more identified with French composers, I discuss his work in the section (above) devoted to France.

UNITED STATES   The first cello concertos composed in the United States were by Victor Herbert (1859–1924), at approximately the same time (1884–1894) that Ricardo Castro was composing his concerto in Mexico.

Walter Piston (1894–1976) studied at Harvard and later in France with Paul Dukas and Nadia Boulanger. He then became an excellent teacher, whose best-known students were Elliott Carter and Leonard Bernstein. In 1966 he composed his Variations for Cello and Orchestra, dedicated to Rostropovich.

Elliott Carter (b. 1908.) composed a fundamental work in the cello music of the United States: his Sonata for Cello and Piano (1948). The sonata is extremely complex, especially in its rhythm. Carter exploits the different natures of both instruments by providing each with its own melodic content and even a separate tempo, thus creating the impression that both instruments are improvising independently from each other.

Samuel Barber (1910–1981) composed two excellent works for cello: Sonata for Cello and Piano, op. 6 (1932) and Concerto for Cello and

Orchestra (1945), both Romantic or Neoromantic pieces supporting Barber's theory that music should not be difficult to understand. Barber composed for himself, fully convinced that the public would ultimately appreciate good music. The difficult solo part of the concerto highlights the instrument's lyrical quality.

Italian-born Gian Carlo Menotti (b. 1911) has composed the Fantasia for Cello and Orchestra and the Suite for Two Cellos and Piano.

Lukas Foss (b. 1922) was born in Germany, but immigrated to the United States in 1933. His many compositions include his picturesque Capriccio for Cello and Piano (1946), which is dedicated to Gregor Piatigorsky and is radically different from his Concerto for Cello and Orchestra, in which the soloist appears twice and one of the two cello voices is recorded on tape. Mstislav Rostropovich, to whom it is dedicated, premiered the work in 1967.

Leon Kirchner (b. 1919) composed his Music for Cello and Orchestra for Yo-Yo Ma, who took his course on performance and analysis at Harvard. Ma premiered in 1992 with the Philadelphia Orchestra conducted by David Zinman.

George Crumb (b. 1929) wrote a noteworthy piece for the contemporary U.S. repertoire. His Sonata for Cello Solo (1955), a dynamic, emotional work, lasts only ten minutes and requires the utmost technical mastery of the cello.

After studying at Harvard and Princeton, John Harbison (b. 1938) became a professor in MIT's Music Department, where he received the Killian Award (1994) for his "extraordinary professional achievements." So far he has composed two works for cello: a Concerto for Cello and Orchestra (1993), premiered in 1994 by Yo-Yo Ma, Seiji Ozawa, and the Boston Symphony Orchestra, and a short Suite for Cello and Piano (1993).

Stephen Albert (1941–1992), who died tragically in an automobile accident in 1992, was one of the most acclaimed composers of his generation, having received two Rome Prizes, the Pulitzer Prize, and a Grammy, among many others. His music has solid roots in traditional composition techniques, and is characterized by a highly personal contemporary language. One of his last compositions was his Concerto for Cello and Orchestra, commissioned by the Boston Symphony Orchestra for Yo-Yo Ma.

The musical education of Robert X. Rodriguez (b. 1946) included classes with Hunter Johnson, Halsey Stevens, Jacob Druckman, and Nadia Boulanger, as well as master classes with Bruno Maderna and Elliott Carter. Rodriguez has been a "composer in residence" with the Dallas

Symphony Orchestra and the Los Angeles Chamber Orchestra, among others. Among his recent works are *Máscaras* (a concerto for cello and orchestra) and *Lull-a-bear* for cello and piano. As detailed in Chapter 6, I premiered both: the first at the International Cervantes Festival at the end of 1994 and the second in Mexico City in 1995.

Christopher Rouse (b. 1949) composed his Concerto for Cello and Orchestra in 1992, calling it a "meditation on death, on the struggle to deny death and on the inevitability of death." Commissioned for Yo-Yo Ma and the Los Angeles Philharmonic Orchestra, it was premiered in 1994, with David Zinman conducting.

Richard Danielpour (b. 1956), originally from New York, is currently a professor at the Manhattan School of Music. Danielpour's Concerto for Cello and Orchestra (1993) is dedicated to Yo-Yo Ma, who premiered it in 1994. It contains four movements: Invocation (arioso), Profanation (dance), Soliloquy, and Prayer and Lamentation (hymn).

IBERO-AMERICA

As mentioned earlier, Appendix 2 includes 425 works by 189 composers from Latin America, Spain, and Portugal. I must stress once again that this list is not meant to be an exhaustive overview, since it will undoubtedly contain important omissions as well as works that will be eventually discarded by the passage of time.

Here, as in the case of the other countries, I will provide a summary of the principal works.[15] In Chapter 6 I described my relationship with many of the composers from this region as well as many of the works I premiered.

ARGENTINA   Alberto Williams (1862–1952) and Julián Aguirre (1868–1924), both representatives of the national Argentinean movement, composed the earliest cello works in that country. Williams, who studied in France with César Franck, wrote his Sonata for cello and piano, op. 52, in 1906.

Aguirre studied for some time in Spain with Albéniz. His only original work for cello and piano, a sonata in A Major, unfortunately remains an incomplete manuscript. His *Rapsodia Argentina* (1898) and *Huella*, op. 49 (1917), though not original works, are available in excellent transcriptions for cello and piano.

The sonata for cello and piano, op. 26 (1918), by Constantino Gaito (1878–1945) is a frequently played work in Argentina, and cellist Daniel Gassé has performed it in the United States.

Among the composers from the first half of the twentieth century, the Castro brothers—José María, Juan José, and Washington—must certainly be mentioned. José María Castro (1892–1964) and Washington Castro (1909–2004) were also cellists and the authors of several cello works listed Appendix 2. Juan José Castro (1895–1968) was the most influential of the brothers as a composer and teacher, but wrote only one sonata for cello and piano (1916). At Pablo Casals's suggestion, Juan José Castro was appointed dean of the Puerto Rico Conservatory from 1959–1964.

Alberto Ginastera (1916–1983) is a predominant figure in Argentinean music. He composed six works for the cello, probably because his wife—now his widow—Aurora Nátola Ginastera, is a cellist. His *Pampeana* no. 2 for cello and piano (1950), which uses rhythms from the pampas, is a work I have often played, since I regard it as a jewel of the Latin American cello repertoire. Twenty-nine years later, Ginastera composed a new piece for cello and piano, the Sonata op. 49. His two concertos for cello and orchestra (1968 and 1980) are also important works.

For Astor Piazzolla (1921–1992), the reader can refer to Chapter 6, which includes a brief biographical sketch of the composer. Here I will add only that his original cello works are the *Tres piezas breves* for cello and piano, op. 4, composed in his youth, and the celebrated *Le grand tango*, one of his finest chamber works and one in which he combines a tango style with polytonal harmonies and clusters.

Several other composers, perhaps not as well known, are worth citing here. Hilda Dianda (b. 1925) has shown interest in the cello, and this has led her to write several pieces for the instrument. Although Werner Wagner (1927–2002) was born in Germany, his musical career took place in Argentina. His Rhapsody for cello and orchestra (1973, revised 1985) is well worth mentioning. Luis Jorge González (b. 1936) has composed two cello works: *Oxymora* (1973–1975) for cello and piano, and *Confín sur* (1995–1996), a suite for cello and piano. He is now composing a cello concerto.

Two recent orchestral works deserve to be mentioned here: the Rhapsody for cello and orchestra by Máximo Flugelman (b. 1945) and the Concertino for cello and string orchestra (1992) by Esteban Benzecry (b. 1970)

BOLIVIA Alberto Villalpando, born in La Paz in 1940, is probably the most important Bolivian composer of his generation. At the age of seventeen he moved to Buenos Aires to continue his piano and composition studies at the Carlos López Buchardo National Conservatory of

Music, where he studied with Alberto Ginastera. I met him in La Paz in May 1999 when I gave a series of concerts and presented a previous edition of this book. In 1999 he composed the *Sonatita de piel morena* for cello and piano, dedicated to Edison Quintana and me.

BRAZIL   Heitor Villa-Lobos (1887–1959), as prolific as the jungles of his native Brazil, composed over one thousand works in every conceivable musical genre. The cello was very special to him: he began studying it in childhood, and fully mastered it, as he did the guitar. In 1913 he wrote his first series of works for cello and piano, and his editor in Rio, Arthur Napoleão, dubbed them the *Pequena suite*. He wrote two sonatas for cello and piano (1915 and 1916), two concertos (1913 and 1953), and a fantasia for cello and orchestra (1945).

Perhaps his most important cello works, and certainly the most frequently performed, are the first and fifth of his *Bachianas brasileiras*. The concept behind this series of works was, in his own words, to combine a form "inspired by Bach's musical ambiance" with diverse Brazilian musical effects. The first, dedicated to Casals, is for eight cellos, while the fifth is for soprano and eight cellos.

Camargo Guarnieri (1907–1993) was one of the principal exponents of Brazilian music, especially within the nationalistic school mentioned in Chapter 6. I will add only that his cello works include three sonatas for cello and piano (1931, 1955, and 1977), *Chôro* for cello and orchestra (1961), and *Ponteio e dança* (1946), in versions for cello and orchestra or cello and piano.

The music of Claudio Santoro (1919–1989) has been divided into three periods. From 1939 to 1947 his work tended toward the atonal and dodecaphonic (twelve-tone); between 1948 and 1960, his music leaned toward nationalism, in a style derived from Soviet theories about art. Finally, from 1960 to his death, Santoro returned to serialism and the use of aleatory techniques.

He did not compose any work for cello and orchestra. His works for cello and piano include four sonatas (1942–1943, withdrawn by the composer; 1947, 1951, and 1963) and an adagio (1946).

After obtaining his degree from the Pernambuco Conservatory, Marlos Nobre (b. 1939) studied in São Paulo with his compatriot Camargo Guarnieri and later in Buenos Aires with Ginastera. Nobre used the most diverse techniques in his compositions: aleatory music, free serialism, and a combination of rhythmic motifs and indigenous timbres. His cello compositions include *Cantos de Yemanjá*, op. 21, no. 3, for cello and piano; *Desafío II* (in three versions: for cello and string orchestra, for cello and piano, and for eight cellos), op. 31/32 (1968); the *Partita latina* for cello and piano, premiered and recorded by me in 2003; *Poema III*, op. 94, no. 3 (2002), for cello and piano; *Cantoria I*, op. 100, no. 1, for solo cello, dedicated to Antonio Meneses; and *Cantoria II*, op. 100, no. 2, for solo cello, dedicated to me.

José Antonio de Almeida (b. 1943), one of the preeminent composers of his generation, has composed a sonata for cello and piano (2003), premiered by the great Brazilian cellist Antonio Meneses.

CHILE   For almost half a century, from the 1920's to the late 1960's, Domingo Santa Cruz (1899–1987)—composer, professor, founder of musical and educational institutions, and enthusiastic promoter of music—was the principal figure in Chilean music.[16] His musical style is characterized by chromatic linearity and particularly rich counterpoint. His roots lie in the contrapuntists of the sixteenth century and in Bach, but his works also reflect Spanish rhythmic and melodic elements. His only contribution to the cello repertoire—but an important one—is his Sonata for cello and piano, op. 38 (1974–1975).

Juan Orrego-Salas (b. 1919) studied in his own country with Pedro Humberto Allende and Domingo Santa Cruz and then in the United States. He has played an active role as a composer, educator, and promoter of Ibero-American music and musicology. In 1961 he moved to Bloomington, where he taught at Indiana University's Music School and founded the Latin American Music Center.

His relationship with the great cellist Janos Starker, also a teacher at Indiana, led to the creation of two works for the cello: the *Balada* for cello and piano, op. 84 (1982–1983), and the Concerto for cello and orchestra, op. 104 (1991–1992), both premiered by Starker. He has also composed *Cantos de advenimiento* for soprano, cello, and piano, op. 25 (1948), *Dúos concertantes* for cello and piano, op. 41 (1955), *Concerto a tre* for violin, cello, piano, and orchestra, op. 52 (1962), and *Serenata* for flute and cello, op. 70 (1972).

My conversations with Orrego-Salas ultimately resulted in *Espacios*, op. 115 (1998), a new piece for cello and piano. After the premiere in Santiago and Viña del Mar, we played it in Mexico, in South Africa, and at the Kennedy Center, during a concert honoring the composer, who was present. A few months later I received a most touching gift from Orrego-Salas, his *Fantasias* for cello and orchestra, with a lovely dedication; I expect to premiere the work in 2006.

Gustavo Becerra-Schmidt (b. 1925) studied at the at the Santiago National Conservatory, where he was assistant professor in Domingo Santa Cruz's composition class. He was subsequently made full professor at the conservatory, and since 1950 he has devoted himself to the threefold task of being a composer, professor, and researcher. In 1973, after the collapse of Salvador Allende's government, Becerra sought political asylum in the Federal Republic of Germany (what was then West Germany), where he has lived ever since.

His work is exceptionally intense and varied, including his cello compositions: three partitas for solo cello, five sonatas for cello and piano, and a concerto for cello and orchestra, dedicated to the excellent Chilean cellist Arturo Valenzuela.

Becerra-Schmidt did me the honor of dedicating his Sonata no. 5 (1997) to me; Edison Quintana and I played it in Chile in 1998 and Mexico in 1999, and recorded it soon after.

Eduardo Cáceres (b. 1955) has had a brilliant career in Chile as a composer, professor, and tireless promoter of contemporary music, both in his own country and abroad. In 1996 he composed *Entrelunas* for cello and piano.

COLOMBIA   Guillermo Uribe Holguín (1880–1971) was the first director of the National Conservatory in Bogotá, founded in 1909, and the most important composer of his generation. Since he studied with Vincent d'Indy at the Schola Cantorum in Paris, there is a marked French influence in all his work, especially in the pieces written prior to 1930, when his nationalistic phase began. Uribe Holguín composed two sonatas for cello and piano.

Blas Emilio Atehortúa (b. 1933) studied in his own country and later in Buenos Aires with Ginastera, Iannis Xenakis, and Luigi Nono, among others. His cello pieces include *Romanza* (five romantic pieces, op. 85) for cello and piano and a concerto for cello and orchestra, op. 162 (1990). He is currently composing *Fantasía concertante* for cello and piano, which he hopes to complete by 2005.

Claudia Calderón (b. 1959), a pianist and composer, was born in Palmira, Colombia. She studied music in Cali and Bogotá and later in Hanover, Germany. She has also devoted time to researching the ethnic music of Colombia and Venezuela. In 2000 she composed *La revuelta circular*, a work for cello and piano, which I played and recorded in 2001.

CUBA   In Chapter 5 I discussed my visit to Cuba and my relationship with Cuban music and musicians, so here I will only provide a short
list of composers and their works.

Amadeo Roldán (1900–1939) composed *Dos canciones populares cubanas* for cello and piano.

Aurelio de la Vega (b. 1925), who has lived in Los Angeles since 1959,
wrote *Leyenda del Ariel criollo* (1953) for cello and piano.

Leo Brouwer (b. 1939), born in Havana, is a composer, guitarist, and
conductor. He studied guitar with Isaac Nicola, a student of Emilio Pu-
jol's, and specialized in composition, subsequently complementing his
studies at Julliard and at the Hartt College of Music of the University
of Hartford (1959–1960). He was the principal conductor of the Cuban
National Symphony Orchestra, and since 1992 he has also conducted the
Cordoba Symphony in Spain. He has had a brilliant career as a guitarist,
composer, and conductor, and is an enthusiastic music promoter, as well.
His principal cello work is a sonata for solo cello (1960, revised 1994).

Carlos Fariñas (1934–2002) was born in Cienfuegos and began his
musical studies in Santa Clara, Cuba. In 1948 he enrolled in the Havana
Conservatory, where he studied with José Ardévol and Harold Gramatges. In 1956 he attended Aaron Copland's course at Tanglewood, and
from 1961 to 1963 he studied at the Moscow Conservatory.

He was director of the music department at the National Theater of
Cuba and of the García Caturla Conservatory, a member of Teaching
Reform Committee, and head of the Music Department at the National
Library. He composed a concerto for cello and orchestra (see Chapter 6)
and a sonata for violin and cello (1961).

Guido López Gavilán (b. 1944) has composed *Monólogo* for cello
solo.

ECUADOR   In the archives of the Central Bank of Ecuador in Qui-
to, I found two manuscripts of scores composed by the great figure of
Ecuadorian music, Luis Humberto Salgado (1903–1977). Entitled *Ca-
pricho español* (1932) and Sonata for cello and piano (1932), they have
never been performed. Salgado also composed a cello concerto.

MEXICO   In Chapter 6 I referred to my relationship with many
Mexican composers and to the works that I have known, played, premiered, and, in some cases, recorded. Here I will present only a brief
summary of the principal cello works by Mexican composers.

Ricardo Castro (1864–1907) is the author of the first documented concerto for cello and orchestra by a Mexican composer. Written some time in the late nineteenth or early twentieth century, its world premiere took place in Paris in 1902, but the work was soon forgotten. The Mexican premiere was not held until seventy-nine years later, when Jorge Velazco, the Minería Symphony Orchestra, and I performed it in 1981.

Julián Carrillo (1875–1965) was born in a small remote village in the state of San Luis Potosí. He studied composition, conducting, and the violin at Leipzig's Royal Conservatory, and for three years he played in the famous Gewandhaus Orchestra, conducted by Arthur Nikisch. The Royal Conservatory Orchestra premiered his First Symphony.

On his return to Mexico, he was known as a rather controversial figure, which did not prevent him from becoming the conductor of Mexico's National Symphony Orchestra and twice director of the National Conservatory.

From the time he was a young man, he had been obsessed with the idea of dividing musical intervals into fractions smaller than semitones. Ever since Bach's time, the traditional system in western music had been the tempered system, whose scale is divided into twelve equal semitones. After 1924, Carrillo's compositions were characterized by the division of tones into thirds, fourths, octaves, and sixteenths. Because he had exceeded the limit of twelve semitones, Carrillo christened his system "Sonido 13" (Sound 13). His works require special instruments, like the so-called "metamorphosed" pianos; cellos and other stringed instruments can be used as they are.[17]

Manuel María Ponce (1882–1948) composed a sonata for cello and piano (1915–1917) while he was in Cuba, and Three Preludes for cello and piano (1932–1933) during a stay in Paris.

María Teresa Prieto (1896–1982), who was my aunt, was born in Spain, but composed practically all of her work in Mexico. For the cello she wrote Adagio and Fugue for cello and orchestra, and a sonata for cello and orchestra. Both works are also available in versions for cello and piano.

Carlos Chávez (1899–1978) was one of the outstanding figures of twentieth-century Mexican music. In 1975 he started working on his concerto for cello and orchestra, but managed to finish only the initial allegro. I premiered this piece in 1987 with the Orchestra of the State of Mexico under its conductor Eduardo Diazmuñoz and under circumstances described in Chapter 5. Chávez also composed Sonatina (1923) and Madrigal (1922), both for cello and piano.

Rodolfo Halffter (1900–1987) divided his time equally between Spain and Mexico, although he wrote most of his work in Mexico. He was also very active as a mentor, teacher, editor, and music promoter. In acknowledgment of his life's work, he received the National Arts and Letters Award (Mexico, 1976) and the National Music Award (Spain, 1985). Halffter composed his Sonata for cello and piano, op. 26 (1960), commissioned for the Second Inter-American Music Festival in Washington.

Blas Galindo (1910–1993) left an abundance of cello works. Among his most important pieces, I would mention his Sonata for cello and piano (1948) and two that he dedicated to me: the Sonata for solo cello (1981) and his Concerto for cello and orchestra (1984).

As related in Chapter 6, my close friendship with Manuel Enríquez (1926–1994) resulted in four works: Concerto for cello and orchestra (1984), Fantasia for cello and piano (1991), and his own cello transcriptions of Miguel Bernal Jiménez's *Danzas tarascas* and Silvestre Revueltas's *Tres piezas*, both originally written for violin and piano.

Enríquez composed other excellent cello works: Poem for cello and small string orchestra (1966), Sonatina for solo cello (1962), and Four Pieces for cello and piano. With the exception of Poem, I have recorded all of his works on compact discs.

Joaquín Gutiérrez Heras (b. 1927), a great composer, has written the following works for the cello: Duet for alto flute and cello, *Canción en el puerto* for cello and piano (1994), Two Pieces for cello and piano, and Fantasia Concertante for cello and orchestra (2005), which I premiered in September 2005.

Manuel de Elías (b. 1939) has composed the Concerto for cello and orchestra that I premiered in Mexico in 1993, as well as other works for solo cello.

Mario Lavista (b. 1943) has written several excellent works for cello: *Cuaderno de viaje* (1989; two pieces for solo cello), Quotations (1976), and Three Secular Dances (1994), the last two for cello and piano. At the time of this writing, he is composing a work for cello and orchestra, which I hope to premiere in 2007.

I met Federico Ibarra (b. 1946) in 1988, and up to now our friendship has resulted in two very successful pieces that I have commissioned: the Concerto for cello and orchestra (1989), which I have played in many countries and has been widely acclaimed both by the public and critics, and the Sonata for cello and piano (1992), which has met with similar success. He has also composed a sonata for two cellos and piano (2004).

Arturo Márquez (b. 1950) has written a piece for cello and piano (1999) and a concerto for cello and orchestra (1999–2000).

Marcela Rodríguez (b. 1951) has composed a concerto for cello and orchestra (1994), which I premiered in 1997 during the Twenty-fourth International Cervantes Festival, as well as *Lumbre* (1990), a piece for solo cello.

Eugenio Toussaint (b. 1954) has, to date, composed seven works for cello: *Pour les enfants* for cello and piano (2000); Concertino for cello and guitar (1993); two cello concertos (1982–1991 and 1999); a piece for solo cello (1992); a tango for cello and piano (1999); and *Bachriations* for solo cello (2005).

Samuel Zyman (b. 1956) has written one cello concerto; Chapter 5 describes its nerve-racking world premiere at Lincoln Center in 1990. Since then, Zyman has composed five other excellent works for cello: a sonata and a fantasia, both for cello and piano; the Suite for Two Cellos; *Reflection*, a piece for eight cellos (2001); and a suite for solo cello (2006).

The career of Javier Álvarez (b. 1956) has flourished mostly in Europe, principally in England and Sweden, but his works are being played worldwide. He composed *Serpiente y escalera* (1998), a work for cello and piano that I commissioned.

PERU   Since Peru and Mexico were the most important centers during the Spanish colonization of America, it is natural that Peru, like Mexico, developed an active musical life, particularly in Lima and Cuzco. This activity declined considerably after independence from Spain was achieved, and it was not until the twentieth century that several eminent figures emerged on the musical scene.

Among present-day composers is Celso Garrido-Lecca (b. 1926), who is discussed at length in Chapter 5. He is the author of a cello concerto—also available in a version with piano as *Sonata Fantasía*—and *Soliloquy* for solo cello. I premiered these works in 1991 and 1997, respectively.

Edgar Valcárcel (b. 1932) studied in Lima, at Hunter College in New York, at the Torcuato di Tella Institute in Buenos Aires, and at the Columbia-Princeton Electronic Music Center. In 2003 he composed the *Concierto indio* for cello and orchestra, premiered in 2004 by Jesús Castro-Balbi.

PORTUGAL   Fernando Lopes-Graça (1906–1994) studied in Lisbon and Paris. His work is usually divided into three distinct periods. The first (1932–1936) clearly reflects the influence of Stravinsky, Schoenberg, and Bartók, whereas during his second phase (1937–1961), which began during his stay in Paris, he gravitated toward the nationalistic style based on the melodic and rhythmic characteristics of Portuguese music. In

1961, he embarked on his third period, in which his language, now devoid of the direct influence of Portuguese music, expanded its tonal and rhythmic possibilities, with a greater focus on structure. It was during this period that Mstislav Rostropovich commissioned and premiered his *Concerto da camera* for cello and orchestra (1965).

The first compositions of Luis Filipe Pires (b. 1934) clearly denote a neoclassical tendency, but by 1961 his style had undergone a radical transformation that caused him to be labeled "avant-garde." He has composed only one cello piece, the Sonatina for cello and piano (1954).

PUERTO RICO   Roberto Sierra (b. 1953), who lives in the United States, is, in my opinion, one of the most important composers of the Americas. In 1981 he wrote a small piece, whimsically entitled *Salsa on the C String*, for cello and piano. As I mentioned in Chapter 6, in 1999 he composed an excellent cello concerto entitled *Four Verses for Cello and Orchestra*. In 2003 he composed Sonata no. 1 for cello and piano, and in 2006, the *Sonata elegiaca* for cello and piano, which I expect to premiere in 2007.

SPAIN   As can be seen in Appendix 2, there are so many works for cello by Spanish composers that I will only mention those I know best and consider the most relevant.

Among the early works of Manuel de Falla (1876–1946) are two pieces for cello and piano: *Romanza* (1899) and *Melodía* (1897–1899). His most frequently played work for cello and piano is the *Suite popular española*, a transcription of his *Siete canciones populares españolas*.

Enrique Granados (1867–1916) composed several works of a light but agreeable character for cello and piano.

Gaspar Cassadó (1897–1966) was a great cellist who composed a good number of works for this instrument, all of them distinguished for their grace, virtuosity, and melodic character, as one might well expect from this master. Among his best-known works, we should include his *Sonata en el estilo antiguo español* (1925), a suite for solo cello (1926), a concerto for cello and orchestra (1926), and diverse pieces such as *Requiebros* (1931), *Lamento de Boabdil* (1931), and *Danza del diablo verde* (1926), as well as his transcription of Frescobaldi's Toccata (1925).[18]

Among the cello works composed by Joaquín Rodrigo (1901–1999) are two concertos for cello and orchestra, the *Sonata a la breve* for cello and piano (1977), *Siciliana* for cello and piano (1929), and *Como una fantasía* for solo cello (1979).

Roberto Gerhard (1896–1970) was Schoenberg's only Spanish student, having studied with him in Vienna and Berlin from 1923 to 1928. Gerhard is the author of an excellent sonata for cello and piano (1956), structured in three movements, in which we discern serialism and Spanish melodic motifs.

The independent, eclectic musical approach of Xavier Montsalvatge (1912–2002), lying somewhere between the nationalistic and the avantgarde, steered him to a series of works of great musical quality, such as his *Sonata concertante* for cello and piano (1972). In 1995 he composed a short piece entitled *Evocación*. In Chapter 6 I describe the origin of the charming piece entitled *Invención a la italiana* for cello and piano, which I premiered in Mexico in September 2000 and recorded in New York in January 2001.

Carmelo Bernaola (1929–2002) wrote *Clamores y secuencias* for cello and orchestra (1993), premiered by the outstanding Spanish cellist Asier Polo.

Cristóbal Halffter (b. 1930), one of Europe's leading musicians (see Fig. 55 on page 282), has written three works for cello and orchestra, each linked to a particular cellist. The first, Partita for cello and orchestra (1957), commissioned by Gaspar Cassadó, is the composer's final tribute to neoclassicism. It consists of four movements: *Preludio a la madrigalesca, fiamenga, courante, chacona.*

At the request of the National Music Commission, Halffter wrote his first cello concerto (1974) for Siegfried Palm and completed it in time for the Granada Festival. His Cello Concerto no. 2 (1985) was the result of Rostropovich's persistence and the composer's desire to honor Federico García Lorca. The concert's subtitle is a quote from the poet: "Nothing remains but silence."

Luis de Pablo (b. 1930), one of Spain's most important composers, wrote *Frondoso misterio* for cello and orchestra, and it was premiered by Asier Polo.

Manuel Castillo (b. 1930) studied in Seville and then in Madrid with Lucas Moreno and Conrado del Campo and in Paris with Lazare Levy and Nadia Boulanger. In 1959 he was awarded the National Music Prize, and in 1964 was appointed director of the conservatory in his native city. In 1992 the Education and Science Council added the name "Manuel Castillo" to the conservatory in Seville. His works for cello include a concerto for cello and orchestra, a sonata, and *Alborada* for cello and piano, for which I gave the world premiere in 1995.

Claudio Prieto (b. 1934) studied with Luis Guzmán, Samuel Rubio, and Ricardo Dorado in Spain; in Italy with Goffredo Petrassi, Boris Porena, and Bruno Maderna; and in Germany with György Ligeti, Karlheinz Stockhausen, and Earle Brown. His command of compositional technique, coloring, and instrumental timbre, along with the expressive power of his work, soon earned him a rightful place as one of the most important names in Spanish music; he has won countless national and international awards. He is also the author of the *Concierto de amor* for cello and orchestra, a sonata for cello and piano, and other works for cello.

Tomás Marco (b. 1942), a multifaceted figure of great relevance to the European cultural scene, is the composer of works in diverse genres, the author of important books and essays, and a highly respected musical critic and promoter. He has composed numerous works for the cello (see Appendix 2), including five that I have had the privilege of premiering: the *Primer espejo de Falla* for cello and piano (1994); the *Partita Piatti* for solo cello (1999); the *Laberinto marino* for cello and strings (2002), described in Chapter 6; the *Ensueño y resplandor de Don Quijote* for violin, cello, and orchestra (2004), which violinist Manuel Guillén and I premiered in Spain in 2004 with the Bilbao Orchestra conducted by Pedro Halffter; and a yet untitled piece for solo cello (2005).

The musical training of José Luis Turina (b. 1952) began at the conservatory in Barcelona and later continued at the Royal Conservatory of Music in Madrid and the Spanish Academy of Fine Arts in Rome. He has received numerous awards, such as the Queen Sofía International Prize for Composition from the Ferrer Salat Foundation in 1986 and the National Music Prize from the Ministry of Education and Culture in 1996. In the winter of 1997–1998 he concluded the composition of *Concierto da chiesa* for cello and string orchestra, which I premiered in St. Petersburg, Russia in 2003.

URUGUAY   The cello does not seem to be especially popular among Uruguayan composers, as can be seen from this rather meager list.

León Biriotti (b. 1929), a composer, an oboist, and a conductor, belongs to the avant-garde of the 1960s; he wrote a concerto for cello and chamber orchestra (1980). Jaurés Lamarque Pons (1917–1982) composed Piece for cello and piano, which I recorded with Edison Quintana in 1998.

VENEZUELA   Between the late nineteenth and early twentieth centuries, the most famous names in Venezuelan music were Teresa Carreño

(1853–1917) and Reynaldo Hahn (1874–1947). Carreño, born in Caracas, was a world-renowned pianist, composer, singer, and conductor.

Two later musicians who had an important impact on Venezuelan music were Vicente Emilio Sojo (1887–1974)—the most influential composer and musician between 1920 and 1960—and Juan Bautista Plaza (1898–1965), an educator, conductor, nationalistic composer, and expert on colonial music. Plaza left us only his *Diferencias sobre un aire venezolano* for cello and piano and the Melody for cello and piano.

Although Venezuela ventured into classical music much later than other Ibero-American countries, it has since become one of the most dynamic musical centers in the entire region; for more on this subject, see Chapter 6. Here I will discuss the principal Venezuelan composers whom I know to have written works for cello.

Aldemaro Romero (b. 1928) is a composer and pianist who has successfully explored concert music and popular music. He wrote a suite for cello and piano (1976) and a cello concerto called *Concierto del Delfín* (2003).

Alfredo Rugeles (b. 1949, Washington, D.C.) studied music in Caracas and in Germany (at the Robert Schumann Institute in Düsseldorf and at the Courses for New Music in Darmstadt). He has conducted orchestras in several countries, and his works have been performed throughout Europe, the United States, and Latin America. Since 1991 he has been the associate musical director of the Símon Bolívar Symphony Orchestra, and he is also the director of the annual Inter-American Music Festival in Venezuela. To date he has written only one piece for solo cello, *Inventio* (1983), a transcription of his 1976 piece for clarinet of the same name.

Paul Desenne (b. 1959,), a cellist and composer, was born in Caracas and studied composition (with Iannis Ioannidis) and cello at the Paris conservatory. He spent ten years in Europe, where he played classical music, contemporary music, and even tangos and salsa, with many Ibero-American groups. He devotes himself to composing mostly chamber music in what he calls the "galeónico" style, which combines influences from Spanish, African, and indigenous Venezuelan music, along with music from the rest of the continent, often using Venezuela's national instrument, the *cuatro*. He has composed a work for three cellos called *Pizzi-Quitiplás* (1989), a suite for solo cello (1999), and a cello concerto (2001).

Ricardo Lorenz (b. 1961) was born in Maracaibo and is one of Venezuela's brightest young talents. He received his musical training in

55. With Spanish composer and conductor Cristóbal Halffter and the National Orchestra of Spain. Madrid, 1994.

Caracas and studied with pianists Elizabeth Marichal and Harriet Serr. He obtained his MA in composition from Indiana University and his PhD in music from the University of Chicago. From 1987 to 1992 he was interim director of Indiana University's Latin American Music Center, following in the footsteps of Juan Orrego-Salas, with whom he studied. His symphonic works have been performed by many renowned orchestras in Europe, the United States, and Latin America. As I mentioned in Chapter 6, in May 1998 I premiered his *Cecilia en azul y verde* for cello and piano, in Caracas. In 2005 he composed a piece for solo cello, which is as yet untitled.

56. The author receiving the French Order of Officer of the Arts and Letters, from Bruno Delaye, French Ambassador in Mexico, 1999.

57. Carlos Prieto and dancer Pilar Rioja, recipients of the 1999 Mexican Cultural Institute of New York Award in New York City. LEFT TO RIGHT: J. García Oteyza, Ambassador Jorge Pinto, Pilar Rioja, Carlos Prieto, Clark B. Winter (Chairman of the Mexican Cultural Institute of New York), and Peter Rockefeller.

58. The author receiving the Cultural Leadership Award from Robert Blocker, Dean of the School of Music of Yale University. New Haven, Connecticut, 2002.

59. With Portuguese writer and Nobel Prize winner José Saramago on the occasion of the presentation of the Portuguese edition of THE ADVENTURES OF A CELLO. *Lisbon, 2002.*

These pages, written in 2009, are accounts of some of my activities and travels subsequent to the initial publication of this book.

A NEW TOUR OF RUSSIA, APRIL 2005

In Chapter 5, I described my long relationship with Russia between 1962 and 2003. In 2005, I returned to Russia with a twofold purpose: to give a series of concerts in Moscow and the vast territory of Siberia, and to present the Russian version of this book, *Priklyucheniya Violoncheli*.

For me, this trip was the fulfillment of a childhood dream. I had always wanted to visit Siberia, ever since I read Jules Verne's book about Michel Strogoff, courier for Tsar Alexander II, and his extraordinary journey from St. Petersburg to Irkutsk. As I grew older, *The House of the Dead* by Fyodor Dostoevsky—exiled to Siberia in 1849—and the works of Aleksandr Solzhenitsyn—*A Day in the Life of Ivan Denisovich*, published in 1962 when I was studying in Moscow, and *The Gulag Archipelago*—only intensified my eagerness to visit the region.[1] During the one-month tour, we traveled many thousands of kilometers by plane, train, and automobile, according to the following itinerary: Moscow—Chita—Ulan-Ude—Irkutsk—Novosibirsk—Tomsk—Novokuznetsk—Kemerovo—Mezhdurechensk—Biysk—Chemal—Novosibirsk—Akademgorodok—Novosibirsk—Moscow. The tour of Moscow and several Siberian cities included fourteen concerts and presentations of this book's Russian version.

Rehearsals began on April 3 in Moscow with the superb pianist Mikhail Arkadiev, "honored artist of the Russian Republic," who for thirteen years was the frequent accompanist of the famous Russian baritone Dmitri Hvorostovsky.

Prior to our night flight to Siberia, Enrique Arriola, Mexico's cultural attaché in Russia, arranged a visit to the magnificent exhibit titled

"Chagall: Tribute to the Homeland at the Tretyakov Gallery." It consisted of paintings from Paris's Centre Pompidou, as well as from Russian private and public collections. It brought back memories of my first visits in 1962 to this gallery and to Leningrad's Hermitage Museum, when Chagall's paintings were hidden from view in the warehouses of both museums, banned since Stalin's time for being "modernistic and decadent." In 1987, thanks to Gorbachev's "glasnost" campaign, a major Chagall exhibit was held in Moscow's Pushkin Museum.

CHITA: THE REGION BEYOND LAKE BAIKAL

On April 5, we set out on our Siberian tour. That night, María Isabel, Mikhail Arkadiev, and I departed for what was then called Chita, the capital of the oblast. In 2008 it was restructured and renamed the Zabai-kalie Oblast, the "region beyond Lake Baikal," on the easternmost tip of Siberia, over 6,000 kilometers from Moscow. After a six-and-a-half-hour flight, we arrived in Chita at 9 a.m. (3 a.m. Moscow time).

The Zabaikalie region is adjacent to the Mongolian and Chinese borders. Although it encompasses an area as vast as France, its population is barely 1.3 million, while Chita, its capital, has fewer than 400,000 inhabitants. Chita's university boasts an outstanding linguistics department. Oxana Lantsova, the Spanish teacher, invited us to get together with her students, who were eager to meet Spanish-speaking people. One student, who addressed us in surprisingly fluent Spanish, declared that reading García Márquez's *One Hundred Years of Solitude* marked a turning point in his life.

During the Soviet period, foreigners were forbidden to go to Chita, and even today, except for some Chinese merchants, there are still very few. Our arrival in Chita created quite a stir; few Westerners and even fewer Mexicans reach that area. The region subsists on its lumber trade and on its commerce with China.

Chita is surrounded by the taiga, the beautiful subarctic evergreen forest. Wolves are so abundant that annual quotas have been established as incentives to their eradication. Although the legendary Siberian tiger occasionally ventures into Chita, it usually remains in the neighboring Far Eastern region.

During the 1827 uprising against the tsar, eighty-five of the "Decembrists," aristocrats and intellectuals who defied the oppressive regime, were exiled to Chita as punishment. Several concentration camps operated near the capital during the Soviet period. Mikhail Khodorkovsky, once Russia's most prominent businessman, is currently imprisoned in this region.

Our recital in the Philharmonic Hall marked the beginning of our Siberian tour. I reproduce its program here because it served as the basis for our subsequent recitals in Siberia:

Sonata for Cello and Piano	Shostakovich
Sonata for Solo Cello	Kodály
Tres piezas	Revueltas/Enríquez (Mexico)
Canción en el Puerto	Gutiérrez Heras (Mexico)
Le Grand Tango	Piazzolla (Argentina)

The next afternoon, we boarded a train that followed the Trans-Siberian route to Ulan-Ude. The 580-kilometer trip westward took ten hours. We stayed in a comfortable sleeping compartment; María Isabel and I occupied the lower berths while Cello Prieto and our luggage were stored in the upper berths.

UNEXPECTED ACCOMMODATIONS IN ULAN-UDE, AND TWO CONCERTS WITH THE NATIONAL ORCHESTRA

We arrived in Ulan-Ude, capital of Buryatia, or the Buryat Autonomous Republic, at 2:30 a.m. Chita time, 1:30 a.m. local time. The Buryat cultural authorities who welcomed us at the station led us to an imposing building that, to our great surprise, was not a hotel at all but rather the consulate general of Mongolia, where we were assigned to no less than the presidential suite, which houses the president of the neighboring republic of Mongolia during his state visits.

The official languages of Buryatia—an area with a considerable Mongol population—are Russian and Buryat, which closely resembles the Mongolian language. Our hosts proudly informed us that this land was the birthplace of Genghis Khan's mother.

Ulan-Ude's history museum houses an interesting exhibit on Buddhism, which today is no longer persecuted and is embraced by a considerable number of Buryats. The city's downtown area, for pedestrians only and lined with lovely houses belonging to ancient merchant families, recalls the period when Ulan-Ude was the crossroads for the trade routes among Russia, China, and Mongolia. The city, once called Verjeudinsk (On the Ude River) was renamed Ulan-Ude (Red City) in 1926. A gigantic head of Lenin presides over the city's main square.

The Ethnographic Museum is located in the wooded area 60 kilometers from the city. It exhibits replicas of the buildings, the church, the school, and the homes first inhabited by the Buryats and then the Russians—the Cossacks, and later the Orthodox Russians. (Known as the "Old Believers," the Orthodox Russians arrived from European Russia after refusing to accept the reforms introduced by Patriarch Nikon during the mid-seventeenth century.)

I expressed my desire to visit a fortress near Ulan-Ude with an extremely interesting historical past, but, unfortunately, not even its ruins remain. It was built around 1727 by an African called Ibrahim Gannibal, who was purchased as a slave when he was a boy in Constantinople and was presented to Peter the Great as a gift. The tsar, astonished at the child's intelligence, gave him the opportunity to study in Russia and in France. Eventually, Gannibal became a celebrity due to his outstanding achievements in military engineering, such as designing the fortress of Buryatia, built in order to defend the Russo-Chinese frontier. Gannibal's additional claim to fame was as the great-grandfather of the poet Alexander Pushkin, who never concealed his pride in his African ancestor. Pushkin even compiled material for a biography of Gannibal that he never completed.

The program for the concert in Buryatia's Opera and Ballet Theater was rather unusual. During the first part, I played works for cello and piano with Arkadiev, and, after the intermission, Shostakovich's Concerto No. 1 for Cello and Orchestra with the National Orchestra of Buryatia, conducted by Valery T. Galsanov. Galsanov and the orchestra's first cello, M. L. Baldayev, mentioned that during the Soviet period, artists of such stature as S. Knushevitsky, M. Rostropovich, D. Shafran, and S. Richter would often perform in Ulan-Ude. They asked me to convey their warmest regards to their friend and great cellist M. Rostropovich, who had never returned to Buryatia.

We repeated the same program the following day, after which we sampled a "fourchette," a cold buffet served in the theater's vestibule. From there we left for the station, where we boarded the night train to Irkutsk, an eight-hour trip, once again moving westward.

IRKUTSK AND A STROLL OVER LAKE BAIKAL

We were met in Irkutsk by the cultural authorities of the oblast, among them Rita Karysheva, assistant director of the conservatory. As soon as we were settled in the delightful Rus Hotel, Rita drove María Isabel and me to visit Lake Baikal. The seventy-kilometer highway we traveled on was built for President Eisenhower's projected visit, at Premier Nikita Khrushchev's invitation, to the Soviet Union—a trip that would include a visit to Lake Baikal. However, when a U2 spy plane was shot down over Soviet territory in 1960, the trip was cancelled. The highway, however, remains.

Lake Baikal, the deepest lake in the world, accounts for one-fifth of the world's fresh water, and is considerably purer and larger than the five Great Lakes in the United States combined. Numerous peoples have marveled at this immense lake, among them the Buryats, Mongols who settled along its banks long before Genghis Khan's conquests during the thirteenth century. Russian fur traders started arriving around 1640, taking advantage of the rich animal life in the region that provided them with ermine, sable, and mink.

It was early April, and we were overwhelmed by the sheer beauty of the pine, cedar, and larch forests all along the Angara River. If we had any qualms about walking over the frozen lake, they quickly dissipated when we saw a heavy truck filled with fishermen making its way over the surface.

Rita bought a delicious fish called omul, which, like many other fish, can only be found in Lake Baikal. The locals capture it by perforating the ice, then they smoke it in rather rudimentary wood stoves and sell it on the riverbanks. Because of the intense cold, we ate inside the van and Rita welcomed us to this land by producing a bottle of vodka.

In Ulan-Ude and in Irkutsk we purchased and drank bottled water of exceptional purity, extracted from the lake at a depth of over four hundred meters. But Russian entrepreneurs are now exploiting the banks along the lake by building huge condominiums and luxury homes that will probably pollute the purity of the water, as is the case with the cellulose plant on the southernmost tip of the lake.

Irkutsk is such a beautiful city that, at one time, it was known as "The Paris of Siberia." As we strolled along stately Lenin Avenue, we came upon streets with magnificent late nineteenth-century and early twentieth-century buildings, in addition to the typical Irkutsk wooden dwellings, many of which were badly deteriorated through years of neglect.

We visited the Sukachev Art Museum, the richest in Siberia. Among its many outstanding works, it houses paintings by Repin, Kramskoy, Vasnetsov, Savrasov, and Shishkin, besides Eastern European pieces and collections from Japan and China. A 1951 painting by Arkady Plastov,

Tractor Drivers' Supper, so displeased the Socialist Realism advocates, because it depicted an everyday family country scene instead of a collective theme, that the painting was exiled to Siberia. The museum's director reported that Nikita Khrushchev, who visited the museum in 1961, was so enchanted by the painting that had been "condemned to Siberia" that he wanted to take it to Moscow. The museum's authorities refused to part with it, but the artist painted a copy for Moscow's Tretyakov Gallery. The museum also has its share of officially acceptable paintings from the Stalinist period. Rendered during the dreadful famine of 1935, some of them portray smiling, well-fed farmworkers counting the money earned that day.

Our recital took place before a packed house at 2 p.m. at the Irkutsk Music Institute. We played encore after encore until we were ordered to stop, lest we miss the 5 p.m. train to Novosibirsk.

THIRTY-TWO HOURS ON THE TRANS-SIBERIAN ROUTE (IRKUTSK—NOVOSIBIRSK), AND FIRST VISIT TO NOVOSIBIRSK

Siberia is so vast that Novosibirsk is three different time zones and 1,450 kilometers from Irkutsk. We spent the afternoon and night of April 12, plus the entire next day, on the train—at one point crossing the imposing Yenisei River, the longest in Russia. After our thirty-two-hour journey, we arrived in Novosibirsk, capital of the oblast of the same name, the administrative center of the Federal District of Siberia and the third most populated city in Russia after Moscow and St. Petersburg. It was 12:40 a.m. Irkutsk time, and 9:40 p.m. local time.[1] We had expected to get a good night's sleep, but it was not to be.

We were welcomed at the station by a delegation headed by Aleksandr Marchenko, director of the Novosibirsk Music Institute Conservatory, where many distinguished musicians of the former Soviet Union and the Russia of today have studied. After greetings were made, we had barely enough time to check into the Sibir Hotel and change our clothes; then we immediately set out for the restaurant at the Philharmonic Theater, where the cultural minister of Siberia and his entourage offered a delicious meal, sprinkled with effusive vodka toasts—all this, after a thirty-two-hour train ride!

The following day we had a full schedule. In the morning, I gave a master class at the Music Institute, and in the afternoon, as a Mexican citizen, I was asked to represent my country by formally inaugurating an exhibit by the celebrated Mexican photographer Casasola at the art museum. In the evening, I had my recital with Mikhail Arkadiev at the Novosibirsk Music Institute.

A few days later, we were to return to Novosibirsk.

BY ROAD FROM NOVOSIBIRSK TO TOMSK, AND THE EDISON DENISOV FESTIVAL

From Novosibirsk, our station wagon took us two hundred kilometers north to Tomsk, the capital of the oblast of the same name. In the late nineteenth century, when the Trans-Siberian railroad route was laid out, the inhabitants of Tomsk objected to the train passing through their city, thus depriving Tomsk of the expansion that characterized Novonikolaev (renamed Novosibirsk in 1925). Perhaps it was this circumstance, combined with the presence of a university in Tomsk, that allowed the city to preserve its serene provincial charm. Its main street is dotted with numerous pleasant cafés and restaurants that we frequented during our stay.

The prominent composer Edison Denisov (1929–1996), one of the most outstanding Russian composers of his period, was born in Tomsk. He had studied mathematics before he decided to take Shostakovich's advice and devote himself to composing music. During the late 1950s, Denisov cultivated an "unhealthy" interest in music composed outside the Soviet Union, especially the works of Pierre Boulez and the Second School of Vienna. The innovative character that soon permeated Denisov's compositions clashed with the type of music advocated by the conservative Soviet system. Denisov, who had always been enthralled by French culture, spent the last few years of his life in Paris, where he died in 1996.

Each year, a major contemporary music festival named after Denisov is held in Tomsk. In 2005, I had the honor of inaugurating this festival as a soloist with the Tomsk Philharmonic Orchestra, conducted by Evgenii Kiss, in the Tomsk Philharmonic Theater's newly restored hall. The program began with a work by Denisov, *Painting for Orchestra*. I then played Shostakovich's Concerto No. 1, followed by the Russian premiere of the Concerto for Cello and Orchestra by the Mexican composer Federico Ibarra, which was greeted with huge ovations by the audience members packed into the concert hall.

The next day, Mikhail Arkadiev and I gave a recital in a magnificent venue, the Organ Hall of the Tomsk Philharmonic.

THREE CONCERTS IN THE OBLAST OF KEMEROVO:
NOVOKUZNETSK, KEMEROVO, AND MEZHDURECHENSK

From Tomsk, we went by road to the site of our next concert, the city of Novokuznetsk—a large steel and industrial center that suffers from considerable atmospheric pollution.

We stayed at a house assigned to guests of the local government. It turned out to be a pleasant change in our tour routine, since all our meals were prepared "at home," where the local authorities would join us for lunch or dinner. One evening we received a visit from the mayor, who happened to be a very cultured man as well as a composer and accordionist. After warming up with several vodkas, he began playing a series of popular tunes and, before long, we witnessed a lively session of singing and dancing.

Novokuznetsk, originally called Kuznetsk, was founded as a Cossack outpost on the banks of the Tom River. As is often the case in Russian cities today, the population of Novokuznetsk is declining. According to the 2002 census, it had 550,000 inhabitants, compared to 600,000 in 1989. Novokuznetsk is located in the Kemerovo Oblast, where I gave three concerts: in the capital Kemerovo, in Mezhdurechensk, and in Novokuznetsk.

60. In the vastness of Siberia, April 2005.

THE "ROCKY ROAD" FROM NOVOKUZNETSK TO BIYSK

When the tour was being organized, I was asked whether I would be interested in giving a concert in Biysk, in the Department of Altai near the Mongolian border. We were informed that the road was not in very good condition; this would prove to be a huge understatement, but I insisted on going ahead, figuring that we could put up with a certain amount of inconvenience for the sake of visiting this remote region.

We set out on the road from Novokuznetsk to Biysk, and it took our station wagon six hours to cover 200 kilometers. On several occasions, barely managing to advance at five or ten kilometers per hour, we would come upon road signs indicating that the maximum speed limit was forty kilometers per hour. (Ironically, the make of the vehicle we were driving was "Gazelle.") The road we were following had at one time been a highway, but now it was nothing but a dirt road filled with potholes. We arrived at our destination completely covered in dust. With my finger, I traced the words "Cello Prieto in Siberia" on the black cello case. Upon our arrival in Biysk, we were greeted by the local TV crew. When I jokingly showed the reception committee and the camera operators what I had written on the grimy case, they hastily offered to clean it by spraying it with water—an offer that we, of course, just as hastily refused.

We gave a concert at the Music Institute in Biysk, one of the principal cities in the Department of Altai.

THE REGION OF ALTAI: A SIBERIAN SWITZERLAND, AND A LONG DAY

The natural surroundings of the Altai mountain range are breathtakingly beautiful. The day after our concert in Biysk, we were treated to a VIP program. It included breakfast in the little village of Cheposh in a private house; a visit to a newly rebuilt monastery across a hanging bridge over the Katun River; and, after a long drive, lunch in another small private house by a lovely river near Chemal. Before lunch, I asked if I could wash my hands, which was not precisely my actual intention. Our hostess, after graciously providing me with a fresh bar of soap and a clean towel, asked me to follow her and guided me to the river. I dutifully washed my hands in the river's freezing water, then wandered off into the woods for a moment.

Upon my return to the house, we enjoyed a delicious meal prepared by a lady who forms part of a private group devoted to "rural tourism." After the meal, we embarked on the long journey back to Novosibirsk.

CONCERTS AND PRESENTATIONS IN NOVOSIBIRSK, AND AKADEMGORODOK OF *PRIKLYUCHENIYA VIOLONCHELI*

The following afternoon, Aleksandr Marchenko, director of the Music Institute, and I took part in the presentation of the Russian version of this book at the Novosibirsk Philharmonic Theater. Later on, we departed for Akademgorodok, a city nestled in a privileged spot in the middle of the forest, half an hour from Novosibirsk. It was created half a century ago to provide the most favorable living conditions for the finest scientists of the Soviet period. After the collapse of the Soviet Union in 1991, Akademgorodok was somewhat neglected, but Prime Minister Putin, who realizes the advantages of supporting and promoting scientific investigations, is giving new impetus to this city.

At 6:45 p.m. Arkadiev and I gave a recital at the beautiful Dom Uchionnikh (House of Scientists), and at 8:30, I presented the Russian edition of my book. Then Akademgorodok's cultural authorities offered us a memorable dinner held at the private restaurant in the House of Scientists, a club with a warm, friendly atmosphere.

MOSCOW: BOOK PRESENTATION AND CONCERT

The next morning we headed for the Novosibirsk airport and boarded the 8 a.m., four-hour flight to Moscow, where, due to the three-hour time difference, we landed at 9 a.m. Moscow time.

Our last activity during this long tour of Russia was a presentation of the book and a concert with Mikhail Arkadiev in Moscow's Tchaikovsky Cultural Center. Oleg Smolensk, Director of the Tchaikovsky Cultural Center; Luciano Joublanc Montaño, Mexico's Ambassador to Russia; Aleksei Selezniov, Professor Emeritus of Cello at Moscow's Tchaikovsky Conservatory; and I all took part in the event.

NEW CONCERTS AND DISCOVERING A NEW CHINA, MAY 2006

As I mentioned in Chapter 5, my first concerts in China took place in 1979, barely three years after the death of Mao Zedong and the end of the Cultural Revolution. When I returned in 1985, the first fundamental changes brought about by Deng Xiaoping's reforms were already evident.

In May 2006, twenty-one years after our previous visit, María Isabel and I returned again to China, this time with pianist Edison Quintana, in order to participate in the 2006 "Meet in Beijing" international arts festival and also perform in Shanghai. The country's transformation could not have been more spectacular. From 1978, when the earliest reforms were introduced, to the present (2009), the Chinese economy, in terms of its GDP, has grown at the highest rate in the world—an average of almost 10 percent per year. In 2005, the Chinese economy was the fourth largest in the world, calculated in dollars at current exchange rates. In 2007, China's GDP surpassed Germany's, ranking third after the United States and Japan.

At first glance, Beijing appears to be an exemplar of uncontrollable urban sprawl. However, the city follows a carefully planned layout, with huge avenues running east to west through the city, traversed by south to north streets. This pattern was derived from Beijing's original design, in which the Forbidden City, oriented south to north, was surrounded by districts of *siheyuan*s, courtyards with houses on all four sides, and *hutong*s, narrow streets or alleys, running from south to north and east to west. Despite massive reconstruction work in the capital, the streets and avenues adhere to this original pattern. Beijing's principal thoroughfare is Chang'an Avenue, which passes in front of the entrance to the Forbidden City and constitutes the northern boundary of Tiananmen Square.

In 1979, Beijing more closely resembled a very large village than a capital city. With the exception of the Forbidden City and a few new buildings, the large *siheyuan* and *hutong* neighborhoods were distributed on both sides of the avenue. In 1985, the predominant view from our place of lodging, the Hotel of Nationalities, was still of these particular districts, with their dirt roads and their walled-in houses surrounding the central courtyards. The contrast in 2006 could not have been greater. Both sides of Chang'an Avenue now feature the ultramodern buildings and lovely, tree-lined gardens that proliferate throughout the city's many new avenues. I have never seen a city with such an intense construction rate. One can easily understand why Beijing, as well as Shanghai, attracts the attention of architects all over the world, and why some people call Beijing "the oldest city still under construction."

The old *siheyuan* and *hutong* neighborhoods are rapidly disappearing, replaced with housing projects that leave ample room for the new thoroughfares. Their residents have preferential rights to the new apartments, whose dimensions are at least equivalent to those of their previous abodes. Some residents complain that, with their new, rather impersonal, apartments, they have lost the community spirit and the close ties with friends and families that once prevailed in their picturesque neighborhoods.

Additionally, the *siheyuan*s and *hutong*s are vanishing at such a rate that it has become a source of concern for Chinese urban developers and historians. They believe that the extinction of these ancient neighborhoods, so closely associated with Beijing's ancestral history, has contributed to the loss of an important part of the city's essence and its personality by transforming it into a new Tokyo or another New York.

That evening, we arrived at the Beijing Concert Hall to rehearse before our performance. A few weeks prior to our trip to China, the concert organizers had sent me an e-mail requesting my confirmation of the concert's program. The message was written in perfect English, and in very gracious terms. At that time, I happened to be in New York, where I played on April 20 and 21. I replied, providing the information they requested and ending my message with the words, "Warm greetings from New York."

When the organizers welcomed us at the Beijing Concert Hall, they showed me the attractive printed program. It was all in Chinese, naturally. However, the musical program itself was also in English, and as I read along, I confirmed that it entirely corresponded to the program I had sent them from New York. However, to my astonishment, I noticed that the concert would end with an additional, unscheduled work.

This was the program:

Sonata for cello and piano	Shostakovich
Sonata for solo cello	Kodály
Intermission	
Three Preludes	Manuel M. Ponce (Mexico)
Song in the Harbor	Gutiérrez Heras (Mexico)
Le Grand Tango	Astor Piazzolla (Argentina)
Warm Greetings from New York	

When the organizers noticed the surprised expression on my face as I read the title of the last work, they hastened to say, "We are sorry that we did not mention the name of the composer of *Warm Greetings from New*

York, since you omitted this information in your message," adding that they assumed it was a work in the same vein as "New York, New York."

We played to a full house at the Beijing Concert Hall. The audience's response required us to play several encores. At the organizers' request, I had prepared a brief description of each work, which was translated into Mandarin and read by an interpreter. Since it seemed appropriate to include a Chinese work in our first concert, the first encore was a piece by the eminent Chinese composer Chen Yi, *Romance of Hsiao and Ch'in*. Before the concert started, I had informed the interpreter that we would cancel "Warm Greetings from New York" and play *Romance of Hsiao and Ch'in* instead. It was very warmly received.

BEIJING—SHANGHAI

In seventy-five minutes, a China Eastern Airlines Airbus flew us to Shanghai's Hongqiao Airport. We were welcomed by Mexico's Consul General in Shanghai, Mauricio Escanero, and a delegation from the Shanghai Arts Center.

We stayed at the Heng Sen Hotel, in a wooded area of Shanghai, once part of the French concession. We left the cello and our luggage at the hotel, then, in Escanero's car, went for coffee on the terrace of a building located on an avenue once known as the Bund, with an ample promenade along the Huangpu River. The terrace afforded a magnificent view of the city, including the Huangpu River upon which we saw innumerable boats loaded with minerals, coal, and other products. We recalled witnessing this same scene in 1985.

However, what really astonished us was what we discovered on the other side of the river. What a few years earlier had been nothing but farmland had burgeoned into an impressive city. Pudong, conceived as one of China's leading technological and commercial centers, seems like a futuristic city of the twenty-second century. It is already a center of worldwide attention, particularly from architects interested in studying its buildings.

CONCERT AT THE SHANGHAI ORIENTAL ART CENTER

Pudong's Shanghai Oriental Art Center, inaugurated in 2005, is perhaps the most important cultural project conceived over the past few years, not only in China but in all of Asia. It comprises a series of geodesic glass domes, that, during the day, appear to float over the water, while at night they emanate a soft, blue glow. The complex contains a huge orchestra hall, a lyric theater, a chamber music theater—where we performed—several libraries, a multimedia center, an exhibition room, a café, and a restaurant. It was the work of renowned French architect Paul Andreu, who also designed Osaka's Maritime Museum in Japan and Beijing's splendid new theater complex near Tiananmen Square.

Our concert program included works by Shostakovich, Kodály, Manuel M. Ponce (Mexico), Chen Yi (China), and Astor Piazzolla (Argentina). This time, the mysterious piece *Warm Greetings from New York* was nowhere to be found.

OBSERVATIONS ON THE NEW ERA OF MUSIC IN CHINA

I will not repeat here what I wrote in Chapter 5 about the Cultural Revolution (1966–1976) and its dreadful consequences. I will only note that, in 1977 and 1978, when the music conservatories were reopened, many young, talented musicians assigned to manual labor during the Cultural Revolution—such as the composers Tan Dun, Chen Yi, Zhou Long, Xu Shuya, and Chen Qijan—finally resumed their studies, and have since attained dazzling international success. Chinese composers have conquered a prominent niche in the current panorama of world music, and are no longer identified only by the "Chinese" nature of their music but rather by the quality and importance of their works.

Tan Dun is perhaps the best-known Chinese composer in the West. In 2000, his music for the film *Crouching Tiger, Hidden Dragon*, with the prominent participation of cellist Yo-Yo Ma, won the Oscar for best film score. In January 2007, I had the opportunity to see and hear his most recent work, the opera *The First Emperor*, at New York's Metropolitan Opera. The central character is the cruel, ruthless Qin Shi Huang, a key figure in the history of China. Only seven months before, I had stood before the tomb of the First Emperor in Xian, and had spent hours admiring the legendary terracotta warriors buried along with their ruler to protect him after his death. How was I to know that I would eventually see him come to life in Tan Dun's opera, in the glorious voice of Plácido Domingo?

Few countries have fostered musical education and love of music to the extent that China has. Western classical music enjoys a remarkable prestige and status there. Nine conservatories exist in China: two in Beijing and one each in Shanghai, Chengdu, Guangzhou, Shenyang, Tianjin, Xian, and Wuhan. Each has incorporated its own elementary school, which allows the study of music and musical instruments to start in early childhood.

In addition to Beijing and Shanghai, many other Chinese cities have already inaugurated or are about to inaugurate marvelously equipped performing arts centers. The number of students specializing in Western musical instruments, particularly the piano, has risen to astonishing proportions, and each year a prodigy emerges. One such example is the young pianist Lang Lang, who, in only a few years, has made his mark on the international music world.

Furthermore, China has become one of the leading manufacturers of Western musical instruments. The second largest piano factory in the world is located in Guangzhou, with an annual production of 200,000 instruments. Violins and cellos made in China are now played all over the world.

A BRIEF STOPOVER IN KOREA AND TAIWAN

In August 2007, I traveled to Pyeongchang, South Korea, to serve on the panel of judges for the Aldo Parisot International Cello Competition, named after the great Brazil-born cellist and teacher. At the conclusion of this exciting competition, won brilliantly by Serbian Maya Bogdanovic, we flew to Taipei, capital of "the other China," the island of Taiwan.

One important stop on this trip was the Chi Mei Museum and Foundation, located in Tainan, almost on the southernmost tip of the island and less than 300 kilometers from Taipei. To get there, we boarded the recently inaugurated high speed train and arrived in Tainan about an hour later. Mr. Win-Lu Hsu, chairman of the foundation, greeted us in the museum's huge vault, where he was trying out his latest acquisition, a violin by the great Venetian maker Domenico Montagnana. The foundation's instrument collection is one of the finest in the world. We admired four violins by Antonio Stradivari, two by Guarneri del Gesù—including the famous 1744 "Ole Bull"—several violins by the Amati dynasty, Petrus Guarneri of Mantua, and Petrus Guarneri of Venice, and two Stradivarius cellos, the 1709 Boccherini—named after its owner, the composer and cellist Luigi Boccherini (1743–1805)—and the 1730 De Pawle. I was then escorted to an imposing auditorium where I tried out six cellos, among them the Stradivari De Pawle, a Gofriller, a Maggini, and a Grancino. Chairman Hsu and his staff requested that I play something for them. I then enjoyed the unique luxury of playing a Bach

61. *With Yo-Yo Ma, playing the Suite for Two Cellos by Samuel Zyman. Monterrey, October 2006.*

suite with six marvelous instruments, changing cellos from movement to movement.

The Chi Mei Cultural Foundation does admirable work. The foundation stresses that "good instruments should be played by good musicians and the music they play must be shared with all mankind." This is why the foundation often lends its instruments to distinguished Chinese artists, beginning with, of course, the Taiwanese themselves. Furthermore, this institution is also dedicated to restoration work on instruments that have suffered damage over several centuries.

CONCERTS WITH YO-YO MA AND COMMENT ON *EL SISTEMA*

Chapter 8 describes the story—in five scenes—of the fruitful encounter between Yo-Yo Ma's cello and mine, and the subsequent birth of Samuel Zyman's Suite for Two Cellos. The story, however, is not limited only to these five scenes, since additional episodes were written over the next few years.

In October 2006, Yo-Yo Ma and I took part in a recital held at the

Monterrey Museum of Contemporary Art. The program included Samuel Zyman's suite. We played the suite again in Mexico City in March 2007, during a benefit concert that Yo-Yo generously dedicated to the Conservatorio de las Rosas, and on June 11 and 12 at the Palace of Fine Arts.

In June 2009, Yo-Yo and I arrived in Caracas, where we had been invited by José Antonio Abreu, chairman and founder of FESNOJIV—the National Network of Youth and Children's Orchestras of Venezuela, known as "El Sistema." Yo-Yo was well aware of the organization's remarkable achievements but had never had the opportunity to witness them for himself in Venezuela. Maestro Abreu scheduled an amazing number of activities and events, such as visits, master classes with Yo-Yo, and concerts by the Cello Ensemble as well as by the children's and youth orchestras, culminating on June 28 when Yo-Yo Ma and the Simón Bolívar Orchestra, conducted by Gustavo Dudamel, played Dvořák's Concerto for Cello and Orchestra. Previously, on June 26, Yo-Yo and I had played Zyman's suite in the presence of El Sistema's founders, teachers, and 1,000 young students in Bolívar Hall, housed in Caracas's Social Action Center for Music.

El Sistema has been such a success that 300,000 children and young people now participate in over 150 youth orchestras and 70 children's orchestras in every state across the country.

THE INTERNATIONAL CARLOS PRIETO CELLO COMPETITION, 2006 AND 2009

Two Carlos Prieto cello competitions took place subsequent to the initial publication of this book: in 2006 and in 2009, as always at the conservatory in Las Rosas, Mexico. Their purpose, as with the previous competitions, was to foster cello activities and attract worldwide attention to cello music in Ibero-America. At each competition, one of the program's special features is that, in order to expand and promote the cello repertoire, it includes the performance of a work expressly composed for this competition. In 2006, it was *Lejanía Interior* by Arturo Márquez of Mexico, and in 2009, it was *Of Broken Bells and Shadows* by Jimmy López of Peru.

In 2006, the first prize went to Patrick Jee (Korea–United States); the second prize went to Pavel Gomzyakov (Russia); and the third prize was shared by Mihai Marica (Romania) and Sophie Shao (United States). Special awards went to Georgina Sánchez Torres (Spain), Gabriel E.

Cabezas, age 14 (Costa Rica–United States), and Santiago Cañón, age 11 (Colombia).

In 2009, the winner was Dmitry Volkov (Russia); second place went to Marion Platero and Alexandre Castro-Balbi (both from France); and no third place was awarded. A special award went to Rolando Fernández Lara (Mexico).

On both occasions, the judges were Jesús Castro-Balbi (Peru–United States), William Molina (Venezuela), Philippe Muller (France), Aldo Parisot (Brazil–United States), Asier Polo (Spain), José Luis Gálvez, and me (Mexico).

The aforementioned cellists gave a number of recitals and a series of master classes.

Some Principal Works for Cello from the Twentieth and Twenty-first Centuries (Excluding Ibero-America)

Note: Ibero-American works appear in Appendix 2. Works marked with an asterisk (*) were commissioned by or dedicated to Carlos Prieto.

AUSTRIA

Arnold Schönberg (1874–1951)	Two concertos (1913 and 1932; after Monn)
Anton von Webern (1883–1945)	Two pieces (1899) Three small pieces for cello and piano, op. 11 (1914) Sonata for cello and piano (1914)
Egon Wellész (1885–1974)	Two suites for cello solo
Ernst Toch (1887–1964)	Sonata, op. 50 Concerto for cello and chamber orch., op. 35 (1925) Impromptu, op. 90, for solo cello
Ernst Krenek (1900–1991)	Concerto for cello and orch. Capriccio for cello and orch. Suite for cello solo, op. 84 (1939)

AZERBAIJAN

Frangis Ali-Sade (b. 1947)	*Habil-sajahand* for cello and piano

BELGIUM

Eugène Ysaÿe (1858–1931)	Meditation, op. 16, for cello and orch. Sonata for solo cello, op. 28 (1924) Poem-Nocturne for violin, cello, and orch.

CANADA

John Weinzweig (b. 1913)	Sonata ("Israel") for cello and piano (1949)

CZECHOSLOVAKIA

Leoš Janáček (1854–1928) — *Pohadka* for cello and piano (1910–1923)

Bohuslav Martinu (1890–1959) — Two concertos for cello and orch. (1939, 1946)
Sonata da camera for cello and chamber orch. (1940)
Three sonatas for cello and piano (1939, 1941, 1952)
Variations on a Theme by Rossini, cello and piano (1942)
Variations on a Slovak Folksong, cello and piano (1959)
Various pieces for cello and piano

ESTONIA

Arvo Pärt (b. 1935) — *Concerto italiano* for violin, cello, and orch. (1978)
Fratres, for 4, 8, 12 cellos (1977–1983)
Fratres, transcription for cello and piano
Spiegel im Spiegel for cello and piano

FINLAND

Jean Sibelius (1865–1957) — Malinconia, op. 20, for cello and piano (1901)
Four pieces for cello and piano, op. 78 (1915)
Solemn melodies for violin or cello and orch., op. 77

Leif Segerstam (b. 1944) — Seven concertos for cello and orch.

FRANCE

Gabriel Fauré (1845–1924) — Two sonatas, op. 109 and 117 (1918 and 1922)
Six pieces for cello and piano; among the most famous: *Elégie*, op. 24 (1883), *Papillon*, op. 77 (1898), and *Sicilienne*, op. 78 (1898)

Vincent d'Indy (1851–1931) — Lied for cello and orch. (1885)
Sonata, op. 84 (1926)

Claude Debussy (1862–1918) — Sonata (1915)

Albert Roussel (1869–1937) — Concertino for cello and orch. (1936)

Maurice Ravel (1875–1937) — Sonata for violin and cello

Jean Huré (1877–1930) — Three sonatas

André Caplet (1878–1925)	*Epiphanie d'après une légende ethiopienne* (1923)
Jacques Ibert (1890–1962)	Concerto for cello and wind instruments (1926)
	Etude-Caprice pour un tombeau de Chopin for solo cello (1949)
	Ghirlarzana for solo cello
Arthur Honegger (1892–1955)	Sonata for cello and piano (1920)
	Concerto for cello and orch. (1929)
Darius Milhaud (1892–1974)	Two Concertos for cello and orch. (1935 and 1947)
	Suite cisalpine for cello and orch. or piano (1954)
	Élégie for cello and piano (1945)
	Sonata for cello and piano (1959)
Francis Poulenc (1899–1963)	Sonata
Henri Sauguet (1901–1989)	Sonata for cello and piano
	Balada for cello and piano
	Mélodie concertante for cello and orch. (1964)
	Sonata for solo cello
André Jolivet (1905–1975)	Concerto for cello and orch.
	Concerto no. 2
	Suite en concert for solo cello (1966)
Jean Françaix (1912–1997)	Fantasia for cello and orch. (1934)
	Variations sans thème for cello and piano (1951)
Paul Tortelier (1914–1990)	Two concertos for cello and orch.
	Concerto for two cellos
	Sonata (1946)
	Suite for solo cello (1944)
Henri Dutilleux (b. 1916)	*Tout un monde lointain . . .* for cello and orch. (1968–1970)
	Trois strophes sur le nom Sacher for solo cello (1982)
Pierre Boulez (b. 1925)	*Explosante fixe* for solo cello
Claude Bolling (b. 1930)	Suite for cello and jazz trio

GEORGIA

Suljan Tsintzadze (1920–2000)	Twenty-four preludes for cello and piano
Giya Kancheli (b. 1935)	SIMI ("Thoughts without happiness") for cello and orch. (1995)
	Kottos, cello solo, 1977

GERMANY

Max Reger (1873–1916)	Four sonatas for cello and piano (1892, 1898, 1904, 1911) Three suites for solo cello (1915)
Paul Hindemith (1895–1964)	Two sonatas for cello and piano (1922 and 1948) Three pieces for cello and piano, op. 8 (1917) Sonata for cello solo, op. 25, no. 3 (1923) Various pieces for cello and piano Concerto for cello and chamber orch., op. 3 Concerto for cello and orch. (1940)
Boris Blacher (1903–1975)	Concerto (1964)
Bernd Alois Zimmermann (1918–1970)	Concerto for cello and chamber orch. (1953) *Canto di Speranza* for cello and chamber orch. (1957) Sonata for cello solo (1960) Concerto for cello and orch. (1965–1966) *Intercommunicazione* for cello and piano (1967)
Hans Werner Henze (b. 1926)	*Oda al viento del este* for cello and orch. (1954) *Serenata* for cello solo (1949) *Capriccio per Paul Sacher* for cello solo

GREECE

Iannis Xenakis (1922–2001)	*Nomos Alpha* for solo cello (1965)

HUNGARY

Emanuel Moor (1863–1931)	Seven sonatas for cello and piano Two concertos for cello and orch. Concerto for two cellos and orch., op. 69 (1908) Two rhapsodies for cello and orch. Many additional pieces for cello and orch. and for cello and piano
Ernst von Dohnányi (1877–1960)	Sonata, op. 8, for cello and piano *Konzertstück*, op. 12, for cello and orch. (1906)
Béla Bartók (1881–1945)	Rhapsody for cello and piano (transcription of his own violin and piano rhapsody) (1928)

Zoltán Kodály (1882–1967)

Sonata, op. 4, for cello and piano (1909–1910)
Duo for violin and cello
Sonata, op. 8, for cello solo (1915)
Capriccio for solo cello (1915)
Transcription of three choral preludes by Bach
Rondo Magyar for cello and piano (1917)

György Ligeti (b. 1923)

Concerto for cello and orchestra (1966)

IRELAND

Brian Boydell (1917–2000)

Sonata for cello and piano, op. 24 (1945)

John Kinsella (b. 1932)

Music for Cello and Chamber Orch. (1971)
Concerto for cello and orch.* (2000)

Philip Martin (b. 1947)

Suite for solo cello (1996–1997)

Kevin Volans
    (b. 1949 in South Africa)

Concerto for cello and orch. (1997)

Kevin O'Connell (b. 1958)

Sonata for cello and piano (1993–1994)

ITALY

Ildebrando Pizzetti (1880–1968)

Sonata for cello and piano (1921)
Tre Canti for cello and piano (1924)
Concerto for cello and orch. (1934)

Gian Francesco Malipiero
    (1882–1975)

Sonata for cello and piano (1907–1908)
Sonatina (1942)
Concerto for cello (1937)
Fantasie concertanti III, for cello and orch.

Alfredo Casella (1883–1947)

Sonata no. 1 for cello and piano (1907)
Sonata no. 2 (1927)
Concerto for cello, op. 58 (1934–1935)
Triple Concerto for violin, cello, piano, and orch.

Mario Castelnuovo Tedesco
    (1895–1968)

Sonata for cello and piano (1928)
I nottambuli, Variazioni Fantastiche, cello and piano (1928)
Concerto for cello (1935)

Luigi Dallapiccola (1904–1975)

Dialoghi for cello and orch.
Ciaccona, intermezzo e adagio, solo cello (1945)

Luigi Nono (1924–1990)	*Diario polacco*, solo cello (1982)
Luciano Berio (1925–2003)	*Ritorni di Snovidenia* for cello and orch. (1976) *Les mots sont allés* (1976)

JAPAN

Hisatada Otaka (1911–1951)	Concerto (1944)
Yasushi Akutagawa (1925–1989)	Concerto (1969)
Akio Yashiro (1929–1976)	Concerto (1960)
Michio Mamiya (b. 1929)	Six Popular Japanese Songs for cello and piano Sonata for solo cello Concerto (1975)
Takemitsu Toru (1930–1996)	*Orion* for cello and piano (1984) *Orion and Pleiades* for cello and orch. (1984)
Yuzo Toyama (b. 1931)	Concerto (1966)

POLAND

Witold Lutoslawski (1913–1994)	Concerto for cello and orch. Grave for cello and piano *Sacher-Variationen* for solo cello
Henryk Jablonski (1915–1989)	Six capriccios for solo cello
Krzysztof Penderecki (b. 1933)	Two concertos for cello and orch. Concerto for three cellos and orch. *Capriccio per Siegfried Palm* (solo cello)

ROMANIA

Georges Enesco (1881–1955)	*Symphonie concertante* (1909)

RUSSIA AND THE USSR

Alexander Glazunov (1865–1936)	*Chant du Ménestrel*, op. 71, for cello and orch. (1901) *Concert-Ballata*, op. 108, for cello and orch. (1933) Various pieces for cello and piano
Sergey Rachmaninov (1873–1943)	Sonata, op. 19 (1901) *Prélude et danse orientale*, op. 2 (1892)

Reinhold Glière (1875–1956)	Ballade for cello and piano, op. 4 (1902) Twelve pieces for cello and piano, op. 51 (1910) Ten duos for two cellos, op. 53 (1910) Concerto for cello and orch., op. 87 (1946)
Nikolai Roslavetz (1881–1944)	Meditation for cello and piano
Nikolai Miaskovsky (1881–1950)	Two sonatas for cello and piano, op. 12 and 81 Concerto for cello and orch., op. 66 (1945)
Igor Stravinsky (1882–1971)	*Suite italienne* for cello and piano (1954)
Sergei Prokofiev (1891–1953)	Ballade for cello and piano, op. 15 (1912) Sonata, op. 119, for cello and piano (1949) Concerto no. 1 for cello and orch., op. 58 (1938) *Sinfonia concertante* for cello and orch., op. 125 (1952) Concertino for cello and orch., op. 132 (finished by D. Kabalevsky and M. Rostropovich)
Vissarion Shebalin (1902–1963)	Sonata, op. 51, no. 3, for cello and piano Concerto for cello and orch. (1950)
Aram Khachaturian (Armenia) (1903–1978)	Sonata for cello and piano Concerto for cello and orch. (1946) Concerto-Rhapsody for cello and orch. (1963)
Dmitry Kabalevsky (1904–1987)	Two concertos for cello and orch. (no. 1, 1949; no. 2, 1964) Sonata, op. 22, for cello and piano Sonata, op. 71, for cello and piano
Dmitry Shostakovich (1906–1975)	Three pieces, op. 9 (1924; lost) Sonata, op. 40 for cello and piano (1934) *Moderato* for cello and piano (1934?) Concerto no. 1, op. 107 (1958) Concerto no. 2, op. 126 (1966)
Moishei Vainberg (1919–1996)	Sonata no. 1 for cello and piano, op. 21 (1945) Cello Concerto, op. 43 (1948) Fantasy for cello and orch., op. 52 (1951–1953) Sonata no. 2 for cello and piano, op. 63 (1958–1959) Sonata no. 1 for solo cello, op. 72 (1960)

	Sonata no. 2 for solo cello, op. 86 (1965)
	Twenty-four preludes for solo cello, op. 100 (1968)
	Sonata no. 3 for solo cello, op. 106 (1971)
	Sonata no. 4 for solo cello, op. 140 (1986)
Edison Denisov (1929–1996)	Suite for cello and piano (1961)
	Three pieces for cello, op. 26 (1967)
	Concerto for cello and orch. (1972)
	Variations on a Haydn Canon for cello and orch. (1982)
	Concerto for bassoon, cello, and orch. (1982)
	Variations on a Schubert Song for cello and piano (1982)
	Cadences for cello concertos by Haydn (1982)
Sofia Gubaidulina (b. 1931)	*Detto II* for cello and 13 instruments (1972)
	Detto III for cello and instrumental ensemble (1974)
	Ten preludes for solo cello (1974)
	Seven Words for cello, bayan, and orch. (1982)
	Partita for cello (1990)
	"And: The Festivities at their Height," cello concerto (1993)
Alfred Schnittke (1934–1998)	Two sonatas for cello and piano
	Two concertos for cello and orch.
	Hymnus I for cello, arpa, and percussion
	Hymnus II for cello and double bass
	Hymnus III for cello, bassoon, cembalo, and glocken
	Hymnus IV for cello and various instruments
	Madrigal in Memoriam Oleg Kagan, solo cello (1991)
	Improvisation for solo cello (1993)

SOUTH AFRICA

Horace Barton (1872–1951 born in England)	Various pieces for cello and piano: Ballade, Hebrew Song of Supplication, Invocation, Impromptu, Sarabande, To Proteas Stefans
	Sonata for cello and piano
Stefans Grove (b. 1922)	Sonata for cello and piano
Graham Newcater (b. 1941)	Concerto for cello and orch.

Jeanne Zaidel-Rudolph (b. 1948)	Four Minim (Citron, Pal Branch, Myrtle, Willow) for cello and piano *Suite afrique* Variations for Cello and Piano on a Chassidic Theme
John Reid Coulter (b. 1958)	Two sonatas for cello and piano
Waldo Malan (b. 1964)	Sonata for cello and piano Sound Diffusion for cello and piano
Herman Jordaan (b. 1975)	Piece for cello and piano

Note: My thanks to the South African Music Rights Organization (SAMRO) for its help in compiling this list.

SWITZERLAND

Ernest Bloch (1880–1959)	*Schelomo*, Hebraic Rhapsody for cello and orch. (1916) *Hebraic Meditation* (1925) *Three Sketches of Jewish Life* (1924) *Voice in the Wilderness*, for cello and orch. (1936) Three suites for solo cello (1957–1958)
Frank Martin (1890–1974)	Ballade for cello and piano (1949) Concerto for cello and orch. (1966)

UNITED KINGDOM

Edward Elgar (1857–1934)	Cello concerto, op. 85 (1919)
Frederick Delius (1862–1934)	*Romanza* for cello and piano (1896) Double Concerto for violin, cello, and orch. (1915) Sonata for cello and piano (1917) Capriccio and Elegy for cello and orch. (1925) Concerto for cello and orch. (1921)
Ralph Vaughan Williams (1872–1958)	Six Studies in English Folksongs, for cello and piano
Gustav Holst (1874–1934)	Invocation for cello and orch. (1911)
Donald F. Tovey (1875–1940)	Sonata, op. 4 (1900) Elegiac Variations for cello and piano (1909) Sonata for two cellos (1912) Sonata for solo cello, op. 30 (1914) Concerto for cello and orch. (1935)

Frank Bridge (1879-1941)	*Oration, concerto elegiaco* (1930)
John Ireland (1879–1962)	Sonata (1924)
Arnold Bax (1883–1953)	Sonata (1923) Concerto for cello (1932)
William Walton (1902–1983)	Concerto for cello and orch. (1957)
Benjamin Britten (1913–1976)	Sonata for cello and piano, op. 65 (1961) Symphony for cello and orch., op. 68 (1963–1964) Three suites for solo cello (1964, 1969, 1972) *Tema Sacher* for cello solo
Alun Hoddinott (b. 1929)	*Noctis equi* (Scene for cello and orch.; 1989)

UNITED STATES

Walter Piston (1894–1976)	Variations for cello and orch. (1966)
Virgil Thomson (1896–1989)	Concerto for cello and orch. (1950)
Henry Cowell (1897–1965)	Four Declamations with Hymn and Fuguing Tune
Quincy Porter (1897–1966)	Fantasia for cello and small orch. (1950) Poem for cello and piano
Ross Lee Finney (1906–1997)	Chromatic Fantasy in E (1957)
Elliott Carter (b. 1908)	Sonata for cello and piano (1948)
Samuel Barber (1910–1981)	Concerto for cello and orch., op. 22 (1946) Sonata, op. 6, for cello and piano (1932)
William Schuman (1910–1992)	*Song of Orpheus*, for cello and orch. (1963)
Alan Hovhaness (1911–2000)	Suite, op. 193
Gian Carlo Menotti (b. 1911)	Fantasia for Cello and Orch. Suite for Two Cellos and Piano
John Cage (1912–1992)	*Etudes boreales* (I–IV) for solo cello (also for cello and piano)
Morton Gould (1913–1996)	Suite for cello and piano (1981)
Norman Dello Joio (b. 1913)	Sonatina (1943) *Duo concertante* for cello and piano (1945)
David Diamond (1915–2005)	Sonata for cello and piano (1938) Concerto for cello and orch. (1938) Sonata for solo cello
Leonard Bernstein (1918–1990)	Three Meditations from Mass (1977) for cello and orch.

Leon Kirchner (b. 1919)	Music for Cello and Orchestra
Lukas Foss (b. 1922)	Capriccio for cello and piano (1947?) Concerto (1967)
Peter Mennin (1923–1983)	Concerto cello and orch. (1956)
Gunther Schuller (b. 1925)	Fantasy, op. 19
George Crumb (b. 1929)	Sonata for cello solo (1955)
John Harbison (b. 1938)	Concerto for cello and orch.
Joan Tower (b. 1938)	Music for Cello and Orchestra (1984)
Stephen Alpert (1941–1992)	Concerto for cello and orch.
Robert X. Rodríguez (b. 1946)	*Máscaras* for cello and orch.* (1993) *Lull-a-Bear* for cello and piano *Tentado por la Samba,* for cello and piano* (2006)
John Adams (b. 1947)	Sonata (1987)
Christopher Rouse (b. 1949)	Cello concerto
Richard Danielpour (b. 1956)	Concerto for cello and orch. (1994)
Gabriela Frank (b. 1972)	Manhattan Serenades for cello and piano Rios Profundos for cello and piano Quartet for four cellos, "La Sombra de la Apus" Double Concerto for cello, piano, and orchestra (2006) Suite of Dances for solo cello (2006)

ſ *Some Principal Works for Cello from the Twentieth and Twenty-first Centuries (Spain, Portugal, and Latin America)*

Works marked with an asterisk (*) were commissioned by or dedicated to Carlos Prieto.

ARGENTINA

Alberto Williams (1862–1952)	Sonata, op. 52, for cello and piano (1906)
Julián Aguirre (1868–1924)	*Rapsodia Argentina* (1898), transcr. for cello and piano by C. Marechal *Huella*, op. 49 (1917), transcr. for cello and piano by A. Schiuma
Constantino Gaito (1878–1945)	Sonata, op. 26, for cello and piano (1918)
José María Castro (1892–1968)	Sonata for cello and piano Sonata for two cellos Concerto for cello and seventeen instruments (1946) Three studies for cello and piano (1946) *Tres Piezas* for cello and piano (1947)
Juan José Castro (1895–1968)	Sonata for cello and piano (1916)
Washington Castro (1909–2004)	Sonata for cello and piano (1943) Rhapsody for cello and orchestra (1965) *Monólogo* for solo cello (1966) Tangos for cello and piano (1969)
Carlos Guastavino (1912–2000)	*La rosa and el sauce*, for voice and piano, transcr. by Aurora Nátola
José Bragato (b. 1915)	*Graciela y Buenos Aires Tango* (cello and string orch. or cello and piano)
Alberto Ginastera (1916–1983)	Concerto no. 1, op. 36 (1968) Concerto no. 2, op. 50 *Pampeana* no. 2, op. 21 for cello and piano

	Puneña no. 2, op. 45 for solo cello (1976) Sonata, op. 49, for cello and piano (1979) *Serenata* for cello, baritone, and orch. (1973) *Triste*, transcr. by Pierre Fournier
Marcelo Koc (b. 1918)	Concerto for cello and orch.
Astor Piazzolla (1921–1992)	*Milonga* in D, orig. for voice and piano *Tres piezas breves*, op. 4 *Le grand tango* Seven tangos: *Michelangelo 70, Balada para mi muerte, Escolaso, Tristeza de un doble A, Río Sena, Adiós Nonino, Contrastes* (transcr. by E. Quintana)
Dianda Hilda (b. 1925)	Adagio-Allegro for cello and piano *Concertante* for cello and orch. (1955) *Estructuras* nos. 1–3 for cello and piano (1960) *Núcleos* (1963) *Ludus I–II* (1968–1969)
Werner Wagner (1927–2002)	Rhapsody for cello and orch. (1973, rev. 1985)
Jorge Arandia Navarro (b. 1929)	*Variantes de la pena negra* for cello solo (1999)
Mauricio Kagel (b. 1931)	Match, for two cellos and percussion (1964)
Mario Davidovsky (b. 1934)	*Synchronismus* for cello and cinta
Gerardo Gandini (b. 1936)	*Sarabande et double* for solo cello (1973)
Luis Jorge González (b. 1936)	*Confín sur*, suite for cello and piano (1995–1996) Cánticos del Esperar for cello and piano* (2005) Concerto for cello and orch.* (2006)
Máximo Flugelman (b. 1945)	Rhapsody for cello and orch.
Carlos Gratzer (b. 1956)	*Alquimia* for cello and piano (1983)
Pablo Ortiz (b. 1956)	*Crocodile Tears* for two cellos (1987)
Esteban Benzecry (b. 1970)	*Toccata y misterio* for cello and piano (1991) Concertino for cello and string orch. (1992) Rhapsodia Andina for cello and piano (2001)

Note: The information on Argentinean composers comes from my own research and from the doctoral dissertation of Eugenio Gassé (Ohio State University, Columbus, 1993). My thanks to Gerardo Dirié of the Latin American Music Center at Indiana University for providing me with Dr. Gassé's work.

BOLIVIA

Alberto Villalpando (b. 1940)	*Sonatita de piel morena* for cello and piano* (1999)

BRAZIL

Henrique Oswald (1852–1931)	Sonata, op. 21, for cello and piano *Sonata fantasía*, op. 44, for cello and piano (1916) Berceuse for cello and piano Elegy for cello and piano
Franciso Braga (1868–1945)	*Toada* for cello and piano
Bento Mossurunga (1879–1970)	*Divagando*
Heitor Villa-Lobos (1887–1959)	Two chôros for violin and cello Elegy for cello and piano (1916) Sonhar-Melodia, op. 14, for cello and piano (1914) Grand Concerto for cello and orch. (1915) Fantasia for cello and orch. (1945) Concerto no. 2 for cello and orch. (1955?) Small suite for cello and piano (1913) Two sonatas for cello and piano (1915, 1916) *Assobio a Jato* for flute and cello Various duets for violin and cello *Bachianas brasileiras* (no. 1 for eight cellos, no. 5 for eight cellos and soprano) *Divagaçao* for cello, piano, and tom-tom (ad lib) Various pieces and transcriptions for cello and piano (*O Canto do Cisne Negro, O Canto de Capadocio, O Trensinho de Caipira*, etc.)
Luciano Gallet (1893–1931)	Elegy for cello and piano
Oscar Lorenzo Fernandez (1897–1948)	*Nocturno elegiaco* for cello and piano
Francisco Mignone (b. 1897)	*Serenata campestre* *Modinha* (1939) Sonatas for cello and piano (no. 1, 1967; no. 2, 1976))

Armando Albuquerque (1901–1986) Music for cello and piano (1955)

Burle Marx Walter (1902–1991) *Samba-tango de concerto* for cello and piano
Concerto for cello and orch.

Radamés Gnatalli (1906–1988) Concerto for cello and orch. (1941)
Concerto for cello and piano
Three sonatas for cello and piano
Sonata for viola and cello
Modinha e Baião for cello and piano

José Guerra Vicente (1907–1976) *Cenas cariocas* for cello and piano

José Siqueira (1907–1985) Concerto for cello and orch. (1952)
Tres cantigas for Iemanjá for solo cello
(c. 1960)

Camargo Guarnieri (1907–1993) Chôro for cello and orch. (1961)
Three sonatas for cello and piano
Ponteio e dansa (two versions: with piano
and with orch. 1946)
Adagio for cello and piano (1946)
Sonatas nos. 2–4 for cello and piano (1947,
1951, 1963); see note below
Encantamiento

Tsuna Iwami (b. 1923 in Japan) Sonata for cello and piano (1978)

Osvaldo Lacerda (b. 1927) Aria for cello and piano
Chôro seresteiro for two cellos

Ernst Mahle (b. 1929) Sonata for cello and piano (1968)
Eight *Duetos modais* for two cellos (1974)
Sonatina for cello and piano (1976)
Concertino for cello and orchestra (1976)

Emilio Terraza (b. 1929) Tango M. 32 for cello and piano

Aldo Taranto (b. 1933) Various cello and piano pieces

Eduardo Bértola (1939–1996) *Um no outro* for two cellos

Marlos Nobre (b. 1939) *Cantos de Yemanjá*, op. 21, no. 3, for cello
and piano
Desafío II, op. 31, for cello and string orch.
(1968)
Desafío II, op. 31, for cello and piano
Desafío II, op. 31, for eight cellos
Partita latina, op. 92, for cello and piano*
(2001)
Poema III, op. 94, no. 3, for cello and piano
Cantoria I, op. 100, for solo cello (2005)
Cantoria II, op. 100, no. 2, for solo cello*
(2005)

José Antonio de Almeida (b. 1943)   Sonata for cello and piano (2003)

Ronaldo Miranda (b. 1948)   *Três momentos* for solo cello (1986)

Ernani Aguiar (b. 1950)   *Meloritmias* for solo cello (1975)
Ponteando

Jaime Zenamon (b. 1953)   *Suite iguatú* for solo cello

Paulo Costa Lima (b. 1954)   *Corrente de Xangô* (1993)

Sérgio di Sabbato (b. 1955)   Concerto for two cellos and orch. (1997)
Sonata for two cellos (1993)

Harry Crowl (b. 1958)   *Aethra I* for solo cello with piano obbligato
Solilóquio II (2000)
Lumen de Lumine for cello and five
   instruments
Visões noturnas* (2002)

Guilherme Schroeter (b. 1960)   Fantasia for cello and piano

Dimitri Cervo (b. 1968)   *Papaji*, op. 11, for cello and piano (1997)

Alberto Andrés Heller   *14 bis* for violin, cello, and orch.* (2002)
Onze momentos for cello and *piano* (2005)*

Note: Santoro withdrew his first sonata for cello and piano (1942–1943).

CHILE

Adolfo Allende (1885–1959)   Concerto for cello and orch. (1915)

Domingo Santa Cruz (1899–1977)   Sonata for cello and piano, op. 38 (1974–
1975)

Juan Orrego-Salas (b. 1919)   *Canciones de advenimiento* for mezzo-
soprano, cello, and piano, op. 25 (1948)
Dúos concertantes, cello and piano, op. 41
   (1955)
Triple concerto, op. 52, for violin, cello,
   piano, and orch. (1962)
Balada, op. 84 for cello and piano (c. 1984)
Serenade for flute and cello, op. 70 (1972)
Concerto for cello and orch. (1994)
Espacios for cello and piano* (1998)
Fantasías for cello and orch.* (2000)

Alfonso Montecino (b. 1924)   Three pieces for solo cello, op. 28 (1989)

Gustavo Becerra-Schmidt (b. 1925)   Sonatas nos. 1–5 for cello and piano (1950,
1954, 1956, 1990, 1998*)
Partitas nos. 1–3 for solo cello (1957, 1957, 1983)
Concerto for cello and orch. (1984)

Pelayo Santa María (1950–1971)   Sonata for cello and piano (1969)

Joakin Bello (b. 1953)   Suite for violin and cello in five mvmts. (1975)

Eduardo Cáceres (b. 1955)   *Entrelunas* for cello and piano (1996)

Estela Cabezas   *Saudade* (1981)

COLOMBIA

Guillermo Uribe Holguín (1880–1971)   Two sonatas for cello and piano

Blas Emilio Atehortúa (b. 1933)   *Romanza,* from *Cinco piezas románticas,* op. 85 (1979, rev. 1987)
Concerto for cello and orch., op. 162 (1990)
Fantasía concertante for cello and piano* (2005)

Miguel Pinto Campa (b. 1945)   Symphony-Concerto for Cello and Orch., op. 4 (1993)

Claudia Calderón (b. 1959)   *Preludio y revuelta circular* for cello and piano* (2000)

CUBA

Joaquín Nin y Castellanos (1879–1949)   *Seguida española,* for cello and piano
Suite española, for cello and piano

Amadeo Roldán (1900–1939)   *Dos canciones populares cubanas*

Alejandro Garcia Caturla (1906–1940)   *Danza del tambor,* for cello and piano (1929)

José Ardévol (1911–1981)   Sonatina (1950)
Variaciones sinfónicas for cello and orch. (1951)

Nilo Rodríguez (1921–1997)   *Ámbitos V, monólogo* for solo cello

Aurelio de la Vega (b. 1925)   *Leyenda del Ariel criollo* (1953)

Carlos Fariñas (1934–2002)   Sonata for violin and cello (1961)
Concerto for cello and orch.* (1995–1996)

Calixto Alvarez (b. 1938)   *Guajira* for cello and piano (1986)
Five short pieces for solo cello (1987)

Leo Brouwer (b. 1939)   Sonata for solo cello (1960; rev. 1994)
Triple Concerto for violin, cello, piano, and orch. (1995)

Tania León (b. 1943)	Four pieces for solo cello (1996)
Guido López Gavilán (b. 1944)	*Monólogo*, for solo cello Variantes, Coral, Leyenda for violin, cello, and piano with alternating percussion (1986)
Jorge López Marín (b. 1949)	Concerto for cello and small orch.
José Antonio Pérez Fuentes (b. 1951)	Toccata for cello and piano

ECUADOR

Francisco Salgado (1880–1970)	*Balada* for cello and strings (1915–1920) Nocturne for cello and piano (1920)
Luis Humberto Salgado (1903–1977)	*Capricho español* for cello and piano (1930) Concerto for cello and orch. (1974–1975) Sonata for cello and piano (1962)
Claudio Aizaga (b. 1925)	Fantasia in E Minor for Cello and String Orch. (1992)
Lucía Patiño	Fantasia for cello and piano (2004)

GUATEMALA

Rodrigo Asturias (b. 1940)	Concerto for cello and orch. (1975)

MEXICO

Ricardo Castro (1864–1906)	Concerto for cello and orch.
Julián Carrillo (1875–1965)	Concertino in quarter, eighth, and sixteenth tones, for violin, cello, harp, and orch. (1926) Concertino in quarter, eighth, and sixteenth tones, for cello and orch. (1945) *Horizontes*, symphonic poem for violin, cello in quarter tones, harp in sixteenth tones, and orch. (1947) Triple Concerto for violin, cello, flute, and orch., in a new six-tone scale (1950) Six sonatas in quarter tones for solo cello (1959)
Manuel María Ponce (1882–1948)	Sonata for cello and piano (1915–1917) Three preludes for cello and piano (1932–1933) *Estrellita* for cello and piano

José Rolón (1883–1945)	Lied
Rubén Montiel (1892–1985)	*Cantinela* and various pieces for cello and piano
Antonio Gómezanda (1894–1961)	*Lagos*, symphonic poem for cello, piano, and orch.
María Teresa Prieto (1896–1982)	Adagio and Fugue for cello and orch.* Adagio and Fugue, version for cello and piano Sonata for cello and orch. Sonata for cello and piano
Silvestre Revueltas (1899–1940)	*Tres piezas* (transcr. by Manuel Enríquez)*
Carlos Chávez (1899–1978)	Madrigal for cello and piano (1921) Sonatina for cello and piano Concerto (unfinished) for cello and orch.
E. Hernández Moncada (1899–1995)	Piece for cello and piano*
Rodolfo Halffter (1900–1987)	Sonata for cello and piano (1961)
Alfonso de Elías (1902–1984)	Three pieces
Luis Sandi (1905–1996)	Sonatina for cello and piano (1958) *Hoja de album* for cello and piano (1958) Sonata for oboe and cello (1984)
Simón Tapia Colman (1906–1993)	Sonata for cello and piano (1959)
Gerhart Muench (1907–1988)	*Out of Chaos* (1973)
Roberto Téllez (1909–2001)	*Destellos* for solo cello (1968) *La tarde*, for cello and piano (1968)
Miguel Bernal Jiménez (1910–1956)	*Tres danzas tarascas* (transcribed by M. Enríquez)*
Blas Galindo (1910–1993)	Suite for violin and cello (1933) Quartet for cellos (1936) Sonata for cello and piano (1948) Sonata for solo cello* (1981) Concerto for cello and orch.* (1984) Duo for violin and cello (1984)
Salvador Contreras (1912–1982)	Sonata for violin and cello (1982)
Carlos Jiménez Mabarak (1916–1994)	Two pieces for cello and piano (*Paisaje con jacintos, Nana*; 1966)
Armando Lavalle (1924–1994)	Sonata for cello and piano (1973) Concerto for violin, cello, and orch.

Manuel Enríquez (1926–1994)   Four pieces for cello and piano
                               Sonatina for solo cello
                               Poem for cello and chamber orch.
                               Fantasia for cello and piano* (1991)
                               Concerto for cello and orch.*
                               Ambivalencia for cello and violin (1967)

Joaquín Gutiérrez Heras (b. 1927)   Duet for alto flute and cello (1964)
                               Canción en el puerto for cello and piano*
                                  (1994)
                               Two pieces for cello and piano (1999)
                               Fantasia concertante for cello and orch.*
                                  (2005)

Mario Kuri Aldana (b. 1931)   *Canto de cinco flor* for cello and chamber
                                  orch.
                               Tarahumara, concerto for cello and orch.*
                               Macui xochitl for cello and piano (1957)

Hermilio Hernández (b. 1931)   Sonata for cello and piano

Raúl Ladrón de Guevara (b. 1934)   *Movimiento concertante*

Emanuel Arias (b. 1935)   *Cantilena*, op. 9
                           Concerto, op. 25, for cello and orch.*

José Antonio Alcaraz (1938–2001)   *Otros cellos, otros ámbitos*, for narrator, cello,
                                  and piano* (1995)

Manuel de Elías (b. 1939)   Concerto for cello and orch.* (1991)
                             Preámbulo (1992?)
                             Fantasia (1962)

Eduardo Mata (1942–1995)   Sonata (1966)

Julio Estrada (b. 1943)   *Canto alterno* for solo cello (1978)

Mario Lavista (b. 1943)   *Quotations* for cello and piano
                           Tres danzas seculares for cello and piano*
                              (1994)
                           Cuaderno de viaje, two pieces for solo cello
                              (*Como un canto*, *Volátil*)
                           Work for cello and orch.* (2006; not yet
                              titled)

Graciela Agudelo (b. 1945)   *Invocación* for solo cello (1993)

Federico Ibarra (b. 1946)   Concerto for cello and orch.* (1988)
                             Sonata for cello and piano* (1992)
                             Sonata for two cellos and piano (2004)

Radko Tichavsky   *Kiddush*, piece for solo cello

Max Lifchitz (b. 1948)   *Transformations*, for solo cello (1979)
                          Voces nocturnas, concerto for cello and orch.*
                             (1993)

Arturo Márquez (b. 1950) Piece for cello and piano (1999)
"Mirrors in the Sand," cello concerto (2000)
Piece for cello and piano (2006)

Marcela Rodríguez (b. 1951) *Lumbre*, for solo cello
Concerto for cello and orch.* (1994)

Federico Alvarez del Toro (b. 1953) *El constructor de los sueños*, for baritone, mezzo-soprano, cello, and harp

Jorge Córdoba (b. 1953) *Contra el tiempo*ic* (1992)

Eduardo Díazmuñoz (b. 1953) *Zonante*, piece for solo cello (1980)
Four Humoresques, op. 11A (1980)

Ramón Montes de Oca (b. 1953) *Elegía** (1994)

Eugenio Toussaint (b. 1954) Concerto for cello and orch. (1991)
Piece for cello solo (1994)
Variaciones concertantes for guitar, cello, and instrumental ensemble (1994)
— Concerto no. 2 for cello and orch.* (1998)
Tango for cello and piano (1999)
Pour les enfants, for cello and piano* (2000)
Bachriations for solo cello* (2005)

Leandro Espinosa (b. 1955) Duo for cello and piano
Transcriptions of op. 22 of Schumann

Arturo Salinas (b. 1955) *Netík 1*, for cello and piano

Javier Alvarez (b. 1956) *Serpiente y escalera*, for cello and piano* (1995)

Samuel Zyman (b. 1956) — Concerto for cello and orch.*
Sonata for cello and piano
Fantasia for cello and piano* (1994)
— Suite for two cellos* (1999)
Reflections for eight cellos
Triple Concerto for violin, cello, piano, and orch. (2006)
Suite for solo cello* (2006)

Ana Lara (b. 1959) *Koaiá* for cello solo
Tribulaciones for two cellos and piano (2004)

Gabriela Ortíz (b. 1964) *Things like That Happen*, for cello and tape (1994)

Hebert Vázquez (b. 1965) Concerto for cello and orch. (1994–1995)

Horacio Uribe (b. 1970) *Introspecciones* for cello and piano (1991)
Tres diálogos for violin and cello (1991–1992)
*Alborada** (2001)

José Luis Elizondo	*Suite barroca* for two cellos* (1997) *Danzas latinoamericanas* for two cellos* (1997)
Alexis Aranda (b. 1974)	*El violonchelo rojo** (2003)

Note: The information on Julián Carrillo comes from Lolita Carrillo, *Catálogo por orden cronológico de las composiciones musicales de Julián Carrillo* (Mexico City [San Ángel], 1989).

PANAMA

Roque Cordero (b. 1917)	Sonata for cello and piano (1963)

PERU

Celso Garrido-Lecca (b. 1926)	*Sonata-Fantasía* for cello and piano (1988) Concerto for cello and orch.* (1988) *Soliloquio II* for solo cello* (1996)
Armando Guevara Ochoa (b. 1926)	*Bronce andino*, for cello and piano
Edgar Valcárcel (b. 1932)	*Concierto indio* for cello and orch. (2004)
Gabriela Frank (b. 1972)	(*See* United States)

PORTUGAL

Fernando Lopes-Graça (1906–1994)	*Adagio ed alla danza* for cello and piano Three pieces for cello and piano *Quatro invençoes* for solo cello *Página esquecida* for cello and piano *Concerto da camera* for cello and orch. (1965)
Luis Filipe Pires (b. 1934)	Sonatina for cello and piano (1954)

PUERTO RICO

Roberto Sierra (b. 1953)	Salsa on the C String for cello and piano (1981) Concerto for cello and orch.* (1999) Sonata no. 1 for cello and piano (2003) Sonata no. 2 (“*Elegiaca*”) for cello and piano* (2006)

SPAIN

Enrique Granados (1867–1916)	Madrigal for cello and piano *Danza Gallega* *Pequeña Suite*

Manuel de Falla (1876–1946)	Two pieces for cello and piano
	~ *Suite popular española* for cello and piano
	    (transcr. by M. Maréchal)
	Danza ritual del fuego and *Danza del terror*
	    for cello and piano (transcr. by G.
	    Piatigorsky

Pablo Casals (1876–1973) ~	*Cant dels ocells*, Catalan folk song arr. for cello and orch. *Sardana* for cello ensemble (1951)
Joaquín Nin (1879–1949)	*Seguida española* for cello and piano
Roberto Gerhard (1896–1970)	Sonata for cello and piano. (1966)
María Teresa Prieto (1896–1982) ~	*See* Mexico

Gaspar Cassadó (1897–1973) ~	Concerto for cello and orch. (c. 1927)
	Rapsodia catalana for cello and orch. (1928)
	Sonata en el estilo antiguo español (1925)
	Sonata for cello and piano
	Partita for cello and piano
	Suite for cello solo (1907)
	Various pieces for cello and piano:
	    Requiebros, Lamento de Boabdil, Ser-
	    enata, Danza del diablo verde
	Various transcriptions for cello and piano
	    (toccata by Frescobaldi, works by Cou-
	    perin, etc.)

Salvador Bacarisse (1898–1963)	Concerto in A Minor for cello and orch.,
	    op. 22 (1935)
	Toccata for cello and piano, op. 54 (1964)
	Introduction, Variations, and Coda, op.
	    102, for cello and piano (1956)
	L'ours et le petit ourson for solo cello, op. 132
	    (1962)

Rodolfo Halffter (1900–1987)	*See* Mexico
Joaquín Rodrigo (1901–1999)	*Siciliana* for cello and piano *Sonata a la breve* for cello and piano *Concerto galante* for cello and orch. *Concerto como un divertimento* for cello and orch. *Como una fantasía* for solo cello*
Ernesto Halffter (1905–1989)	*Fantasía española* for cello and piano *Canzona e pastorella* (orig. for violin)
Xavier Montsalvatge (1912–2002)	*Sonata concertante* for cello and piano *Evocación* for cello and piano

	Invención a la italiana, for cello and piano* (2000)
Ramón Barce (b. 1928)	*Sonata Leningrado* for cello and piano
Manuel Castillo (b. 1930)	Concerto for cello and orch. Sonata for cello and piano *Alborada* for cello and piano* (1994)
Cristóbal Halffter (b. 1930)	Partita for cello and orch. (1957) Concertos for cello and orch. (no. 1, 1974; no. 2, 1985) Variations on a Theme by Sacher, for solo cello
Luis de Pablo (b. 1930)	*Ofrenda*: Six Pieces in Memory of Manuel Azaña, for solo cello *Frondoso misterio* for cello and orch.
Joan Guinjoan (b. 1931)	Duet for cello and piano (1970) *Cadencia*, for solo cello (1980) *Microtono*, for solo cello Music for Cello and Orch. (1975, rev. 1980) Elegy (monody), for solo cello (1996) *Diptic*, for eight cellos (2000)
Leonardo Balada (b. 1933)	Three Transparencies of a Bach Prelude
Claudio Prieto (b. 1934)	Fantasía for cello and piano (1974) *Lindajara* for violin and cello (1985) Caprice for a Party, for cello and piano (1992) Sonata no. 7, *Canto de amor*, for cello and piano *Concerto de amor*, for cello and orch. (1985–1986) *Caminando por la aventura*, for eight cellos (1996)
Josep Soler (b. 1935)	Concerto for cello and orch.
Jesús Villarojo (b. 1940)	Two concertos
Angel Climent (b. 1942)	Concerto for cello and orch.
Tomás Marco (b. 1942)	*Maya*, piece for cello and piano Concerto for cello and orch. *Primer espejo de Falla* for cello and piano* (1994) *Partita Piatti* for solo cello* (1999) *Laberinto marino* for cello and strings* (2002)

Ensueño y resplandor de don Quijote, for
   violin, cello, and orch.* (2004)
Chelo Prieto, for solo cello* (2006)

José Luis Turina (b. 1952)   Two duos
Concerto da Chiesa for cello and string orch.*
   (1998)

Alberto García Demestres   *Siete canciones de soledad* (1982)

URUGUAY

Jaurès Lamarque Pons (1917–1982)   Piece for cello and piano (1981)

León Biriotti (b. 1929)   Concerto for cello and chamber orch.

René Marino Rivero (b. 1936)   Bagatelles for cello and piano

José Serebrier (b. 1938)   Piece for cello and piano* (2006)

VENEZUELA

Rogerio Caraballo   *Elegía* for cello and piano

Andrés Delgado Pardo (1870–1940)   *Mirando al mar*, dramatic melody

Juan Bautista Plaza (1898–1965)   *Diferencias sobre un aire venezolano*
   Melody for cello and piano

Primo Casale (1904–1981)   *Serenatilla* for cello and piano
   Nocturne

Carlos Teppa (b. 1923)   Two concertos for cello and chamber orch.
   Sonata for cello
   Sonata for solo cello

Modesta Bor (1926–1998)   Suite for cello and piano

Aldemaro Romero (b. 1928)   Suite for cello and piano
   Concierto del Delfín, cello concerto (2003)

Diógenes Rivas (b. 1942)   Work for cello solo

Juan Carlos Nuñez (b. 1947)   Poulet Concerto for cello and orch.
   Yocasta for cello and piano

Alfredo Rugeles (b. 1949)   Invention for cello solo (1978)

Emilio Mendoza (b. 1953)   Four studies for violin and cello (1974)

Pedro Simón Rincón (b. 1953)   Two pieces

Domingo Sánchez Bor (b. 1955)   *Sonotráfico*, for cello solo

Paul Desenne (b. 1959)   *Cuaderno abierto de piezas* for three cellos
   Pizziguasa (1985)

Los ricochelos (1987)
Pizzi-Quitiplas (1989)
Aeroglifos, for eight cellos (1994)
Preludio and *Quitiglass*, both for eight cellos (1995)
Birimbaos, for eight cellos (1986–1987)
Suite for solo cello (1999–2000)
Concerto for cello and orch.* (2001)

Ricardo Lorenz (b. 1961)

Cecilia en azul y verde for cello and piano* (1998)
Michigan es Michoacán, for solo cello* (2006)

Juan Palacios (b. 1961)

Duet for violin and cello (1984)

Note: My thanks to Juan Francisco Sans, president of the Vicente Emilio Sojo Foundation, Caracas, for providing information on Venezuelan composers.

∫ *Carlos Prieto's Discography*

This is a complete list of recordings by Carlos Prieto (as of June 2005), alphabetized by composer. The details of these recordings can be found at www.carlosprieto.com. Works marked with an asterisk (*) were commissioned by or dedicated to Carlos Prieto.

Alvarez del Toro, Federico	*Constructor de Sueños*
Bach, Johann Sebastian	Six suites for solo cello
Becerra-Schmidt, Gustavo	Sonata no. 5 (world premiere)
Bernal-Jiménez, Miguel	*Tres danzas tarascas.* (transcr. by M. Enríquez) (world premiere)
Boccherini, Luigi	Sonata in A major
Bruch, Max	*Kol Nidrei* for cello and orch.
Calderón, Claudia	*La revuelta circular** (world premiere)
Cassadó, Gaspar	*Sonata en el estilo antiguo español*
Castillo, Manuel	*Alborada** (world premiere)
Castro, Ricardo	Concerto for cello and orch. (world premiere)
Chávez, Carlos	Concerto for cello and orch. (world premiere) Sonatina for cello and piano Madrigal for cello and piano
Chopin–Feuermann	*Polonaise brillante*
de Elías, Alfonso	*Chanson triste*
de Falla, Manuel	*Suite popular española*
Enríquez, Manuel	Concerto for cello and orch.* (world premiere) Four pieces for cello and piano Sonatina for solo cello Fantasia for cello and piano* (world premiere)
Fauré, Gabriel	*Elégie*, op. 24

Foss, Lukas	Capriccio for cello and piano
Garrido-Lecca, Celso	*Sonata fantasía** *Soliloquio** (world premiere) Cello Concerto* (world premiere)
Gerhard, Roberto	Sonata
Ginastera, Alberto	*Pampeana* no. 2 *Triste* Sonata
Guarnieri, M. Camargo	Chôro for cello and orch.
Gutiérrez Heras, Joaquín	*Canción en el puerto** (world premiere)
Halffter, Ernesto	*Canzona e pastorella*
Halffter, Rodolfo	Sonata for cello and piano
G. F. Handel–J. Halvorsen	Passacaglia for violin and cello (with Juan Luis Prieto, Jr.)
Ibarra, Federico	Sonata for cello and piano* (world premiere) Concerto for cello and orchestra (world premiere)
Kinsella, John	Cello Concerto* (with the Xalapa S.O. cond. by Carlos Miguel Prieto) (world premiere)
Kodály, Zoltán	Sonata for solo cello, op. 8
Lamarque Pons, Jaurès	Piece for cello and piano
Lavista, Mario	Quotations for cello and piano (world premiere) *Tres danzas seculares** (world premiere)
Lorenz, Ricardo	*Cecilia en azul y verde** (with Edison Quintana, piano) (world premiere)
Mahle, Ernst	*Duos modais* (with Juan Hermida, cello)
Marco, Tomás	*Primer espejo de Falla** (world premiere) *Partita a Piatti** (world premiere)
Márquez, Arturo	*Espejos en la arena*, cello concerto* (world premiere)
Martinu, Bohuslav	Sonata No.2 for cello and piano (with Doris Stevenson)
Mignone, Francisco	*Modinha* (with Edison Quintana, piano)
Montsalvatge, Xavier	*Invención a la italiana** (world premiere)
Nin, Joaquín	*Suite española* (with Edison Quintana, piano)

Nobre, Marlos	*Partita latina** (world premiere; with Edison Quintana, piano)
Orrego-Salas, Juan	*Espacios** (world premiere)
Piazzolla, Astor	*Le grand tango* (with Edison Quintana, piano) *Tres piezas breves*, op. 4 (world premiere)
Piazzolla, A.–J. Bragato	*Milonga* (with Edison Quintana, piano)
Piazzolla, A.–E. Quintana	*Michelangelo 70* (with Edison Quintana, piano) *Balada for mi muerte* (with Edison Quintana, piano)
Ponce, Manuel M.	Sonata for cello and piano (with Edison Quintana, piano) Three preludes for cello and piano (with Edison Quintana, piano)
Rachmaninov, Sergey	Vocalise (with Edison Quintana, piano) Vocalise (with Doris Stevenson, piano)
Revueltas, Silvestre	Three pieces for cello* (world premiere)
Rodrigo, Joaquín	*Siciliana*
Rodríguez, Robert X.	*Lull-a-Bear**
Romero, Aldemaro	Golpe with fandango (with Edison Quintana, piano)
Saint-Saëns, Camille	Cello Concerto no. 1
Shostakovich, Dmitry	Cello Concerto no. 1 Sonata op. 40 (with Doris Stevenson, piano) Sonata op. 40 and Sonata op. 147 (transcribed for cello by C. Prieto; with Doris Stevenson, piano)
Sierra, Roberto	*Cuatro versos* for cello and orch.* (world premiere)
Tchaikovsky, Pyotr	*Pezzo capriccioso*, op. 62 (with Doris Stevenson, piano) *Pezzo capriccioso*, op. 62 (with Edison Quintana, piano)
Toussaint, Eugenio	Concerto no. 2 for cello and orch.* (world premiere) *Pour les enfants*, for cello and piano* (world premiere)
Villa-Lobos, Heitor	Aria from *Bachianas brasileiras* no. 5
Villalpando, Alberto	*Sonatita de piel morena** (world premiere)

Zyman, Samuel   Concerto for cello and orch.* (world premiere)
                          Fantasia for cello and piano* (with Edison
                              Quintana) (world premiere)
                          Suite for Two Cellos* (world premiere; with
                              J. Castro-Balbi)

APPENDIX 4

∫ *Reviews of Concerts*

Renaissance man. But when does he sleep? Edith Eisler asks cellist Carlos Prieto about his astoundingly rich life as a performer, author, globe-trotter and tireless promoter of Latin composers.   *STRINGS*

Prieto knows no technical limitations. His musical instincts are impeccable.

NEW YORK TIMES

Throughout, the cellist produced a consistent stream of pure and articulate sounds in support of stylish music making.

DAN CARIAGA, *LOS ANGELES TIMES*

Prieto is a cellist of high gifts and impressive technical command.

R. BUELL, *BOSTON GLOBE*

Considering the audience enthusiasm, it seems obvious that Prieto will be invited back. It cannot be too soon, for this was distinguished music-making.   HEUWELL TIRCUIT, *SAN FRANCISCO CHRONICLE*

Cellist Carlos Prieto is one of those rare musicians who can cause audiences to cry out with delight as he proved Friday night. He showed the energy and virtuosity of a prodigy.

JIM KOPP, *ATLANTA JOURNAL-CONSTITUTION*

"Cellist Prieto spectacular in 'Premiere Performance.'" Whether the music at hand was vigorous or gentle or something in between, the results were breathtaking.   *ST. LOUIS POST-DISPATCH*

Carlos Prieto is a bold interpreter who commands an imposing sound from his instrument. A cellist of obvious gifts.

DANIEL WEBSTER, *PHILADELPHIA INQUIRER*

Several traits were immediately noticeable in Prieto's playing: a focused tone and strong, nimble fingers that moved swiftly and decisively up and down the fingerboard. He also employed a bowstroke that could confidently phrase melodies in long, lyrical arcs. He could also stitch together little single-stroke passages using the tip of the bow as precisely as a sewing-machine needle.   CARL CUNNINGHAM, *HOUSTON POST*

Prieto's programming and his musicianship gave the concert a gem-like lustre. . . . A cellist with an exceptionally robust tone and a dramatic approach to interpretation. . . . A virtuoso performer with a strong feeling for dramatic and emotional contrast. It was a stunning performance.

GLOBE AND MAIL (TORONTO)

Prieto is a well schooled instrumentalist, one with a surpassing command of his instrument. Doris Stevenson was at the piano, providing expert support for the cellist. The two seem to make an ideal musical team.

JACOB SISKIND, *OTTAWA CITIZEN*

Masterful performance, stimulating and relaxing by turns, admirable and accessible. I hope we see him back in London soon.

ADAM BLAKE, *MUSIC AND MUSICIANS* (LONDON)

We owe Prieto at least 50 percent of the Latin American cello repertoire. He has already made a huge impact in the history of music.

MUSIC NOTES, MICHIGAN STATE UNIVERSITY SCHOOL OF MUSIC

John Kinsella . . . is equally impressed by the player. "Carlos played in the Hugh Lane Gallery on a Sunday morning early in 2000. And even though I'd known his playing from records and from his quartet recital in 1998, I wasn't quite aware of just how good he was until that solo concert. And he's really terrific. An extremely well controlled player, which gave me a lot of mental freedom to say, 'This guy can play anything.'"

NEW MUSIC NEWS (DUBLIN)

The Piatti Strad used by Carlos Prieto is in well deserving hands. Not a poorly sounding note or an unmusical phrase were conceivable in Monday's recital. Beethoven's sonata flowed effortlessly, with the ease of an ever renewed spring.   DOUGLAS SEALY, *IRISH TIMES*

The concert was a unique triumph of a marvelous cello in the hands of an artist of the highest musicality and virtuosity.

SÜDKURIER (GERMANY)

Superb personality with great temperament and expressivity. Hartmut Schneider was an ideal accompanist.   *SCHWABISCHE ZEITUNG*

In a few years Carlos Prieto has jumped into the front ranks of cello playing today; not only a virtuoso but a complete artist.

E. FRANCO, *EL PAIS* (MADRID)

Carlos Prieto: not only his country's outstanding cellist but one of the great international soloists of his generation.

TOMÁS MARCO, *DIARIO 16* (MADRID)

Carlos Prieto: magical cellist.

I. K. SEMENOVA, *LATINSKA AMERIKA* (MOSCOW)

A cello in the hands of a genius.

NOVOKUZNETSKY RABOCHI (RUSSIA)

NOTES

CHAPTER I

1. Adolfo Salazar, *La Música en la Sociedad Europea* (Madrid: Alianza Editorial, 1983), 2:212.

2. Elizabeth Cowling, *The Cello* (New York: Scribner's, 1975), 53.

3. *The New Grove Dictionary of Music and Musicians*, ed. Stanley Sadie (New York: Macmillan, 1980), s.v. "viol," 19:793.

4. Giuseppe Strocchi, *Liuteria: Storia ed arte* (Lugo, Italy: Tipografia Michele Cortesi, 1937), 15.

5. The complete family of the violas de gamba includes the *pardessus de viole* (or *viol contra soprano*), the soprano viola da gamba, the bass viola da gamba, and the *violone* (an augmented viola, or double bass viol).

6. Another intermediate instrument that appeared in numerous paintings at the end of the fifteenth century and throughout the sixteenth century was the *lira da braccio*. It had seven strings and was played with a bow. It looked like a violin, but like the gambas, it had frets.

7. The term *violoncino* comes from the Italian *violone piccino* and, concretely, from *violone cino* (small violone). Still in our days, *cino* is used in Bologna instead of *piccino* (small). Lauro Malusi, *Il Violoncello* (Padua: Edizioni G. Zanibon, 1973), 231.

8. Adolfo Salazar, *Juan Sebastián Bach: Un ensayo* (Mexico City: El Colegio de México, 1951), 233.

9. *The New Grove Dictionary of Music and Musicians*, s.v. "Marais, Marin," 11:640.

10. Curt Sachs, *The History of Musical Instruments* (New York: Norton, 1968), 360.

11. Ibid.

12. Hubert Le Blanc, *Défense de la basse de viole contre les entreprises du violon et les prétentions du violoncel*, reprinted serially in *La Revue Musicale* 9 (1927–1928): 54.

13. It was used for the first time in the opera *Armide* (1686) by Lully. In an aria of the second act, the parts of string instruments have the indication: *Il faut jouer ceci avec des sourdines* (This part should be played with mutes).

14. *Alma* in Spanish and Portuguese, *âme* in French, and *anima* in Italian.

15. Werner Bachmann, *The Origins of Bowing and the Development of Bowed Instruments up to the Thirteenth Century*, trans. Norma Deane (London: Oxford Univ. Press, 1969).

16. Madrid, Biblioteca Nacional, MS Hh 58, fol. 127r.

17. Louis Antoine Vidal, *Les instruments à archet* (Paris: Claye, 1876–1878), 1:271.

18. Joseph Roda, *Bows for Musical Instruments of the Violin Family* (Chicago: William Lewis & Son, 1959), 287.

CHAPTER 2

1. Salazar, *La música*, 2:215.

2. Cowling, *Cello*, 29; Charles Beare, *Capolavori di Antonio Stradivari* (Milan: Arnoldo Mondadori, 1987), 23.

3. Alfred E. Hill, Arthur F. Hill, and W. Henry Hill, *The Violin Makers of the Guarneri Family, 1626–1762: Their Life and Work* (1931; repr., London: W. E. Hill & Sons, 1965), 110.

4. Beare, *Capolavori*, 23.

5. Ibid.

6. Cowling, *Cello*, 30.

7. Beare, *Capolavori*, 25.

8. Ibid., 26.

9. Malusi, *Violoncello*, 15.

10. The information in this section relies heavily on Jacques Français, *Jacobus Stainer and Eighteenth-Century Violin Masters*, a leaflet prepared on the occasion of the exhibit prepared by J. Français at Lincoln Center, New York, October 1981–January 1982.

11. I have relied in this section primarily on Hill et al., *Guarneri Family*.

12. Ibid., 13.

13. Ibid., 33.

14. I have relied in this section primarily on W. Henry Hill, Arthur F. Hill, and Alfred E. Hill, *Antonio Stradivari: His Life and Work, 1644–1737* (London: W. E. Hill & Sons, 1902; repr., New York: Dover, 1963). Citations are to the Dover edition.

15. Ibid., 285.

16. Ibid., 125.

17. Ernest N. Doring, *How Many Strads? Our Heritage from the Master* (Chicago: William Lewis & Son, 1945), 309.

18. Information supplied by Rene Morel, New York, 1998.

19. The recent work by Stewart Pollens has caused a lot of commotion in the world of stringed instruments. According to him, one of the most famous violins by Antonio Stradivari dates from after his death and should be attributed to his son Francesco. The work of Pollens is already known, but is unpublished. Pollens based his research on recent techniques of dendrochronology, the science of dating aged wood. (Source: conversations with Stewart Pollens, New York, July 1998.)

20. Simone Sacconi, *I segreti di Stradivari* (Cremona, Italy: Libreria del Convegno, 1972), 44–45.

21. My main source of information has been Hill et al., *Guarneri Family*.

22. Ibid., 94.

23. Among other works, I consulted *Les Violons: Lutherie Vénitienne, Peintures et Dessins*, catalogue of an exhibition at the Hôtel de Ville de Paris (Paris: Association pour la Promotion des Arts, 1995).

24. Hill et al., *Stradivari*, 251.

25. Duane Rosengard and Carlo Chiesa, "Guarneri del Gesù: A Brief History" in *The Violin Masterpieces of Guarneri del Gesù: An Exhibition at the Metropolitan Museum of Art*

Commemorating the 250th Anniversary of the Maker's Death, ed. Peter Biddulph (London: Biddulph, 1994), 17.

26. Hill et al., *Guarneri Family*, 111.

27. George Hart, *The Violin: Its Famous Makers and Their Imitators* (London: Dulau, 1875), quoted in Doring, *How Many Strads?*, 201.

28. Beare, *Capolavori*, 24.

CHAPTER 3

The only period of time about which I have been unable to obtain any detailed information on the history of this instrument is from its birth in Cremona up until its first years in Cádiz. I have filled in the gaps with a hypothetical but likely history of the cellist Carlo Moro, based, as far as possible, on real historical data. I point to the specific sources in my footnotes. After 1818, all historical facts are well documented.

1. Hill et al., *Stradivari*, 281.

2. Ibid., 140.

3. Ibid., 245.

4. Ibid., 94, 245.

5. This occurred in 1775. Charles III sent Father Brambilla to Cremona. Paolo was already very ill, and Father Brambilla succeeded in acquiring the ornamented quintet for the Spanish crown, thus granting, though posthumously, Antonio Stradivari's wish.

6. Marques de Ureña, *El viaje Europeo del marques de Ureña*, ed. María Pemán Medina (Cádiz, Spain: Unicaja, 1992), 31.

7. Ibid., 34.

8. Ibid.

9. Data provided by María Pemán Medina (Madrid, 1994) and by a letter from violinist Paul Alday to the Reverend Booth (Dublin, Clergy Library, 1832).

10. Pablo Antón Solé, "Un testimonio artístico y religioso de la burguesía gaditana: La Santa Cueva," *Anales de la Real Academia de Bellas Artes de Cádiz* 2 (1984).

11. Robert Stevenson, "Los contactos de Haydn con el Mundo Ibérico," *Revista Musical Chilena* 46, no. 157 (1982): 3–39.

12. Ibid., 11.

13. A. C. Dies, *Biographische Nachrichten von Joseph Haydn* (Vienna: Carmesinaische Buchhandlung, 1810); translated by Vernon Gotwals and contained in his *Joseph Haydn: Eighteenth-Century Gentleman and Genius* (Madison: Univ. of Wisconsin Press, 1963), 288.

14. Preface to the score, published in 1808 by Breitkopf und Härtel. See Karl and Irene Geiringer, *Haydn: A Creative Life in Music*, 3rd ed. (Berkeley and Los Angeles: Univ. of California Press, 1982), 83.

15. *Carta edificante del V. sacerdote o Relación Sumaria de la vida de José Sáenz de Santa María, marques de Valde Íñigo* (1807), in the Biblioteca de Estudios Gaditanos, Cádiz.

16. Geiringer and Geiringer, *Haydn*, 84.

17. Juan Antonio Ruiz Casaux, *La música en la Corte de Don Carlos IV y su influencia en la vida musical española* (Madrid: Real Academia de Bellas Artes de San Fernando, 1959), 16.

18. This story appears, as told by a great-grandson of Boccherini, in Nicolás Solar-Quintes, "Nuevos documentos sobre Luigi Boccherini," *Anuario Musical* (Barcelona) 2, (1947): 91.

19. *La colección artística de Sebastián Martínez, el amigo de Goya* (Madrid: Consejo Superior de Investigaciónes Científicas, Instituto Diego Velázquez, 1978), 201.

20. Ureña, *Viaje Europeo*, 35.

21. *Partición Combencional de los Bienes quedados por muerte del Sr. Sebastián Martínez, Thesorero General del Reino* (1805), II, legajo 5387 (folios 1233–1394), Archivo de Protocolos [Public Records], Cádiz.

22. Hill et al., *Stradivari*, 137.

23. Ramón Solis, *El Cádiz de las cortes: La vida en la ciudad en los años de 1810 a 1813* (Madrid: Silex, 1987), 63.

24. Archivo de Protocolos, Cádiz, vol. 2662, folio 69–72; vol. 5401, folios 778–781.

25. Ibid.

26. *Lista general de los comerciantes establecidos en Cádiz, así nacionales como extrangeros,* Guía Patriótica de España para el año de 1811, Real Isla de León, imprenta de D. Miguel Segovia, impresor de la Real Marina Guía.

27. Hill et al., *Stradivari*, 267.

28. Ibid., 137.

29. I owe knowledge of this document to Professor María Pemán Medina of Madrid and to Professor Bara Boydell of Dublin.

30. Hill et al., *Stradivari*, 138.

31. A document from the Pigott House. I owe the knowledge of this document to Professor Barra Boydell of Dublin.

32. Hill et al., *Stradivari*, 138.

33. Ibid., 139.

34. Ibid., 127.

35. W. E. Whitehouse, "About Piatti," *The Strad*, May 1929, 15.

36. Hill et al., *Stradivari*, 132.

37. Biographical data on Piatti taken from "Alfredo Piatti: A Grand Master of the Cello" (an article based on material from Morton Latham, *Alfred Piatti: A Sketch* [London: W. E. Hill and Sons, 1901]), *Newsletter of the Violoncello Society, Inc.* (New York), May 1978. All quoted material in the rest of this section on Alfredo Piatti is taken from this source.

38. Whitehouse, "About Piatti."

39. Arthur Hill's diary (August 27, 1918), published with the kind permission of Charles Beare, London, who bought the Hill diaries.

40. Gregor Piatigorsky, *Cellist* (New York: Doubleday, 1965), 128.

41. *New York Times*, December 11, 1936.

42. Ibid., December 13, 1936.

43. Charles Beare, conversation with the author, London, February 1998.

44. Thomas Blubacher, conversation with the author, Kronberg, Germany, October 2002.

45. Joe Roddy, conversation with author, New York, 1980.

46. Adolf Busch, *Adolf Busch: Briefe, Bilder, Erinnerungen* [*Adolf Busch: Letters, Pictures, Memories*], ed. Irene Busch Serkin, trans. Russell Stockman (Walpole, N.H.: Arts and Letters Press, 1991), 265n.

47. The Busch Quartet lasted thirty-two years, till Adolf's death in 1951.

48. Busch, *Briefe, Bilder*, xi.

49. Sam H. Shirakawa, *The Devil's Music Master: The Controversial Life and Career of Wilhelm Furtwängler* (New York: Oxford Univ. Press, 1992), 151.

50. Ibid., 272.

51. Ibid., 247.

52. Mrs. Anna Lee Wurlitzer, conversation with the author, New York, January 23, 1998.

53. Ibid.

54. Lynn H. Nicholas, *The Rape of Europa: The Fate of Europe's Treasures in the Third Reich and the Second World War* (New York: Knopf, 1994), 101.

55. Ibid.

56. Busch, *Briefe, Bilder*, 493.

57. The founding members were Rudolf Serkin, Adolf Busch, Hermann Busch, Marcel Moyse, Louis Moyse, and Blanche Honegger Moyse.

58. Wurlitzer, conversation.

59. Ibid.

60. Both the great Spanish violinist Víctor Martín (a friend of Cassadó and an assistant to his courses in Siena) and Felícitas Keller (the prior representative of Cassadó in Spain) confirmed this information in November 1997. They both remember the "Mendelssohn Stradivari" well.

61. Wurlitzer, conversation.

62. Marta Casals Istomin, conversation with the author, New York, January 15, 1998.

63. Wurlitzer, conversation.

64. Roddy, conversation.

65. René Morel, conversation with the author, New York, January 1998.

66. Wurlitzer, conversation.

67. Ibid.

68. Roddy, conversation.

69. José María Corredor, *Conversations avec Pablo Casals: souvenirs et opinions d'un musicien* (Paris: Éditions Albin Michel, 1955; repr. Collection Pluriel, 1982), 288.

70. Jacques Français, conversation with the author, New York, 1978.

71. Ibid.

CHAPTER 4

1. It is not commonly known that MIT has an undergraduate program leading to a bachelor of science in music.

2. Stravinsky assured us that he had enjoyed going to the bullfights since the times of Diaghilev's *Ballets Russes* in Spain, when he had witnessed many in the company of Picasso and Nijinsky. He claimed that both these artists were very familiar with bullfighting. When the bullfight began, we realized that the composer had exaggerated somewhat. "What are those pillows for?" he asked when he saw the protective covering on the horses. The next question, which he asked as the bull entered the ring, left us speechless: "C'est un monsieur, ou c'est une dame?"

3. Carlos Prieto, *De la URSS a Rusia: Tres décadas de Observaciones y Experiencias de un Testigo* (Mexico City: Fondo de Cultura Económica, 1993 and 1994).

CHAPTER 5

1. Carlos Prieto, *Alrededor del mundo con el violonchelo* (Mexico City: Alianza Editorial Mexicana, 1987).

2. Roxane Witke, *Comrade Chiang Ch'ing* (Boston: Little, Brown, 1977), 386; Ross Terrill, *Mao: A Biography* (New York: Harper and Row, 1980), 315.

3. Jay and Linda Matthews, *One Billion: A Chinese Chronicle* (New York: Random House, 1983), 245–256.

4. Ross Terrill, *Madame Mao: The White-Boned Demon* (New York: Bantam, 1986), 250–251.

5. Witke, *Chiang Ch'ing*, 459.

6. The name "Persia" derives from "Pars." "Persis" is the hellenized form of "Pars."

7. Prieto, *URSS a Rusia*.

8. Now we know that these canals have caused an ecological disaster of colossal magnitude.

9. I remind the reader that this text was written in 1991.

10. *Ogonëk* 21 (1989), 4–5, 30–32.

11. Richard Pipes, *The Russian Revolution* (New York: Knopf, 1990).

12. Note published by John Kinsella for the program of the National Symphony Orchestra, March 15, 2002.

CHAPTER 6

1. The composer always signed his name "Sumaya." However, in the chapter records of the cathedral in Mexico City, his name appears as "Zumaya."

2. Note by Craig H. Russell in his edition of Sumaya's *Lamentaciones* (Los Osos, Calif.: Russell Editions, 1993).

3. Periodicals Library, National Archives, Mexico.

4. Jorge A. Mendoza Rojas, "The Cello Concerto by Mexican Composer Ricardo Castro," PhD dissertation, University of Texas at Austin, 1994. Mendoza has recently undertaken a comprehensive critical revision of the score and parts.

5. Jorge Velazco obtained a copy of the manuscript from the Edwin A. Fleisher Collection in the Free Library of Philadelphia.

6. For a more detailed account of the subject, see Robert L. Parker, "Carlos Chávez's 'Opus Ultimum': The Unfinished Cello Concerto," *American Music* 11, no. 4 (Winter 1993): 473–487.

7. Napoleón Cabrera, *Clarín* (Buenos Aires), May, 23, 1991.

8. Horacio Salas, *El tango* (Buenos Aires: Editorial Planeta, 1986).

9. Ibid., 36.

10. Estéban Pichardo, *Diccionario provincial de voces cubanas* (Matanzas, Cuba: Real Marina, 1836); quoted in Salas, *Tango*, 36.

11. Salas, *Tango*, 52.

12. Cited in Salas, *Tango*, 82.

13. Nicolas Slonimsky, *Music of Latin America* (New York: Crowell, 1945), 61.

14. Ibid.

15. Salas, *Tango*, 115.

16. According to certain Argentinean sources, Gardel claimed he was Uruguayan to avoid military service in Argentina.

17. Astor Piazzolla, *A manera de memorias*, comp. Natalio Gorín (Buenos Aires: Editorial Atlántida, 1990), 80.

18. Ibid., 45.

19. Ibid., 56.

20. Ibid., 31.

21. The details of this story were provided by Efraín Paesky and Mstislav Rostropovich.

22. Efraín Paesky, conversation with the author, 1999.

23. Renato Almeida, *História da música brasileira*, 2nd ed. (Rio de Janeiro: Briguiet, 1942), 298.

24. Celso Garrido-Lecca, conversation with the author, 1997.

25. Alejo Carpentier, *La música en Cuba*, vol. 12 of *Obras Completas* (Mexico City: Siglo XXI, 1987), 171.

26. Quote from the official program for the concert and award ceremony, Madrid, October 31, 1997.

27. Notes written by the composer for the Urtext Digital Classics recording (JBCC 015, 1997).

28. Program notes for the Urtext Digital Classics recording (JBCC 047, 2001)

29. Ibid.

30. Ibid.

31. Carlos Prieto, *As aventuras de um Violoncelo: Historia e Memorias* (Rio de Janeiro: Top Books, 2000).

32. For those interested in such facts, the five largest countries by land area are Russia, Canada, China, the United States, and Brazil.

33. See Chapter 9 for more detailed information on Ricardo Lorenz.

34. Note sent by the composer for the program notes of the concert of November 21, 2003.

CHAPTER 7

1. A sonata was a piece to be played (from the Italian *sonare*, "to play"); a cantata, a piece to be sung (from the Italian *cantare*, "to sing").

2. Leopold Mozart, *A Treatise on the Fundamental Principals of Violin Playing*, trans. Editha Knocker (London: Oxford Univ. Press, 1948 [orig. pub. in Augsburg, 1756]), 10n.

3. Salazar, *Juan Sebastián Bach*, 142.

4. Robert Stevenson, "La música en el México de los siglos XVI a XVIII," in *La música de México: I. Historia*, vol. 2, *Periodo virreinal (1530 a 1810)*, ed. Julio Estrada (Mexico City: Universidad Nacional Autónoma de México, 1986), 27.

5. The *scordatura* was not unusual at that time, when widespread experimentation with the tuning process and even with the number of strings of an instrument was common. In 1618 Michael Praetorius observed that the cello was called—as we have mentioned—basso de viola da braccio and had five strings: F, C, G, D, A, although its tuning was variable. Praetorius himself added, "Attention: the way that someone tunes his violin or viola is not of great importance as long as he plays with precision, clarity, and in tune" (quoted in Hans Vogt, *Johann Sebastian Bach's Chamber Music: Background, Analysis, Indvidual Works* [Portland, Ore.: Amadeus Press, 1988], 48).

6. Vogt, *Bach's Chamber Music*, 21.

7. Cowling, *Cello*, 67.

8. For information in this section I have consulted, among other works: Ugo Biagioni, *Boccherini* (Madrid: Instituto Italiano di Cultura, 1993); Germaine de Rothschild, *Luigi Boccherini: His Life and Work*, trans. Andreas Mayor (New York: Oxford Univ. Press, 1965); Ramón Barce, *Boccherini en Madrid* (Madrid: Instituto de Estudios Madrileños, 1992).

9. Cowling, *Cello*, 112.

10. H. C. Robbins Landon, ed., *The Mozart Compendium: A Guide to Mozart's Life and Work* (New York: Schirmer, 1990), 343.

11. Ibid., 355.

12. This "numbered" writing is the equivalent of a kind of musical shorthand.

CHAPTER 8

1. Sonata form consists of three sections—exposition, development, and recapitulation—and is used especially in the first movement of sonatas, quartets, concertos, symphonies, etc.

2. Joseph Schmidt-Görg and Hans Schmidt, eds., *Ludwig van Beethoven* (New York: Praeger, 1969), 153.

3. Wilhem von Lenz, quoted in Schmidt-Görg and Schmidt, *Beethoven*, 152.

4. Lev Ginsburg, *History of the Violoncello*, ed. Herbert R. Axelrod, trans. Tanya Tchistyakova (Neptune City, N.J.: Paganiniana Publications, 1983), 109.

5. The music critic who covered the event wrote: "I believe that no cellist has ever dared perform this difficult task, for which Herr Popper deserves to be doubly thanked. This work is not intended for the general public, but a connoisseur would appreciate its outstanding musical merits . . ." (quoted in Ginsburg, *Violoncello*, 92).

6. Ginsburg, *Violoncello*, 129.

7. Malcolm MacDonald, *Brahms*, Master Musicians Series (New York: Oxford Univ. Press, 2001), 437.

8. This version was published in 1897 as "Edition for cello and piano," but was subsequently lost. A copy was discovered in 1974, and a new edition was subsequently published (International Music Co., 1975).

9. McDonald, *Brahms*, 320–321.

10. The manuscript for this concerto was discovered in Würtemberg in 1925. See John Clapham, "Dvořák's First Cello Concerto," *Music and Letters* 37 (1956): 350–355. It has been played by the Czech cellist Milos Sadlo in an orchestral version by Jan Burghauser.

11. John Clapham, "Dvořák's Cello Concerto: A Masterpiece in the Making," *Music Review* 40, no. 2 (May 1979), 136.

12. Ibid., 123.

13. Brahms to Simrock, letter dated January 27, 1896, in *Dvořák and His World*, ed. Michael Beckerman (Princeton, N.J.: Princeton Univ. Press, 1993), 80.

14. Donald Francis Tovey, *Essays in Musical Analysis*, vol. 3, *Concertos* (Oxford: Oxford Univ. Press, 1978), 148.

CHAPTER 9

1. For further information on this subject one can consult the excellent book by the cellist and professor Elías Arizcuren, *El violonchelo: Sus escuelas a través de los siglos* (Barcelona: Editorial Labor, 1992).

2. Pablo Casals, *Joys and Sorrows: Reflections by Pablo Casals*, as told to Albert E. Kahn (New York: Simon and Schuster, 1974), 69–70.

3. The Gagliano family, founded by Alessandro Gagliano (1640–1720), was Naples's most distinguished dynasty of violin makers.

4. Casals, *Joys and Sorrows*, 98.

5. Ibid.

6. José García Borrás, *Pablo Casals: Peregrino en América* (Mexico: Talleres Gráficos Victoria, 1957), 96.

7. The winners of the competition were Rama Jucker, from Switzerland; Anner Bijlsma, from Holland; and Josef Chuchro, from Czechoslovakia.

8. Emanuel Feuermann, "Cello Playing: A Contemporary Revolution," *Newsletter of the Violoncello Society, Inc.* (New York), Spring 1972, 2.

9. Piatigorsky, *Cellist*, 49.

10. Soviet criticism was unanimously negative, partly for ideological reasons, but the composer himself was not satisfied with the concert and chose to withdraw it. See Harlow Robinson, *Sergei Prokofiev: A Biography* (New York: Viking, 1987), 356.

11. Piatigorsky, *Cellist*, 144.

12. Elizabeth Wilson, *Shostakovich: A Life Remembered* (Princeton, N.J.: Princeton Univ. Press, 1994), 324.

13. Michael Scammell, *Solzhenitsyn: A Biography* (New York: Norton, 1984), 603.

14. Professor Daniel Homuth drew up a list of 4,600 cello works since 1960: 2,119 for cello and piano, 1,541 for solo cello, 695 for cello and orchestra, 125 for cello and string orchestra, and 120 for cello and chamber orchestra. Naturally, because of a lack of information he included few works by Latin Americans. See Daniel Homuth, *Cello Music since 1960: A Bibliography of Solo, Chamber, and Orchestral Works for the Solo Cellist* (Berkeley, Calif.: Fallen Leaf Press, 1994).

15. I am very grateful to the Latin American Music Center at Indiana University (Bloomington), and in particular to Carmen Téllez and Gerardo Dirié for the information they provided me.

16. Among his numerous contributions to music, in 1945 he founded the *Revista musical chilena*, perhaps the most important Latin American publication of this type.

17. When violinists and cellist do not play in tune, it is usually because they are inadvertently venturing into "Sonido 13"!

18. Perhaps the transcription of Frescobaldi's *Toccata* is an original work by Cassadó, in the style of works by Fritz Kreisler.

EPILOGUE

1. All train schedules follow Moscow time. Due to the sheer size of the country, there are eleven time zones, so it is more practical to follow a system that is familiar to everyone. We spent a great deal of time figuring out the time difference!

BIBLIOGRAPHY

"Alfredo Piatti: A Grand Master of the Cello." *Newsletter of the Violoncello Society, Inc.* (New York), May 1978. An article based on material from Morton Latham, *Alfred Piatti: A Sketch* (London: W. E. Hill and Sons, 1901).

Alcaraz, José Antonio. *En una música estelar: De Ricardo Castro a Federico Álvarez del Toro.* Mexico: INBA, 1987.

Almeida, Renato. *História da musica brasileira.* 2nd ed. Rio de Janeiro: Briguiet, 1942.

Arizcuren, Elías. *El violonchelo: Sus escuelas a través de los siglos.* Barcelona: Editorial Labor, 1992.

Bachmann, Werner. *The Origins of Bowing and the Development of Bowed Instruments up to the Thirteenth Century.* Translated by Norma Deane. London: Oxford Univ. Press, 1969.

Baines, Anthony. *Musical Instruments.* Harmondsworth, England: Penguin, 1961.

Baruzzi, Arnaldo. *La Casa Nuziale: The Home of Antonio Stradivari, 1667–1680.* London: W. E. Hill & Sons, 1962.

Barzano, Annalisa Lodetti, and Christian Belisario. *Signor Piatti: Cellist, Composer, Avant-Gardist.* Text in German and English. Kronberg im Taunus, Germany: Kronberg Academy Verlag, 2001.

Beare, Charles. *Capolavori di Antonio Stradivari.* Milan: Arnoldo Mondadori, 1987.

Beckerman, Michael, ed. *Dvořák and His World.* Princeton, N.J.: Princeton Univ. Press, 1993.

Bein & Fushi. *The Miracle Makers: Stradivari, Guarneri, Oliveira.* Chicago: Bein & Fushi, 1998.

Biagioni, Ugo. *Boccherini.* Madrid: Instituto Italiano di Cultura, 1993.

Biddulph, Peter, ed. *The Violin Masterpieces of Guarneri del Gesù: An Exhibition at the Metropolitan Museum of Art Commemorating the 250th Anniversary of the Maker's Death.* London: Biddulph, 1994.

Borrás, José García. *Pablo Casals: Peregrino en América.* Mexico: Talleres Gráficos Victoria, 1957.

Bowden, Sidney. *Gand-Pajeot: A Letter of Instruction.* New York: Morel & Gradoux-Matt, 2000.

Busch, Adolf. *Adolf Busch: Briefe, Bilder, Erinnerungen [Adolf Busch: Letters, Pictures, Memories].* Edited by Irene Busch Serkin; translated by Russell Stockman. Walpole, N.H.: Arts and Letters Press, 1991.

Carmona, Gloria. *Periodo de la Independencia a la Revolución, 1810–1910.* Vol. 3 of *La Música de México.* Series editor: Julio Estrada. Mexico: UNAM, Instituto de Investigaciones Estétitcas, 1986.

Carpentier, Alejo. *La música en Cuba.* Vol. 12 of *Obras Completas.* Mexico City: Siglo XXI, 1987.

Carta edificante del V. sacerdote o Relación Sumaria de la vida de José Sáenz de Santa María, marques de Valde Íñigo (1807). In the Biblioteca de Estudios Gaditanos, Cádiz.

Casals, Pablo. *Joys and Sorrows: Reflections by Pablo Casals.* As told to Albert E. Kahn. New York: Simon and Schuster, 1974.

Casaux, Juan Antonio Ruiz. *La música en la Corte de Don Carlos IV y su influencia en la vida musical española.* Madrid: Real Academia de Bellas Artes de San Fernando, 1959.

Chiesa, Carlo, and Duane Rosengard. *The Stradivari Legacy.* London: Peter Biddulph, 1998.

Chiesa, Carlo, John Dilworth, Robert Hargrave, Peter Klein, Stewart Pollens, Duane Rosengard, and Eric Wen. *Giuseppe Guarneri del Gesù.* Two Volumes. London: Biddulph, 1998.

Clapham, John. "Dvořák's Cello Concerto: A Masterpiece in the Making." *Music Review* 40, no. 2 (May 1979): 123–140.

———. "Dvořák's First Cello Concerto." *Music and Letters* 37 (1956): 350–355.

Comas, Ramón Pinto. *Los Luthiers Españoles.* Barcelona: Libreria Herder, 1988.

Corral, Manuel Antonio del. *Andante con variaciones.* Edited and with an introductory study by Ricardo Miranda. Mexico: Instituto Nacional de Bells Artes/Centro Nacional de Investigación, Documentación e Información Musical Carlos Chávez, 1998.

Corredor, José María. *Conversations avec Pablo Casals: souvenirs et opinions d'un musicien.* Paris: Éditions Albin Michel, 1955; repr. Collection Pluriel, 1982.

Cowling, Elizabeth. *The Cello.* New York: Scribner's, 1975.

Dalos, Anna, et al. *Von Budapest nach Bloomington. Janos Starker und die ungarische Cello-Tradition.* Kronberg im Taunus, Germany: Kronberg Academy Verlag, 1999.

David, Hans T., and Arthur Menzel, eds. *The Bach Reader.* New York: Norton, 1966.

De'ak, Steven. *David Popper.* Neptune City, N.J.: Paganiniana Publications, 1980.

Dies, A. C. *Biographische Nachrichten von Joseph Haydn.* Vienna: Carmesinaische Buchhandlung, 1810. Translated by Vernon Gotwals and contained in his *Joseph Haydn: Eighteenth-Century Gentleman and Genius.* Madison: Univ. of Wisconsin Press, 1963.

Doring, Ernest N. *Matteo Gofriller of Venice.* Chicago: William Lewis and Son, 1959. Reprints of articles published in the magazine *Violins and Violinists* from January 1942 to July 1943.

———. *The Guadagnini Family of Violin Makers.* Chicago: William Lewis and Son, 1949.

———. *How Many Strads? Our Heritage from the Master.* Chicago: William Lewis & Son, 1945.

Feuermann, Emanuel. "Cello Playing: A Contemporary Revolution." *Newsletter of the Violoncello Society, Inc.* (New York), Spring 1972.

Français, Jacques. *Jacobus Stainer and Eighteenth-Century Violin Masters,* a leaflet prepared on the occasion of the exhibit prepared by J. Français at Lincoln Center, New York, October 1981–January 1982.

Geiringer, Karl, and Irene Geiringer. *Haydn: A Creative Life in Music.* 3rd ed. Berkeley and Los Angeles: Univ. of California Press, 1982.

Ginsburg, Lev. *History of the Violoncello.* Vol. 4 of the original Russian edition. Edited by Herbert R. Axelrod; translated by Tanya Tchistyakova. Neptune City, N.J.: Paganiniana Publications, 1983.

Ginsburg, Lev. *Istoriya violonchelnogo iskusstva.* Vols. 1–IV. Moscow, 1950, 1957, 1965, 1978.

Goodkind, Herbert K. *Violin Iconography of Antonio Stradivari, 1644–1737: Treatises on the Life and Work of the Patriarch of Violinmakers.* Larchmont, N.Y.: privately printed, 1972.

Henley, William. *Antonio Stradivari: His Life and Instruments.* Revised and edited by Cyril Woodcock. Brighton, England: Amati, 1961.

Hill, Alfred E., Arthur F. Hill, and W. Henry Hill. *The Violin Makers of the Guarneri Family, 1626–1762: Their Life and Work.* London: W. E. Hill & Sons, 1931; repr., London: W. E. Hill & Sons, 1965.

Hill, W. Henry, Arthur F. Hill, and Alfred E. Hill. *Antonio Stradivari: His Life and Work, 1644–1737.* London: W. E. Hill & Sons, 1902; repr., New York: Dover, 1963.

Homuth, Daniel. *Cello Music since 1960: A Bibliography of Solo, Chamber, and Orchestral Works for the Solo Cellist.* Berkeley, Calif.: Fallen Leaf Press, 1994.

Huggins, Margaret. *Gio: Paolo Maggini. His Life and Work.* London: W. E. Hill & Sons, 1892; new material compiled and edited by William Ebsworth Hill, William Hill, Arthur Hill, and Alfred Hill, published in London by W. E. Hill & Sons, 1976.

Itzkoff, Seymour W. *Emanuel Feuermann, Virtuoso: A Biography.* Tuscaloosa: Univ. of Alabama Press. 1979.

La colección artística de Sebastián Martínez, el amigo de Goya. Madrid: Consejo Superior de Investigaciónes Científicas, Instituto Diego Velázquez, 1978.

Laurie, David. *Reminiscences of a Fiddle Dealer.* Boston: Houghton Mifflin, 1925; repr. Cape Coral, Fla.: Virtuoso Publications, 1977.

Le Blanc, Hubert. *Défense de la basse de viole contre les entreprises du violon et les prétentions du violoncel.* Originally published in Amsterdam, 1740; reprinted serially in *La Revue Musicale* 9 (1927–1928).

Leopold Mozart, *A Treatise on the Fundamental Principals of Violin Playing.* Translated by Editha Knocker. Originally published in Augsburg, 1756; reprinted London: Oxford Univ. Press, 1948.

Les Violons: Lutherie Vénitienne, Peintures et Dessins. Catalogue of an exhibition at the Hôtel de Ville de Paris. Paris: Association pour la Promotion des Arts, 1995.

Lista general de los comerciantes establecidos en Cádiz, así nacionales como extrangeros. Guía Patriótica de España para el año de 1811. Real Isla de León, imprenta de D. Miguel Segovia, impresor de la Real Marina Guía.

MacDonald, Malcolm. *Brahms.* Master Musicians Series. New York: Oxford Univ. Press, 2001.

Malusi, Lauro. *Il Violoncello.* Padua: Edizioni G. Zanibon, 1973.

Markevitch, Dimitry. *Cello Story.* Princeton, N.J.: Summy-Birchard Music, 1984.

Matthews, Jay, and Linda Matthews. *One Billion: A Chinese Chronicle.* New York: Random House, 1983.

Mendoza Rojas, Jorge A. "The Cello Concerto by Mexican Composer Ricardo Castro." PhD diss., University of Texas at Austin, 1994.

Menuhin, Yehudi. *The Violin.* Paris: Flammarion, 1996.

Millant, Roger. *J. B. Vuillaume: Sa Vie et Son Oeuvre.* Edition in French, English, and German. London: W. E. Hill & Sons, 1972.

Munrow, David. *Instruments of the Middle Ages and Renaissance.* London: Oxford Univ. Press, 1977.

Nicholas, Lynn H. *The Rape of Europa: The Fate of Europe's Treasures in the Third Reich and the Second World War.* New York: Knopf, 1994.

Parker, Robert L. "Carlos Chávez's 'Opus Ultimum': The Unfinished Cello Concerto." *American Music* 11, no. 4 (Winter 1993): 473–487.

Partición Combencional de los Bienes quedados por muerte del Sr. Sebastián Martínez, Thesorero

General del Reino (1805), II, legajo 5387 (folios 1233–1394). Archivo de Protocolos [Public Records], Cádiz.

Piatigorsky, Gregor. *Cellist.* New York: Doubleday, 1965.

Piazzolla, Astor. *A manera de memorias.* Compiled by Natalio Gorín. Buenos Aires: Editorial Atlántida, 1990.

Pichardo, Estéban. *Diccionario provincial de voces cubanas.* Matanzas, Cuba: Real Marina, 1836.

Pipes, Richard. *The Russian Revolution.* New York: Knopf, 1990.

Pleeth, William. *Cello.* Compiled and edited by Nona Pyron. New York: Schirmer, 1983.

Prieto, Carlos. *Alrededor del mundo con el violonchelo.* Mexico City: Alianza Editorial Mexicana, 1987.

———. *As aventuras de um Violoncelo: Historia e Memorias.* Rio de Janeiro: Top Books, 2000.

———. *De la URSS a Rusia: Tres décadas de Observaciónes y Experiencias de un Testigo.* Mexico City: Fondo de Cultura Económica, 1993 and 1994.

Racster, Olga. *Chats on Violoncellos.* London: T. Werner Laurie, 1907.

Robbins Landon, H. C. *Haydn at Esterháza,* Vol. 2 of Haydn: Chronicle and Works. London: Thames & Hudson, 1995.

———, ed. *The Mozart Compendium: A Guide to Mozart's Life and Work.* New York: Schirmer, 1990.

Robinson, Harlow. *Sergei Prokofiev: A Biography.* New York: Viking, 1987.

Roda, Joseph. *Bows for Musical Instruments of the Violin Family.* Chicago: William Lewis and Son, 1959.

Rothschild, Germaine de. *Luigi Boccherini: His Life and Work.* Translated by Andreas Mayor. New York: Oxford Univ. Press, 1965.

Russell, Craig H., ed. *Lamentaciones* by Sumaya. Los Osos, Calif.: Russell Editions, 1993.

Sacconi, Simone. *I Segreti di Stradivari* (Cremona, Italy: Libreria del Convegno, 1972.

Sachs, Curt. *The History of Musical Instruments.* New York: Norton, 1968.

Salas, Horacio. *El tango.* Buenos Aires: Editorial Planeta, 1986.

Salazar, Adolfo. *Juan Sebastián Bach: Un ensayo.* Mexico City: El Colegio de México, 1951.

———. *La Música en la Sociedad Europea.* Vol. 2. Madrid: Alianza Editorial, 1983.

Samuel, Claude. *Entretiens avec Mstislav Rostropovich et Galina Vishnevskaïa.* Paris: Robert Laffont, 1983.

Sandys, William, and Simon Andrew Foster. *The History of the Violin and Other Instruments Played On with the Bow.* London: John Russell Smith, 1864.

Scammell, Michael. *Solzhenitsyn: A Biography.* New York: Norton, 1984. (Includes references to Rostropovich.)

Schmidt-Görg, Joseph, and Hans Schmidt, eds. *Ludwig van Beethoven.* New York: Praeger, 1969.

Shirakawa, Sam H. *The Devil's Music Master: The Controversial Life and Career of Wilhelm Furtwängler.* New York: Oxford Univ. Press, 1992.

Silverman, William Alexander. *The Violin Hunter.* Neptune City. N.J.: Paganiniana Publications, 1981.

Slonimsky, Nicolas. *Music of Latin America.* New York: Crowell, 1945.

Solar-Quintes, Nicolás. "Nuevos documentos sobre Luigi Boccherini." *Anuario Musical* (Barcelona) 2, (1947).

Solé, Pablo Antón. "Un testimonio artístico y religioso de la burguesía gaditana: La Santa Cueva." *Anales de la Real Academia de Bellas Artes de Cádiz* 2 (1984).

Solis, Ramón. *El Cádiz de la cortes: La vida en la ciudad en los años de 1810 a 1813*. Madrid: Silex, 1987.

Starker, Janos. *The World of Music according to Starker*. Bloomington: Indiana Univ. Press, 2004.

Stevenson, Robert. "La música en el México de los siglos XVI a XVIII." In *La música de México: I. Historia*, vol. 2, *Periodo virreinal (1530 a 1810)*. Series editor: Julio Estrada. Mexico City: UNAM, 1986.

———. "Los contactos de Haydn con el Mundo Ibérico." *Revista Musical Chilena* 46, no. 157 (1982): 3–39.

Strocchi, Giuseppe. *Liuteria: Storia ed arte*. Lugo, Italy: Tipografia Michele Cortesi, 1937.

Terrill, Ross. *Madame Mao: The White-Boned Demon*. New York: Bantam, 1986.

———. *Mao: A Biography*. New York: Harper and Row, 1980.

The New Grove Dictionary of Music and Musicians. Edited by Stanley Sadie. New York: Macmillan, 1980.

Tovey, Donald Francis. *Concertos*. Vol. 3 of *Essays in Musical Analysis*. Oxford: Oxford Univ. Press, 1978.

Ureña, Marques de. *El viaje Europeo del marques de Ureña*. Edited by María Pemán Medina. Cádiz, Spain: Unicaja, 1992.

Vidal, Louis Antoine. *Les instruments à archet*. 3 vols. Paris: Claye, 1876–1878.

Vishnevskaya, Galina. *Galina: A Russian Story*. Translated by Guy Daniels. New York: Harcourt Brace Jovanovich, 1984.

Vogt, Hans. *Johann Sebastian Bach's Chamber Music: Background, Analysis, Indvidual Works*. Portland, Ore.: Amadeus Press, 1988.

Weschler-Vered, Artur. *Jascha Heifetz*. New York: Schirmer, 1986.

Whitehouse, W. E. "About Piatti." *The Strad*, May, 1929.

Wilson, Elizabeth. *Shostakovich: A Life Remembered*. Princeton, N.J.: Princeton Univ. Press, 1994.

Witke, Roxane. *Comrade Chiang Ch'ing*. Boston: Little, Brown, 1977.

INDEX

From Bach to Piazzolla

CARLOS PRIETO, CELLO

LIST OF WORKS PERFORMED BY CARLOS PRIETO ON ACCOMPANYING CD

1. J. S. Bach, Courante from Suite no. 6 in D Major for solo cello
2. J. S. Bach, Gavotte from Suite no. 6 in D Major for solo cello
3. Dmitry Shostakovich, Allegro from the Cello Sonata in D Minor, op. 40. Doris Stevenson, piano
4. Dmitry Shostakovich, Scherzo from the Viola Sonata, op. 147; transcribed for the cello by Carlos Prieto. Doris Stevenson, piano
5. Manuel de Falla, "Nana" from *Suite popular española*. Edison Quintana, piano
6. Manuel de Falla, "El Paño Moruno" from *Suite popular española*. Edison Quintana, piano
7. Astor Piazzolla, *Milonga*. Edison Quintana, piano
8. Astor Piazzolla, *Le grand tango*. Edison Quintana, piano
9. Joaquín Gutiérrez Heras, *Canción en el puerto*. Edison Quintana, piano
10. Marlos Nobre, Appassionato from *Partita Latina*, op. 92. Edison Quintana, piano
11. Marlos Nobre, Vivo from *Partita Latina*, op. 92. Edison Quintana, piano
12. Samuel Zyman, Danzando from the Suite for Two Cellos, with Jesús Castro-Balbi, cello
13. Samuel Zyman, Allegro energico from the Suite for Two Cellos, with Jesús Castro-Balbi, cello
14. Roberto Sierra, Vivo from *Four Verses for Cello and Orchestra*. Orquesta de las Américas, Carlos Miguel Prieto, conductor
15. Mario Lavista, Allegro giocoso e leggiero, the second of *Three Secular Pieces*. Edison Quintana, piano
16. Federico Ibarra, Presto from the Cello Concerto. Orquesta de las Américas, Carlos Miguel Prieto, conductor
17. Alberto Ginastera-Fournier, *Triste*. Edison Quintana, piano
18. Eugenio Toussaint, Presto with swing from Cello Concerto no. 2. Orquesta de las Américas, Carlos Miguel Prieto, conductor

COURTESY OF URTEXT DIGITAL CLASSICS. DAVID FROST, PRODUCER.